Divine Providence

DIVINE PROVIDENCE

God's Love and Human Freedom

Bruce R. Reichenbach

CASCADE *Books* • Eugene, Oregon

DIVINE PROVIDENCE
God's Love and Human Freedom

Copyright © 2016 Bruce R. Reichenbach. All rights reserved. Except for brief quotations in critical publications or reviews, no part of this book may be reproduced in any manner without prior written permission from the publisher. Write: Permissions, Wipf and Stock Publishers, 199 W. 8th Ave., Suite 3, Eugene, OR 97401.

Cascade Books
An Imprint of Wipf and Stock Publishers
199 W. 8th Ave., Suite 3
Eugene, OR 97401

www.wipfandstock.com

PAPERBACK ISBN 13: 978-1-4982-9285-6 /
HARDCOVER ISBN 13: 978-1-4982-9287-0
EBOOK ISBN: 978-1-4982-9286-3

Cataloging-in-Publication data:

Name: Reichenbach, Bruce R.

Title: Divine providence : God's love and human freedom / Bruce R. Reichenbach.

Description: Eugene, OR: Cascade Books, 2016 | Includes bibliographical references and index.

Identifiers: ISBN 13: 978-1-4982-9285-6 (paperback) | ISBN 13: 978-1-4982-9287-0 (hardcover) | ISBN 978-1-4982-9286-3 (ebook)

Subjects: 1. Providence and government of God—Christianity. 2. Free will and determinism. 3. God (Christianity)—Omniscience. 4. Philosophical theology. I. Title.

Classification: BT135 R44 2016 (print) | BT135 (ebook)

Manufactured in the U.S.A.   AUGUST 31, 2016

Scriptures taken from the Holy Bible, Today's New International VersionTM TNIV®. Copyright © 2001, 2005 by International Bible Society®. All rights reserved worldwide.

Thanks are due to the following for permission to reprint sections of my articles, with revisions.

"Hasker on Omniscience." *Faith and Philosophy* 4.1 (1987) 86–93.

"Freedom, Justice, and Moral Responsibility." In *The Grace of God, the Will of Man*, edited by Clark Pinnock, 277–303. Grand Rapids: Zondervan, 1989.

"God and Good Revisited." *Philosophia Christi* 16.2 (2014) 319–38.

For Sharon Lee Harvie Reichenbach
Loving wife, faithful partner, remarkable companion for fifty years,
Devoted helpmate, patient provider, humble caregiver,
Caring mother and proud grandmother,
who listens to and sees things from others' point of view;
who puts the concerns and welfare of others before her own
for the glory and honor of God.

And for our parents,
Robert C. and Alberta M. Reichenbach
C. Thomas and Gertrude M. Harvie
In deep gratitude for the love, care, support,
training, and inspiration they provided for us,
until we meet again.

Table of Contents

Preface ix

Chapter 1: Providence and Sovereignty 1
Chapter 2: Providence and Freedom 16
Chapter 3: Freedom and Agency 51
Chapter 4: God and Goodness 81
Chapter 5: God as Omnipotent 118
Chapter 6: God as Almighty 134
Chapter 7: God's Knowledge 151
Chapter 8: The Open View of God's Knowledge 171
Chapter 9: When Providence Seems Absent 207
Chapter 10: Providence and Petitionary Prayer 233
Chapter 11: Providence and Miracles 262
Chapter 12: Enjoying the Provider 300

Bibliography 307

General Index 315

Scripture Index 319

Preface

Praise the LORD.
How good it is to sing praises to our God,
  how pleasant and fitting to praise him.
The LORD builds up Jerusalem;
  he gathers the exiles of Israel.
He heals the brokenhearted
  and binds up their wounds.
He determines the number of the stars
  and calls them each by name.
Great is our Lord and mighty in power;
  his understanding has no limit. . . .
He covers the sky with clouds;
  he makes grass grow on the hills.
He provides food for the cattle
  and for the young ravens when they call. (Ps 147:1–5, 8–9)[1]

IN RECOUNTING HOW GOD providentially engages the world, the Psalmist brings into play God's essential characteristics. God is providentially good in gathering the exiled, healing the afflicted, and provisioning. God exhibits providential omniscience in that by calling each thing by its name he deeply knows and understands everything. God displays that he is providentially almighty because he can do what he wants in his created earth.

Christian theology forms a complex web with numerous rich and critical concept-strands radiating from the center. The center that holds all together is divine love. God loves what he created so much that he deeply involves himself in and with it to promote its good for his glory. The implementation of divine love runs out providentially along each supporting radius, bestowing life, reconciliation, and significance. The themes I explore

---

1. Biblical references in this book use *Today's New International Version* (Grand Rapids: Zondervan, 2005).

in this book presuppose this providentially radiating love rooted in God's properties. Using C. S. Lewis's distinction, we will study and analyze the themes (what Lewis terms "contemplation") and the significant theological and philosophical problems or issues they generate, while at the same time looking along the themes (what Lewis terms "enjoyment") to appreciate how richly they manifest divine providence.[2]

Love flows providentially along the radius of creation. Creation manifests God's faithfulness and loving care for everything, including for those most vulnerable or needy: "Blessed are those whose help is the God of Jacob, whose hope is in the Lord their God" (Ps 146:5). One might reasonably conjecture that to dispense his providential love is the important reason why God created.

> He is the maker of heaven and earth,
>   the sea, and everything in them—
>   he remains faithful forever.
> He upholds the cause of the oppressed
>   and gives food to the hungry.
> The Lord sets prisoners free.
>   The Lord gives sight to the blind,
> the Lord lifts up those who are bowed down,
>   the Lord loves the righteous . . .
> but he frustrates the ways of the wicked. (Ps 146:6–9)

God creates the world for himself, for us, and for both interacting together. Its non-sentient contents compose, establish, and nourish the environment for the righteous and wicked alike. Indeed, without the non-sentient there could be no sentient beings, for we are constituted of their very elements and play in their fields. Although God has interests in the non-sentient, the sentient receives his greatest attention, for a world without sentient creatures would lack beings with whom God can engage in meaningful, personal, covenant relationships. Providence conveys creation love to us.

Divine love also streams providentially along the radius of reconciliation and healing. Even though God's repeated endeavors to establish covenants with individuals, groups, and nations often were and are frustrated, God's unfailing love brings his mercy to the fore.

---

2. Ward, *Planet Narnia*, 16–17. I will return to the themes of contemplation and enjoyment in the final chapter.

> Because of the LORD's great love we are not consumed,
>> for his compassions never fail.
> They are new every morning,
>> great is his faithfulness. (Lam 3:22–23)

God's love and providence lie behind his reaction to Eve and Adam's rejection of him when they set up themselves as their own gods and arbiters of good and evil. God responds with deserved punishment, but it is both mitigated (exclusion from the garden replaces immediate physical death) and tempered with a promise of reconciliation. The garden story recounts not the end but the beginning. In subsequent stories God pursues reconciling covenants with individuals such as Cain, Noah, Abraham, Saul, David, Solomon, and with groups like Israel and, later, the gentiles.

> In my faithfulness I will reward my people
>> and make an everlasting covenant with them.
> Their descendants will be known among the nations
>> and their offspring among the peoples.
> All who see them will acknowledge
>> that they are a people the Lord has blessed. (Isa 61:8–9)

After countless failures and rejections, out of love God the Father sends his Son to provide the once-for-all grand basis for reconciliation. Providential love underlies both the incarnation and the atonement. "For God so loved the world that he gave his one and only Son, that whoever believes in him shall not perish but have eternal life" (John 3:16). Love motivates Jesus' miracles, when in his healing ministry he tangibly demonstrates God's concern for those distressed. Jesus looks on the needy with compassion (Matt 15:32) and heals them (Matt 14:14; Luke 7:13) both physically by his word and spiritually through forgiveness (Matt 9:1–8). God displays his ultimate providential action in Jesus' sacrificial death that brings us healing, forgiveness, and reconciliation. Manifesting God's desire to bring us into a personal, covenantal relationship with him, God makes his ultimate sacrifice for our own and his good (Heb 7:27).

Providential love manifests itself in the radius of ecclesiology (the doctrine of the church). "Christ loved the church and gave himself up for her to make her holy, cleansing her by the washing with water through the word, and to present her to himself as a radiant church, without stain or wrinkle or any other blemish, but holy and blameless" (Eph 5:25–27). Love perfects the church, sometimes through its blood-stained persecution and terrible suffering; at other times through its both little and spectacular triumphs.

Providence also directs the course of eschatology (the doctrine of the end times). When God restores a new heaven and the new earth, "God's dwelling place is now among the people, and he will dwell with them. They will be his people, and God himself will be with them and will be their God. He will wipe every tear from their eyes. There will be no more death or mourning or crying or pain, for the old order of things has passed away" (Rev 21:3-4). In the end, God will accomplish his long-sought purpose of intimate covenantal relationship.

The centrality of the doctrine of providence in Christian theology and faith is a given. At the same time, the doctrine generates a slew of theological, philosophical, and ethical issues. These challenging issues form the structure and content of what we will consider. In chapter 2 we will note that in order to achieve a covenantal relationship, God had to create significantly free beings. We will explore how to understand the freedom God gives us and how it comports with his sovereignty and providence. In chapter 3, we take the contention from chapter 2 that we are free and explore philosophically how it is that physical human beings can be free. In particular, we are concerned with how the mental—our beliefs, desires, feelings, intentions—can influence, affect, or cause the physical, and vice versa, in ways consistent with contemporary scientific anthropology. Since providence stems from God's perfect goodness, in chapter 4, we will reflect on what it means to say that God is good in a way consistent with a meaningful understanding of moral goodness. Since providence is possible only where God is powerful enough to enact his will, we will consider God's power and what it means to be omnipotent or almighty in chapters 5 and 6. A providential God needs to know something about the future; otherwise we must wonder why we should trust God to reliably guide us. In chapters 7 and 8 we will discuss the difficult issue of God's knowledge, especially about the future, whether such knowledge is possible, and how this knowledge connects with providence. In chapter 9 we will ask how a loving, powerful, and knowing God can not only allow but also at times *cause* the pain, suffering, and dysfunction present in our world. If God loves us so much, why do we suffer? In chapter 10 we will address the issues surrounding petitionary prayer: if out of his goodness God seeks our good, why do we need to petition repeatedly, and why are so many prayers seemingly unanswered. In chapter 11 we will consider the nature, possibility, and occurrence of miracles, by which God works to achieve his providential plans and purposes in the world. The final chapter addresses practical implications that follow from our discussion of divine providence.

The task of reconciling all these themes and ideas is enormous. The endeavor has similarities to reconstructing a huge jigsaw puzzle. Puzzles are both magnetic and enigmatic. I recall my elderly father finding it difficult to pass by his dining-room table where puzzle pieces lay scattered and not to be drawn into putting in place a piece or two or three . . . , until he ended up hooked, wanting to find just one more piece toward solving the puzzle before he moved on. Puzzles also present enigmas. When we purchase a puzzle, we consider not only the beauty or artistry of the puzzle picture, but also the challenge the puzzle presents. If we desire a serious test, we select puzzles with a large number of pieces, substantial areas of similar shading, and repetitive design. In this way the puzzle presents us with captivating and often frustrating challenges. The box affirms that the pieces all fit neatly together; the trick is to discover that fit as we construct the final picture.

The central topic of this book—divine providence—presents an intellectual and spiritual puzzle that is both magnetic and enigmatic. Because of its magnetism, theologians, philosophers, and Christians over the centuries have been drawn to address the critical questions that providence raises. Some have touched on the problems merely in passing; others have treated them in great detail. In this book I will consider how we can fashion a coherent, finished picture from the individual pieces that we have been given. Unfortunately for us, we do not have access to the complete picture; we possess only the individual puzzle pieces and no overall revealed representation on a box cover enabling us to know how the finished product should look. Only the Puzzlemaker knows the finished masterpiece. We are thus limited to humanly determining how the joined pieces that we put together reasonably form a coherent picture. Nevertheless, as serious inquirers we accept the appointed task to complete the puzzle as best we can. We will argue for a particular picture of God's providence, realizing that the cut, shape, or color of the puzzle pieces at times is somewhat ambiguous, such that others might try to reconstruct the puzzle in a different way. We will also find that some of the pieces are difficult and challenging to fit into the puzzle, for they can yield paradoxical or problematic conclusions. Some pieces link uneasily or in seemingly diverse ways. Although only God ultimately knows how all the pieces conform, in the meantime he has given us hints in his general and special revelation about what the overall picture might be like and has bequeathed us the rational abilities to thoughtfully figure out a possible, coherent picture. These tools—revelation, reason, and experience—will assist us in our quest for understanding divine providence. Yet our intellectual endeavor will be tempered with serious humility at the difficulty of the daunting task facing us and wisdom of those who have worked at the puzzle before us.

In the end, my readers will have to decide how successfully I have crafted the puzzle of God's loving providence. Some might conclude that

I have forced pieces together that do not properly belong or link together, or that they fit together in very different ways than I suggest. I hope that many others will conclude that I have made notable progress in resolving the providence puzzle. Each puzzler will decide, but whatever the decision, our attempt to work out the puzzle is itself worthwhile, not merely for the contemplative intellectual challenge, but to bring to our awareness and enjoyment the magnitude, wonder, and extent of God's providence. Through our study of providence not only will we look *at* the individual pieces, we also will look *through* them to appreciate the loving kindness that the caring Puzzlemaker manifests to us. No matter how all the concepts are analyzed and arranged, what remains is the fact that God greatly loves and cares for us, created us to be in covenant relationship with him, went to great extremes, including the death of the Son, to restore that relationship, and involves himself daily in our lives to bring about our good and holiness for his glory. That alone justifies the great endeavor that I undertake. I invite you to take up the thought-provoking, challenging, creative, and rewarding task of puzzle-solving with me in the following chapters.

As I get older, I reflect on the trajectory of my life and think about the people I have met over the years. Many of them were blessings to me as they introduced me to new experiences, new people, new ideas, new feelings, new opportunities, and new directions. I would not be the same had I had different parents, not met my future wife in college over a chess board, not married her shortly thereafter and enjoyed fifty years of marital happiness, or not fathered two creative and energetic children. I would be very different had not a philosophy professor had confidence in me and hired me to teach philosophy at a Lutheran college in Minneapolis after another school turned me down; I would have missed out on the joys of knowing and working with all the particular students I have taught. I would be very different in my interests and experiences if my father-in-law had not needed language training in Mexico to become a short-term missionary teacher after his successful and distinguished military career in Germany and Korea, and had I not traveled there to visit my in-laws and consequently developed a deep passion for engaging people in other cultures in the places where they live. The list of experiences is great. Some people created hardships that forced me to compensate in various creative ways outside my comfort zone. These people unwittingly provided opportunity in ways I had not anticipated for growth and development, at times very painful, but in the end substantially rewarding. Although I cannot point to definitive, miraculous events in my life, as a believer in a good and powerful God I hold that it is at least reasonable to think that along my path God secretly involved himself at some if not many points. As we providentially provide for the daily welfare of our family and the benefit of others, often without their awareness of our doing so, so it is reasonable to think that much of what God does lies behind the scenes and sometimes is realized only in thoughtful hindsight. What seems at times extraordinary serendipity might well be divine intervention.

I have also listened to and read stories from others who have discovered God's providence in their lives, some in dramatic settings of physical healings, unexpected rescues, and spiritual encounters. Their passion and fervor, the physical evidence they have adduced, and above all, the difference these events have made in their lives, cause me to pause and reflect more generally about God's greater involvement in our lives. One has to take seriously their witness accounts, while thoughtfully turning to the issues they raise.

In the spring of 1997 I was looking for a place overseas to volunteer to teach for my sabbatical. I had heard of an organization called DaystarUS, headed by a person named Bob Oehrig, that might connect prospective faculty with a university in Kenya. I attended a conference on Christian-Muslim dialogue at the University of Minnesota at which I believed he might be present. Standing in the lobby, I asked a stranger if he knew Mr. Oehrig. From behind me came a voice, "Hello, I am Bob Oehrig." From that chance meeting came opportunities for me to teach, first at Daystar University in Kenya, and over a decade later, at ABC University in Liberia. Some years later, Ebola having closed universities in Liberia, we again looked for a place to volunteer. My wife exercised with other women at Curves, where she discussed our experiences in Liberia and the unlikelihood of our going back there. "Have you thought about Slovakia?" a co-exerciser asked. Several years before, she had been there for two weeks on a mission trip with St. Andrews Lutheran Church teaching vacation Bible school and enjoyed the experience. No, we replied, we did not know of any opportunities there and so had not thought about the country; we were interested in going somewhere in Africa. As we explored the option of going to Slovakia, we sat one afternoon in the backyard at an open house of a high school graduate with a couple we had never met. As we talked we discovered that she coordinated short-term mission work for Roseville Lutheran Church sending people to Martin, Slovakia, and could put us in touch with people who recently returned from there, one of whom, it turned out, was a former student of mine, and another a co-worker of one of our good friends. Eight months later, after some questioning and exploring, we were teaching at the

Lutheran Academy in Martin. Happenstance, maybe; divinely providential, likely.

These reflections and experiences, and more like them, have led me to write on the theme of divine providence, for as a Christian I believe that God did not simply create the universe and deistically disappear but remains continuously involved in the world and in our lives. God acts in the world for our good, disciplines us to develop and grow in our moral and spiritual character, and ultimately patiently bids us to choose to enter into a personal, covenantal relationship with him. To make this possible God created us with significant freedom. Without significant freedom we can neither develop the qualities of character and spiritual maturity that enrich us as moral people, enter into a meaningful personal relationship with God and others in the human community, nor engage morally with our threatened and threatening environment. God does not force us to accept his providence, but lures, persuades, invites, seduces, and entices us to willingly accept him and his acts of goodness—the kingdom banquet—on our behalf. God is gracious, although at times the Lord of Severe Mercy. Providence is the theological way of talking about the ways in which God manifests his gracious love in our lives.

In my years of teaching philosophy of religion, I slowly came to realize that the abstract, analytical treatment of topics in that discipline rarely connected with students. They wanted to see how reflective, analytical philosophy connected with their religious beliefs and traditions. This book is written with a full understanding of philosophy of religion from a Christian perspective in mind. It intentionally connects Scripture, theology, and philosophical reflection. Scripture provides a context that for the Christian highlights God's providential involvement in creation, history, redemption, and human affairs. Its multiple authors affirm providence without analytically or critically reflecting on the significant theological or philosophical issues that arise from the doctrine. Rather, they rightly look to the existential significance that it has for individual and corporate relational living. Thus, the following chapters often commence with the scriptural discussion of the dimension of providence being reflected on and reflect the fact that the book is rooted in the biblical tradition. From there I proceed to the theological and philosophical dimensions of providence. Theology provides reflection on the scriptural texts that allows for comparison between authors, development of ideas over time, anticipation and integration, and attempts at coherence. Philosophy provides the basic framework through careful analysis of the meaning of terms and concepts used in the discussion, questioning the truth and consistency of the claims made, attempting to create a synthesis that incorporates reasoned reflection and experience, and evaluating the constructed justifications for and critique of the claims made. My purpose is not only to engage in the analytical discussion, but to do so without losing sight of the synthetic and existential. Scripture and experience will provide an entrée into the discussion and will not be overlooked, but for the most part the primary focus of the chapters will be on theological/philosophical issues that the doctrine of providence raises.

Chapter 1

Providence and Sovereignty

To reach the distant mountain of Moriah required a grueling three-day trek by foot. Abraham loaded the dusty donkey with provisions sufficient for the trip and rough firewood to burn on the altar to be constructed from coarse mountain stones. Two servants carried the remaining accoutrements needed for the arduous journey and the unspoken event. Again and again Abraham played out the sacrifice scenario in his mind as they determinately walked. A long climb up the steep mountain; unrelenting thorn bushes grabbing at the billowing robes; loose rocks sliding under foot and tumbling haphazardly down the slope behind them; the gathering heat of the day turning their heavy clothes damp with sweat. Together the father and son struggled up the mountain with the wood, brazier, and knife. Hauling on his back the dry wood for the burnt offering, Isaac read Abraham's mind and asked the hitherto unspoken question, "The fire and wood are here, but where is the lamb for the sacrifice?" Abraham had prepared for that inquiry, circling around it in his mind for the three days and nights since God spoke to him in a startling dream. "God himself will provide the lamb for the sacrifice, my son" (Gen 22:8).

God provides. God's last minute intervention to provide a sacrificial lamb exhibited it. In naming the place Jehovah Jireh, Abraham affirmed it. "And to this day it is said, 'On the mountain of the Lord it will be provided'" (Gen 22:14). The destiny of the two participants in their roles as providing the blessing for all nations on earth established it. Among all his glorious titles affirming presence, strength, and observation, Yahweh is named "provider."

The central theme of providence

Scripture repeatedly recounts the intentional actions of the providential God. The instances are too numerous to record here, but a sampling affords evidence of the diversity with which the biblical writers interpreted God's hand in the events they experienced. They see divine providence spreading a wide umbrella over both natural and human events.

God provides for nature and through nature for humans. For the earth and its living things God sends rain (Job 5:10; Isa 43:20; Matt 5:45); for the birds and animals, wild and domestic, he provides food (Job 38:41; Ps 147:9). Even the lowly common sparrow cannot fall without God knowing and consenting (Matt 10:29). Scripture does not inform us about the means by which God cares for nature, only that nature's features indicate that it falls under God's knowledge, power, and provision.[1]

God provides for all nations and peoples. For all, God produces rain and storms, "crops in their seasons," and "food in abundance" (Job 36:31; Acts 14:17). The Old Testament writers reiterate that God directs his care most particularly, but not exclusively (Egypt is his people, Assyria his handiwork [Isa 19:23–25]), toward Israel. In the often-recounted exodus story, God sends inarticulate Moses to the Israelites to deliver them from slavery (Exod 3), provides a Passover lamb as protection from the deathly plague that struck dead the Egyptian firstborn (Exod 12), guides by a pillar of fire at night and a concealing cloud of protection during the day (Exod 13:21), drops manna in the desert (Exod 16), gushes water from the rocks where there seems to be none (Exod 17:5–6), and brings decisive victory on the battlefield (Deut 7:17–24). God blesses the Israelites with fertile land (Ezek 34:29), with rain for their crops, plentiful harvests, pasture land, and healing (Isa 30:23–26). God brings peace and prosperity (Jer 33:9).

Biblical stories tell that God especially cares and provides for individuals. On the murderer Cain God placed an undeserved mark of protection (Gen 4:15); gave Noah and his family plans for the wooden ark, whereby they could save themselves and representative animals to re-populate the world (Gen 6:14–17); preserved David from the violent madness of Saul (1 Sam 23:14); saved the life of fleeing Jonah by means of a great fish when he was tossed overboard into the roiling sea (Jonah 1:17); and rescued the apostles from prison (Acts 5:19) and Peter from the deadly clutches of Herod (Acts 12:6–11).

God provides not only for our physical but also for our spiritual needs, offering redemption (Ps 111:9), a savior (John 3:16), and adoption into God's family (Eph 1:5). Providential escape from temptation (1 Cor 10:13), the Spirit to guide us into truth (John 16:13), and the Scriptures for our teaching, training, and correction (2 Tim 3:16) supplement the Christian inventory. From our birth to death (Ps 139) God sees and cares, assuring us of his sufficiency through the metaphor of knowing the number of hairs

---

1. Humans are assigned a stewardly role in this. See Reichenbach, *On Behalf*, ch. 3.

on our head (Matt 10:30). Paul aptly sums it all up: God "richly provides us with everything for our enjoyment" (1 Tim 6:17).

These intentional, providential actions flow from God's goodness (his benevolence), power, and knowledge, and are manifested in his actions toward us. From beginning to end, God providentially intervenes, both indirectly through nature (e.g., Paul and Silas are rescued from prison through an earthquake—Acts 16:25–26) and directly in our affairs. Providence lies at the core of the biblical text. Although the biblical writers see God's guiding and caring hand in many events, two repeatedly stand out as central. The Old Testament most frequently refers to the providential rescue of Israel from slavery in Egypt (Pss 105 & 136). In the exodus story God provides for his covenant people liberation from bondage through Moses and Aaron, sustenance through manna and water in the desert, and the possibility for a prosperous future in a new rich environment. The providence exhibited in the exodus foretokens God's rescue centuries later of a remnant from captivity in Babylon. Matthew recalls it to shape in part his Jesus birth story. The other is the theme of the New Testament, presaged in the Abrahamic story with which we began this chapter. God's incarnational, deadly, atoning provision majestically but terribly reveals divine providence. Christ's death brings salvation from sin, healing from the effects of sin, and restoration of the relationship with God destroyed by sin. In short, God's love, care, provision, and protection constitute the running theme of the biblical text; from the beginning, where the creator God sees everything as good, they form the undeniable center around which the biblical stories, psalms of praise, interpreted historical events, prophetic pleas, theological teachings, and deeds of Jesus weave their web of narrative, songs, and discourse.

Providence and plans

Although "providence" literally means "to foresee," as applied theologically to God it refers more broadly to God's active loving care for, beneficial actions on behalf of, and guidance of his creation than to any passive observation or witnessing. Divine providence exhibits at least three dimensions of God. First, it proclaims God's goodness insofar as God declares what he makes to be good and through love and grace seeks the good of blessing for what he created. God in his goodness is the source of blessing or happiness.[2]

---

2. The Greek term usually used for "happiness" in the New Testament is μακάριος or "blessed." This duality indicates that God blesses us for happiness, not for abnegation of life. For an historical discussion of the shift from happiness as a state, measured in lifetimes or eternal well-being, not independent of suffering, to an emphasis on painless

Second, providence presupposes God's power by which God realizes his purposes by his actions in the cosmos and, more especially, in the affairs of humanity. Third, providence invokes God's wisdom revealed in his plans and purposes, to his understanding of the present and future, by which God directs us to what is good for us. (We will address God's goodness in chapter 4, God's power in chapters 5 and 6, and God's knowledge in chapters 7 and 8.)

Scripture reveals that God has purposes for the universe as a whole, for groups and nations, and for particular individuals. For the cosmos God intends "to sum up all things in heaven and on earth in Christ" (Eph 1:10). What this means practically is unclear, but perhaps the thought is that Christ will not only be the head of the continuing church (Eph 1:22; 4:15)[3] but also the cosmic focal point in the end times. According to Paul, God also has intentions or purposes for groups of individuals, for nations, and for his church. For example, God intended to bring the gentiles into the family of God to be joint heirs with Israel (Eph 2:13–22). For human persons God wills that all be saved (2 Pet 3:9), so that they conform to Christ's image (Rom 8:39) and God can show "the immeasurable riches of his grace in kindness toward us" (Eph 2:7). The content of the providential plan for people emphasizes salvation, healing, sanctification, and blessing. For particular individuals God has special purposes and callings. God selected reluctant Moses to deliver Israel and hiding Saul to be the first king of Israel (Exod 3; 1 Sam 9:15), chose Jeremiah as a prophet to deliver the word of the Lord (Jer 1:5–9), dramatically called Saul (later, Paul) to be God's messenger to the gentiles (Acts 9:15–16), and commissioned Peter to feed Christ's flock (John 21:15–17).

To realize his providential purposes, God institutes plans of action that might involve particular individuals or, corporately, nations. In Abraham he intended to bring about a nation through which all nations would be blessed (Gen 12:1–3). God worked through Pharaoh to release Israel from captivity (Exod 9:16), through Nebuchadnezzar and the Babylonians to punish Judah for abandoning God, and through Cyrus to restore the Jews to their land (Isa 44:28). Through the Messiah, God instigates and carries out his plan to redeem humanity and destroy the works of the devil (1 John 3:8).

One has to be careful, however, to discern how much one can generalize from these particular cases of individual callings to the claim that all individuals are specifically called to particular tasks. In many instances we might understand what we do as God's calling in the sense that we

---

momentary feelings, see McMahon, *Happiness*.

3. Schlier, "ἀνακεφαλαιόομαι," 682.

incorporate the presence of God into the task, situation, and community. This understanding can be termed our vocation or calling: God calls us to bring him into what we do, making him an essential aspect of our being and doing, wherein we take pleasure in our doing and serve others. We can discern our calling in a variety of ways: through a realistic understanding and assessment of our talents and abilities, through the insightful guidance and astute counseling of others, but most of all through the joy we find in our work or avocation. We truly have found our vocation or avocation when what we do productively coincides with what brings us delight, when we would rather not be doing anything else to fulfill ourselves in relating to, serving, and meeting the needs of others. But generally vocation is not to be understood in the sense that God wants you to do this particular task in contrast to everything else, such that engaging in any other task runs counter to God's will for you. This latter, when pressed, can lead to guilt and despair when the circumstances militate against or remove opportunities to do what we think is God's will for us or when we find what we do unfulfilling but cannot escape it.

We might put our point this way: to say that God has purposes and plans for his creation says nothing about their scope. Does God's plan or purpose cover every detail of human history and personal experience, or are his plans often more general and only at times specific? The former is referred to as meticulous providence: nothing happens apart from specific divine planning; everything accords with God's will. According to this frequently articulated view, God has a master plan or blueprint filled in complete detail, not only for the universe but also for each of us. All events that we experience express features of what God has carefully conceived for our lives; our role is to discover as best we can how all the diverse events fit into the whole of God's plan and what we can do to perfectly conform to his program for us and others. God predetermined his plan and as all-powerful controls all aspects of our existence as he capably works to realize that plan. Thus, believers in meticulous providence say that *whatever* happens to them—good, bad, or indifferent—is part of God's plan; God has and works his purpose in each event that he realizes.

Many often support their broad view of the detailed scope of God's plans by citing Jeremiah 29:11: "For I know the thoughts (*machashebeth*) that I think (*chashab*) toward you, says the Lord, thoughts (*machashebeth*) of peace (*shalom*), and not of evil, to give you an expected end (*acharith*)." The passage is ambiguous, as the various translations exhibit. *Machashebeth* comes from *chashab* (to think, account, or plan). The KJV translates *machashebeth* as "thoughts," as it does the similar passage of Psalm 40:5 (see also Ps 33:11). The TNIV translates both instances as "plans" (but "purposes" in

Ps 33:10–11). The RSV and the English Standard Version translate *machashebeth* in Ps 40:5 as "thoughts," while they render it in Jeremiah 29:11 as "plans." The two—"thoughts" and "plans"—convey very different meanings and connotations, such that how the versions render the passage depends upon the determinate perspectives of the translators. The context of the Jeremiah passage is a letter sent from Jeremiah to the exiles dwelling in Babylon, telling them to make the best of their situation, since they will reside there for seventy years. By the end the exiled adults will have died and new generations will take over. But, Jeremiah assures them, God will fulfill his promise to bring the exiles back to Jerusalem; this is the expected and promised end. To eventually return them to their homeland and to reestablish them in peace are the good thoughts or plans that the Lord has.

If divine thoughts are in view in this passage, there is little to support meticulous providence. The thoughts present no worked-out scenario of repatriation, no list of who will and who will not return, and no details about how God will orchestrate it all. The point of the passage is the reassurance that God has not forgotten them even though they live in distant exile, hundreds of miles away from their former homes in Judah. Faithful to his promise, God will certainly restore the exiles—not those taken captive, but through their corporate identity he'll restore the exiles through their descendants—to their longed-for homeland.

Even if one follows the TNIV and RSV and translates *machashebeth* as "plans," there still is little to recommend meticulous providence rather than a general plan in the Jeremiah (or Psalms) text. We get no indication here that the Lord has a plan all worked out how the descendants will return, which descendants (since more stayed in Babylon than returned), under what conditions, and at exactly what date. Rather, although the plan is general, Jeremiah assures his listeners that God's promises are part of his overall purpose to restore exiled Judah. The purpose is there; the means are sketchy.

Although in one sense a belief in meticulous providence—that nothing happens apart from what God has planned, intended, and willed for the good of us, others, and indeed, all creation—is comforting, this view encounters serious difficulties when we think about the significant number of dysteleological events that we find difficult to consistently reconcile with a meticulous divine plan for our good. Some events bring unrelieved pain, serious suffering, and dysfunction that seem individually unrequited. Other events introduce obstacles to our realizing our perceived vocation. On the large scale it is difficult, if not impossible, to think that Stalin's ruthless pogroms and murders in the Katyn Forest, the deadly deportation marches of the Armenians, Hitler's racial cleansing and hideous concentration camps, Pol Pot's massacres of his Cambodian people, the brutal Hutu genocide against the Tutsis in Rwanda, the Serbian massacres of Bosnian Muslim men and boys at Srebrenica, and the tragic slaughters by ISIS in Syria and Iraq are part of God's plan for the good of the people affected. It is difficult, if not impossible, to think that the colonial, degrading plantation enslavement and mistreatment of Africans and the American willful destruction of Native American cultures, the demeaning segregation of Blacks, Indians, and Coloreds by white South Africans, the trafficking of women and children for prostitution in India, and mass murders in a Colorado theater and a Connecticut elementary school are part of God's plan for the good of those so maltreated. And on the individual level, it is difficult to believe that contracting pancreatic or brain cancer, macular eye degeneration, Parkinson's and Alzheimer's diseases, schizophrenia and bi-polar disorders, and so much more are part of God's detailed plans for an individual's good and not harm. To many, many more examples we could appeal; each reader could supply instances known to him or her where harm seemed to outweigh the good for the individuals involved. In short, not only is it difficult to believe in meticulous providence in the face of this evil, it demeans the sufferers themselves to say that this seemingly gratuitous suffering is part of God's best plan of blessing for them.

This is not to say that justification can never be given for some of the pain, suffering, and dysfunction that we experience. Indeed, in chapter 9 we will face head on the enormous problem of providing justification for evil or suffering in the context of divine providence. But our argument will not be that all evils are justified by any good achieved for the sufferer; such a case simply cannot be made empirically. It would smack of cosmic sadism. Too many died in Auschwitz and the Soviet gulags, Andersonville and Robin Island, Nanking and Hiroshima, the Trail of Tears and the Bataan death march, Bull Run and Iwo Jima, London and Dresden, Monrovia and medieval Europe, the tsunami-struck beaches of south Asia and earthquake devastated villages of the Himalayas, the bubonic and small pox ravaged towns of Europe and the Americas, and other places famous and obscure, to make this remotely plausible.

Meticulous providence also conflicts with God's granting us freedom. If God has every event scripted as part of his meticulous providence for each individual, where does human choice and human free action fit in? If God has planned every event in detail, we lack the freedom to determine our own destiny and relationships. Even our own assent would be part of the meticulous providential structure of the world

The view that God's plans are often general, although at times in certain regards specific, fits better with our understanding of the existence and role of human choice. On this view, although God at times has specific plans for persons (God's call of Paul to evangelize in Macedonia in Acts 16:9), it more often is the case that God has general plans to which we are asked to adapt using the wisdom and resources God has given us. For example, Paul writes that God "wants all people to be saved and to come to a knowledge of the truth" (1 Tim 2:4). To realize this general plan, God instituted a salvation narrative that included the obedience of the innocent Son to go to the cross, even though it was not what Jesus wanted (Matt 26:39, 42). But the full realization of this plan depended upon the *willing* obedience of the Son and the *free* cooperation of those who arrested, tried, and crucified him. Likewise, fulfillment of God's salvific desires depends on the faith and acceptance of those whom Christ came to save. Without faith and willing acceptance—God knows that many will not accept, for though having ears to hear they do not hear—they will not experience the salvation God planned for them (Mark 4:11–12). Not all invited to the banquet choose to come (Luke 14:16–20).

This understanding of providence allows that the success of God's plans, even when specific, depends in part upon those he created, and as free beings we have the divinely-bestowed power to resist or cooperate with God's plans. This power is possessed by nations (Israel continually resisted God's pleading to respond with active and faithful participation in the covenant relationship) and individuals (the history of Moses and King Saul are cases in point). In the next chapter we will discuss whether God's purposes necessarily will be realized (whether God's purposes can be thwarted) and whether humans can resist God when we discuss freedom and predestination. We will emphasize God's initiative and his responsiveness to human free choices and actions in his sovereign, providential realization of salvation history.

Providence and miracles

To say that God has purposes and plans usually of a general nature leads to the question how God governs or to the ways he realizes these purposes and plans. Will God realize them directly or indirectly? God operates in both ways, providing for us and creation both indirectly and directly. On the one hand, God frequently works through the natural laws and the matter they govern that he established in creation. The creation story recounts God bringing about and affirming its goodness, that it meets the purposes intended. Jesus affirms God's working through natural laws when he says that God causes the sun to shine and the rain to fall on both the just and the unjust (Matt 5:45). It is not that God manipulates each rain cloud to achieve his end; rather, cosmic forces are part of the overall plan of nature that makes life possible and good for all. Yes, agriculture involves sweat and toil, as recognized in Genesis 3. Yet Scripture sees that the bounty of the land, productive in its natural course, manifests God's providential goodness.

On the other hand, God can and does act at times in ways that intervene on natural events. Jesus' miracles are just such interventions. Jesus' healings alter the natural course of diseases; he restores disrupted physical functions for the blind and lame; he reverses the effect of death; he provisions groups of people by reversing shortages of food and drink. John highlights Jesus' intervention as part of God's work, where the miracles (called signs—σημεῖος) were intended to authenticate not only Jesus' ministry but also his claims to his identity as "the Messiah, the Son of God" (John 20:31). Other persons also were mediums of divine intervention in nature. Moses, the prophets Elijah and Elisha, and the apostles Peter and Paul are noteworthy examples of persons through whom God worked. It is not that they performed miracles; only God does the miracle. But they were the media through which God worked. And we have no reason to think that miracles came to an end with the departure of the apostles; God continues to work by miracle on and within nature and through people to implement his providential purposes.

At the same time, we have good reason to think that God does not run or operate the universe by miracles. If God consistently intervened in the operation of natural laws, the world would become a chaos in which human rational and moral action would be impossible. Without regularity and order, we could not rationally plan or calculate what actions to take to achieve particular goals. Predictions about the results of our actions and those of others would be impossible. Suppose we see a person thrashing about and calling for help in middle of the lake. Should we act, and if so, how should we act? If there are no natural laws or if the events governed by the laws are very frequently affected by God's direct intervention, we would not know whether we need to jump into the water to attempt a rescue. Without natural laws or regularity we would not know whether the water would drown the person, whether the person would be able to get up and walk on the water out of the lake, or whether the person would simply float like a cork.[4] How we act depends on how we can act, and how we can act depends on the way the world is, not only in its particularity, but in its universality or natural structures. How we will act in this case depends on our knowledge

---

4. The story of Peter's attempt to walk on the water of Lake Galilee aptly illustrates how our (and Peter's) reasoned understanding of and reliance on natural laws leads to skepticism about miracles, that outside forces can alter natural norms and processes (Matt 14:29–30).

of the natural properties of water and their relation to the human body. But without this type of knowledge our own activity as rational beings becomes impossible, for we would not know which actions would be possible and hence which we can rationally implement. God's operation of the world by miracle would thus eliminate the possibility of human rational and hence moral action.

Moreover, if God operated the world by miracle we would have no reason to act in any case. If the person calls for assistance from the middle of the lake, then let God save her. And even if we would attempt to rescue the drowning person, our actions would require reliance on God's intervention to help us to succeed. That is, if God operated the world by miracle, we would not be independently-acting agents acting in a rule governed world, but all our actions would depend either upon his directly causing the action or on his facilitating in some fashion our performing the action. In either case, for us to act God would be an active agent as a necessary operative condition to bring about the event, for there would be no natural laws, only divine volition. In such a world what we do would really be what God does in, through, and for us. Again, such a scenario would destroy the kind of human moral response, both willingness and action, that God expects from us.

This does not mean that God cannot act directly in nature. But it does mean that if we are to be morally responsive beings God cannot act in such a way that would result in destruction of the natural order and consequently in our own inability to act rationally, prudently, and morally. This suggests that the world God created is central to God's providence. God generally acts through nature and its laws to achieve his purposes. But this does not eliminate the possibility of God acting providentially through direct intervention. Miracles are tools of God's arsenal of providence. We will discuss miracles in greater depth in chapter 10.

Providence and sovereignty

Sovereignty invokes the political relationship of governance. It implies that at least two classes of individuals exist, governors and the governed, between which an ordered relationship holds. The governor or sovereign has both authority and power. The authority is either legislative or executive, or both. In their legislative roles, sovereigns create laws by which they rule those they govern. Sovereigns may create the basic laws (for example, write the constitution) or may write or dictate subsequent laws that support, develop, or implement prior laws (what might be called secondary or enabling laws) or their own subsequent desires. In their executive role, sovereigns exercise their authority by seeing to the implementation of those laws in the lives of the governed. These two are frequently supplemented with exercised judicial power. Sovereigns also have power, with or without limitations. The relation of sovereigns to fundamental structural laws and the source of the sovereigns' authority help determine the kinds of powers the sovereigns have, their limits, and the ends to which their powers may be deployed. If the social and legal structure is weak, their authoritarian powers are magnified. If the social and legal structure is strong and independent, laws delineate and limit the sovereigns' power. When sovereigns derive their power from the consent of the governed, the governed, who may withdraw their consent under particular circumstances, limit that power.

To be sovereign does not automatically mean that everything that occurs accords with the will of the sovereigns or that they can bring about anything they want. The ability of sovereigns to determine the outcomes depends, in part, on the type and amount of freedom granted to the governed. If those subject to the sovereigns possess significant freedom, then the sovereigns are limited in what they can do. For example, sovereigns cannot make the subjects freely acknowledge their sovereignty. Sovereigns can compel their subjects to bow in their presence, but they cannot compel them to bow freely; to pay taxes, but not to pay them willingly. On pain of threats sovereigns can coerce their subjects to do their will, but they cannot coerce free obedience. The more freedom sovereigns award their subjects, the less sovereigns can control their subjects' behavior without withdrawing or circumscribing the very freedom granted. In granting significant freedom to their subjects, sovereigns make it possible for their authority and will to be freely obeyed and also freely resisted. If sovereigns command their subjects to do some act and if the subjects are free, they can refuse—although at the same time they must bear the consequences of their refusal. Sovereigns might be able to make their subjects act as sovereigns desire, but only at some great cost to other aspects of the sovereigns' program. For example, if sovereigns seek to eliminate certain evils that resulted from granting freedom of expression (for instance, writing and distributing obscene material) they might at the same time have to limit in some more general way the expression and dissemination of thoughts and ideas. In short, sovereignty is a relational notion and must be so analyzed complexly.

Christians hold that God is sovereign; God has both authority and power over his creation. We find indicators of this in the Old Testament—the Nile, the livestock, even the amphibians and insects in Egypt either are instruments of or fall under God's plagues (Exod 7–10); God makes the sun to stand still and hailstones to rain destruction on the enemy (Josh 10); "You are the ruler of all things. In your hands are strength and power"

(1 Chr 29:11–12). In the New Testament we read the Parable of the Rich Householder in Matt 20:1–16 and the analogy of the potter in Rom 9:19–24. The foundation for God's authority over nature and over us is not a social contract but the fact that God created and sustains the universe. Sovereignty is rooted in creation: God made and continues to uphold the universe and everything in it by "his word of power" (Heb 1:3; see also Neh 9:6; Ps 104:29; Col 1:17).

A heightened concept of social contract comes into play when Scripture discusses how divine sovereignty plays out in God's dealings with humans. It is not that God's sovereignty itself results from the contract; we do not make or appoint God the sovereign, as if God were sovereign only if we elect him to be so. Judeo-Christian theism is not a form of democracy; objectively God is sovereign over creation. But the personal application of Christian theism is democracy: it is up to us to decide whether to make God sovereign in our lives. He becomes subjectively sovereign in our lives when we acknowledge him so. Idolatry occurs when we create our own gods, replacing God with ourselves or other things to which we give priority or obeisance. The contract, or better, covenant, God makes with us delineates the character of the relationships that he desires to hold between us. God chose to make covenants with specific people, wanting them to be instruments of his grace. Through them lineages of all living creatures would be saved, the nations of the earth would be blessed, a long line of descendants would occupy and rule the land, and the gospel would be preached throughout the world. In Israel's initial theocratic state the laws were presented as having divine origin. Through the covenants divine sovereignty was exercised more directly over those who put themselves under the covenant. When the Israelites wanted a human king to emulate the nations around them, God expressed dissatisfaction, for God alone was to be Israel's monarch (1 Sam 8:7–9). Under the new covenant (Heb 7:22; 8:13), established by the death and resurrection of Jesus, the church stands in a similar relationship to God's special sovereignty as Israel experienced (Gal 6:15–16). It acknowledges a covenant signed and sealed with Jesus' blood, through which we are now adopted by grace into the royal family.

One must be very clear to distinguish the sovereign from the novelist. Novelists create their own characters, plot, setting, and outcomes. All of the participants in the storyline do exactly what the author determines. All have their traits laid out by and have no existence apart from the author. The plot moves inexorably, though at times convolutedly, to the end determined by the author. What the author desires is precisely what occurs; neither characters nor plot can resist the will of the author. It is true that novelists often speak as through the characters themselves wrote the plot and carried it out, developed their own qualities of character, and dictated the scenes. And though in one sense this is true in that once the writing begins, certain features or inevitabilities seem to arise out of the flow. But ultimately there would be no characters or storyline without the fertile minds of the authors, and the authors must take responsibility for the contents of the texts. Gatsby is Fitzgerald's, not Salinger's, Gatsby.

We frequently confuse God in his role as sovereign, having control over creation, with the novelist. If viewed as a novelist, God would be able to determine what or who is created, what the created are like, what they will do in all circumstances, the detailed plot, and how the story will turn out, not just in general, but for each individual. As we noted above, we term this view "meticulous providence." God has a foreordained master plan for everything and everyone.

This is an inadequate view of divine sovereignty, for what would those over whom God is sovereign be like? On this view of meticulous providence God is not sovereign over creatures who can freely respond to him. Indeed, in this scenario creatures have no freedom to make real, meaningful responses to God as a person. As in the novel, the participants at best would have an apparent or illusory freedom, a freedom within the confines of the novel. They might think that they are free and that their choices are their own. But in fact God has brought it about that they cannot but choose in a given fashion since God has caused directly or indirectly their motives, intentions, thought patterns, and desires from which they act.[5] With

---

5. The doctrine of middle knowledge has been introduced to overcome this. According to this doctrine, God knows not only what is possible under all circumstances but also what each person would actually do in each circumstance in which the person could possibly find him- or herself. It is important to be clear; on the view of middle knowledge what God knows is not what each free person *might* choose or do in all circumstances (although God knows this as well) but what they *actually would choose* were that person in that situation. In more philosophical language, God possesses knowledge of all counterfactuals of free will (if-then statements of choices and actions where the antecedent is false because what it asserts never occurs). God knows what I would choose from the menu were I in a restaurant tonight in Mumbai, Islamabad, Cairo, Monrovia, Havana, or Bogota, although I will be in none of these. Based on this knowledge, God brings about the world in which people freely choose as God knows they would. God decides whom or what to create, what events he will allow or cause to happen in the actual world, and what circumstances we will face. The world that results is God's ordained world, although the choices people make and the actions they perform are free because persons actually choose them. It is just that this actual world that is known by God is the world God (weakly) brings about or actualizes by his creative acts.

The major problem with this view is that there are *no grounds* for God to know what possible persons would chose to do under particular circumstances that never happen. No grounds exist for saying that I would or would not have visited Sacra de Coeur had I visited Paris this past summer, since I did not go there this past summer. Yet,

meticulous providence creation consequently turns out to be a well-orchestrated novel, deceptive at best in giving an illusion of freedom, rather than a story of divine sovereignty over responsive and responsible creatures. A sovereign without respondents is not a sovereign but a novelist or a player with toys. One can move the toys to do what one wants, but genuine response or action is absent. One can line up the toy soldiers, but they do not really fight or look to the general for guidance; one can race the Matchbox cars, but they are not competing.

Significant sovereignty between free persons, then, is more like a dance between two partners. They need not be equal in skill or ability, power or knowledge. They may be very, very different from each other. Yet each needs and chooses the other to perform the dance. In our case, it is the covenant dance of life. The key to the dance is God's desire to be in a covenant partnership with those he created. God invites us to be partners in the dance, to respond to his advances and to follow his lead. The dance occurs in the embrace of mutual love, where ideally the one partner willingly follows the lead of the other, seeking to emulate the leader, and where the God who takes the lead makes the partner beautiful for God's own glory. In creating a covenant, God desires an ongoing relationship of love, fellowship, and obedience in return for his salvific action. In the dance, the sovereign God responds to his created partner, not in the sense that the created controls God or vice versa, but that God truly respects and responds to the free choices and actions of the covenant partner, and in the relationship works out his plans in creation and specifically in humans to bring us by grace to himself. Since the valuer determines the good, and without a valuer there is no good, the sovereign's goal is to see that whatever happens is good, for the glory of God.

---

on middle knowledge God would allegedly know this. But no one, not even God, can say what my choice would have been. One might conjecture what I might have done based on my character or past choices when I actually went to Paris, but there is no ground for establishing what my choice would actually have been. To be part of God's knowledge, counterfactual conditionals of free will must be true. But they are not true because they do not correspond with anything that actually happens; as counterfactuals they describe events that never occur. Neither are they true because they follow necessarily from particular causal conditions, for this is inconsistent with their being about possible free choices or actions. Neither do they follow necessarily from my character, for character only influences but does not determine or necessitate actions. In short, God's knowledge of created persons is unlike that of the novelist, for counterfactual conditionals about free acts of possible persons lack grounds for being true and hence cannot be part of God's knowledge.

The journey

In what follows we will take providence as a central or core belief and organize concepts essentially related to it into a coherent whole. In the preface I likened our task to putting together a marvelous puzzle of many intricately cut pieces. We also can liken our task to undertaking a journey, adventure, and pilgrimage. We *journey* intellectually into understanding and appreciating the divine initiatives. We cannot remain static in our understanding of God's truths. God calls us to go "farther up and farther in." It is an *adventure*, for we do not know what twists and turns the path of understanding will take. It will lead into confusing thickets as well as to broad plains with sweeping vistas, steep hills to climb, and soaring peaks from which we can better view and appreciate the theological landscape. Exploring providence exudes excitement, for we discover that God manifests himself in all the corners of life in both expected and unexpected ways. He is the God of traditions as well as of novelty. As a *pilgrimage*, we seek in the end to discover, indeed, encounter the God who initiates his providence. Providence is not an end in itself, but one means by which God in love takes action to relate to us and to bring us to relate to him. God is the initiator, the agent, and the goal of providence. In his mercy he aims to bring us all to him and initiates caring actions. Providence establishes the covenant framework on which divine-human interaction builds. I hope that through this book the reader appreciates both the majestic properties of God and his love and concern for his creation as he seeks, loves, lures, persuades, incarnates, dies, and rises so that we might have a fuller life in relation to him and bring him the deserved praise of returned love.

Chapter 2

Providence and Freedom

PROVIDENCE IS ESSENTIALLY RELATIONAL. God's providential relationship with nature involves creation (bringing the world into existence), preservation (keeping the world in existence), and sustenance (bringing forth its potential goodness).[1] Nature points beyond itself and brings glory to God:

> The heavens declare the glory of God;
>> the skies proclaim the work of his hands.
> Day after day they pour forth speech;
>> night after night they display knowledge.
> They have no speech, they use no words;
>> no sound is heard from them.
> Yet their voice goes out into all the earth,
>> their words to the ends of the world. (Ps 19:1–4)

But nature, as magnificent and "noisy" as it is, cannot respond in any personal or morally responsible way to God. That is reserved for humans who, although embodied and embedded in nature, can respond to God with speech and action in love and adoration. God desires that we seek him with our whole being—mind, heart, emotions, and will. God wants us to be in covenant with him, not because we are compelled to do so but because that is what we deeply desire. God chooses, invites, calls, allures, persuades, even seduces us to respond to his solicitation to dance with him. For our covenant relationship to be meaningful to us and to God, our response must be free, for if it is coerced nothing is returned except what has been programmed into our being. Human freedom, then, is not the goal of God's creation, but a prerequisite for establishing the kind of partnering relationship and for becoming the moral creatures God wants. This chapter is about the freedom that is so essential to our being persons and to the possibility of our being in covenant relationship with our creator.

---

1. Helm, *Providence*, 22.

Freedom of choice and action

We can discuss human freedom in terms of both choice and action.[2] To say that we are free with respect to our *choices* means that, in a given set of circumstances, including all the causal conditions up to the time of choice, we (to put it in the past tense) could have chosen otherwise than we did. Causes either internal to ourselves over which we have no control (genetic structure, irresistible drives) or external (other human persons, God) did not compel us to choose as we did. Even if the obtaining causal conditions had been the same, we conceivably could have chosen to do otherwise than we did. Obviously particular causal conditions are present and necessary for us to choose. We must have the requisite neurological structure to consider the options, desires to motivate us, and a physical and psychological environment that presents us with options. But if we are free, these past and present conditions are not sufficient to cause us to choose one way or another. The fact that we can choose differently does not mean that it is likely or probable that we will do so. We recognize that we have causal influences that generally dispose us to choose in one way rather than another. These causal conditions operate with varying degrees of force or influence. In many cases we give ourselves up to our dispositions, since it is easier to function in this way rather than having to consciously deliberate about every choice. However, it is possible for us to resist or choose contrary to our dispositions. Further, many times we are not consciously aware of the reasons for choosing one way rather than another, though often we could supply reasons if we were asked to do so. Having reasons, whether or not they are good reasons or really are the reasons for the choice we made (we may be self-deceived about our reasons for choosing as we did), provides the possibility of constructing a rational basis for our choice. Acting from those reasons suggests that if those reasons were present and functional in an identical situation, and if we are rational, it is likely that we would choose as we did before. But neither dispositions nor reasons remove our freedom; when we are free ultimately the individual is the sufficient condition for the choice made. It is important to be clear: our claim concerns not the likelihood but the *possibility* of choosing otherwise. The primary cause of the choice is the agent: the agent has "the power to be the ultimate creator and sustainer of [his or her] own ends or purposes."[3]

When we understand freedom in terms of *actions*, we say that we are free when given the circumstances, including all the causal conditions

---

2. For an excellent collection of materials on human freedom, see Kane, *Oxford Handbook*. See also O'Connor, *Agents*.

3. Kane, "Rethinking Free Will," 381.

up to the time, we could have acted otherwise than we did. We were not compelled or prevented by causes either internal to ourselves over which we have no control (genetic structure, physical or mental limitations, or irresistible drives) or external (other human persons, God) to act as we did. Even if the causal conditions had been the same as obtained, it is possible that we acted otherwise than we did. Again, causal conditions are present and necessary for us to act. In any action, the physical environment, our physiological and psychological states, and our interactions with other persons are factors that significantly condition our actions. However, if we are free, these causal conditions are insufficient to cause us to act or to prevent us from acting in a particular way, although again they might predispose us to act in a certain way. It is important to be clear: the claim is not about likelihood but about possibility of acting otherwise. The conditions exercise considerable influence, often influences of which we are unaware, but when we are free the primary cause of the action is ourselves.

We might put this in another way. When we hold that we perform an act voluntarily or freely, several conditions must be met. First, the action results from our choices, and we choose to act in a certain way because of our wants, desires, and intentions over which we can exercise a measure of control. We intend to act or not act in a particular way. Second, something or someone other than ourselves does not compel or coerce our actions. The action is unforced, although not unconditioned.[4] Third, we could have acted differently than we did, given the circumstances or conditions present at the time.[5] Even if the causal conditions that obtain were the same as when we performed the action, the action we performed we could have not done. The first addresses the source of our choices and actions; the second the absence of determining causal conditions (and by inference the identification of ultimate responsibility), and the third the opportunities available to us.

Suppose a chocolate cookie rests on the table in front of me. If I am free, I can either choose to eat the cookie or choose not to eat it at the moment. Of course, certain conditions are present that will affect my choice: I must be aware of the cookie, I should like chocolate (although this need not

---

4. From this usually an inference about responsibility is drawn: We are ultimately responsible for our actions.

5. John Martin Fischer suggests that "there are two ways in which it might be true that one couldn't have done otherwise. In the first way, the actual sequence compels the agent to do what he does, so he couldn't have initiated an alternate sequence; in the second way, there is no actual-sequence compulsion, but the alternative sequence would prevent the agent from doing other than he actually does." "Responsibility and Control," 33. In the second case, I am not free if the contemporary causal conditions are such that I would be unable to do otherwise should I attempt to exercise the other option.

be the case; I might choose to eat it just so that my brother does not get it), I need to have a working mouth where my jaw is not wired shut to repair a break, and so on. But in those cases where I am free, although the cookie is present and I really like chocolate cookies, neither the mere presence of the cookie nor my liking of chocolate cookies causes or determines me or necessitates that I choose to or actually eat it. Exerting great will power I could have resisted. On the other hand, if there were something in my genetic constitution that made eating chocolate a compulsion (chocomania), such that the mere presence of a chocolate cookie was enough to cause me to eat it no matter what my resolution, then I would not be free with respect to eating the cookie. Similarly, if someone were stuffing it down my throat or threatening me to eat it or else, I would not be free.

Freedom of choice differs from freedom of action. I might have the freedom to choose without being able to act on that choice. For example, paralyzed persons might be free to choose what they want to eat for dinner, even though they cannot act on that choice. Someone has to feed them. Even non-paralyzed persons can face a similar situation; they might be given a menu to choose from in a restaurant, and once they have freely chosen the chicken pot pie the waitress informs them that the chicken pot pie they wanted is no longer available. The menu gave them choices, but their action on that choice was restricted. Usually, however, we combine the two: freedom of action manifests freedom of choice. Or consider the case where I decide to stay at home and work on this chapter rather than go to the bank. The decision to stay at home is free even though I could not have driven to the bank, for unbeknown to me the car I needed for the trip had a dead battery. In this case my choice to stay at home and work rather than go to the bank remains free because my choice did not involve actualizing the limiting condition.

It should be quite clear from the above account, first, that I am not describing or advocating a radical freedom where our choices are made and actions performed completely independent of causal conditions or reasons or where no restraints are placed on us. Freedom as we experience it is not the absence of influences or causal conditions that affect the choice or action, either external or internal. Liking and desiring chocolate would be a reason for choosing to eat chocolate cookies. Cookies must be present and I must have a digestive system in order for me to eat them. Rather, to be free means that the causal influences and reasons do not completely determine my choice or action. The fact that conditions always structure, limit, circumscribe, and facilitate our actions in one way or another but generally do not compel us to choose or act in a particular manner shows that in real life we are free in varying degrees. That is, in any circumstance we are more or less free to choose and free to act, depending on how and the degree to which the conditions affect our choices and actions. Understanding freedom in terms of degrees is important, for the freedom actually found in our experience is relative: since the freedom we exercise is conditioned, we experience varying degrees of freedom. But where we experience any freedom, we could have done other than we did, even though it might have been very difficult to do so (as it is for me to resist warm, homemade chocolate cookies).

Second, to view our choices and actions in terms of degrees of freedom does not mean that our choices are arbitrary or that the acts we perform result from chance.[6] Usually we can give reasons for the choices we make and the actions we take. These reasons vary in soundness, rationality, and accuracy, but are reasons nonetheless. These reasons might include ends we desire to achieve. For example, to fill my car with gasoline would be a reason for turning right at the freeway exit and proceeding to the gas station. Reasons can also include a person's likes and dislikes. For instance, I ordered tilapia at the local restaurant because I prefer fish over beef. Liking fish did not compel me to order it; I could have ordered chicken or even beef. But my preferences factored in and may have strongly influenced what I ordered. Free persons can accept reasons that are sound and rationally persuasive, they can reject the most telling reasons and choose according to others, or they can give the most inane or irrelevant reasons (rationalizations) for their action. In fact, at times we fabricate or construct reasons to suit what we have already chosen or done.[7] Whether the reasons are good or bad, simple or complex, accurate or falsely constructed, we usually are able to explain our choices and actions if requested to do so. Even rationalizations

---

6. Freedom is not quantum indeterminacy, although some attempt to make this connection, for this would make a particular free choice or action random in the sense of being only statistically probable. For a discussion of how quantum physics might bear on the issue, see Hodgson, "Quantum Physics," 57–83.

7. Experimenters showed pairs of pictures of female faces to 120 participants, from which the participants were to choose which face they found more attractive. After fifteen such choices, they were shown some of the face cards they selected and asked to verbally give the reasons for choosing the face they did. Unbeknown to the subjects, the experimenters switched some of the rejected faces for the chosen ones. Only 13 percent of the switches were detected. In the undetected cases the subjects gave reasons for the choices, reasons that had to be fabricated since the picture shown and for which they were to give reasons was not the one they chose. Johansson, "Failure to Detect Mismatches," 116–19. However, that we later on fabricate reasons does not show that we did not have reasons, even cogent ones, at the time. In the experimental case, it is possible that the subjects forgot those reasons, particularly in the absence of the paired face card.

are attempts to provide reasons for action. Free choices and actions, then, are not arbitrary simply because they are made freely.

Indeed, the very presence and adherence to reasons helps account for the consistency of our free actions. They help make our actions understandable to ourselves, often reasonable, and able to be communicated meaningfully to others. But being reasonable is not contrary to being free to choose or act. Both reasons and causes are consonant with voluntary acts, so long as they are not totally conditioning but leave us with the ability to choose between reasons or options or to take different courses of action even with the presence of the same reasons (we can act non-rationally or irrationally). Again, it is possibility, not likelihood, that is in view.

Third, an action can be voluntary and intentional even though limiting or facilitating conditions exist of which we may not be aware. In choosing to act often we are aware to some degree of the facts of the case and the general principles that apply. We consider some of the conditions that are present and the options available to us. However, we need not be aware of all or even of many of the causal conditions that operate and that affect or condition our choices. Indeed, rarely if ever are we aware of all or many of the operative conditions that affect our choices and actions. But although many of the causal conditions might be unknown to us, our act would still be termed voluntary where we have significant knowledge regarding the choice so that we can do something of what we want and we could have done otherwise. We act, not despite these conditions, but often because of or through them, for they make our choices and actions possible.

This point about our knowledge of the causes, however, implies that there may be times when we may think that we are free when we are not. We may believe that we have freedom of choice and action but actually do not because causal conditions unknown to us compel us to choose or act in particular ways. People suffering from mental illnesses such as schizophrenia or dementia can fall into this category, but so might people not so afflicted. We may believe that we have a greater degree of self-knowledge than we actually have. We will return to the significance of this in the next section.

In short, we are free to some extent in many of our choices and actions, although both of these are constrained and enabled by conditions, some of which we know and others of which we are ignorant. Our choices and actions are free when our actions result from our choices and we choose to act in a particular way because of our wants or desires, when our actions are not compelled or coerced by something or someone other than ourselves but rather we have ultimate responsibility for them, and when we could have acted differently, given the internal and external circumstances or conditions present at the time.[8]

Evidence for human freedom

At least two kinds of evidence support this view of human freedom. On the one hand, we have universal, introspective, experiential evidence. We feel that in our daily lives and activities we have real choices—I could have chosen to play racquetball today rather than work on this chapter; I could have put slices of ham rather than turkey into my sandwich; I could have disregarded the mechanic's advice to install new front wheel bearings in my car. But choice makes sense only if we can meaningfully select between the options, if we could have chosen or acted differently than in fact we did, given the circumstances in place. It is possible, of course, that we are wrong or deluded when we think that we could have chosen or done otherwise than we did. We might think that we have a real choice between options when in reality we do not. We might be in error about our introspective evidence regarding whether we could have performed differently than we did, given the extant causal conditions, when in fact we could not have done so. Simply put, what seems to be the case might not really be the case. It is difficult to validate introspective evidence. We cannot introduce as evidence what would have happened had we not chosen or acted as we did or had we chosen and acted differently, since we cannot in any possible way establish what would have happened had we not chosen or acted as we did or chosen differently. The counterfactual situation does not obtain: what allegedly would have happened did not happen. And what does not happen provides no evidence that it would have happened and that we are free. Yet, the best explanation of these daily experiences of choice and action is that we really are to some degree free, that we really have meaningful choices between options, and that although we are bombarded by numerous external

---

8. Joshua Knobe and Shaun Nichols suggest that how we understand freedom ties to how we understand our self, and that understanding is complex. We might understand the self from a bodily point of view; if one asks who built the tool shed, I can reply that I did it—as an embodied person, and that I as an embodied self did it as a physical being. We also entertain a psychological conception of the self, where our psychological features—memories, desires, beliefs—constitute the self. Here our free choices emerge from ourselves insofar as they reflect our desires and beliefs. A third concept, the executive conception of the self, focuses on the agent that has some control over both bodily and psychological processes. The agent or person, who takes into account his beliefs, desires, hopes, and so on, is the ultimate chooser, decision-maker, or doer. Persons are more than the interaction of their physical and psychological states. "Free Will," 536–41. We will explore this further in the next chapter.

and internal features that influence us to choose or act in a particular way, ultimately in the vast majority of cases it is we who make the decision to act as we do.

Keith Lehrer argues that there is reason to doubt this skepticism about being able to present evidence for counterfactuals of free choice.[9] To this end he presents an inductive argument to show that we can provide empirical evidence to support the claim that we could have acted differently. Lehrer first suggests four epistemic conditions that, if satisfied, will provide the requisite empirical evidence for the contention that someone can do something even though we do not see the person do it. These conditions are temporal propinquity, circumstantial variety, agent similarity, and simple frequency. Regarding the first, if we saw the person do A at time t, we have reason to believe the person can do A at t_1 if t and t_1 are close to each other. Generally, although not always (for example, rerunning a marathon three hours later), the closer together the two times are, the more likely it is that the person also can do A at t_1. Regarding the second, if we see a person doing A in diverse circumstances, we have reason to believe the person can do A in other like circumstances. Regarding the third, if the person has not changed significantly from what the person was like at t and we saw the person do A at t, we have good reason to think the person can do A at t_1 as well. Finally, the more frequently we see a person do A, the more we are justified in believing that the person can do A when we do not observe the person. Given these conditions, we have empirical reason to believe a person can perform an action when we are not present or do not see the person doing it. And since "can" is a form of "could," we have empirical evidence that a person could do otherwise, even if we are not present or even if we are present but the person does not do it. The fact that the person does not perform an action that we expect in other circumstances does not provide evidence that the person cannot do it. If we have reason to think that the person did not try to do an action, and if the conditions warrant the judgment that the circumstances are favorable to doing the action, then the failure of the action to occur does not support the hypothesis that the person cannot do it. In this way we have inductive reasons to think that the person could have done otherwise.

It would seem that if Lehrer is correct, we have good inductive evidence against causal determinism and in support of a libertarian view of human freedom. However, Lehrer denies this. He writes, "But this evidence hardly seems sufficient to justify the hypothesis that his behavior was not causally determined! To put the matter another way, the experimental evidence that

---

9. Lehrer, "Empirical Disproof?" 172–95.

renders highly probable the hypothesis that the subject could have done otherwise fails to render highly probable the hypothesis that his behavior was not causally determined. This fact provides the basis for a proof that the statement that a person could have done otherwise is consistent with the statement that his behavior was causally determined."[10] Lehrer is correct that the evidence doesn't establish anything about the causes because it does not talk about the causes, only about the effects; all we have are reasons to think the person can do or repeat an action even when we are not present. But the determinist and indeterminist (libertarian) theses contain references to the causal conditions. Thus, it seems that Lehrer's argument is irrelevant to the issue of causal indeterminism and freedom.

Lehrer, however, continues. If the evidence E renders it probable that O (the person could have done otherwise), but establishes no probability with respect to the causal indeterminism of the event (non-D), then E does not make non-D probable. From this he concludes that O is logically consistent with D (the event was causally determined). That is, being able to do otherwise does not count against causal determinism.

But the reason that it establishes no probability with respect to the causal indeterminism of the event is simply that it is silent on the causal aspect. This can be seen from the fact that the evidence E also establishes no probability with respect to the causal determinism of the event (D). It establishes no probability at all with respect to either D or non-D because it does not address or take into consideration the causal conditions at all.

How does Lehrer understand determinism? Determinism holds that all of our actions are caused, indeed, ancestrally caused in that the determinative causal chain for any action extends prior even to our birth. And

> to say that something is caused does entail that what happened could not have happened otherwise. For example, if a brick has been dropped from a fifty-story building and there is nothing to prevent it from falling toward the ground, it is surely the case that certain natural forces will cause the brick to fall toward the ground, and it is surely also the case, not only that the brick will not do otherwise, but also that it could not do otherwise. Moreover, the example will not be altered in any relevant respect if we substitute a man for a brick.[11]

Consequently, "something is causally determined if and only if it is causally impossible for it not to happen," which is the thesis of determinism. What Lehrer does is differentiate the "could" related to free will from the

10. Ibid., 192–93.
11. Ibid., 184.

"could" of causal determinism, and then inquire whether one can affirm the first "could" of free will and at the same time the "could not" of causal determinism.

But both the libertarian and the determinist reject the notion that these present two different senses of "could." The libertarian holds not simply that the free person could have done otherwise, but that the person could have done otherwise *given the same causal conditions*. In effect, the libertarian agrees with the determinist in affirming that a free person can do otherwise. Where they disagree has to do with whether doing otherwise is possible given a particular set of causal conditions. If, as the determinist holds, the causal conditions necessitate an action, then it simply follows for the determinist that the person (causally) could not have done otherwise given the extant causal conditions. Hence, the person is not free; freedom is an illusion. The libertarian, on the other hand, holds that the causes condition but do not determine an action, such that the person when free (causally) could have done otherwise given the extant causal conditions. In effect, we cannot separate the two senses of "could," as Lehrer does. The sense of "could" relevant to freedom for both the determinist and the libertarian invokes the role or relevance of causal conditions. Accordingly, if Lehrer's evidence has a causal condition, it provides evidence against determinism. If Lehrer's evidence says nothing about causal conditions (which is his position), then it is irrelevant to the question asked by the libertarian whether there is evidence for a libertarian as over against a determinist view of freedom. And coincidentally, it does not commit the determinist to holding that a person could do otherwise in the sense relevant to freedom. (We will return to consider the compatibilist position, of which Lehrer provides an example, later in the chapter.)

The other kind of evidence is more philosophical. Someone who read a draft of this chapter said to me that, yes, we have "cookie freedom," but when it comes to important things, we have no such freedom. Yet this cannot be farther from the truth, for freedom touches essential dimensions of our being. Persons are essentially capable of performing actions that are right or wrong (what we term morally significant actions), actions for which they can be held morally accountable or for which they are especially morally praiseworthy. But if persons are to be held morally accountable or are especially morally praiseworthy for their actions, they must have been able to have acted differently. If persons are to be held accountable for stealing, it must have been possible for them not to steal under those circumstances. If persons are to be praised for contributing to the poor, it must have been possible for them not to have contributed. Put generally, to be able to act morally requires that we could have acted differently, that is, we must to some extent be free. We have already noted that our freedom comes in degrees. Correspondingly, moral accountability varies by degree. In part we hold people morally accountable in respect to the degree that they are free to choose or to act.

Moral responsibility disappears if our choices are compelled or coerced. We cannot be morally accountable if an action taken by another person—human or divine—compels us to think, will, or act in a certain manner. In such cases we are not truly agents and hence cannot truly be morally responsible or praiseworthy. Likewise, if our internal features—drives, mental illness, or neuronal network—leave us without choices, we cannot be held morally accountable or praiseworthy. For example, some schizophrenics suffer from hallucinations but are unable to understand them for what they are; instead they form beliefs, make choices, and take actions on these experiences. Having no voluntary control over their actions, they are not free. Their beliefs, choices, and actions are determined by their neurophysiology, and although we hold them responsible for their actions since they did them, we do not hold them morally accountable for what they do. The treatment prescribed for such persons differs radically from the treatment prescribed for those who would do the same actions but are morally accountable for their actions. With people so determined by their physiology, we want to cure, not blame or punish.

A related field bears out this differential approach to moral behavior. The law makes distinctions between murder (where intentions play a critical role and the person could have acted differently) and manslaughter (where some critically relevant factors were beyond the person's control, as when a driver cannot avoid hitting a child who suddenly darts out from between parked cars). We also invoke the insanity plea to excuse persons who commit murder. That they committed the act is not in question. What is in doubt is whether they did so freely or whether their psychological or neurological state was such that they could not have done other than they did. The rarity with which we allow this plea in courts testifies to our belief that fundamentally most of us to some degree or another generally are free and hence morally responsible for our actions.

Freedom and Scripture

Scripture does not discuss human freedom *per se* (although it does discuss freedom in relation to other aspects of our lives, for example, in relation to the law and to sin). But instances of posed choices that presuppose the ability to have chosen and done otherwise permeate Scripture. This theme appears in the beginning stories of Genesis. In the story of the fall from innocence God presents Adam with a definite choice: "You are free to eat from any tree in the garden, but you must not eat from the tree of the knowledge of good and evil" (Gen 2:16–17). Although the serpent influenced Eve, who also knew of the restriction (Gen 3:2–3), still they had the choice: they could eat or not eat of the forbidden fruit. And when they ate, they were held morally accountable for their action: "Because you listened to your wife and ate from the tree," Adam is told, he would toil working the ground (3:17).

In the story of his farewell address Moses presents choices to the Israelites.

> Now what I am commanding you today is not too difficult for you or beyond your reach. It is not up in heaven, . . . nor is it beyond the sea. . . . See, I set before you today life and prosperity, death and destruction. For I command you today to love the LORD your God, to walk in obedience to him, and to keep his commands, decrees, and laws; then you will live and increase. (Deut 30:11–16)

Moses offers two options: life and death, prosperity and destruction; the choice is theirs. In his final speech concerning service Joshua repeats this theme. "Now fear the LORD and serve him with all faithfulness. . . . But if serving the LORD seems undesirable to you, then choose for yourselves this day whom you will serve, whether the gods your ancestors served beyond the River, or the gods of the Amorites. . . . But for me and my household, we will serve the LORD" (Josh 24:14–15). Joshua presents the Israelites with the choice to obey or not obey God's commands; whichever they chose, they could have done otherwise. Throughout the Old Testament, choice lies at the heart of the theme of Israel's rejection of God's covenant.

Some might suggest that these events are formulaic of a kairotic event, where the encounter with the offer is so compelling that in fact the Israelites had no choice in the matter. They could not help but agree to choose to serve God. But even as significant kairotic events that seemingly overpowered choice, it does not follow that they had no choice. It might not have been likely at the moments when the challenges were posed that the Israelites would have chosen other than God, given the significant nature of the event in question and the powerful personality of the poser. But from that it does not follow that they lacked the possibility of choice, as evidenced by the choices that they subsequently made—Joshua is followed by Judges.

An excellent example of freedom is presented in Ezekiel 33. The prophet speaks of the choices available to the watchman either to blow or not to blow the warning trumpet when he sees the enemy approach. Similarly, the citizen has the choice to heed the warning or not if the watchman blows his warning trumpet. Each, the watchman and the citizen, has the choice between options, of doing one action when they could have done the other. Moreover, this choice has great significance, for in case the citizen is killed moral accountability accrues to the watchman or to the citizen depending on their choices.

> If anyone hears the trumpet but does not take warning and the sword comes and takes his life, his blood will be on his own head.... If he had taken warning, he would have saved himself. But if the watchman sees the sword coming and does not blow the trumpet to warn the people and the sword comes and takes the life of one of them, that man will be taken away because of his sin, but I will hold the watchman accountable for his blood. (33:4–6)

Jesus too presents numerous options: he sketches out choices between how to and not to worship at the altar, how to or not to take oaths, whether or not to take revenge or to love our enemies, and to take the broad or narrow way (Matt 5–7). These commands to obey, believe, choose, love, think, and walk, and the rewards promised for right choices and sanctions imposed on improper belief and conduct make sense only if humans have freedom to choose between morally significant options, so that in the given circumstances we can truly do one or the other. God places before us his obligations and at the same time created us free to accept or reject them.

It is important to see that although God does not want us to reject him and his commands, throughout history people have done this. God "wants all people to be saved and to come to a knowledge of the truth" (1 Tim 2:4). Yet the history of Israel and subsequent peoples is one of rejection of God as much as acceptance. Israel is unfaithful. "Let her remove the adulterous look from her face and the unfaithfulness from between her breasts" (Hos 2:2). Despite God's love, they turn to other gods. "There is no faithfulness, no love, no acknowledgement of God in the land. There is only cursing, lying and murder, stealing and adultery" (Hos 4:1–2). Jesus mourns over those who reject him. "Jerusalem, Jerusalem, you who kill the prophets and stone those sent to you, how often I have longed to gather your children together, as a hen gathers her chicks under her wings, and you were not willing" (Matt 23:37). Jesus offers the rich young man a choice: "If you want to be perfect, go, sell your possessions and give to the poor.... Then come, follow me," and is disappointed when the young man "went away sad, because he had great wealth" (Matt 19:21). The young man had a choice between two options and, considering his desires and his possessions, chose not to follow Jesus, although he could have followed him. Jesus invites Saul to cease his persecution of the believers and change his life. "Saul, Saul, why do you persecute me? . . . I am Jesus, whom you are persecuting. . . . Now get up and go into the city, and you will be told what you must do" (Acts 9:4–6). Saul has a choice and, contrary to action taken by the rich young man, became a follower, although again he could have done otherwise (at the same time it should be noted that the temporary blindness Saul suffered provided a powerful incentive to choose one way over another). "God stakes the odds against himself in favor of human freedom, and the very fact that the Bible includes Job, with its powerful arguments against God's injustice, underscores that pattern."[12]

We need not multiply endlessly the scriptural instances of choices between options, where persons apparently can meaningfully choose and do other than they choose or do, or where the commands are such that we are given options. Our choices are meaningful because the options presented to us are real options, and they are significant, for at times the consequences of what we choose to do are life-changing. Our choices are not predetermined or causally determined; often we are asked to choose contrary to our previous desires, to repent, mend our ways, move in a new direction, and change our dispositions and tendencies. Sometimes we fail in this regard; at other times we change our desires to take on new paths of behavior.

Foreordination and freedom

We recognize that while human freedom permeates Scripture in the structure of posed choices between options where people could do one or the other, given their conditions and circumstances, and that the Christian Scriptures as religious texts often see these choices as morally and religiously significant in expressing moral and spiritual accountability in response to God and God's laws and commandments, a few Scriptures present an apparently contrasting aspect of divine initiative that must be addressed. These Scriptures suggest that God foreordains events and selects (or predestines) persons and nations according to God's will for some specific purpose.[13] At the outset it is important to distinguish between plans and foreordination. Isaiah describes God as having plans—the freeing of Israel from Assyria (Isa

---

12. Yancey, *Bible Jesus Read*, 10.

13. Millard J. Erickson distinguishes between predestination and foreordination. Foreordain is the broader term, used to "refer to God's decisions with respect to any matters within the realm of cosmic history. 'Predestination' will be reserved for the matter of eternal salvation or condemnation." *Christian Theology*, 373.

14:26), terrifying the nations on behalf of Judah (Isa 19:17), the building of a reservoir (Isa 22:11–12), the destruction of cities (Isa 37:26), to "summon a bird of prey" (Isa 46:10), and plans that we do not know about (Isa 5:19). Other writers speak of plans for punishing those who depart from the covenant (Zech 1:6) and for setting national boundaries (Acts 17:26). It is perfectly in line with conceiving of God as personal and as acting providentially while granting freedom to us to believe that God has plans and acts intentionally to implement them.

Language about divine plans is consistent with the libertarian view of freedom developed above. In each of these (and other) passages the plans referred to are what God proposes and intends to carry out. "I planned it and now have brought it to pass" (Isa 37:26). This in no way entails that all events are foreordained, only that God intends to do some very general and, at times, very specific things, and that he has the power to bring these about, frequently in conjunction with and through the cooperation of persons. Since God's plans involve persons, persons significantly contribute to the plans in diverse ways. Sometimes persons contribute positively to facilitate God's plan, as King Nebuchadnezzar played a role in God's judgment of idolatrous Judah by capturing Jerusalem and forcibly transporting the captured inhabitants to distant Babylon. Sometimes persons work against God's plans, and God has to adapt his plans (Balaam and his donkey, Num 22–24) or initiate one of the options that he indicated might happen when wrong choices are exercised (God predicted that contrary to his desires and plan for Israel, Israel would turn to apostasy, "forsake [him] and break the covenant [he] made with them" [Deut 31:16]).

Scripture also asserts that whatever God has planned will come about. "For the LORD Almighty has purposed, and who can thwart him? His hand is stretched out, and who can turn it back?" (Isa 14:27. See also Job 42:2: "No purpose of yours can be thwarted."). No individuals such as Pharaoh or nations such as Egypt or Assyria can ultimately stand up against God. "Many are the plans in a human heart, but it is the LORD's purpose that prevails" (Prov 19:21; see 20:30).

Yet, as we already noted, people do frustrate divine plans. God planned to build a great nation out of the exiles from Egypt, but when he saw their unfaithfulness in the desert he told Moses that he would destroy the exiles and start anew with Moses (Exod 32:9–10; Num 14:11–12). Moses, however, successfully interceded twice with the Lord to talk him out of abandoning the recalcitrant Israelites. God intended that the emancipated Israelites march victoriously into the fruitful land promised to them, but upon their rebellion on hearing the mixed report of the spies God changed the plan so that only Joshua and Caleb among those adults who left Egypt would enter the new land (Num 14:20–31). God planned that he himself would be the king of theocratic Israel yet yielded to the Israelite leaders' request to have a human king to lead them "'as all the other nations have'" (1 Sam 8:4–5). God selected reluctant Saul to be the king, with his family inheriting the role in perpetuity, but impetuous Saul did not turn out as expected. He failed in delivering Israel from the warring Philistines (1 Sam 9:16) and took up a wrongful role in offering sacrifices to the Lord (1 Sam 13:9), so that despite his pleas God took the kingdom from him (13:13–14). Even during Jesus' ministry, in rejecting John's baptism "the Pharisees and experts in the law rejected God's purpose for themselves" (Luke 7:30).

With this conflicting data we can conclude that, on the one hand, God's plans are malleable. They are conditioned upon the responses of the people with whom God deals, so that in the short run God's purposes face challenges to which God adapts in realizing his ultimate purpose of calling people to himself. On the other hand, the promise remains that God will realize in one way or another his overall purposes and plans. As Paul notes, God's plans and their realization are mysteries that God gradually reveals to us (Eph 3:2–6).

But the Bible contains passages that present a stronger view of God's planning than that found in the previous passages. The relevant themes emerge especially in Acts, Ephesians, and Romans.[14] The writer of Acts records Peter's speech in which Peter affirms that "This man was handed over to you by God's deliberate plan and foreknowledge, and you, with the help of wicked men, put him to death by nailing him to the cross" (Acts 2:23). Here foreknowledge is involved in the plan, although its precise connection with and role in the plan is left unspecified. Peter prays, affirming that Herod and Pontius Pilate "did what your power and will had decided beforehand should happen" (Acts 4:28). Peter affirms a relation between power and will, "will" presumably addressing God's deciding whereas "power" concerns God's ability to carry out what God wills. Acts also addresses God's selection of individuals to be saved; at Peter's preaching, "the gentiles . . . were glad and honored the word of the Lord; and all who were appointed for eternal life believed" (Acts 13:48). Whereas God appointed those saved, they were glad, honored the word of the Lord, and believed. Appointment is coupled with human voluntary action. All three passages in Acts indicate collaboration between a divine plan that is deliberate and appointing and human choice and action. God handed Jesus over, but the Jews who rejected him, Herod and Pilate who condemned him, and the Roman soldiers who nailed

---

14. But see also Ps 139:16: "All the days ordained for me were written in your book before one of them came to be"; and Isa 37:26: "Long ago I ordained it, in days of old I planned it, now I have brought it to pass."

him to the cross determined the details of his death. God appointed people to be saved, but the people gladly and freely believed. The events "fit into the boundaries of what God willed."[15]

Two other extended passages flesh out the themes of foreknowing, choosing, predestination, plan, and purpose. Ephesians 1 has an interesting structure. Besides being an extremely long and convoluted sentence, verses 3–14 develop key themes in parallel. God chose us, predestined us, and had a plan for all things. We might put it this way.

> God's action: chose individuals (4), predestined individuals (5), purposed or had a plan to be put into effect at the right time (9)
>
> Medium of God's action: chosen in Christ (4), adopted through Christ (5), purposed and realized in Christ (9)
>
> Purpose: to make us holy and blameless before God (4), to adopt us as children and heirs (5), to unite everything in the universe under the authority of Christ (10)
>
> Ultimate purpose: for the praise of God's grace and the glory of God (6, 12, 14)
>
> When did this take place? before the foundation of the earth (4)
>
> How did this take place? according to (the pleasure of) God's will (5 & 9)

The summation occurs in 11: we are chosen or predestined according to the plan of God, who acts to achieve his purposes, and are allotted a destiny, to bring praise to the glory of God. This all occurs in, through, by, and under Christ. Throughout the passage the emphasis rests on God's plan or purpose; it is God who takes the initiative to bring us to the place of redemption and forgiveness that God lavishes on us. "For it is by grace that you have been saved, through faith—and this not from yourselves, it is the gift of God—not by works, so that no one can boast" (2:8–9). God has plans, part of the mystery previously hidden but now revealed, to bless us in the ways mentioned above. What is unclear in this passage is the extent of these divine plans or purposes; do they encompass every human event or aspect of human life, or are they directed specifically to particular aspects of salvation history—redemption, forgiveness of sins, riches of grace, guaranteed inheritance—through which we are blessed? Is God's initiative generalizable even further to all events, including nonhuman ones? Since

---

15. Sanders, *God Who Risks*, 105.

the emphasis lies on "every spiritual blessing," we can suggest that the more limited interpretation provides the proper understanding: Ephesians 1 presents us with God's active role in salvation history: God chooses, predestines, and works out the redemption story and its application to us. There is no doubt that this is a strong, theologically deterministic passage relating to God's salvation-history.

At the same time, Paul recognizes human response. The chosen, having "put [their] hope in Christ," "were included in Christ when [they] heard the word of truth," and "when [they] believed ... were marked ... with a seal" (1:12–13). These are active verbs of human response to God's initiative of grace. Paul is thankful for the faith of his readers and for their "love for all the saints" (1:15). God's initiative calls for an appropriate response of belief and trust, faith and love.

The other passage is Romans 8:28—11:36. We do not have room to consider all the important but challenging themes Paul presents in this rich passage, but four themes relevant to our discussion of the nature of freedom demand our attention. First, Paul provides us with a nexus of justification concepts in what seems to be a logical sequence (Rom 8:28–30), bookended by God's calling (divine initiative) and our love of God (our free response). Those whom God foreknows (will love him) he predestines to be like the Son; these God calls, and the called God justifies; these in turn God glorifies. The sequence reflects God's initiating actions on our behalf. It begins with God's foreknowledge of us (a theme repeated in 1 Peter 1:2: "who have been chosen according to the foreknowledge of God the Father"; see also Rom 11:2).[16] The passage asserts that God employs foreknowledge, although precisely how Paul leaves unexplicated. If we treat "foreknowledge" in the sense of knowing ahead of time what will occur, this understanding leaves us with an unresolved tension, for here foreknowledge takes precedence as the basis for predestination, whereas in a subsequent passage Paul rules out God's foreknowledge of what we have done as providing a basis for divine selection. God's election or choice is not based on what Isaac and Ishmael (9:7–9) or Jacob and Esau did but solely on God's purpose (9:10–11). In effect, a tension clearly arises here. To resolve this tension, some commentators suggest that "foreknowledge" should be understood in an experiential sense of knowing beforehand. That is, God establishes personal contact with individuals or nations and in doing so predestines, calls, and elects them. So understood, commentators see no distinction between foreknowledge and

---

16. See also Rom 11:28, where God's love manifested in Israel's on-going election is grounded in the root of the olive tree, the patriarchs.

foreordination; the former in its breadth encompasses the latter.[17] But as Dunn admits,[18] this broad interpretation of foreknowledge relieves predestination of any real additional function in the verse. Why then does Paul use two terms? The response of those who reduce the two terms to one is that it is simply to emphasize the point of God's determination. The contrary response of others to the two terms is that, although the passage does not discuss the relationship between their respectively different roles, a difference exists, for establishing an experiential relationship requires the existence of both parties, something predestination does not demand. However one resolves this dilemma, although this passage commences with God's foreknowledge of our free return of love to him, Paul's clear emphasis is on God's actions on our behalf.

Second, we also hear of God's disappointment with the responses of some to his calling. People can repudiate God's calling and offer of a covenant relationship. By rejecting the Messiah, to which the law pointed, Israel rejected the righteousness that comes through faith in Christ in favor of trying to obtain righteousness through obeying the law (9:31–32; 10:3). Paul writes that they heard and understood the message of good news, but still resisted—all this despite God's waiting for them with open arms (Rom 10:21). God does not respond to human rejection with rejection; nothing can "separate us from the love of God that is in Christ Jesus our Lord" (8:39). God's call is irrevocable (11:29); he continues to love us. It was not God but Israel and their lack of faith that created the stumbling. They rejected God. Even though God foreknew that Israel would react as it did, God did not spurn them; grace remains available to them (11:2, 5–6). In spite of Israel's rejection, God's word (covenant with Israel) has not failed (9:6), for not only will an elect remnant be saved by grace (11:4–5), but the way has now been opened to the gentiles to enter by faith into the covenant community (11:11). Even human rejection fits into God's larger plan (9:23). Thus, although we might reject God, God finds ways to realize his ultimate purpose (9:6–9) of people being in covenant relationship with him. These ways, incorporating among other things sending preachers and preaching the message (10:12–15), will lead to the inclusion of the elect of Israel and

---

17. Bultmann, "προγινώσκω," 715.
18. Dunn, *Romans 1–8*, 482.

the Gentiles.[19] Yet, although many believe, many will be lost when they stumble over Christ.[20]

Third, God's purposes contain both compassionate acceptance and stern discipline (11:22), and both come at God's good pleasure or will. This is more clearly affirmed later, where some were hardened, blinded, and deafened (11:7–10). It is even theoretically possible that God created "objects of his wrath—prepared for destruction" (9:22), although here Paul does not expressly affirm that this hypothetical has been realized. But—and here is the difficult part—if it were, God cannot be held to account for either his gracious acceptance or his stern "preparation for destruction," for God as creator has the right to do what he wants with what he made—"to make out of the same lump of clay some pottery for noble purposes and some for common use" (9:21). This raises an important issue whether creators of something have the right to dispose of it as they wish. This issue applies to physical things (for example, do artists have the right to dispose of their works of art as they wish, including destroying them?), but more particularly and problematically to created conscious beings, for not only do we belong to God, but God has untethered us to be able to reflect God's love. Although we are made of earth, we are more than mere inanimate clay. By comparison, we cannot do to our progeny simply as we wish without being held to account. Does God face different moral standards or none at all?

But there is another side here. Although God brings judgment, mercy is demonstrated throughout (9:24–29; 11:32). Even those who were hardened and disobedient will receive mercy (11:30–32). Selection to disobedience leaves the door open to repentance and forgiveness. This testifies to God's grace amid his sternness (11:22). But many who stumble were not hardened or rejected by God but rather themselves rejected God. Although they faltered, their fall was not beyond recovery; hope remains, for they are accepted as bringing life out of death (11:11, 15). What is required is confession that Jesus is Lord and belief in his resurrection (10:9–13). Amazingly,

---

19. The contrast between the remnant in Israel and the reference to "all Israel" in Romans 11 has been the source of much commentary and theorizing, not the least between advocating particular and universal salvation and the problem of identifying "Israel" in 11:26. Some commentators suggest that "all" in "all Israel will be saved" (Rom 11:26) refers to the elect remnant. Others suggest that "all" should be understood as a group term rather than an inclusive universal term. "'All Israel' is a recurring expression in Jewish literature where it need not mean 'every Jew without a single exception, but Israel as a whole'" (Bruce, *Letter of Paul*, 209). Yet these interpretations clash with Paul's contention that since God has "bound everyone over to disobedience," he will show "mercy to all" (πάντας ἐλεήσῃ) (11:32).

20. Dunn, *Romans*, 581.

God gives even Assyria and Egypt hope after the desolation he pours on them.

> When they cry out to the LORD because of their oppressors, he will send them a savior and defender, and he will rescue them. ... They will turn to the LORD, and he will respond to their pleas and heal them. The Egyptians and Assyrians will worship together. In that day Israel will be the third along with Egypt and Assyria, a blessing on the earth. The LORD Almighty will bless them, saying, "Blessed be Egypt my people, Assyria my handiwork, and Israel my inheritance." (Isa 19:20–25)

Rejection,[21] acceptance, and restoration come from God, who both takes the initiative and also responds to people who believe and call.

Fourth, in contrast to the strong emphasis on divine selection of chapters 8 and 9, chapter 10 places an equally strong emphasis on faith and human response. "The word is near you, ... that is, the word of faith we are proclaiming: That if you confess with your mouth 'Jesus is Lord,' and believe in your heart that God raised him from the dead, you will be saved. ... 'Anyone who trusts in him will never be put to shame.' ... 'Everyone who calls on the name of the Lord will be saved'" (Rom 10: 8–9, 13). Free response lies at the heart of chapter 10: "Brothers and sisters, my heart's desire and prayer to God for the Israelites is that they may be saved" (Rom 10:1). We hear the message of invitation, of calling, to all. The theme here is that salvation is open to all who have faith and believe. Free response tempers election; all that is needed is that people call "on the name of the Lord." Belief requires not that God determine or cause our desires and intentions, but that we hear, understand, and respond. So, whereas God's calling can be rejected, God graciously offers it to all for their free response.

This discussion highlights several key biblical themes, all of which center around God's mercy and acceptance and the Christological focus that implements them. Foreknowing is paired with predestining. Divine choice or election is paired with human freedom of response of anyone to accept or reject. God's grafting and irrevocable call pairs with not persisting in unbelief. God desires acceptance of his overtures, but even rejection can fit into the larger plan of God creating and entering into covenant relations with everyone. God can create vessels "prepared for destruction," but

---

21. Paul does say that God rejects or, better, puts aside some (Rom 11:15), and the grounds are both that it may (note the hypothetical) stem from his "choosing to show his wrath and make his power known" (9:22) and also because of unbelief (11:20). But the putting aside (perhaps by hardening) is a temporary state, for not only the remnant and the ingrafted gentile branches but "all [regrafted?] Israel will be saved" (11:26–32) by the mercy of God.

even this is not irrevocable; confession and change towards reinstatement remain possible in a theology of hope and blessing; even the most dissolute can repent, engage in true worship, and transform by renewing their mind, intentionally fitting into God's will.

Compatibilist freedom

One way to absorb these texts in Acts, Ephesians, and Romans while holding on to freedom is called compatibilism or soft-determinism. This represents a view that many Christian theologians have held; the later Augustine, Thomas Aquinas, Martin Luther, and John Calvin espoused it, and it is alive and well in Catholic, Reformed, and Lutheran Christian traditions. Compatibilism is not only a theological position but is also commonly espoused in naturalistic philosophical circles. Compatibilists hold both that we are free and that we are causally determined: being free is compatible with being caused. Non-theological compatibilists affirm that the universe is deterministic, with the result that causes necessitate all events, including events that constitute our choices and our actions. They hold in consonance with classical physics that nothing happens without a determining cause.[22] Theological compatibilists hold that an omnipotent, omniscient, perfectly good God ultimately predetermines, foreordains, causes, or controls everything. God, as we noted above, is the potter, molding his creation clay as he sees fit to accomplish his own ends and purposes. At the same time, compatibilists affirm that we are free; we engage in voluntary actions and thereby are morally responsible for the voluntary choices we make and the actions that we perform. We are free so long as we are not *externally* compelled to act or prohibited from acting against our will. We are free, that is, if we can act on our desires: if we can do what we want to do. And when this is the case and when the action has moral significance, we are morally responsible for our actions. In short, for compatibilists we can both be caused to act and yet be able to act voluntarily.

Since all events are caused, our mental states, will, emotions, and desires are among what is caused. For the non-theological compatibilist, this results from the causal structure of the universe, whether its laws are necessary or probabilistic, normative or descriptive. For the theistic compatibilist

---

22. We will bypass discussion of the role that quantum physics plays in questioning the strict deterministic interpretation of the universe. In noting the quantum effects that operate on the subatomic level, although determinable within statistical frequency, quantum physics challenges any claim to total causal determinacy. See Bishop and Atmanspacher, "Causal Closure," 101–11.

this cause is God in the primary sense that God exercises control or sovereignty over all things. But God also uses secondary causes, the material structure of the created world exercising its causal powers. "[T]hese two sorts of cause are not in competition with each other. The primary cause is an enabling and sustaining cause, making possible secondary causes and setting bounds to them.... [T]he primary cause is not an event in time, as the secondary causes are, but is an eternal cause which has the whole of creation as its effect."[23] As Paul Helm writes, "Divine primary causation ensures the performance of the action of typing this page, from the point of view of the divine order, while my own causal power ensures the performance at the secondary level."[24] In effect, two sets of necessary and sufficient conditions, operating at different levels, serve to structure or cause my choices and actions.

God exercises his sovereignty in and through us in that he causes us to desire or to will to do something. In this way God ensures that moral agents do what he wants. "God ... ordains those factors which determine human free agency."[25] By God's predetermining or foreordaining actions God controls whatever we do, since we act from our wills and desires.

Although no external causes force us to act or prevent us from acting, since God infallibly foreordains or causes our wills and implants desires in us, and since our actions stem from what we want or desire to do, it follows that we cannot do anything except what God determines or ordains us to do. The causal stream goes from God to our desires to our acting on our desires. This has the consequence that for our actions there is a shared responsibility. With regard to moral actions, God is responsible in that he causes our desires, and we are morally responsible in that we act on our desires.

John Calvin affirms this very point. The fall of our first parents was no accident; it was not unexpected, but God predetermined it as part of his eternal plan. "For the first man fell because the Lord had judged it was so expedient; why he so judged is hidden from us. Yet it is certain that he so determined because he saw that thereby the glory of his name is duly revealed.... Accordingly, man falls according as God's providence ordains, but he falls by his own fault."[26] Not only did God foreordain the fall of our first parent, he also foreordained our own sins. God ordains and commands each event. "All events are governed by God's secret plan."[27] God regulates

---

23. Helm, *Providence*, 86.
24. Ibid., 178.
25. Ibid., 174.
26. Calvin, *Institutes*, III.23.8. See also III.23.4.
27. Ibid., I.16.2.

and directs the actions of each individual creature to the specific and proper end by his will, so that everyone's every action is disposed by each person's deliberate will, ultimately to achieve the divine purpose. Even inanimate objects are "directed by God's ever-present hand."[28] "'[T]he will of God is the necessity of things,' and . . . what he has willed will of necessity come to pass."[29]

It would seem that this view is deterministic, and whether it is natural causal determinism or supernatural determinism, our power over the future is removed. In effect, we have no freedom of action. For the compatibilist we have no power over the past and its conditions and over the laws of nature, and for the theological compatibilist no power over God. If we have no power over what determines us, and if what determines us causes or foreordains whatever happens, that is, if the line of causation extends prior to our existence, then it seems that we have no power over what those causes bring about. They are, as Calvin correctly sees, necessary. And if they are necessary and we have no power over what these determinants cause, namely, the future, what will happen necessarily will happen and we are not truly free.[30]

If this implication holds, this view raises some serious questions. If God foreordains us to sin and if God by his omnipotence is causally efficacious in bringing this about through our wills and desires, it is impossible for us to not sin. As Augustine put it, *non posse, non peccare*. But can the God who predetermined that we choose and act thus hold us morally accountable? To do so seems unjust, for it was God who foreordained what we choose and who caused our desires. If God foreordained or caused the desire out of which we act to do evil to further God's will, how can God be innocent and we be guilty? If our very passions and desires are directed by the secret inspiration of God,[31] if God operates on our minds, desires, and wills to direct our deliberations and endeavors as he pleases, so that these serve his foreordaining will, God is morally responsible for our choices and actions. God is equally, if not more or entirely, culpable for the evil we choose or perform.

Calvin demurs, for although we do evil according to God's determinate will, plan, and causation, we are not "serving God's will. For we shall not say that one who is motivated by an evil inclination, by only obeying his

---

28. Ibid.
29. Ibid., III.23.8, quoting Augustine, *On Genesis in the Literal Sense* V. I. xv. 26.
30. Ginet, "Might We Have," 87–104.
31. Calvin, *Institutes*, I.18.2.

own wicked desire, renders service to God at his bidding."[32] Sinners do not obey the will of God but only their own passions and thereby are culpable. Evildoers "serve his just ordinance by doing evil," but God knows how and intends to use this evil to do good. For Calvin and other theological compatibilists, moral accountability derives not from the cause of the action but from the character and will of the actor and the breaking of God's law. Since we are sinners in the eyes of God, whatever the cause of our sinful character, we rightly are subject to God's retributive justice because we *voluntarily* follow our evil desires and passions into evil ways. Of our own accord, we act wrongfully because we want to. In short, being necessitated by God and other causes is compatible with our moral accountability that is based on our voluntary action.

Calvin argues that we must distinguish between an act done out of necessity and one that is done under constraint or compulsion.[33] On the one hand, acting out of *necessity* (or its opposite, free will) refers to the causal structure of our acts. An act that is necessary has a sufficient causal antecedent, either in terms of a specific set of causal conditions or in terms of God's foreordination and continuing omnipotent intervention, whereas an act done out of free will has no such determining antecedents. Calvin rejects acting out of free will on the grounds that it would make our actions irrational. On the other hand, acting out of *constraint* (and its opposite, acting voluntarily) refers to whether we are able to do what we want. If I am acting against what I want or being prohibited from acting for what I want to do, I am acting under constraint or involuntarily. When I am able to do what I want, I act voluntarily.

For Calvin and compatibilists, the freedom moral accountability presupposes does not refer to the necessitating conditions of our action. It is not free will, the ability to do otherwise than we do, given a particular set of causal conditions. "Freedom is not an equal power to do or to think either good or evil, but merely that we are freed from compulsion."[34] Freedom deals with acting voluntarily. In those cases where we can be held morally accountable we must be able to act voluntarily, to act unconstrained and unrestrained by external forces operating on us against our will. To be free is not to be prevented from doing what we want to do. Thus, it is perfectly possible and actually the case for persons to be determined or act necessarily to do evil and yet be morally accountable for that evil because they did it voluntarily. To be free is not the contradictory of acting under necessity; it is

---

32. Ibid., I.17.5.
33. Ibid., II.3.5; II.5.1.
34. Ibid., II.2.6.

being able to do what one wants. And only for voluntary acts can we be held morally responsible, regardless of the causal conditioning.

Compatibilists want to restrict coercion to external conditioning. But coercion can be internal as well when it extends to our desires and wants. When something coerces our *actions*, we are prevented from doing anything other than it was determined by another that we do. When something coerces our *will*, we are prevented from making any choices other than those determined by persons or internal circumstances. We will what we must or are caused to will and cannot will otherwise. The causal conditions cannot be different from what they are, for their nature and order is either part of the total causal structure of nature or, for the theological compatibilist, part of God's predetermined plan. Restricting freedom to voluntary action fails to account for the deeper coercion that extends into the depths of our being and choosing. It is true that a free act is one that is done by an agent not acting under external constraint or restraint. But that is only *part* of freedom; what the compatibilist fails to recognize is that constraints can internally cause as well as restrict action. That over which we have no control can so cause our beliefs, desires, and intentions that we are unable to will in any fashion other than we do. This deeper constraint means that ultimately we cannot act in any way other than what God has sovereignly predetermined. God, not the individual person, is the ultimate causal source of choice and action. We contribute to the action by doing what we will, but ultimately it is the causal conditions that bring about the action. And the causal conditions make no reference to the persons themselves but to God, who is the ultimate or primary cause of all events.

Jonathan Edwards, defending the Calvinist view, replies that this is an uncommon use of "constraint" and "unable." To be unable to do what one wants presupposes that the agent already has a "present will or inclination to the things, with respect to which [he] is said to be unable."[35] That is, if persons are unable to do something, it means that they have already willed to do it and that circumstances have prevented or now prevent their acting on their choice. In this case it makes sense to say that the persons were not free. But to speak of persons as unable to make a decision other than they are determined to make does not presuppose that they have a "present will or inclination." Here, then, it does not make sense to say that the persons were not free, for there is no choice to be countermanded. Hence, whether their particular act of will was causally determined is irrelevant to their being unable to do the act. Whatever the source of the strongest motive, that motive or inclination will determine the action taken. Thus, for Edwards,

---

35. Edwards, *Freedom*, 1:4.

what is significant for determining issues of freedom and moral accountability is not the source of the volition or its causal status, but whether the persons were able to act in accord with their volition.

Now it is true that being unable to carry out our will is one sense of the word "unable." We are not free (to act) if we are unable to act on our choices because of some external constraint. However, there is another sense of the word that is also relevant to the freedom required for moral responsibility. We are not free (to choose) if we are unable to choose to do other than we did. We say, for example, that a person acting under the influence of strong drugs or hypnosis or who is insane is not free. By this we do not mean that these persons are externally restricted so that they cannot carry out their choices. Rather, we mean that they are in such a position that they are unable to will or choose other than they are determined to do by factors beyond their control. Their very desires lie beyond their control. As such, they cannot properly be held morally accountable for the acts that follow from these desires (even if their acts are not constrained by another person).[36]

To this Edwards might respond that such persons, although capable of actions that are either harmful or beneficial, are not moral agents, not because they are determined to act as they do by factors beyond their present control, but because they cannot be influenced by moral inducements. Their reason or understanding is so affected by drugs, insanity, or whatever that reason cannot guide their choice about what is morally proper or improper.

This response, however, will not work because of Edward's theory of motivation. Edwards holds that the strongest motive causes or determines the choice made (the act of the will). That is, persons always and necessarily act for what they deem good, that is, most agreeable or pleasing. It is not that persons evaluate their inducements or select between competing motives. If persons selected between motives, they would have to have a stronger or strongest motive according to which they would select, and if they in turn had to select this motive, this would lead to an infinite regress. Rather, the strongest motive determines the action chosen. Consequently, what causes the motive is what causes our choice, and this in turn causes our action. Persons, then, are determined to act as they do by whatever motive determines the volition.

---

36. This way of putting it is not entirely correct. It must be qualified to distinguish between persons who knowingly and willfully put themselves under the power of drugs and those who do not do so either knowingly or willingly. Although the former do not act freely at the time, they still are morally accountable for their actions because they freely and knowingly put themselves in that state. Freedom at the time of the act, then, might not be a necessary condition for moral accountability, although freedom understood in a broader time span, e.g., one that includes a historical relationship between a prior free act and the state out of which the agent acted, is necessary.

However, this has the devastating consequence of precluding moral agents. For Edwards, a moral agent is not only a being "capable of those actions that have a moral quality" and having a "moral faculty, or sense of moral good and evil," but also one who possesses a capacity "of being influenced in his actions by moral inducements or motives, exhibited to the view of understanding and reason, to engage in a conduct agreeable to the moral faculty."[37] But as we have seen, according to Edwards, moral agents do not consider the motives and choose which ones they will accept as determinative of their actions; reason does not guide choice but only registers it. Rather, actions necessarily follow from the strongest motive. That is, when it comes to the determining power of motives, reason and understanding are irrelevant; the strongest motive necessarily determines the act, whatever it is and whatever its source. But this means that Edwards assimilates being influenced by motives to being determined by them. If the influences are not the strongest, they are powerless to motivate action; if they are the strongest, the volition necessarily occurs as they dictate. The person has no say in the affair. But then there is no room for the self to be influenced in its actions by moral inducements and hence the self is not a moral agent.

Contrary to Edwards, the freedom necessitated by our concept of moral agency applies to more than simply our actions (where our action is voluntary when we can carry out what we have chosen to do). It also applies to our choices. Persons are free when they could have chosen to do otherwise than they did. The compatibilist fails to grapple with the very nature of choice. To choose means to select among alternatives what one is going to do. If that selection process is not genuine, there is no genuine choice. If no alternatives are available, there can be no choice, only the implementation in action. If the alternatives are apparent only, in that we (mistakenly) think there is more than one alternative available to us, we have only the illusion of choice, not genuine choice. It is not genuine because so long as we choose the possible, we can act on the choice. But if we choose the impossible, it becomes evident that although the choice in itself seemed to present a real choice in that we could have chosen other than we did, the choosing carries the aura of illusion, for being able to act on the choice was illusory in that at least one option could not have been realized. At least one option was not really an option. Choice implies that persons can select among genuine alternative courses of action, and persons are free when they are not necessitated, either by external or internal coercion, in their choices and actions.

We have already hinted at the further, significant theological or ethical problem that arises from compatibilism. While theological compatibilists

---

37. Edwards, *Freedom*, 1:5.

accept that God ordains and hence is responsible for the desires, they reject the claim that God is *morally* responsible or accountable. And well they might, for if we do evil, then not only would we be morally responsible for the evil that we perform from our desires, but God also would be morally responsible for the evil that we do, for it is God who ordained or caused the desires in us out of which we do evil. And if God ordains all things, God ordains our acts as well, good and evil. In effect, God would be morally co-responsible for all the moral (and natural) evil that is done in the world, something that would seriously compromise God's goodness. Theological compatibilists must hold that whereas God is responsible for foreordaining or causing our desires and thereby our actions, God is not *morally* responsible for the actions themselves. God is responsible, yes, but moral responsibility rests solely on us because we did the evil that we wanted to do.

But as Helm admits, "God so arranges and orders reality that whatever intention the creature has carries the divine intention in a wider context of meaning. ... [I]n some sense God causes the specific intention of Judas, and indeed of every lower level causal event."[38] How, then, can God escape moral accountability? Compatibilists suggest several responses.

First, God's "will is so much the highest rule of righteousness that whatever he wills, by the very fact that he wills it, must be considered righteousness."[39] We simply cannot hold God to any account because his reasons are his own. God is the potter; we the clay. Thus, God as the sovereign artist has the right and privilege to do as he pleases with the pots he makes (Rom. 9:22–24). The problem with this view is that any divine action or divinely commanded action must then be considered right because God willed or commanded it, which itself could turn out to be a morally reprehensible position. One way of escaping this is to suggest that God has two wills, a will for what God intends (what ought to happen) and a will for what God permits (what does happen).[40] But the appeal to dual wills does not resolve the difficulty, for both what God permits and what God intends fall under God's causal power. God could prevent what God permits (here, evil), such that whether or not God intends the evil, God as having control over everything has causal control over the evil that occurs, and hence since causality is a factor in moral responsibility, God has moral responsibility for what he permits as well as for what he intends. It is true that God does not prescribe that we should act to produce evil, but God has control over the

---

38. Helm, *Providence*, 181.
39. Calvin, *Institutes*, III.26.2.
40. Helm, *Providence*, 131.

desires out of which we necessarily act and hence could alter them by his divine initiative.

A second suggested solution is that God does not perform the evil; the person does. Hence God cannot be morally accountable for this action.[41] But this distinction does not free God from moral accountability, for God causes the desires and motives, and causation connects with accountability. If I intentionally cause an event, even indirectly, I am responsible for that event. Compatibilists attempt to separate internal causation from accountability, and in doing so have failed to understand the relation of accountability to internal causation. Suppose I had the power to manipulate a person's desires by giving him or her a particular drug. I could make the person irresistibly crave chocolate. Would I not be responsible for that person's choosing chocolate? Now there is nothing moral or immoral here, but suppose I could make that person irresistibly crave sexual relations with members of the opposite sex and this craving led to rape. Would not I as the cause of these irresistible desires necessitating the action thereby be morally accountable for them? Despite Calvin's protestations, it is undeniable that the ultimate moral responsibility would lie with me as the cause of the desires, especially if those desires were irresistible or necessitating. The very causal connection is sufficient to establish not only responsibility but, where the action is a moral action, moral accountability.

Put more generally, if our choices necessarily stem from our desires, and our desires are deterministically caused by another, then the other is responsible for both our choices and the actions that follow from them. If that selection process is not genuine in the sense that we have no control over our desires and will, there is no genuine choice. Our desires are causally determined, such that we really don't have options; they are only apparent. If the alternatives are apparent only, in that we mistakenly think there is more than one alternative available to us, we have only the illusion of choice, not genuine choice. Choice implies that persons can select among genuine alternative courses of action, and agents are free when they are not necessitated, either by external or internal coercion, in their choice and action. It seems inconsistent in this regard that compatibilists are willing to accord God praise for the good that results but not the evil. They do this on the ground that God does not intend evil but intends good.[42] But if God causes these desires in us that God knows will lead to evil, it is difficult to see that he does not intend this.

---

41. Ibid., 184.
42. Ibid., 190.

Third, the suggestion is made that since all things work for good, the evil that is done or suffered ultimately will work out for the greater good.[43] There is no such thing as gratuitous evil, evil for which there is no justifying greater good which it necessarily serves. Evil necessarily always serves the greater good.[44] However, though this is sometimes true, it seems very unlikely in each and every case; each of us knows too many evils that *prima facie* appear to serve no purpose in themselves. And it is just as wrong to justify the suffering of one person to benefit another (e.g., to help or encourage them to become more compassionate). This introduces the problem of evil, which we will take up in detail in chapter 9.

A final response is advanced by the apostle Paul himself: he simply rules out the question and the questioner. "But who are you, a mere human being, to talk back to God" (Rom 9:20). Calvin reiterates the same argument. "It is not fitting that God's will should be dragged down into controversy among us. . . . Let us not be ashamed, following Paul's example, to stop the mouths of the wicked, and whenever they dare to rail, repeat the same thing; 'Who are you, miserable men, to make accusation against God?' . . . Consider the narrowness of your mind, whether it can grasp what God has decreed with himself. . . . Ignorance that believes is better than rash knowledge."[45] Election, reprobation, and hardening are all in "God's hand and will, just as much as mercy is [Rom 9:14ff.]. And Paul does not . . . labor anxiously to make false excuses in God's defense; he only warns that it is unlawful for the clay to quarrel with its potter [Rom 9:20]."[46] Paul's and Calvin's response to those who question whether God can still hold us morally accountable is that those who are created should not argue with God, for the potter has the right to do what he wants with the clay, all for his own glory (Rom 9:19–26). As mere vessels created from and composed of earth we have no standing to query the Potter.

But this is either an *ad hominem* argument against the absent objector or a deeper argument to suggest that moral properties do not apply to God at all. The former fails to take seriously the objection; the latter more significantly and controversially affirms God's transcendence of moral properties. In either case, however, the counter argument is advanced in the second part of Genesis 18. Calvin misses that the writer of Genesis pictures Abraham querying God's justice and receiving a divine reply (Gen 18:20–28). We

---

43. Ibid., 184.
44. Ibid., 202.
45. Calvin, *Institutes*, III.23.5.
46. Ibid., III.23.1.

will consider in detail the second option—the propriety of ascribing moral properties to God—in chapter 4.

The compatibilist doctrine of freedom, then, will not suffice to account for moral responsibility. If we are to be free, not only must we be able to act according to our choices, but we must also be able to choose to act otherwise than we did. We need to have some control over our desires, motives, and will. External forces cannot compel us to choose or act as we do. Neither can internal forces, such as an inherited nature or the effects of a foreordaining God, compel or determine us to choose or act as we do. We must not be under complete causal compulsion, either external or internal, to choose or act in a given way. In short, persons are free if and only if, given a certain set of circumstances or causal conditions, persons could have chosen or done otherwise than they did and do not choose or act under coercion.

Again, this does not mean that no causal conditions operate on the agent. Nor does it mean that the agent will have no biases, dispositions, or tendencies to act in particular ways, or that desires and wants are conditioned. Freedom is not the absence of influences, either external or internal. Here Calvin, Augustine, and other theologians of compatibilist convictions are correct in their description of the freedom-removing aspects of sin. The more we sin, the more we are bound in slavery to sin. It creates a disposition or bias in us. And we often act out of this bias, for our biases form part of the causal conditions that influence our decisions. But although we do not act in our freedom from complete neutrality or from a dispositionless state, we still can act contrary to those dispositions and choose not to follow their leading. Aligning our dispositions and doing good might not be entirely in our individual power but might be part of the empowering general work of the Holy Spirit. But since we can resist the Holy Spirit, we have some power or control even here.

Return to Scripture

We have excellent philosophical reasons to reject compatibilism in favor of a libertarian or indeterminist view of human freedom. But what do we have to say to the scriptural passages noted above? This is not an easy question, for it presumes that a totally consistent, philosophically considered, and theologically vetted way of correlating all these scriptural themes can be constructed. Were this so, the long-running debates between libertarians and compatibilists, Calvinists and Armenians, Catholics and Protestants, would have been resolved and terminated long ago, to the peace and unity of all. Although Paul was not a philosopher, we will say something about these passages, nonetheless. Taking foreknowledge and predestination or election first, assuming that the terms "foreknowledge" and "predestination" have different meanings, we have seen that in Paul's order (Rom 8:29; 11:2; also 1 Pet 1:2), foreknowledge precedes predestination and election. If this reflects a logical ordering between independently-meaning concepts, selection and calling depend upon what God knows will happen, so that God has knowledge not only of the present (Rom 8:27) but also of the future. This coincides with a libertarian emphasis on freedom. Yet this presents only one side of Paul's story. He goes on to compare our election with God's selection of Israel, wherein God affirms that God did not select Israel because of its status or standing or what it would do. God chose Israel because he loved them and their patriarchs (Rom 11:28; Deut 4:37; 7:7–8). Similarly, God chose Jacob over Esau before either performed any action—which technically is consistent with foreknowledge—but more significantly, not because of anything good or bad that each of them would do (Rom 9:11–12). The selection was by God's own will for God's own glory and the showing of mercy (Rom 9:15): "It does not, therefore, depend on human desire or effort, but on God's mercy" (Rom 9:16). The upshot is that, while both foreknowledge and God's will are involved in God's salvific election, unless foreknowledge is reduced to or made synonymous with predestination, it is unclear precisely how scripturally both smoothly fit together in a way that satisfies Paul's conceptual structure. Foreknowledge, as truly knowing beforehand and not as predetermining, preserves freedom but conflicts with the contention that election is by grace alone and not based on human effort or actions (Rom 11:5–6). Predestination not grounded in foreknowledge but as independently determining protects workless election but conflicts with human freedom necessary for meaningful response.

Election is part of God's irrevocable action. God's love cannot be lost; nothing we, others, or circumstances can do can alter that love (Rom 8:35–39). God's love for us is abiding and unchanging; it is one thing of which we are assured. Yet, despite all that we are given (Rom 9:4–6), we can reject that love and attempt to pursue our own righteousness (Rom 9:30–32; 10:3, 16). Ultimately, God lovingly elects, but the choice to respond to it is ours. God calls us back into that love. We are invited to confess and believe, "For it is with your heart that you believe and are justified and it is with your mouth that you confess and are saved" (Rom 10:10). We are invited to take action, to make a response to the offer of mercy made to everyone. But history reveals both acceptance and rejection of that invitation. Both divine initiative and human response collaborate in the salvific dance.

When it comes to the matter of desires, Paul quotes Exodus to the effect that God hardened Pharaoh's heart. God stiffened his resolve to make him unyielding. "[T]o look for reasons for God's hardening in Pharaoh's 'evil dispositions' or previous self-hardening is a rationalizing expediency. . . . Such a thought clearly has no place in Paul's exposition and in fact contradicts what Paul has been so careful to stress in vv. 11 and 16."[47]

At the same time, nowhere in all this discussion does it arise that God determines *all* our desires, so that everything we choose and do is predetermined. Rather, God allows us to tailor and follow our desires (Rom 1:24-32). God ordains but allows for change on our part. Confession and repentance can lead to a change of our mind and a renewed pattern of life (Rom 12:1-2). This is not something that we can achieve simply on our own, by our own attempts at righteous deeds. Given who we are, Paul sees this attempt as a fruitless struggle (Rom 7:14-24). But through Jesus Christ, by the power of the Spirit, we can be set "free from the law of sin and death" to set our minds on what the Spirit desires for us to choose and do (Rom 8:2, 5).

The model for Paul is God's selection of Israel. Their calling was not the end of the story but only the beginning. They were chosen, not because of who they were, but because God loved them. But God's choice and the offering of the covenant to them called for a response of willing obedience. Whereas the calling of Israel was selective, one nation out of many to bless all nations, Paul now sees everyone, Jew and gentile, as called to be conformed to the image of Christ, heirs of the kingdom, and to lead holy lives. The calling is of God's mercy, and even though we are bound in sin, there is hope in the grace provided for us. Our freedom to affect our desires is not removed but enhanced when we attempt to live the life of the Spirit.[48]

What one can reasonably conclude is that with respect to theological and, in particular, salvific themes, Paul takes a compatibilist stance—advocating both human freedom and divine election. But he has no philosopher's

---

47. Dunn, *Romans 9-16*, 555.

48. "Paul is thinking solely in terms of salvation-history, of God's purpose for Israel. . . . A more extensive doctrine of election is not to be found here. Nor should the antithesis of v. 16 be overdrawn, as though Paul were advocating an ethical attitude of total passivity. He has already emphasized the believer's obedience and moral responsibility far too much for such a corollary to be possible (e.g., 1:5; 6:12-23; 8:13). The contrast too is limited to the point at hand and the alternatives posed are God's election on the one hand and Israel's widespread belief that their obedience to the law (whether in intention or in fact) was a factor in sustaining their covenant status before God. It is the latter which Paul disputes on the basis of Israel's own Scriptures dealing with their election. Beyond that we should not push Paul's argument at this stage. . . . It is the recognition that Paul refuses to be drawn into a discussion of the fairness or unfairness of God's judgment, and that he is intent on using Israel's history to illuminate God's purpose in salvation-history, which provides the key to the difficult verses 22-23/24." Ibid., 562-63, 566.

eye to resolving the conceptual difficulties of compatibilism. And most importantly, he has no desire to do so, for such an engagement would introduce something he rejects: the possibility of questioning the potter. His authoritative use of the Old Testament would not countenance that. What is unclear is the degree to which we can legitimately extrapolate or generalize from Paul's specific salvific concerns, presented within the Jewish context of his discussion, to advocate a robust view of either philosophical or theological compatibilism.[49] To espouse a philosophical compatibilism would require such an extensive extrapolation. We will have much more to say in chapters 4 about divine goodness and in 7 and 8 about foreknowledge and the difficult—some say intractable—issues it poses.

Conclusion

In what follows we will adopt the incompatibilist or libertarian view as best accounting for the freedom presupposed by moral responsibility. The philosophical and theological difficulties facing compatibilism are too great to reasonably overcome. From this it should be clear, however, that freedom is not given to us as a good in itself. God gives us freedom not simply so that we can choose; it is given so that we can choose rightly. We are created free so that we can be responsible moral agents who respond to God's invitation to covenant relationships and holy living. It is God's desire for our responsiveness to him that leads him to give us the freedom that we have. Without this freedom we would be programmed or caused to do what we do but would lack meaningful, moral responsiveness to God's invitation and solicitation. While God providentially seeks our good, the ultimate good is to glorify God and enjoy him forever. Glorifying and enjoying are mutually relational and presuppose God's freedom to invite us and our freedom to respond to his invitation, his commands, and his covenant. Unfortunately, in pursuing our own selves as gods we do not always desire God; we choose to separate ourselves from God. Fortunately, in his grace God always desires us; nothing can make God love us less.

---

49. See, for example, Dunn, who tempers the discussion of predestination by terming it "an in-house Jewish argument." Ibid., 555.

Chapter 3

Freedom and Agency

IN THE PREVIOUS CHAPTER I indicated that we have good reasons for holding to a libertarian view of freedom. I noted three features or conditions of a libertarian perspective: first, the action results from our choices, and we choose or intend to act in a particular way because of our wants, desires, and intentions. Second, something or someone other than ourselves does not compel or coerce our choices and actions. The action stemming from our choice is unforced, although not unconditioned. Third, we could have acted differently, given the circumstances or conditions present at the time. This does not mean that it is likely or probable that we would have acted otherwise, only that it is possible that we did so. Human behavior is predictable to a significant extent, but this is not inconsistent with particular actions being free to various degrees. That reasons can be given for choices and behavior, and that those reasons establish fairly consistent behavioral patterns, is consistent with human freedom. I also contended that neither a determinist nor a compatibilist view provides an adequate account of freedom and hence of moral responsibility because they fail in regard to at least one of these three features.

However, we are still not out of the woods, for the libertarian view of freedom faces particular difficulties when it comes to spelling out *how* humans can act freely in the world. That is, it is one thing to advocate for a libertarian view of freedom. It is quite another to lay out how libertarian freedom is possible. With regard to condition one, if our wants, desires, and intentions are rooted in our brain activity, and if our neural activity, as physical, is determined solely by physical causes, and these physical causes are part of causal chains that extend prior to our existence, what sense can be made of the claim that we have control over our desires and intentions? As physical events, neural actions are caused by prior physical causal conditions, so that it is the physical and not the mental (wants, desires, intentions) that brings about the action. While it appears that the events are "our" own, consciously chosen and rationally deliberated, in reality they are events resulting from complex physical causal chains that extend beyond and prior to us. If the libertarian model is to be believed to be true, it must provide an understanding of the ways in which the mental—our wants, desires, intentions—plays a significant factor in our behavior. With regard to condition two, how are we to understand "myself" as the decision maker and agent? Is "myself" my physical structure, rooted centrally in the brain? Are we solely the product of genetics and environmental input? If so, we are merely part of complex physical causal conditions, so that to talk about us making intentional choices is misleading. The "we" that initiates decision-making is merely rhetorical, a place-holder for complex neurological events. Under this scenario it is difficult to see how to escape physical causal determinism. With regard to condition three, how is it possible for us as psychophysical beings to act differently in a causally conditioned physical world? The mental is realized by the physical, and the physical is causally determined by precedent physical conditions. Whatever occurs in the physical realm has solely physical causes. If we are physical beings, then we fall under the physical causal chain. If effects follow necessarily from their causal conditions, how could something different occur given the same causal conditions? How, we need to ask, are human free choice and free action possible in a physical world out of which we are constructed and that we as physical beings inhabit?

Some suggest that we are more than physical beings; we have a spiritual dimension manifested in a spiritual substance. The existence in us of a spiritual substance, influenced and conditioned but undetermined by the physical, allows us to make free choices and take free actions. But that suggestion does not free us from the same difficulty, namely, of specifying *how* it is possible for the nonphysical to interact with the physical in ways that facilitate human free choice and action. The problem is not new; philosophers point to the lack of success that even the most notable dualists, including Descartes, have had in describing the mechanics of the process of physical-nonphysical interaction. In short, simply appealing to the spiritual or mental is insufficient to relieve us of the apparent need to posit an explanation for how we can be free; the ontological questions regarding how freedom can occur in a physical world inhabited by a non-physical or spiritual reality remain to be explored. In effect, the moral arguments for human freedom must be supplemented by reasoned ontological descriptions and accounts. Whereas deterministic and compatibilist accounts of freedom are more amenable to such accounts, for a libertarian view of freedom the challenge is significantly greater. If we are spiritual beings, how does the spiritual connect with the physical and how can one account for the overwhelming evidence of the causal role the physical brain plays in human cognitive functioning and decision making? If we are physical beings, how can the mental possess any causal role whatsoever, in bringing about either further mental processes or events or internal physical neural processes?

We have every indication that we (along with numerous other animals) possess both physical and mental properties. Our behavior and that of many animals exhibit the influences of perception, thought, recognition, classification or categorization, deliberation, memory, and choice. Like us, animals recognize members of their own family, their own species, their masters, and their enemies. They choose with whom to mate and remain mated, whom to defend, what to eat, and where to go, among much else. They have desires and feelings upon which they act. They engage in problem solving and in tool creation and use. They communicate in complex and intentional ways, and can even learn to communicate in languages not natural to them. Animals, such as dogs, elephants, and dolphins, whose brain mass as compared to expected body weight given their size exceeds the norm, manifest by their behavior higher levels of cognitive activity.

Furthermore, few deny that our mental properties or abilities arise in some way from or depend upon our physical properties. Neural activity in the brain is responsible not only for our mental abilities to perceive, think, learn, discriminate, choose, create, or will, but it roots particular perceptions, thoughts, memories, desires, and choices. Through fMRIs, we can correlate activity in particular cortical regions with specific mental processing. This correlation provides the basis for claims that although mental properties differ from physical properties, they depend for their existence and activity upon physical properties. Given the overwhelming correlative evidence that the brain is not only necessary but possibly, if not probably, sufficient for mental activity, the more controversial and challenging aspect concerns whether the mind has causal powers with respect to the physical world, not only on our own body but via it also on the world around us. What sense can be made of the claim that our thoughts, desires, and intentions affect the choices we make, and the choices affect the physical world, both outside and inside of us?

Consider, for example, worry. I might worry whether or not my child will survive a serious skiing accident, whether or not I will pass an important examination or interview, or whether a particular job will be offered to me. The brain not only makes it possible for me to worry, the very worry and the ideas associated with that particular concern are realized in the neural conditions in the brain. The worry may be linked with a particular memory of my own skiing accident, which is rooted in particular neurons in the spatial memory area of my brain.[1] But the worry, in turn, affects not

---

1. de Lavilléon, et al., "Explicit Memory."

only other ideas I might have or choices I might make (for example, leading me to pray that I will pass the examination), but also can affect my physical being. It can be effective in producing additional stomach acid leading to ulcers, headaches, or shortness of breath. So our question: how can I as a person be both physical and free, requires an answer to two other questions, who am I, and how can my mental life, including my free choices or will, affect or effect changes in the physical world?

Who am I?

At first sight it might be obvious who I am as a human being. We quickly and easily identify people with their bodily existence. When we see Susan across the room, we recognize that the envisaged human being is Susan, biologically different from other non-human things around her. Susan is "everything from the skin in,"[2] to whom we assign a name and who acts in the world with all of her physical and (presumed) mental qualities. She interacts with the world and with what is in it, including other beings, human and nonhuman, in multiply divergent ways. This is the *everyday, holistic view* of humans whom we encounter, observe, sense, and communicate with. This biological, behaviorist view is undoubtedly the most common approach we take to other human beings, distinguishing them from other beings or things.

At the same time, one might think that this view of human beings does not really get at the person or self that we are. We move from the concept of a human being to something more relational, that is, to the concept of a *person*. Here we note that some features "from the skin in" are more constitutive of the person than other things; these constitute our personal identity. We might term this the *identity view* of the self. It focuses on what is essential to making us the persons we are, giving us the identity we have. It centers on what cannot be dispensed with for us to maintain our personal identity. Philosophers have long sought for what it is that constitutes our identity. Many have located this identity in our psychological features, events, and properties, for the physical features are malleable and seem capable of inorganic or artificial replacement and even disappearance. The self of identity intimately connects to the body but is much more than, maybe even other than, the body. The physical "us" is not one given thing, but a continuity of passing, contiguous properties and events, held together by a conceptual "apparatus" capable of calling what belongs to me "mine."

---

2. Knobe and Nichols, "Free Will," 537. The following modifies their suggested approach.

Particular physical properties change or fall away, and yet the person, with his or her identity, continues. We identify the person or agent that is me with my ideological categories, thoughts, memories, intentions, desires, feelings, and beliefs. Memories especially are central to our personal identity. My memories are not another's; they flow from my personal experience and are indicative of it. My memory of Niagara Falls implicates my own experience and not that of another. Another might replicate my memories in terms of content, but cannot have *my* memories.

However, this psychological perspective, though central and important, also might be challenged for its adequacy, for the connection between certain parts of the body, in particular the neural structures in the brain, and the mental or psychological life, is close indeed. To identify the person or self with the psychological cannot evade the role of the physical in producing, bringing about or causing, or realizing the psychological. The physical roots the mental, such that the physical and mental coordinate and act integrally. Moreover, even the psychological is malleable and capable of replacement or disappearance. Particular thoughts and categories change over time; ideas are learned, held, and forgotten. Memories disappear or change over time. No irreducible, unchanging psychological core constitutes our identity; the psychological also is richly transitional. Rather, we experience a connectedness and continuity of psychological and physical properties.[3]

A third view of the self or person derives from the contention that something organizes our mental life and executes it in the physical. Something provides unity to our experience and consciousness, mental life, and physical being. The "me" is some organizing center that brings all the psychological characteristics and features into a coherent unity. Which particular categories, memories, or thoughts I have is less germane to me than the self that is their central locus. The self controls, is affected by, and manages our mental and physical life. It might be referred to as the *executive self*, as that in terms of which we are considered agents.[4] It is not a thing but rather functions at the center of *self-consciousness*. It is our first-person perspective.[5] It is both that which understands itself and the self that is understood. As both knower and known, in reflecting on my self I am both subject and object; as implementing my mental states of desiring, believing, and intending I am a conscious agent.[6]

3. This is developed to an extreme event view in Parfit, *Reasons and Persons*.
4. Knobe and Nichols, "Free Will," 539.
5. Baker, *Persons and Bodies*, 4.
6. We cannot turn aside here to consider but can only point to the seriously insightful phenomenological analyses of the dialectic between prereflective self-consciousness (a first-order cognition), various modes of reflective self-consciousness (second-order

In some contexts we think of human beings (other than ourselves) from a biological or bodily perspective that includes physical and assumed or inferred psychological properties. In other contexts we think about the identity of the person (especially ourselves) and identify this with particular psychological features such as core memories and a conceptual perspective. In the third sense the self is manifested in self-consciousness; from a first-person perspective the self functions executively as the agent. We shift between these differing perspectives depending on how it is that we are addressing or considering people: as humans, persons, or agents.

How do these three views connect with human freedom as we have understood it? When it comes to free choice and action, all these dimensions—psychophysical wholeness of being, psychological personal identity, and executive agency—play critical roles. The holistic view of freedom emphasizes the second condition of freedom noted above: that something or someone other than ourselves does not completely compel or coerce our choices and actions. The freedom that we have is found in our independence from total external coercion of the physical beings that we are. The identity view of the self emphasizes the first condition of freedom. Since the identity view focuses on our psychological identity through its emphasis on our psychological features such as memories and conceptual categories, we are free when our action results from our choices, and we choose or intend to act in a particular way because of our unique wants, desires, and intentions. Freedom is found in our choosing and deciding—exercising our intentions in the world—that invoke the causal dimension of our psychological self. The executive view of the self affirms that we as agents could have acted differently, given the circumstances or conditions present at the time. Of course, in each of the three views of who I am all three of the conditions invoked by the libertarian concept of freedom are operative, but the feature that is emphasized differs depending upon the context in which human freedom is considered. This, in part, helps explain some of the diverse perspectives about freedom that we find in the literature.

Agency

If we are to claim that we make free choices in a libertarian sense, the relation between thinking, believing, desiring, evaluating, deciding, and choosing, which are mental acts involved in human agency, and the physical world that both affects and is affected by our choosing should be clarified.

---

cognition), and the self reflected on. See Gallagher and Zahavi. "Phenomenological Approaches."

Given the executive and psychological views of the self, the rationality of the libertarian view of freedom seems to rest on being able to provide some reasonable account of how as intentional agents we could have chosen to do otherwise in a causally structured physical world.[7] A libertarian perspective on freedom affirms that mental states can and do affect both physical states (such as evidenced by our behavior) and other mental or psychological states. There is little argument that, from a common sense or ordinary perspective (what some philosophers disparagingly refer to as folk psychology), we believe that the mind or mental has such causal powers. Our experience of sharp pain causes us to move our muscles and consequently our arms away from the stinging yellow jacket. Our desires affect our intentions, which in turn alter our behavior. We want to read Kane's book on human freedom lying on the shelf, so we reach for it rather than Hasker's book on the problem of evil standing next to it. Our beliefs play a significant role in our deliberation, which in turn affects how we act. I believe that today is Tuesday, that I have a racquetball game at noon, and that it takes twenty-two minutes to drive to the Augsburg gym; so I get in my car at 11:30 to drive to the gym from home. Our feelings motivate us to behavioral responses. My feeling of love leads me to reach out to my wife to kiss her in the morning. In all such cases, we appeal to psychological conditions like desires, beliefs, and emotions to help explain what has occurred. "[I]f it isn't literally true that my wanting is causally responsible for my reaching, and my itching is causally responsible for my scratching, and my believing is causally responsible for my saying, . . . if none of that is literally true, then practically everything I believe about anything is false and it's the end of the world."[8]

What is at issue is not whether in a pretheoretical way we *believe* that the mental, with its specific content, causes or affects physical states. It is clear that we give the mental a significantly large explanatory role in our behavior. And since we generally ground explanation on causation, our explanations are strengthened when we can verify the causal conditions the explanations invoke. To explain why my ironwood tree fell in the backyard I might note the surreptitious chewing of black ants in hollowing out the tree trunk. The objective causal conditions of their entry into the tree's inner tissues root my explanation of the tree's fall. The same is suggested for psychological explanation; I explain why I turned left at the intersection in terms of my belief about the location of the grocery store and my desire to shop for fresh fruit there. If my explanation is accurate, it is grounded in real causal conditions that hold between mental and physical (desires

---

7. We will address this key assumption at the end of the chapter.
8. Fodor, "Making Mind Matter," 77.

played a causal role in my turning the car's steering wheel) or mental and other mental conditions (beliefs played a causal role in my choice of direction in which to steer). These causal conditions may be variously described. They constitute at least sufficient conditions for my driving behavior of turning left, although not necessary conditions. Other beliefs, desires, or intentions—for example, to avoid hitting the child I saw running out into the street from the right sidewalk—may have led to my left-turning behavior. We also may describe causal conditions in ways other than as being necessary or sufficient for the event to occur. For example, some see mental conditions as triggering the events, as when the conscious experience of pain triggers bodily avoidance. Other mental conditions, such as beliefs, provide structural necessary conditions for behavior but are not properly envisaged as triggering or as energy-transferring events, since we may have the relevant belief that chocolate cookies are in the jar but not desire them.[9]

The issue we face, then, is how to understand what we term as mental causation, whether the mental *really* can causally affect the physical, and hence whether causally efficacious mental events happen. That is, although we normally have a predisposition to believe that mental states can causally affect or effect both physical and other mental states, does it happen, and if so *how* is such possible, and *how* are mental states causally effective?[10] Do mental states cause or bring about physical states in virtue of being mental or in virtue of the physical states on which they depend or supervene? And do mental states cause other mental states or behavior in virtue of being mental or in virtue of the physical states on which they depend, supervene, or which realize them? The answers to these questions are critical to helping us not only to understand human free agency but also to defend agency as a free endeavor in the current context of a generally physicalist view of the world.[11]

---

9. Dretske, "Mental Events," 121–36.

10. John Heil takes the strong stance; "[T]hose philosophers [who hold to non-reductive physicalism] owe us an account of how mental causation *could* work if the non-reductivist picture is correct" ("Mental Causation," 19). "Non-reductive physicalists hold that, although mental properties are in some way wholly dependent on physical properties, mental properties are nevertheless distinct from physical properties" (Ibid., 18). For our purposes and discussion, we will presuppose a background of non-reductive physicalism in this chapter.

11. Physicalists hold that although "at first glance [many items in the world] don't seem physical—items of a biological, or psychological, or moral, or social nature, . . . nevertheless that at the end of the day such items are either physical or supervene on the physical." Daniel Stoljar, "Physicalism," 2009.

Physical and mental properties

The libertarian view presumes that mental properties differ from physical properties. Thinking, believing, desiring, feeling, and intending are of a different sort than physical, chemical, and biological properties. For one thing, physical properties are spatially locatable, whereas mental properties are not. We can locate neurons in the brain, but the attempt to spatially locate the mental lends what we now consider ludicrousness to Descartes's suggestion that the pineal gland houses the mind. It simply makes no sense to attempt to answer the query as to *where* mental properties are located; they do not possess the spatial characteristics of physical properties. For another, whereas natural, necessary physical laws govern the physical, the same kinds of laws do not govern the mental. If there are universal laws governing the mental—and this may be doubted—they would be what might be termed psychological laws. But psychological laws, if they exist, lack the necessity structures characteristic of physical laws.[12] Rather, many would be telic in nature, governing action for ends or purposes. Third, reasons and evidence play a role in mental explanations but are not terms appropriate to physical causation (we will say more about this shortly). It is not because of reason that a group of neurons signals one response rather than another through their synapses (though we might seek a reason in terms of a cause for it happening). In short, the mental is believed to be causally effective in ways that differ from the physical. Psychologists study mental processes and suggest operative features, but the connections governing psychological states and processes differ in kind from those governing physical states and processes.

However, a significant number of contemporary philosophers deny that mental and physical properties ultimately differ. For them, mental properties are either identical to or can be reduced to physical properties. This is the thesis of the so-called identity theory, according to which mental processes or states are not caused or brought about by the physical brain but are identical with its processes. Consciousness, as U. T. Place put it, is a brain process.[13] One can think of parallel cases in the physical world. The physicist will speak about lightning as an electrical discharge of a certain voltage, whereas the ordinary observer will use language about bright flashes illuminating the stormy sky. Although the physicist and the ordinary person will

---

12. The degree to which this is true may well be debated. The nomic connection between physical events might not have deterministic certainty, as evidenced by quantum physics. Other sciences, such as biology, are much less subject to this necessity-type structure in their causal relations. But the telic dimension would still be absent.

13. Place, "Is Consciousness?" 44–50.

use noninterchangeable language systems, both genuinely report the same physical occurrence.

The identity theory encounters several difficulties. First, it conflicts with our phenomenal accounts of our own control over our events. If our behavior results solely from physical causes, these find their place within the deterministic (or probabilistic) causal chain that extends prior to our existence. This leaves little room for behavior resulting from our own intentions, beliefs, desires, and the like, unless they likewise are part of the physical causal chain. Of course, we may be mistaken about our own phenomenal experiences; what seems to be the case regarding the origins of and our intentional control over our behavior might well not be the case. We can be, and indeed at times are, deceived about the role that the mental plays in our lives and the control we can exercise over our behavior. But if we are to abandon our beliefs about the role of the mental, good reasons should be given.

Second, the identity theory faces the problem of how to account for this cross-category (mental/physical) identity. Defenders claim that mental and brain states are not causally related or constantly correlated; they are strictly identical. According to Wilhelm Leibniz's principle of the identity of indiscernibles, two things are identical if and only if every property of the one is a property of the other. But the properties of mental states and of brain states differ, not the least in that mental states are nonspatial and private whereas brain states are spatial and publicly accessible. Neuroscientists can trace brain patterns and measure electrochemical discharges but lack direct, unmediated access to what the observed patient is thinking. An identity theorist might respond that Leibniz's principle does not apply to cross-category identities. In particular, one cannot expect total property identity when the application of the property to one of the categories would be meaningless, which would be the case if we applied spatial predicates characteristic of physical states to mental states. But given this reply, what criteria do two things with different category-sets of properties have to meet to be identical? In the case of the mind and body, although we have mental events and brain events occurring simultaneously, something more than simultaneity is necessary to show that they are identical rather than causally related.

Third, the same mental properties can be realized by differing physical properties or physical systems. It is possible that beings with somewhat or wholly different physiological constitutions can perceive, be consciously aware, think, and entertain beliefs and desires. For example, the feeling of pain could be realized or produced by very different neural structures, not only in individual humans, but among diverse species. The neurons and their structures or functions associated with pain in a bird might differ from those in a dog or human. Accordingly, there can be no identity between the mental and the physical, for if they were identical all instances of a particular mental type would have the same physical realization or presentation.

Finally, when an event occurs, one can ask whether the event occurred because of the mental or the physical. If I move my arm away from a hot surface, do I move it because of the pain that I experienced or because of the neural action in my brain? Do I choose a book from my shelf solely because of physical brain processes? This seems unlikely since it is not merely or, in most cases, even the physical properties of the book that determine my choice but the non-physical content of the book that I am seeking. Although the content is conveyed by physical features such as the printed words with a particular syntax, it is mentally understood, such that the choice arises from mental and not strictly physical features. If the mental is identical with the physical, the descriptions of the choice in mental terms would be identical with the physical description of what occurred when the particular book was removed and hence would have nothing to do with the semantic or meaning dimension or basis of the action. It is difficult to think that we can accord the impersonal the same kind of explanatory powers as the personal and intentional.[14] We will say more about this in the next section.

In short, it is most reasonable to contend that a difference really exists between mental and physical properties or states. At the same time, this leaves open the question concerning what relations hold between them. The Cartesian solution was rejected because it presupposed a common causal nexus in which they both operated. As we proceed, we will have to keep in mind whether a common causal nexus is necessary to understand their relation, and whether this assumption might be an unwarranted thesis or demand that *a priori* mitigates against a possible resolution of the difficulties that arise.

Mental causation

Most important for our purposes is the causal relation that holds between minds and the physical. We need to assess whether the mind and hence our choices produce or bring about effects in the physical and the psychological worlds. Mental causation must be possible if we are to defend our libertarian perspective on free choice and action and its implications for moral accountability. "Our conception of ourselves as conscious, intentional agents

---

14. Hornsby, "Agency," 161–85.

capable of perception, memory, and reasoning is tied up with the assumption of the reality of causal processes involving cognitive phenomena."[15]

Our ordinary world experience gives credence to the view that minds are causally effective. My desire for the granola bar causes me to reach for it. Because I desire the item, I choose to act to acquire it, and that choice is conveyed physically into the world by nerves stimulating my muscles that move my arm to untwist the jar lid. I see my friends across the street and that perception, with the accompanying recognition, leads me to use my vocal chords to call out a greeting to them. The experience of the faces of my friends has a meaning that I do not find in the faces of others. I see not merely physical facial features but my friends, which category of recognition brings about a unique behavioral response. I twist my ankle on the racquetball court and cry out in pain as I hobble to the corner. My mental images of my physical space help me to navigate my environment in the dark of the night. Categories of foe and friend imposed on a perception enable the soldier to take instantaneous action to pull or not to pull the trigger in an unanticipated confrontation.

> Mental causation—the mind's causal interaction with the world, and in particular, its influence on behavior—is central to our conception of ourselves as agents. Mind-world interaction is taken for granted in everyday experience and in scientific practice. . . . In each case, a mental occurrence appears to produce a series of complex and coordinated bodily motions, which then have additional downstream effects in the physical world. Instances of apparent mental causation are so common they often go unremarked, but they are central to the commonsense picture we have of ourselves. . . . [I]f minds did not influence behavior, in what sense would anyone truly *act*? Sounds would be made, but no one would *mean* anything by them. Bodies would move, but no one would thereby *do* anything.[16]

A denial of mental causation is found in epiphenomenalism. The epiphenomenalist agrees that mental properties differ from physical properties but holds that mental properties are epiphenomenal in that they are given off by or produced by physical properties but have no causal powers of their own. Physical brain events cause mental events, but not vice versa. We act when neural impulses motivate our physiological features, but mental events play no causal role in this process: they make no difference to the physical world. The neural processes in and of themselves are causally

---

15. Menzies, "Mental Causation," 58.
16. Robb and Heil, "Mental Causation."

sufficient to produce physical effects or behavior without invoking mental states. Without causal powers, mental events are causally inefficacious and irrelevant. Hence, we have no good ontological reason to give independent, psychologically-based causal accounts of behavior; behavior results from the operative physical conditions.

This epiphenomenalist view encounters several difficulties. First, epiphenomenalism, in denying any causal activity to the mental, runs counter to our phenomenal experience because it asserts that our perceptions, pains, thoughts, beliefs, intentions, and the like, as being mental, have no effect on our behavior. Only if they are identified with the physical (which is the thesis of the reductionist identity theory noted above) can they have any such effects. This position seems patently wrong. I take pain-relief medicine not because my C-fibers are firing but because I am in the conscious state of *feeling* pain. I wait on the train platform at 9:20 because I *believe* that the commuter train will stop here to pick me up in five minutes. I *desire* to get to the theater and so hail a taxi by waving my hand. Although the particular way my hand is waved might be causally described in purely physiological terms, my beliefs about taxis and how to attract their attention and my desire for a ride motivates the hand waving, and my understanding of culture explains the particular way I wave. My feelings, beliefs, desires, and intentions causally affect my behavior to a very significant degree.

Moreover, on an epiphenomenalist account how can one determine whether other physical objects have a mind? We generally determine this through observing and making inferences from the individual's behavior, discriminating it from the behavior of objects that we infer does not stem from mental activity. Whereas we infer that the being hailing the taxi by waving its arm in the windstorm has a mind and is acting intentionally, we make no such claim for the tree waving its branches, even if we cannot sense any wind (we might be watching the tree through a window). But this ability to differentiate presupposes a causal relation between minds and behavior. Minds possessed by the right sorts of beings can operate intentionally, whereas other sorts of nonconscious beings lack minds and hence desires, beliefs, and intentions. Without the contention that minds are causal, all we can infer from the actions of something is the operation of physical or, more specifically in regard to humans and animals, neural processes, but nothing such as acting intentionally or from beliefs and desires. It is the belief that beliefs and other mental acts make a difference that leads us to ascribe meaning and telic significance to behavior.

Perhaps the strongest philosophical argument for the causal effectiveness of the mental is that the mental makes a real difference. In particular, there must be a real difference between a choice that results from mere physical causes and a choice that results from rational deliberation, that is, a choice that we make for good reasons. Only the second allows us to assess the rational value of our choices. In our daily life we are interested not only in the fact that we make choices, but in whether our choices are rational or not. To make good choices presupposes that we deliberate carefully about the options. When we deliberate we look at and evaluate the evidence before us, and if our deliberation is rational, we make our decisions based on what we take to constitute the best evidence. We deliberate by evaluating the supporting evidence in terms of its strength. We reason toward conclusions that we think follow from sound and cogent argumentation, and then use these conclusions to make our informed decisions and choices.

If our mental processes are caused, determined, or realized by arational neural events, we can account for the choosing causally, but we cannot account for our drawing a *rational* conclusion or making *rational* deliberation or choice based upon the strength of the support we find in the evidence. The physical, electro-chemical transferences in the brain are entirely arational, governed by physical laws encompassing energy transfer and *not* by reason. Whereas the neural firings are determined in terms of deterministic or probabilistic physical laws, rational deliberation works with norms. We introduce values when we speak about assessing the evidence and engaging in sound or cogent reasoning. The causal laws simply describe the factual, dominant causal conditions operative in each case, and these causal conditions are arational, non-normative facts. The processes they govern are not bound by the laws of *good* reasoning; neither do they conform to the demands of rationality. The physical, we might say, works with what is; the deliberative with what ought to be.[17]

> Once a complete mechanistic explanation has been given, no room is left for the reasons one might have for an action to play a role in bringing it about that one performs the action. If this is so, then the doctrine that all actions have complete neurophysiological explanations entails that no one *ever* does anything because she has reason to do so—that is, no one ever performs an intentional action.[18]

The mental, then, plays a very different role in deliberation and choice than the physical. This does not mean that the mental can dispense with the physical; as we will argue below the mental is essentially grounded in the physical. But it does mean that in rational decision making we cannot dispense with the significant contribution of the mental. The mental and the

17. Lowe, "Substance Causation," 170.
18. Hasker, *Emergent Self*, 64.

physical clearly function in different ways in our deliberation and decision-making. The one appeals to the deterministic or probabilistic laws of physical causation; the other makes normative judgments about good reasoning.

If we draw conclusions to arguments merely on the basis of neural input, there appears to be no such thing as good (as over against mere) reasoning. Neurons cannot distinguish whether or not one has followed the laws of good or sound reasoning, whether the premises are relevant to the conclusion, or whether the argument is cogent or valid. But these features are necessary to distinguish good reasoning from mere reasoning when we engage in deliberation and make rational choices. In short, a critically important difference exists between making a choice and making a good or rational decision or choice. A purely physical system can account for events occurring in one way rather than another, but it cannot account for the latter unless it allows for a significant distinction between physical and mental properties.

To rationally reject this argument one must appeal to evidence that counts against it. Not just any evidence, but *good, relevant* evidence. One might be able to supply a physical, causal account of a person's rejection of the argument's (e.g., their dyspepsia), but if it is to constitute a rational refutation of the argument just presented, this evidence must be not merely physically causal but rational in nature. If one rejects this argument for deterministic or probabilistic causal conditions, the rejection by its very nature would have to be arational and hence irrelevant to the rationality of the argument. Physicalists who disagree with this argument cannot reject it on the grounds that the argument is not cogent or that the conclusion does not follow logically. The argument may in fact be unsound, but a physically causal rejection of the argument does not reject it because it is unsound but because of the neural causal conditions operative at the time of consideration. The causal account may come to the "proper" conclusion regarding its soundness, but it does so accidentally and not for reasons having to do with rationality of the argument.

It is epiphenomenalism, not mental causation, then, that we should hold in doubt. The mental has powers of some sort or other to bring about effects in the physical and psychological realms. What these are remain to be explored.

The principle of physical closure

The major argument against the causal efficacy of the mental is formulated in terms in the principle of physical closure. According to this principle, every physical event has a sufficient physical cause. Physical events are caused solely by physical events. This principle allows for uncaused events (which some, questionably to be sure, have seen as a feature of quantum phenomena), although it does not affirm their existence either. But whenever physical events occur, the cause is solely physical.

The principle is sometimes stated more boldly as the principle of exclusion: "A state that is causally sufficient for some effect excludes any mental state that supervenes on it from being causally efficacious with respect to the effect."[19] This principle follows from the principle of closure. The point of this principle is that if any physical event can be explained in terms of other physical events, there is no point in introducing another set of causal conditions, namely, mental conditions. The physical conditions are sufficient in and of themselves to bring about the event. Where this metaphysic holds sway, no room exists for the causal influence of psychological states except through their physical surrogates.

If the principles of physical closure and exclusion hold, the physical realm is causally closed to mental events. Physical events only have physical causes; the physical is causally sufficient to bring about the physical effect. No room remains for psychophysical causal activity. Clearly, if the principle of physical closure is true it would seriously undermine our usual or ordinary explanatory practices that invoke beliefs, desires, intentions, and the like to explain our behavior. To the extent that physical causation underlies explanation, mental causation would lack explanatory power. Consequently, it is important to ask why one should think that the principle of causal closure is true.

The reasoning for this position is less an argument than an appeal to a materialist metaphysic, which sees all causation as being physical causation. It is founded on the presumption that science can proceed only with physical closure, and by "science" is understood the hard sciences. The issues, then, are whether we should adopt this type of materialistic metaphysic and whether the hard sciences in fact invoke this brand of materialism.

---

19. "A state that is causally sufficient for some effect excludes any [mental] state that supervenes on it from being causally efficacious with respect to the effect." Menzies, "Mental Causation," 60. Heil terms it autonomy: the physical realm is causally self-contained. "Mental Causation," 22.

No systematic overdetermination

One attempt to reconcile mental causation with causal physical closure is through the appeal to overdetermination.[20] Overdetermination allows multiple causes to produce a single effect. With overdetermination, although ultimately physical effects are brought about by physical causes (causal closure), one can properly also allow and even appeal to mental causation in an explanatory role.

At times a physical effect may result from two simultaneous causes. For example, two hunters may simultaneously shoot a deer. The death of the deer is causally overdetermined in that either shot independently would have killed the deer. It is impossible to say which shot was fatal or to whom the kill belongs. Or again, adding to the weight of materials stored at a particular point on a highway bridge might be sufficient to cause it to collapse, while at that very moment an earthquake moves the supporting bridge pillars. Either the added excess weight on the bridge or the earthquake by itself would be sufficient to bring down the bridge.

If the mental is to function at all on the physical in a causal sense, given causal closure, which claims that physical events have a sufficient physical cause, overdetermination would have to be a regular or normal pattern, not an occasional event. Every time a mental event is seen to be causally effective overdetermination would be in play. Each mental event would bring about through overdetermination a physical event that was already sufficiently caused by prior physical events. But the mental would be otiose; it would not contribute anything over and above what would happen without it.

But why disallow regular overdetermination? For one thing, most instances of causation are causally specific: a specific effect occurs as the result of a specific cause, such that we can properly infer the cause from the effect. Causal specificity is the basis for the cogency of inductive causal reasoning; it enables us to discern what actually caused the collapse of the interstate highway bridge in Minneapolis. Were overdetermination a regular occurrence, inductive causal reasoning from effect to cause would prove extraordinarily difficult; the causes inferred from the effect would be indeterminate. However, perhaps the main reason is that a healthy dose of William of Occam's principle of simplicity rules it out, for when we provide an explanation in terms of one set of operative conditions, it is otiose then to introduce a second set, especially on a systematic basis. It would be, as one philosopher put it, a case of bad engineering to have overdetermination

---

20. Some seem to beg the question by making a more stringent claim that "Mental causes do not overdetermine their effects." Árnadóttir and Crane, "Exclusion Problem," 253.

regularly and, it would seem, unnecessarily.[21] We simply would not need, or even have room for, mental causation.

One might conclude that although causal overdetermination in the world of our experience can occur, it is rare. A general scenario of systematic causal overdetermination seems neither likely nor reasonable and hence fails to provide an adequate solution to the problem of mental causation in light of the principle of closure.

Dependence of the mental on the physical

Before we critique the principle of closure and the type of materialist metaphysic underlying it, we need to say something about the causal relations that hold between the physical and the mental. Not only is it difficult to spell out how minds can affect the physical, but it is equally challenging to specify how the physical can causally affect or bring about the mental. How do electrochemical transferences between neural synapses enable or cause us to form mental pictures, conduct a logical argument, imagine a scene, intend to take action, feel pain, or comprehend the meaning of something? There is little contesting of the claim that mental properties, although distinct from physical properties, depend in some way upon physical properties. Results from brain research, using such tools as fMRIs and PET scans, repeatedly confirm this. For example, our ability to physically position our body in the world is made possible by nerve cells located in a specific region of the brain called the hippocampus. Some of these cells, called place cells, help us construct maps of the places where we are located and store them, whereas other cells, termed grid cells, located in a nearby part of the brain called the entorhinal cortex, allow us to determine our position and to navigate in our environment. However, although dependence of the mental on the physical is accepted as the standard view by those who accept the existence of both mental and physical properties, precisely how this dependence is to be explicated is a matter of significant discussion and disagreement.

One way to explicate this dependence is causally: our physical properties are the cause of our mental properties. But this likewise is vague, for in what sense is "cause" to be understood?[22] The physicalist would probably not explicate this relationship causally, for then as the physical effects of the physical causes have causal powers, so the mental effects of the physical

---

21. Schiffer, *Remnants of Meaning*, 148.

22. Causal analyses range everywhere from understanding the relation as production, as constant conjunction, as making a difference, as stating covering laws, or in terms of counterfactuals. Exploring these options will have to occur at another time.

causal powers could have causal powers. If x produces or causes y, there is no reason to think that y cannot itself be a cause, brought about by but acting to some degree independently of x. If this principle applies to the physical realm where the effects such as magnetism and light supervene on physical properties, it might be able to occur in the mental realm as well. The causal power of the mental would be inherited from or grounded in the physical, but not reducible to it.[23]

In physicalist philosophical circles it is common to explicate this relationship between mental and physical using the language of supervenience. The mental supervenes on the physical just in case the mental cannot vary without the physical varying; the mind cannot vary independently of the relevant neural features. There cannot be any change in the one without a corresponding change in the other. Any physical events that are alike will have identical mental events supervening on them, and any two alike mental events will supervene on identical physical events. Technically speaking, while this view of supervenience only speaks to covariation and does not require dependence,[24] most philosophers who speak about supervenience understand it as a form of dependence.[25]

The problem with understanding the relation between mental and physical in terms of supervenience is that it leads to epiphenomenalism, which as we have seen denies that the mental has any causal role to play in bringing about physical events. Although mental properties are distinct from physical properties, if they are wholly supervenient upon physical properties, they cannot vary without a corresponding physical variation. Anything mental that would change in a particular way would have a correspondingly similar physical variation. Since the mental cannot have any causal influence apart from the physical conditions that realize it, we are back to epiphenomenalism and the problems we noted above with it

Critique of physical closure

The principles of closure and exclusion, if followed consistently, lead to a situation where even macro-physical properties would lack causal efficacy.

---

23. Reductive physicalists would reject this analysis of dependence, for since causes and effects differ, the causal understanding implies a real distinction between physical and mental properties. We have given reasons for questioning this strict reductionism above.

24. McLaughlin and Bennett, "Supervenience."

25. Audi, "Mental Causation," 61–62; Baker, "Metaphysics," 79; Kim, "Non-Reductivism," 195.

If the principle of closure is formulated generally (without any specific reference to the mental *per se*), then even neural states cannot function causally, for they supervene on or are realized in lower-level molecular arrangements and processes. What brings about the neural effects are the molecules and, in turn, atoms out of which neurons are composed, so that these atomic elements and their subatomic components, which are sufficient causes for the neurons and their processes, are thereby sufficient for the behaviors in the world. According to this application of the exclusion principle, it is not neurons but the atomic and subatomic particles that cause physical events and behaviors. This reductionism, which would result in the view that the only causal powers are those held by the atomic and sub-atomic components or building blocks of the physical, would be unacceptable even to physicalists, for it would make all molecular properties and states merely epiphenomenal. Causal efficacy would only be found in micro-particles, with the result that not only psychological but scientific explanation in sciences like biology and chemistry, grounded in causation, would be otiose.[26]

Jaegwon Kim identified this as a problem for non-reductive physicalism and emergentism. "[W]ithin the stratified world of non-reductive physicalism and emergentism, 'same-level' causation can occur only if 'cross-level' causation can occur. It will not be possible to isolate and confine causal chains within levels; there will be inevitable leakage of causal influence from level to level."[27] But the argument above shows that this inevitable causal leakage applies even to Kim's reductive physicalism. Kim attempted to avoid this problem by affirming that the exclusion principle only applies to objects where the object and its supervenient properties are on the same level.

> In general, supervenient properties and their base properties are instantiated by the same objects and hence are on the same level. . . . So the microphysical, or mereological, supervenience does not track the micro-macro hierarchy; the series of supervenient properties, one mereologically supervenient on the next, when we go deeper and deeper into the micro, remains at the same level in the micro-macro hierarchy. . . . This means that the supervenience argument, which exploits the supervenience relation, does not have the effect of emptying macro-levels of causal powers and rendering familiar macro-objects and their properties causally impotent.

---

26. Baker, "Metaphysics," 75–95.
27. Kim, *Mind*, 206.

Kim's point is that the supervenience relation holds only with respect to properties occurring in the same object and on the same level. Since the mental and physical properties belong to the same object, they are on the same level. Reduction to the micro-level would occur only if the neural and its subatomic realizers belonged to the same object. But, he argues, they do not: the neural components differ from the subatomic particles. They are different objects. Since causal "leakage" can occur only within a supervenience relationship in the same object, it would not affect multi-level metaphysical structures and hence the exclusion principle would not apply.

To refute this "draining of causal power" criticism of the closure principle Kim has to show that the relationship between mental and physical differs from that which holds between neurons and their components. That is, the one relation is within one object on the same level, while the other relation is between objects at different levels. In the latter case, Kim argues, the relationship is not one of supervenience but mereological (part-whole). But Kim's reasoning appears to beg the question by assuming that the mental and the physical relations are intralevel, belonging to the same object, and not really operative on different levels. That is, he assumes at the outset that between mind and body there is no downward causation. But this contention is what is at issue. The causal closure argument is advanced to establish this contention, but then this contention cannot be employed to shore up the causal closure argument.

Furthermore, it would seem that causal drainage can occur across levels. In supervenience the alteration of properties in one cannot occur without alteration of properties in the other. Supervenience in this sense can hold across levels, not only in the same object. Neurons would be realized in the atomic and subatomic particles, such that an alteration in the micro-components could not occur without alteration in the macro-components. Since neurons (the higher level) can supervene on its components (lower level), they are subject to the drainage of their causal powers.[28] In effect, given this view of supervenient relationship, drainage of causal powers can occur even across levels.

In short, adopting the causal closure principle would eliminate macro-scientific causal explanation, and this would have the significant effect of largely putting the respective natural sciences out of business. If the causal drainage problem is as severe as suggested, the closure principle is hardly a principle that science would adopt at all. It would drain science of much of its causal and explanatory power.

28. Menzies, "Mental Causation," 70.

How does mental causation occur?

We may properly conclude, then, that there is good reason to reject the causal closure principle and to think that the mental plays an important causal role. However—and here is the difficult and seemingly intransigent problem—it is extremely difficult to spell out clearly the causal relation that holds between the mental and the physical. This difficulty goes both ways: how do the physical conditions of the neural components of the brain and the transfers of chemical energy therein bring about the mental processes and states, and how can the mental affect the physical, both neural and motor? That is, although we have good reasons to believe *that* the mental affects the physical, the question remains as to *how* this is accomplished.

The problem is easily resolved if the mental is identical with the physical. The physical causes bring about physical effects, and we merely address the physical using mental categories and language. Mental categories simply provide another way of looking at the physical, just as descriptions of flashes of lightening constitute another way of thinking about the transfer of electrical energy. But we have already rejected the identity theory, not only because of the possibility of multiple realizations of the psychological but also because it does not comport with our phenomenal experience. Hence, we need to think seriously about the causal role of the psychological on the physical, assessing the evidence pro and con.

One often-used argument against psychological causation relies on the law of the conservation of matter and energy, according to which the total matter and energy of any closed system is conserved. Physical change occurs or is brought about by the transfer of energy. If the mental is to produce effects in the physical realm, some energy needs to be transferred from the mental to the physical. But according to the law of conservation of matter and energy, the amount of energy in the physical universe is fixed and cannot be supplemented or lost. Hence, no mental energy can be infused into the physical realm.[29] In effect, there can be no psychological causation of the physical.

Several replies are in order. First, the law of energy conservation does not exclude the possibility of energies other than physical energy. The principle of conservation of matter and energy does not restrict itself to physical energy, only to the energy found in the closed system. It does not say what that energy is. Thus, in applying the law, one must take account of the entire or complete energy system, and this might include energy other than physical energy, that is, mental energy. If mental energy exists and is included,

---

29. Dennett, *Consciousness Explained*, 35; Fodor, "Mind-Body Problem," 25; van Inwagen, *Metaphysics*, 196. See Averill and Keating, "Interactionism," 102.

then the introduction of mental energy into the physical system does not violate the law of the conservation of energy. Mental causation would violate this law only if the energy considered under the law of the conservation of matter and energy only includes physical energy.

Is there mental energy? Defenders of the conservation-of-energy-critique of mental causation argue inductively for excluding so-called mental energy from the total energy bucket. They claim that if there were mental energy, we should have evidence of it. But science has been unable to detect any such energy. "If there were such forces, they could be expected to display some manifestation of their presence. But detailed physiological investigation failed to uncover evidence of anything except familiar physical forces."[30] For example, if energy were supplied by souls then physiological calculation should reveal this. It would have discovered anomalies in us where events would have insufficient physical causes. But, it is argued, detailed investigation of human processes does not reveal the presence of these energy anomalies.

Perhaps the difficulty of detecting mental energy results from problematic measurement criteria. The objection seems to presuppose that mental energy can be measured, probably in the same way that physical energy can be measured. However, mental energy is likely to be of a sort different from physical energy, such that we cannot measure it with calibrating tools that are geared to standards of physical measurement. If so, it is reasonable to think that mental energy is immeasurable, at least in any ordinary or physical way. This does not establish the existence of such energy or even make it probable, but it does indicate that the measurability objection lacks teeth in presupposing physiological-like conditions of and types of energy measurement.

Some suggest that measurement taken indirectly is possible. One finds this in reports of psychological experiments. To give just one such example, researchers studying what is termed mental mobilization studied how mental processes such as mental contrasting (comparing desired objectives with impeding conditions) affect performance.[31] They framed the study in terms of energization, which is the activation or arousal of the organism as a whole, and can both be felt (a mental activity) and objectively measured by physiological standards. They calculated how the activity of mental contrasting gets translated into the physical mobilization by measuring changes in systolic blood pressure. Because effort mobilization leads to energization, which results in increased bodily demand of oxygen and nutrients,

---

30. Papineau, *Thinking about Consciousness*, 254.
31. Sevincer et al., "Mental Contrasting," 139.

and since the cardiovascular system supplies tissues with energy in the form of oxygen and nutrients, increased energization is manifested in a stronger cardiovascular response. Gearing up mentally to think about achieving a goal creates physiological energy, which in turn is reflected in both blood pressure change and in an increased ability to perform a physical task such as squeezing a lever. Both of the latter can be objectively quantified.

But although the authors speak about "translation" from mental activity such as mental contrasting into physiological energization, and about measuring the latter, what they mean by "translate" remains obscure. They note that "simply thinking about upcoming challenges (e.g., when people anticipate that they will perform complex arithmetic tasks) [has] been linked to increased energy mobilization."[32] Thus, although they do not employ the term "mental energy," they see both the mental and the physical as bringing about energization, which in turn can be measured using physiological methods. But the mechanism of how this translation from the mental to the physical is accomplished lies hidden behind terms such as "triggers," "causes," "produces," and "mobilizes."

Second, returning to the conservation of energy argument, the argument supposes "that the only way the nonphysical can affect a physical system is by affecting the amount of energy or momentum within it."[33] But some suggest that changes in the physical can occur without some sort of energy transfer from the mental to the physical. It might occur, for example, by redistributing the energy already present within the physical system.[34] Examples given of how this can occur within a physical system include how the pendulum string controls the swing without a causal transfer of energy, how the closing of an electrical switch causes the light to go out, and how the interruption of the flow of blood to the brain causes the person to faint.[35] In such types of instances energy is not added or taken from the system but rather redirected within it. Similarly, the suggestion is that the mind can alter the physical in ways that are not reliant on any transfer of energy but employ some sort of redirecting or redistribution action.

In the case of the brain, the redistribution of neural energy need not be on individual neurons but on neural system itself. Although individual neuron firings have their place in the neural chain, how, it might be asked, do the millions of neurons firing individually and independently bring about concerted effort to create unified patterns? On this view the function of the

---

32. Ibid., 141.
33. Gibb, "Closure Principles," 364.
34. Campbell, *Body and Mind*, 52–53.
35. Montero, "Conservation of Energy," 390.

mental is to provide the unity of consciousness that allows for unified intentional mental effort. The mental does not contribute energy to the system but provides structure and unity. It directs and redirects, so that the patterns of firing will have significance beyond any randomization. The mental "orders" the neural system so that we have unified mental experiences of self and its intentionality. This approach circumvents the conservation-of-energy issue entirely by suggesting a structuring rather than a triggering role for the mental.

The problem with this structuring approach is that while the mental does provide a unity of consciousness that might be seen as structuring, the mental also appears to serve a triggering role in our behavior. The conjunction of particular beliefs and desires results in specific behaviors. If I did not want *that* book or *that* sweet I would not have chosen to take the action or make the bodily movements that I did.

A different approach does not address the question of energy at all, but rather observes that different kinds of properties do different kinds of work. The color reflected by a traffic sign does different work than does the shape of the sign. Yellow indicates caution, whereas the shape, for example, a triangle, informs what the caution is about. Or again, the color of a vehicle has no effect on the damage it creates when it impacts another, but the color might signal us about the role or purpose of the vehicle—red on the truck indicating a fire emergency vehicle.

So instead of addressing the "how" question in terms of energy, we might consider thinking about how the mental affects the physical in terms of selective, relevant, unique properties. In particular, what is relevant about the mental is its ability to address semantics. John Searle helpfully emphasizes the diverse roles that semantics and syntax play with his Chinese room example. Searle argues that a person who in a closed room receives messages in Chinese, looks up the inputted symbols on a chart, and sends out the correct translation might get the translation correct (although even here mere translation protocols are often quite inaccurate because they fail to capture the nuances of meaning). However, it cannot be said of the person doing the transcribing that he understands Chinese. The critical feature of understanding Chinese is discerning the meaning of the message in Chinese, and this requires more than syntactical translation according to coded registries. It necessitates the ability to function semantically in Chinese, and functioning semantically requires a mind or mental processes.

The point here is that we explain persons' behaviors to a significant degree by mental processes in virtue of the content of their acts of believing, desiring, willing, or intending. We cannot explain behavior by merely appealing to transfers of electrochemical components in the brain. The reader of the fMRI can determine which areas of the brain are involved when mental processing occurs, but the reader cannot determine what those mental processes mean by observing the highlighted colors and their brain location. Red locations on the scan indicate which area is significantly operative, but an area exhibiting red or yellow cannot inform the observer about the determinate meaning or intention the subject entertains. The meaning correlates with the physical evidence only through some explicit or implicit environment of communication invoking a mental state with a specific content (for example, asking the subject to think, intend, wish, believe, or report about something). Mental states such as believing, desiring, and intending, possessing particular contents, function causally when the mental affects the behavioral.[36] A purely physical system can have syntax, but to have semantics requires the ability to process meaning. And it is in virtue of semantics or meaning that the mental exercises its causal power in a specific way. Our beliefs produce effects not simply by being beliefs but by being beliefs *with a specific content*, which differentiates and individuates mental states of a particular type. We act on our beliefs based on what the beliefs are *about;* otherwise the purported explanation "would be considered only a rationalization":[37] causally produced by physical conditions, but not rational. The same is to be said for our thoughts, feelings, and intentions; these mental states with specific semantic content function through their causal power. "Granted that mental factors might have no causal power apart from their non-mental bases, they might both exercise the power they derive from the latter and, in so doing, direct that power."[38] The presupposition of a common, physical causal nexus now becomes problematic.

Agency and human freedom

We have indicated several possible scenarios in terms of which to understand how the mental affects the physical. But despite the presumption,

---

36. See Audi, "Mental Causation," 54–59. Audi treats these mental states as dispositional, whereas they can be either dispositional or occurrences. Treated as occurrences rather than as mere dispositions their causal function is less problematic. See Reichenbach, *Epistemic Obligations*, ch. 6.

37. Audi, "Mental Causation," 55.

38. Ibid., 66. "Very roughly, my relevant beliefs provide a cognitive map; my governing want indicates a destination on that map; and my action is explained as an effort to reach that destination. Even physical causes can have direction as well as energy. The natural analogy here is to beliefs as providing, with the help of perception, the direction of behavior, and wants providing its energy: the direction requires a kind of instrumental content; the energy requires a conceptualized goal to which that content is connected." Ibid., 57–58.

noted earlier in this chapter, that the rationality of the libertarian view of freedom seems to rest on being able to give some reasonable account of how as intentional agents we could have chosen to do otherwise in a causally structured physical world, perhaps it is not necessary to give an account of how mental causation occurs after all. For one thing, we believe that many physical phenomena occur without being able to give an account of how they come about. We might discover that a particular drug cures an illness without knowing how it does so. That does not stop us from searching for the causal mechanisms, but the fact that we cannot present an operative causal mechanism for the cure does not indicate that we should abandon our belief that physical causation between the drug and the malady occurs. We do not withhold the curative drug on the grounds that we don't know how it works. Knowing how enlightens us when we know that, but it is not a prerequisite for knowing that.

Second, as we noted earlier, the request for an explanation of how the mental causes or affects the physical tends to beg the question, for the explanation sought for or at least deemed acceptable by the physicalist is in terms of a physical explanation. This is what led Descartes into trouble when he invoked a physical, mechanistic explanation for mind/body interaction. But to require a physical explanation to unpack the relation between the mental and the physical is to beg the question. The presumption of a common causal nexus and the determination of this as physical makes the problem irresolvable. If we are not required to provide a physical explanation of how the mental affects the physical, then the door is open to giving meaningful psychological accounts that do not appeal to physical laws.

This means, third, that psychological explanations are not only acceptable in accounting for human behavior but desirable. Indeed, it is in terms of psychological explanations that we generally seek to understand our human affairs. "As long as mentalistic explanation yields knowledge and understanding, and as long as that explanation is (sometimes) causal, we can firmly believe that mind-body causation is a part of the world."[39] The point here is that explanation becomes a primary way of approaching and understanding the world. It is true that explanation often relies on causation; the explanatory account must be rooted in ontology, in something that happens. But that we cannot give a complete causal account does not mean that we cannot give an explanation. "What matters is that our mentalistic explanations work and that they do not conflict with our physicalist explanations. As philosophers, we want a well-founded understanding of how these explanations, and their subject matters, relate to one another. But it

---

39. Burge, "Mind-Body Causation," 117.

serves no purpose to over-dramatize the conflict between different ontological approaches of the merits of the materialist approach."[40]

All of this ties back to our interest in what it is to be a person and what it is to be a person in an executive sense: as an agent. I cannot put it better than Tyler Burge does.

> Much of the interest of psychological explanation, both in psychology and in ordinary discourse, lies in helping us understand ourselves as agents. Causal implications are built into our intentional concepts and intentional modes of explanation. We think that we make things happen because we made decisions or will to do things. We think that we make assertions, form theories, and create cultures, because we think certain thoughts and have certain goals—and we express and fulfill them. In this context, we identify ourselves primarily in terms of our intentional mental aspects—our wants, our thoughts, our values. Our agency consists in our "wants," "willings," "thoughts," "values" as such (under these "aspects") having some sort of efficacy in the world. Our mental events' having the intentional characters that they have is, in individual instances, what we define our agency in terms of. Most of our intellectual and practical norms and evaluations presuppose that we are agents. If our willing or deciding made something happen, but that event's being a willing or deciding were (sic) not causally efficacious (so that the efficacy resided in some underlying neural property) then the agency would not be ours. . . . Most normative evaluations of our intellectual and practical activity would be empty. . . . I am not here asserting that it is inconceivable that psychological explanation could break down—or at least be very much more limited than we conceive it as being. I think that the question of conceivability is quite subtle and complex. The point is that this form of psychological explanation has not in the least broken down. It works very well, within familiar limits, in ordinary life; it is used extensively in psychology and the social sciences; and it is needed in understanding physical science, indeed any sort of rational enterprise. We have reason to believe that it provides explanatory insights. But then as I have noted, there is a deep connection between intentional psychological explanation and the view it provides of ourselves as agents, on the one hand, and the attribution of some sort of causal efficacy to intentional mental states and events as such, on the other.[41]

40. Ibid.
41. Ibid., 118–19 (supplying missing quotation marks).

The point is to determine what it is that will guide our deliberations about freedom and mental causation. The exploration of agency might be focused on causation or on explanation. Clearly, causation and explanation are related, but not identical. If the focus is on causation, then the claim that libertarians must establish the causal mechanism of free agency for their position to be intelligible and accepted leaves us at an impasse, since we cannot specify the mechanisms of mental causation or even of physical causation on the mental. But we are not alone; scientists regularly note correlation, even claim causation, without knowledge of the relevant mechanisms. We have indicated some of the considerations that point to the fact that the mind and body causally interact. And given a physicalist model, they do so in a much more intimate sense than in a Cartesian dualist model. It is not the interaction of two independent substances, but somehow an intense relation between sets or nexus of diverse properties that, in conscious humans, cannot be disengaged from each other. The use of sophisticated technology to show locations accompanying mental processes confirms the intimacy of the connection. We understand a great deal about the neural processes necessary for mental acts. For example, functional MRI (fMRI) can be used to enable persons to condition or activate parts of their brain.[42] But the connection between mental acts and their narrow content and neural processing is still debated and to be investigated. How this causation takes place remains to a great extent mysterious.

If the focus is on explanation, we can find meaningful place for both psychological and physical explanations of our behavior. Psychological explanation works very well, especially when it is coupled with an understanding of the neurophysiology linked with it. Behavior discussed in terms of the telic is more meaningful in many cases than neural explanation. However, the neural often provides a better understanding of aberrant behavior or disease-conditioned behavior (such as found in Tourette's syndrome or in Alzheimer's). For example, in explaining compulsive drug-taking behavior, where addicts develop an almost irresistible craving for drugs while simultaneously developing a dislike of them, one theory is that

---

42. "On occasion, volunteers would see a particular image, and if on seeing that image they successfully increased neural activity in the part of brain concerned with generating hand movements (but without making any real hand movements), then the volunteers would receive a monetary reward. In response to another image, subjects had to instead imagine making a foot movement in order to get the reward. Once subjects had learned to activate the correct area of their brain, we then over time increased the level of activity needed to obtain reward. This had the effect that subjects learned to progressively increase activity in specific brain regions in order to keep attaining the rewards." O'Doherty, "Neural Conditioning."

> it is the activation of this neural system that results in the experience of "wanting," and transforms ordinary stimuli into incentive stimuli.... Drug-associated stimuli become more and more able to control behavior, because the neural system that mediates "wanting" becomes progressively sensitized. "Wanting" evolves into obsessive craving and this is manifest behaviorally as compulsive drug seeking and drug taking. Therefore, by this view, drug craving and addictive behavior are due specifically to sensitization of incentive salience.[43]

But whereas the neural sensitization, located in the mesotelencephalic dopamine system, increases the wanting, it does not increase the liking. The drug-sensitization is so effective that even after long periods of abstinence, the craving can be reignited. Here the explanation begins with the neurophysiological conditions and proceeds to the mental (wanting), all of which factor in an explanation of addictive behavior. The telic and the neurophysiological nontelic both factor in explaining behavior.

Free agency invokes psychological explanations to account for our executive and psychological senses of the self. As we noted in the previous chapter, freedom is a matter of degree, so that in giving explanations of behavior others factors, environmental and physiological, play roles of varying degrees and importance. At the same time, in giving psychological explanations, it should not be forgotten that for them to have cash value, real action of some broadly causal sort must link the mental and the physical. These linkages the biological and psychological sciences explore.

We have not said how agency works. Because our language games and conceptual categories in psychology and physiology are not interchangeable, perhaps it will not be possible to fully connect the two. There simply might not be the linguistic tools and causal nexus that provides the conceptual framework. Not only might we not have the language capacity to do so, the telic versus nontelic structures of the explanations constitute important obstacles. But this recognition leaves open the view that we are psychophysical creatures whose free agency is rooted in, facilitated by, and limited by our physiology, and whose physical behavior can frequently best be understood and explained in terms of human intentional actions stemming from beliefs, desires, and free choices. Free agency remains a most viable category for explanation of our choices and actions.

---

43. Robinson and Berridge, "The Neural Basis," 249.

Chapter 4

God and Goodness

THE DOCTRINE OF DIVINE providence affirms that God loves, cares and provides for, and acts in ways that propitiously carry out his covenant relations with human beings. God acts to benefit both his creation in general and especially human beings for their good and God's glory. Beneficial providence presumes that God is not only good but perfectly good—his goodness endures forever. In this chapter we will explore what it means to say that God is good, discussing two views that people put forward to interpret this claim.[1]

God's manifest goodness

The writer of Genesis begins by portraying God as bringing about what he subsequently deems and declares as good. All that God makes by his word he determines to be good, whether heavenly bodies and the earth, water in and above the earth, dry ground, or plants and animals: all are pronounced as being good. The universe is not value-neutral; God bestows on it its goodness. The writer emphasizes that God's deeds of goodness begin even before humans are created. God's creation of humans completes the saga and brings the final assessment that all are not only good but very good (Gen 1:31). With humans the initial creation is now whole and the Sabbath arrives.

Our creation is only the first of God's plethora of beneficial acts on our behalf. The second creation story soon turns to God's personal concern for the man because being alone is not good for him (Gen 2:18). God's remedy provides an intimate helper. God manifests continuing providence in his surprising protection of a murderer (Gen 3:15) and his protection of a

---

1. Although there are numerous treatments of God's goodness with respect to ethics, especially as it relates to the divine command theory, book-length treatments of goodness itself as a divine property are rarer. For a recent treatment combining both see Baggett and Walls, *Good God*. See also Davies, *Reality of God*.

righteous family and nature's animals from present and future disaster (Gen 6–9). The blessing of goodness extends to all nations, facilitated through God's selection of Abram (Gen 12:2–3). The remainder of the Old Testament story celebrates God's goodness to individuals, the nation of Israel, and surrounding peoples and nations. Blessing is never completely localized, but like water disperses wherever it flows: "He is like a tree planted by streams of water, which yields its fruit in season and whose leaf does not wither. Whatever he does prospers" (Ps 1:3).

The thread of God's providential goodness connects his many loving acts of redemption, whether from Egypt, Babylonia, the hands of enemies, or the dangers of nature. Providence manifests itself in God's self-sacrifice, where "God so loved the world that he gave his one and only son" (John 3:16). The incarnation and death of the Messiah are the ultimate beneficial, sacrificial contribution of a loving, forgiving, saving, and healing God. The portrayal of God's goodness culminates in James's sweeping affirmation: "Every good and perfect gift is from above" (Jas 1:17). God is not merely good; God is the *source* of all good. Whatever good we experience God wills for us.

> Praise the LORD, O my soul;
> > and forget not all his benefits—
> who forgives all your sins
> > and heals all your diseases,
> who redeems your life from the pit
> > and crowns you with love and compassion,
> who satisfies your desires with good things
> > so that your youth is renewed like the eagle's. (Ps 103:2–5)

Not only does God providentially produce beneficial good, the good comes from a good God. Numerous passages, notably in the Psalms, but also elsewhere, affirm God's goodness.

> According to your love remember me,
> > for you are good, O LORD.
> Good and upright is the LORD. (Ps 25:7–8)

> Taste and see that the LORD is good;
> > blessed are those who take refuge in him. (Ps 34:8)

> Give thanks to the LORD, for he is good;
> > his love endures forever. (Ps 106:1)

Jeremiah echoes this last psalm.

> Give thanks to the LORD almighty,
>> for the LORD is good:
>> his love endures forever. (Jer 33:11)

Whether in sorrow or celebration, the writers affirm God's goodness.

> The LORD is good to those whose hope is in him,
>> to the one who seeks him. (Lam 3:25)

Accompanied by trumpets, cymbals, and other instruments, the singers raised their voices in praise to the LORD and sang: "He is good; his love endures forever" (2 Chr 5:13).

The biblical writers recount God's goodness, not in the abstract, but as palpably present and visibly manifested in daily life. God's goodness pours over into the goodness of his actions that result in our benefit. God's goodness brings forth prosperity from the land:

> The LORD will indeed give what is good,
>> and our land will yield its harvest. (Ps 85:12)

> Hear all the good I do for (this city); they will be in awe and tremble at the abundant prosperity and peace I provide for it. . . . I will restore the fortunes of the land as they were before, says the LORD. (Jer 33:9, 11)

God displays his goodness in his love and mercy (Pss 69:16; 86:5), in his deliverance from adversaries and trouble (Ps 54:7), and in his favor and honor—indeed, in all good things (Ps 84:11). The summation, which tacitly affirms God's own goodness, is plain:

> If you, then, though you are evil, know how to give good gifts to your children, how much more will your Father in heaven give good gifts to those who ask him! (Matt 7:11)

The Scriptures present two persistent and prominent themes: God is good and God is the source of all good things.

God as ontologically good because of his being

Some Christians believe that we should not call God good in a moral sense at all. One such thinker is the Thomist Brian Davies, who contends that something's goodness is intimately connected with the kind of thing it is.[2]

---

2. Davies, *Reality of God*, 198.

To understand divine goodness we need to understand God's being. It is not that we have much of an understanding of God. Indeed, "God is not something we can understand as we normally understand what something is."[3] But we know enough *via negativa* to understand that since God is unchanging and unimprovable he is perfect (itself a negative concept) and thus good.[4]

When Davies speaks about God's goodness, he turns to Thomas Aquinas's discussion of God's goodness, noting that God's goodness is not moral goodness but rather a goodness derived from his being and his creative acts.[5] Aquinas constructed two arguments designed to establish God's goodness. In both cases he drew heavily on his Aristotelian philosophical roots. In his first argument, Aquinas contended that God is good because God has no ontological deficiencies; God is complete. Aquinas employed the Aristotelian act-potency distinction to argue that since potentiality to exist is a lack of existence, whatever is merely potential lacks something and is therefore imperfect. But whatever exists, by virtue of its existing, is actual and thus perfect with respect to its existence. When something created exists, its potentiality to exist has been overcome and it possesses the relevant perfection. Since perfection implies goodness, everything that exists is good by virtue of the fact that it exists. God, as pure act, is unique in that his being and essence are identical; God has no potentiality. God never came into existence but has always been actual. God thus participates fully in his being and hence, never having any ontological deficiencies, is most perfect. Put plainly, God is perfectly good because of his being—the self-sufficient being whose essence is to exist fully and completely.[6] We will term this *ontological goodness*, a goodness derived from and co-extensive with being.

Aquinas based his second argument for God's goodness on the Aristotelian contention that everything desires the good and that everything has a natural *telos* or end that specifies what it should appropriately desire. If everything aims at the good, goodness consists in being desirable and desired. God is both the first cause—the origin—and the final cause—the end or goal—of all things. Since the effect desires to be like its cause, all things desire their own perfection, which is the likeness of divine perfection. That is, all things desire to be perfect in that they want to emulate God. They seek

---

3. Ibid., 227.
4. Ibid., 203.
5. Ibid., 101.
6. Thomas Aquinas, *Summa Theologica*, Ia, Q 3, art. 2 and 4; Q 4, arts. 1 and 2; Ia Q 5, art. 3.

after God their creator as their end. Since everything seeks the good and God is that sought end, God is good.[7]

For Aquinas, these two arguments do not really differ. This follows from his argument for the denotative identity of goodness and being. Goodness, being-desirable, perfection, act, and being are all coextensive or identical. They differ in their conceptual meaning, but in reality they are all the same. Specifically, goodness and being are the same reality; only a conceptual, not a real, distinction differentiates them. Since "goodness" and "being" have different meanings but are in reality identical, God in his perfect being is perfectly good.

If sound, Aquinas's arguments establish that, insofar as God is good by virtue of his nature, goodness belongs to his very essence. God is essentially and necessarily good. This follows from both of Aquinas's arguments for God's goodness. It follows from the first argument because for Aquinas, God's essence is to exist; his existence is indistinguishable from his nature. Therefore, perfection of being, and consequently goodness, is part of God's very essence. According to the second argument, God is the end (*telos*) of everything, including himself. But willing God's own being is the only thing that God wills necessarily. God necessarily promotes the good, which is himself. Similarly, what God created necessarily serves this same end in that it necessarily seeks its own perfection, which is found in emulating God as its cause. Thus, desirability and, consequently, goodness are essential features of God's being. In short, God does not merely happen to be good; God is good necessarily. Since God's acts must accord with God's nature, whatever God does must be good. As Aquinas wrote, "God cannot do anything except that which, if He did it, would be suitable and just."[8]

Davies contends that this goodness is not a moral goodness but a goodness of being. "My argument does not rule out seeing human moral goodness as a reflection of good, for what I am saying is that human moral goodness reflects God and shows us something of what God is. So I have no problem in agreeing that human moral goodness reflects what God is. But that is not the same as saying that the goodness of God is, quite simply, moral goodness."[9] Moral agents are individuals who are subject either to moral praise or moral blame. But God radically differs from all that God created and is subject neither to moral praise (e.g., that God is "well-behaved") nor to moral censure (e.g., that God "acts badly"). Since God is not a moral agent, terms of moral agency that allow for moral evaluation do not apply to God. To apply concepts such as engaging in good or bad behavior, virtue or

---

7. Ibid., Ia, Q 4, art. 4; Q 5, art. 4; Q 6, art. 1.
8. Ibid., Ia, Q 25, art. 5, reply 2.
9. Davies, *Reality of God*, 208

vice, duty or obligation to God commits a category mistake.[10] Neither can one ascribe moral character, like virtue, to God, for since character develops and is manifested over time and since God is unconnected to time, it makes no sense to say that God's character changes or develops. For Davies this reflects how God differs from his creation: they differ in their being. Since God is perfectly complete and completely perfect, no sense can be made of God improving; recommendations or commands that he do so are nonsense. Hence, we do not need moral terms to characterize God's goodness or to hold him accountable. Indeed, Davies argues, to do so is to inappropriately judge God according to some moral standard; to call God morally good seriously anthropomorphizes God.

Davies admits that the Bible portrays God as being "holy, or righteous, or just, or faithful, or merciful, or loving." But, he argues, when the Bible uses these terms, "it does not seem to be commending God for conforming to moral standards (or to what we might call 'universal moral requirements')."[11] We have to understand terms like "holy" as metaphysical and not moral terms. The goodness to which "holy," "righteous," and the like point is not moral goodness but ontological goodness, a goodness or perfection of being. "Holy" as applied to God is not a moral concept, but indicates divine transcendence as an "awe-inspiring mystery distinct from creation."[12] Similarly, "righteous" as applied to God is not a moral notion; God's righteousness is understood as God acting in accord with his covenant: God can be relied on to perform what he says he will do, not because God morally has to but because that is what he does. We might say that it is a performance rather than a character term.

Davies does allow us to call God good, but only in the special way that invokes the analogy of attribution, in which God may be said to possess a property formally in that God is able to *cause* that property or command that good happen. For example, God is rich—"rich" is a proper predicate of "God"—not because God owns things, but because he creates a world of untold riches. Similarly, God possesses the property of moral goodness, not actually in that moral goodness is a literal divine property, but analogously in the sense that God is able to cause or command good to happen. God is good or just, not as a morally good or just agent, but as being the cause of the natures of things, giving things the nature they deserve insofar as they are God's creatures. Analogical terms apply to God so long as nothing that is "essentially creaturely can be literally attributed to God."[13]

10. Ibid., 92.
11. Ibid., 101.
12. Ibid., 94.
13. Ibid., 100.

But as we noted at the beginning of the chapter, the Bible understands God's goodness not as an abstract metaphysical concept but as a quality of character manifested in concrete actions. God's goodness is seen in God's love, faithfulness, righteousness, and justice, all of which stem from moral traits in God's character (Ps 36:6). It is because God actually has these qualities of character, understood univocally, that God acts in ways that we recognize as loving, forgiving, correcting, provisioning, protecting, and saving. God also is reliable, which is manifest in God's covenant-making and keeping (1 Kgs 8:56). Being reliable is a recognizable quality of moral character. In short, the biblical view is that God's goodness is a quality of God's character and the basis of his other moral qualities and his moral agency. God has these properties not simply because he can cause them, but univocally, although to an extent far greater than we can comprehend. Moral goodness is appropriately predicated of God.

God as morally good because of his nature

Whereas Davies denies that moral goodness can be affirmed of God and further, that, ultimately, God is incomprehensible, other Christians avow that God is necessarily morally good. The statement, "God is perfectly good" expresses a necessary truth; God cannot be or do anything but good. The argument for this position is fairly straightforward, typically expressed in what is termed Anselmian theology. For Anselm, God is necessarily good because God, who is the greatest conceivable being, necessarily possesses every perfection or great-making property, and goodness necessarily is a perfection.[14] The more evil something is, the farther it departs from perfection. Hence, God is not merely good, God's nature is goodness itself.

Defenders of this view see this as most consistent with the biblical picture of God.

> Far be it from God to do evil, from the Almighty to do wrong . . .
> It is unthinkable that God would do wrong,
>   that the Almighty would pervert justice. (Job 34:10, 12)

The argument here is that since it is inconceivable that God would do evil, it is impossible for God to do evil, for example, to pervert justice. God as just and mighty stands outside any condemnation. God judges us, not vice versa (34:17–28).

A second passage comes from the New Testament: "God cannot be tempted by evil" (Jas 1:15). If God cannot be tempted by evil, then it is

14. Anselm, *Proslogium*, chapter V.

impossible for him to do evil, since the desire to do such cannot arise in him.

Defenders of God's necessary moral goodness invoke this Anselmian *a priori* approach. But before we can assess the truth of the contention that God is necessarily good, we have to first understand what meaning "good" has when predicated morally of moral agents. This will lead us to ask whether we can meaningfully say that God is necessarily good in a moral sense.

Criteria for attributing moral goodness

While the above approaches to divine goodness are metaphysical and *a priori*, developing from analyses of being and perfection, we might pursue another approach to understanding God's goodness that is *a posteriori*, asking what is required for an agent or person to be morally good or morally praiseworthy. If, for example, we were to say of Abraham Lincoln that he was a morally good person, what features would we be looking for? What criteria would he have to meet to be a morally good agent? At least six criteria are necessary.

1. Morally good persons have a morally virtuous character.

We often act out of the habits or dispositions that we have formed in our lifetime. These predispose, although do not necessitate, us to act in one way rather than another. Thus, it is reasonable to hold that good persons must have the disposition or tendency to do what is right.[15]

2. Morally good persons have intellectual virtue.

They act from relevant knowledge and wisdom. They know the empirical facts and general and moral principles that are relevant to the situation in which they make the decision and have the wisdom necessary to make the best and right choice. Intellectual virtue is necessary to translate right intentions into outward moral action.

3. Morally good persons act from right motives or intentions.[16]

Their doing the right does not result from being unmotivated or from being poorly or badly motivated; otherwise what is done is accidentally accomplished and not meritorious. Rather, they intend to do what is right and best in the situation confronted.

---

15. Mark 7:20–23. The New Testament use of καρδία (heart), referring to the many dimensions of the inner person, goes beyond the Greek notion of character; it is "the main organ of psychic and spiritual life, the place in man at which God bears witness to Himself." Behm, "Καρδία," 611.

16. Matt 5:28, 44.

4. The actions morally good persons perform are right acts.

They accord with some justifiable set of moral standards or universal moral principles.[17]

5. Morally good persons choose and act freely.

As we argued in the second chapter, only if a person is free either to perform or to refrain from performing an action can we hold that person morally accountable or morally praiseworthy for that action. For example, we do not commend someone for not beating his wife when he is in one city and she in another, that is, where the necessity is external.[18] Neither do we morally condemn someone if as a result of an epileptic seizure she injures another person; here the necessity is internal insofar as it is a feature of her genetic or physiological composition. In both of these cases, since the action was not done or was done out of necessity, though the action violated an ethical code or created bad outcomes, the agent who performed the action is neither morally praiseworthy nor blameworthy on account of it.

As we also noted in the second chapter, choosing and acting freely should not be equated with choosing and acting apart from any causal conditions. Were causal conditions absent, one could not choose or act at all. Similarly, choosing and acting freely should not be equated with choosing and acting apart from reasons. Were reasons regarding the choice and action absent, one would be choosing or acting, but doing so irrationally or non-rationally, neither of which we laud for moral behavior. Choosing and acting freely involves both not being causally determined by external causes and being able to choose or do otherwise than one did for reasons one accepts.

The nature of the freedom involved in moral choice must be more closely specified.

6. The freedom must be not only with respect to the doing or not doing of the action, but also with respect to whether the choice itself is between right and wrong actions.

Alvin Plantinga makes this point when he notes that "a person is *significantly free*, on a given occasion, if he is then free with respect to an action that is morally significant for him," and "an action is *morally significant* for a given person at a given time, if it would be wrong for him to perform the action then but right to refrain, or vice versa."[19] Others have phrased

---

17. Matt 19:16–20; John 14:15; Deut 27:10.

18. If the person intended to beat his wife (although distance made it impossible to carry it out), this would reflect negatively on the man's moral character because the man had immoral intentions.

19. Plantinga, *Nature of Necessity*, 166.

this condition in terms of the choice between it being right to perform the action and wrong to not do it, or vice versa, or between doing something worse or better.[20]

Applicability to God

Why should we think that these six criteria apply to God? Maybe God's goodness radically differs from ours. God's goodness is not our goodness. The fact that the criteria noted above apply to humans does not immediately entail their applicability to God. The danger, as we noted above when we discussed Davies's view, is in anthropomorphizing God. We give God human properties that God does not possess. Davies contends that the gap between God and the creation is too great to cross this linguistic and conceptual divide. Persons live in the world, but God as creator is radically other than the created and hence is completely incomprehensible using human language.[21] We can know that God exists, is perfect and good, but we cannot say what these concepts mean as applied to God in any positive sense.

An approach emphasizing the inapplicability of language and incomprehensibility of God is neither philosophically nor theologically fruitful. Restricting our theological discourse to negative predicates leaves us conceptually bankrupt. If the meaning of terms applied to God requires complete or significant variance from its application to agents in general, then we are at an impasse to understand what God is like and consequently about what our language about God means. "The word *good*, applied to Him, becomes meaningless: like abracadabra. We have no motive for obeying Him. Not even fear. It is true we have His threats and promises. But why should we believe them? If cruelty is from His point of view 'good,' telling lies may be 'good' too."[22] To address this issue adequately would require a separate extensive treatise on religious language. What we can say is that if we are to make and understand claims or statements about "good" in a moral sense with respect to God, then the fundamental criteria governing the use of the term for God must be comparable with its use for moral agents in general. Our denial of significant criteriological variance does not prevent there being significant differences in the way that the criteria are met, for example, the nature of divine character or God's reason for doing the right, but it does mean that if we are to understand discourse about God's properties, there must be a commonality of essential meaning. "Good" as applied to God

20. Bergmann and Cover, "Divine Responsibility," 386–89.
21. Davies, *Reality of God*, 92.
22. Lewis, *Grief Observed*, 37.

cannot mean something quite different from that applied to humans. As C. S. Lewis notes in his analogical style,

> The Divine "goodness" differs from ours, but it is not sheerly different: it differs from ours not as white from black but as a perfect circle from a child's first attempt to draw a wheel. But when the child has learned to draw, it will know that the circle it then makes is what it was trying to make from the very beginning.[23]

One response to this view is to invoke an analogical understanding of the term "good." But if we adopt analogical predication, how are we to understand this sense of "good"? Above we noted that a term can be analogically predicated of something when that being is able to cause that property. For example, we may call a particular place a health resort, not because it actually has the property of being healthy but because it causes those who visit it to become healthy. Or again, red, ripe peaches are tempting not because they univocally possess this property but because they have the power to tempt us to eat them. The problem is that the analogy of attribution is both too broad and uninformative. It is too broad in that we can appropriately predicate almost any property of God insofar as God is the creating cause of the universe. Analogy understood in this fashion does not help us to pick out or determine those characteristics that are uniquely appropriate to our understanding of God rather than of God's creative activity. Analogical predicates so understood are informative about God's actual properties in that they tell us about what God is capable of doing, but not about what God is.

The analogy of proportionality holds that God possesses his properties in accordance with his nature analogously to the way that humans possess their properties in accordance with their nature. According to the analogy of proportionality, a dog has the property of thinking in relation to its nature, just as humans have the property of being able to think in relation to their nature. The thinking is proportionate insofar as their natures are similar and different. Applied to God, God is good in relation to his nature in the way that we are good in relation to our nature. The goodness is proportionate insofar as God's nature and ours are similar and different (analogous). On this analysis, the six criteria noted above for ascribing goodness to a human person are correlative with human nature; the criteria that apply for ascribing goodness to God will be correlative with God's nature. Thus, if we are to be able to appropriately correlate God's goodness with God's nature we need to know God's nature. But if goodness is necessary or essential to God's nature (which is the view under consideration), to understand God's nature

---

23. Lewis, *Problem of Pain*, 39.

we need prior understanding of the very goodness whose understanding is in question, and to understand this goodness we invoked the analogy of proportionality. The analogy of proportionality does not get us out of this loop.

In short, there must be univocal criteria that control the use of the analogy that are comprehensible to us; otherwise it makes little sense to call God morally good. Although to repeat, the way and extent to which God satisfies them will surely differ from the way we do, it is reasonable to think that these controlling criteria in the case of "good" are what we have specified above in (1–6). To the understanding of and reasons for this we now turn.

Character

When we apply these six criteria to God's goodness, two are particularly relevant to our discussion. Let us begin with character. Since our actions arise out of our character, that good persons have the appropriate virtuous character is necessary to their being good. "It's because God has the recognizably good character he does that it's rational to see him as the entity who satisfies our description of the ultimate Good."[24] How is it that God has a recognizably good character? In virtue of what does God have this character? Traditionally, character was held to be something that one acquires over time by doing good acts. Aristotle wrote that moral virtue is acquired by habit. The more one does the right, the more one is disposed to do the right. "None of the moral virtues arises in us by nature. . . . Neither by nature, then, nor contrary to nature do the virtues arise in us; rather we are adapted by nature to receive them, and are made perfect by habit. . . . The virtues we get by exercising them."[25] One finds hints of this in the New Testament, where we are "to put on the new self, created to be like God in true righteousness and holiness" (Eph 4:24). Character is developed by self-forming actions.[26]

As I noted above, that character develops over time is one reason why Davies rejects ascribing character to God. But for many, God does not possess character by virtue of God's actions; God is immutable and therefore does not acquire his character. God's character has always been perfectly good.

That character can be innate appears counterintuitive, given Aristotle's discussion. At the same time, it is consistent with those strands of traditional

---

24. Baggett and Walls, *Good God*, 93.
25. Aristotle, *Nichomachean Ethics* II, 1.
26. Kane, "Rethinking Free Will," 383.

Christian thought that hold that humans are innately affected with original sin. How original sin gets treated varies. For some it is a disposition: because of Adam's sin, we are born with a disposition or tendency to do evil. For others original sin is more determinative. Augustine understands original sin as rendering us into the state of *non posse non peccare*.[27]

Interestingly, recent studies suggest that babies have not only the innate ability to distinguish right from wrong, but also the roots of moral dispositions to generosity, fairness, justice, and deserts. "A growing body of evidence, though, suggests that humans do have a rudimentary moral sense from the very start of life."[28] "Babies are oriented towards pro-social individuals. They prefer interacting with a pro-social individual over an anti-social individual."[29] But the researcher also notes that babies also demonstrate negative traits, such as bias toward those who are like them and against those who differ from them. The actions of babies do not constitute moral behavior because we associate morality with free, rational choice, not with mere innately-rooted responses. But it suggests the possibility that the roots of moral behavior—innate predispositions to both virtuous and non-virtuous actions—might lie within us from birth.

Defenders of God's innate moral character may believe that character is determinative of God's actions rather than merely dispositional. Impeccable character determines impeccable action. But if the character that determines actions is compatible with God's freedom, is it not possible for God to give humans a character that determines their actions while protecting their freedom?[30] One problem with this suggestion is that whereas the character of God would be innate and not caused by another being, so that God's freedom is not affected, if God imputed character into us, it is not acquired by us through our experience but caused by God. In such a scenario our freedom would be compromised in that we could not do anything but the right.

Leaving the question of freedom aside and focusing simply on the issue of innate character, if God had bestowed on us perfect moral character and if character is determinative, it would seem that we, like God, would be impeccable. We could not but do the right. Given a determinative relation between character and action, the difference between God and

---

27. It must be noted that Augustine's discussion of original sin is not in terms of character but in terms of will. Originally, Adam had the ability to choose either good or evil (freedom of the will). But after he sinned, Adam lost the ability and will to choose good without divine assistance. Augustine, *Enchiridion*, 104–5.

28. Bloom, "Moral Life," *New York Times*.

29. Wynn, quoted in O'Brien and Baime, "Babies."

30. Guleserian raises this issue. "Divine Freedom," 348–66.

humans with respect to performing moral acts then would have to relate to something other than dispositions. Possibly the difference would have to do with knowledge. As omniscient, God possesses such knowledge that God's moral character is always manifested wisely and rightly, whereas humans have finite knowledge, such that their moral errors would not be due to their moral character (on a scenario where God granted humans perfect moral character) but due to their limited knowledge. Whereas in God it is the combination of character and knowledge that makes God's actions impeccable, our human epistemic finitude would be the culprit. We would do evil out of ignorance, not immoral character.[31] This emphasizes the critical importance of our second criterion, namely, that morally good beings possess not only moral but epistemic virtue: the relevant knowledge and wisdom to be able to exercise well their moral judgments.

Libertarians will not see character as determinative of actions but as dispositional. Anticipating our subsequent discussion, it is always logically possible that one act "out of character" or contrary to one's character. If we are correct about human epistemic finitude, in our case it is not only possible but likely that we will act freely not only contrary to our character but wrongly at times. But in God's case acting wrongly is morally and epistemically impossible, given God's combination of God's quality of character and extent of knowledge.

Morally significant freedom

Suppose we grant that for God the moral quality of God's actions follows necessarily from his innate character, that God always and necessarily does right and good. This runs counter to criterion 6 for determining that a person is good. Necessary impeccability is compatible with criterion 5, since God still could choose among various right actions. God is free in that God is not causally determined to do any particular right action. But it is incompatible with 6, which specifies that morally good persons must be free with respect to the *rightness and wrongness* of the action.

The argument for 6 is based on the contention that only if a person is significantly free, that is, free qua the rightness of the action, can we properly term the person good in a moral sense. If it is logically or causally impossible for the individual to perform a wrong action, so that the person can freely perform only acts each of which accords with the ethical standards for right actions, then despite the fact that the person acts freely in choosing

---

31. The follow-up question, which we cannot take up here, would be whether God could give us perfect knowledge, so that coupled with good character we would not do evil.

between right options it would be inappropriate to commend that person morally for performing right actions.[32] The person might be commendable in terms of intellectual virtue in the sense that the person has prudently chosen the best path presented by the respective goods, but since in this case performing any of the actions accords with the moral norm, doing any of them would manifest moral virtue. Although the person is free with respect to performing or not performing any given action, no *moral* significance attaches to the person choosing or doing the right, for the person could not have chosen or done otherwise than the right or the best.

One response would be to deny that 6 is a necessary condition of moral goodness. This position is developed by Thomas Morris, who questions the applicability of 6 to God on the grounds that 6 appeals to a duty ethic and that God does not have any moral duties. Morris holds to a duty ethic for humans, while at the same time freeing God from having any moral duties (and thus from the necessity of keeping and the possibility of breaking a duty). "We can hold that those moral principles which function as either deontically prescriptive or proscriptive for human conduct stand in some other relation to divine conduct. We could even go so far as to claim that they are merely descriptive of the shape of divine activity."[33] Morris distinguishes between acting from duty and acting in accord with moral principles that for humans would constitute duties. In our actions we are bound by moral duties; we ought to keep the moral laws. But God freely acts in necessary accordance with moral principles; as perfectly good he follows moral principles but is not bound by them as constituting his duties. That is, God does what is right not because God is so obligated but as flowing from his character of perfect goodness. For example, God does not engage in promise making, for this would mean he would have a duty to fulfill his promises. What looks to us like divine promise-makings are rather statements of divine intention to act in a particular manner. What appears to be promising is really an affirmation that God will act according to his intention, necessarily, but not from any duty. Similarly with truth telling; God is not obligated to tell the truth; rather, he freely follows his intentions to tell the truth necessarily.

But why is it necessary that God intentionally act in accord with the moral law? Morris cannot give moral reasons for doing so, for that would introduce acting from moral principles back into the equation. The *ought* found in moral duty is replaced with an *is:* it simply is a necessary fact—but not a moral fact—that when God acts, God acts according to the moral law.

---

32. See Pike, "Omnipotence," 215–6.
33. Morris, *Anselmian Explorations*, 36.

One might object to Morris that on this description God is not worthy of praise. Since God has no duties, no basis exists for praising God for carrying out God's duties. Morris replies that this is unproblematic, for praise is given not for performance of duty but for supererogatory acts, and God, insofar as he graciously brings about great providential good that he is not required to bring about or insofar as he communicates with us in our humble estate, can be praised for this. In effect, acts of providence are not duties but gracious acts of supererogation.

But in what sense now is God good? Morris introduces the term "axiological goodness." Axiological goodness, which is appropriate to the kind of being God is, is the goodness found in engaging "in deeds of supererogation and free acts in accordance with moral principles."[34] Acting out of supererogation is a common property between human and divine axiological goodness, whereas acting necessarily in accord with moral principles (and not out of duty) applies only to divine axiological goodness. Of course, this abandons the view that moral goodness (having duties or obligations) applies to God, but for Morris this is inconsequential since axiological goodness captures all that we need to understand about goodness relevant to God's necessarily perfect nature.

Morris thinks that axiological goodness accords with a biblical account of divine activity and with God's relations with humans. But to the contrary, to exchange moral goodness for axiological goodness would deprive many biblical descriptions of God's actions and relations to humans of their moral force. As we saw at the outset of this chapter, God makes promises he is expected to keep, engages in dialogue about the justice expected from him, makes covenants that as confirmed with an oath lead to expectations, and assures that he does not lie. Perhaps the most notable passage is the striking dialogue between Abraham and Yahweh. The question at stake in the conversation is whether God's justice would allow him to destroy in Sodom the innocent along with the guilty. Abraham suggests that God has a duty to not to sweep away the righteous with the wicked. "Far be it from you to do such a thing—to kill the righteous with the wicked, treating the righteous and the wicked alike. Far be it from you! Will not the judge of the earth do right?" (Gen 18:25). In effect, Abraham holds God to account. Similarly with God's covenant-making. Ezekiel 18:21–29 records a similar affirmation of God's justice in light of God's acts and in comparison with human acts of injustice. In the Noahitic story, God not only makes a covenant with Noah, but institutes a sign of his promise—not for Noah's recall but for God's own remembering (Gen 9:12–16). The rainbow reminds God of his covenant and the obligations that covenant-making entails, in this case that God never

34. Ibid., 39–40.

again destroy all life in a flood. God's signs also remind those with whom God made a covenant that he can be expected to be faithful in carrying out what he has promised (Gen 15).

The Psalmist also expects God to fulfill his covenant, to rescue his people from their enemies (Ps 74:20). The Psalmist reminds God of his great love and the faithfulness on which he took an oath (Ps 89:49–50). God took an oath with Abraham that his seed would be as numerous as the stars (Exod 22:11) and that God would rescue Abraham's descendants from their enemies so that they could serve God without fear (Luke 1:73). God's oath to Abraham was based on God's utter truthfulness and reliability (Heb 6:13–18). God also took an oath with David that one of his descendants would occupy his throne (Acts 2:30). The mention of oaths is important in that oaths are used with duties; they are visible signs that one is bound by and will fulfill one's duty.

In a passage we noted earlier, the Psalmist refers to God as good and upright (Ps 25:7–8; see Pss 92:15; 119:137). In the Song of Moses we find,

> His works are perfect,
>   and all his ways are just.
> A faithful God who does no wrong,
>   upright and just is he. (Deut 32:6)

The word for "upright" is *yashar*, which means "straight," "right," "level." Since to determine whether something or someone is straight, right, or level one needs a standard, these verses suggest that it is appropriate to apply standards to God's actions.

In short, many biblical passages describing God's virtues and acts are ambiguous enough to allow alternative readings: either, as Morris suggests, that God in being faithful and just acts according to the moral law or, as we have indicated, in terms of obligation. Yet, we have noted, some critical passages conflict with his contention that God's goodness differs from ours as not being obligatory

Equally problematic with Morris's axiological position is the question whether supererogation can be understood independently of a deontic ethic. Supererogatory actions are good actions that are better to do than an alternative permissible act, optional because costly to the performer but not blameworthy if not performed, and in the doing of which one goes beyond one's duty.[35] What is apparent is the presence of an obligatory framework that underlies this analysis of supererogatory acts. First, supererogatory acts are optional not because persons are not beholden to duties or obligations,

---

35. Young, "God's Moral Goodness," 87.

but because in assessing the total weight of the action considerations apply that have to do with the cost to the agent and that mitigate the duty. The soldier who faces the choice of falling on a hand grenade tossed by an enemy into the crowded foxhole would have a duty to fall on it if he could be assured that he would not be killed or injured by his action (i.e., if he was wearing a suit of impenetrable body armor). But without this assurance, the duty to fall on the grenade is mitigated. Second, supererogatory acts are not blameworthy when not performed. The language of blameworthiness employs duties or goods that have to be assessed. Third, if one performs a supererogatory action, one goes beyond one's duty, for example, a duty to oneself on behalf of others. Thus, supererogation invokes a context where the concept of duty is intrinsically involved. In short, even if Morris is correct that the good involved in God's good actions is axiological good understood as supererogation, he has not circumvented the notion of obligation with respect to God. If one cannot understand and unpack supererogation without invoking obligations, reducing God's goodness to supererogation provides no escape for avoiding the conditions for moral goodness, including criterion 4, we specified above.

In sum, although Morris is correct that God acts in accordance with moral standards, he is not correct in claiming that axiological goodness captures all that we need to understand about goodness with respect to God. There are enough clear scriptural evidences of duty and obligation as applied to God to prohibit us from ruling out the obligatory nature of divine action. And one cannot understand supererogation without invoking duty or obligation.

A defense of divine necessary goodness

Alexander Pruss presents a different argument for the thesis that criterion 6 does not properly apply to God. (I have numbered his statements).

7. "God is the most perfect possible object for human love."

8. "The more deeply committed a love is, the more deeply true it is that the lover would love the beloved *no matter what*."

9. "Love involves an appreciation of a good."

10. "The more permanent, lasting and non-contingent the good, the more committed can the love be insofar as it is an appreciation of this good."

11. "Therefore, ... this love is most strongly committed when this good is one that the beloved has *essentially*, for then the lover can be committed to have had this dimension of love absolutely no matter what had befallen. Even to imagine a logically possible scenario under which the lover *ought not to* have had this dimension of love is to weaken the commitment in the love."[36] (Italics are in the original.)

The argument is insightful but problematic. First, a clarification: 7 is true for God as a title and hence for any being (like Yahweh) who is God. This distinction between "God" as a title and "God" as a proper name is important, and I will return to it below. Second, adding the italicized "no matter what" to 8 raises the question whether 8 is true. It ignores the fact that although person A loves person B unconditionally now and seeing the good in B is fully committed to B, this does not entail that A must love B later should A discover that B is or was not good or is undeserving of that love. If, as Pruss suggests, love responds to the beloved's goodness, then it would be downright inappropriate to love B absolutely if in fact A discovers that B is or was not good or, horribly evil. That one has absolute love now does not commit one to love absolutely later *no matter what*.

Suppose, however, that we grant 8, the argument still does not work, for 8 stands in tension with 10. 10 provides a condition that was absent in 8, with the result that 10 conflicts with 8. 8 says that the deepest love will be found when the lover loves the beloved, *no matter what*. The depth of the love depends on the lover, not the beloved. 10, on the other hand, says that the amount or depth of love depends upon the beloved. Love is better if the beloved cannot not be good: its goodness is non-contingent and permanent. 11 clearly embodies this very tension. Thus, the argument fails to show that criterion 6 does not apply to God. Although 7 is true for any being bearing the title God, it does not follow that any being that is God must be good necessarily.

Agent responsibility and thankfulness

A different attempt to resolve the issue of the apparent inconsistency of divine necessity with morally significant freedom keeps the concept of moral goodness but approaches the discussion through the concept of responsibility. The argument is that even if God is not free with respect to bringing about a better or worse action, God is still the agent-cause of the action, and responsibility accrues from being the agent-cause of the action. A being is

---

36. Pruss, "Free-Will Defense," 221.

an agent-cause just in case nothing, not even its nature, causes the agent to act. As Bergmann and Cover put it, when the buck stops with the agent who exercises its volitional power, no one or nothing else could be responsible. And if the person is responsible, they go on, the person is thankworthy. "If (2) God is responsible for some good act and (b) he performs it for the right reasons, then he is thankworthy even if (c*) he can't do better or worse than what he does."[37] For example, if a mother recognizes that God raised her child from the dead,

> couldn't she sensibly tell God that (i) she acknowledges this as indeed a good act, (ii) she realizes that he is to be credited with performing it, (iii) she is glad and greatly relieved that he performed it, and (iv) she considers herself to be in his debt ... since nothing else caused her son to be raised from the dead? [If so,] she could sensibly thank God for raising her son from the dead.[38]

But to get their conclusion Bergmann and Cover conflate two senses of responsibility. One sense derives from the fact that the agent alone did the action and was not caused by something else to do so, and hence can be thanked for the action. The responsibility here is causal, and the thanking is given for the causal action taken. It expresses gratitude for the beneficial action (as above, raising the child from the dead), recognizing that the particular effects would not have occurred had the agent not acted. For example, one might be thankful that during the picnic the wind came up and blew away all the mosquitoes. That the wind acted as it did satisfies criteria (i)–(iv) above: the action was good because beneficial, the wind and not the mosquito repellent blew the insects away, one is relieved to be free from the pestering insects, and one is "in his debt" in that one could not have accomplished this by oneself. But the thankfulness has nothing to do with moral praiseworthiness, only with assigning causal responsibility.

One might object that the wind is not an agent because it does not act freely but rather from its nature and other causal conditions (that it is caused to act as it does). But that something acts necessarily from its nature is precisely what is at stake in the argument as to whether God's actions that are necessarily good render God morally praiseworthy. And if we apply agency only to agents that are free, then Bergmann's and Cover's arguments regarding the appropriateness of thankfulness to God even if God is not free fade, since their point was that freedom was not necessary for returning thankfulness.

37. Bergmann and Cover, "Divine Responsibility," 402.
38. Ibid., 400.

Whereas the responsibility they present is agent-causal, the responsibility that is relevant to our discussion about divine (and human) goodness is not only agent-causal but moral. And moral responsibility requires more than mere agency. One wants to be able to praise the agent for its moral action. But being morally praiseworthy requires not merely freedom, but morally significant freedom. The wind is neither a free nor significantly free agent, and hence it would be inappropriate to morally praise it for an action that proved beneficial. Similarly, where a personal being is not significantly free, thankfulness understood in a moral sense of recognizing praiseworthiness is inappropriate.

Judging divine actions morally

Criterion 4 above concerns the necessary condition that the person's actions are right. This requires assessing the actions of the person; do the person's actions satisfy the moral standards for rightness in that situation? Critics contend that we cannot judge divine actions; to do so is to treat God anthropomorphically. The implications of such a position are significant. For one thing, the nub of the argument from the existence of pain, suffering, and dysfunction (the problem of evil) to the conclusion that God does not exist or lacks critical divine properties is that these evils in some way count against God's goodness. They are either incompatible with a God of a certain sort, or in their profusion make it unlikely that a God of this sort exists. But if we cannot assess God's actions then the problem of evil disappears. The arguments from the existence of evil assume the moral principle: "Good is opposed to evil, in such a way that a good thing eliminates evil as far as it can."[39] The rejection of the contention that God has duties, as Morris advocates, eliminates the argument from evil, for without such duties one cannot expect God to eliminate evil. God might do it, but God has no such duty or obligation. On this view, instead of agreeing that evil presents even a *prima facie* problem that is worth pondering and addressing, we must conclude that we cannot judge that evil is in any way inconsistent with God's goodness. Of course, this view also prevents Christians from presenting a defense of God's goodness and justice or constructing theodicies that suggest possible morally sufficient reasons for God allowing evil. If there is no problem of evil, then we need not worry about constructing defenses of and theodicies for God's goodness. God's ways and categories are not our ways and categories.

---

39. Mackie, "Evil and Omnipotence," 201.

I find it difficult to dismiss the problem of evil in this fashion. To have read any number of books about suffering, such as Elie Weisel's *Night* or *The Trial of God*, Roméo Dallaire's *Shake Hands with the Devil: The Failure of Humanity in Rwanda*, Philip Gourevitch's *We Wish to Inform You That Tomorrow We Will Be Killed with Our Families*, or Nawuth Keat and Martha Kendall's *Alive in the Killing Fields: Surviving the Khmer Rouge Genocide,* or to hear discussion regarding the everyday difficulties severely ill or abused people suffer, and not to be moved—or think that God is not moved—by the problem of suffering, is difficult to fathom. It is true that a recent flurry of writings espouse divine hiddenness and cognitive limitations as rational ways to address the problem of evil. But this view usually affirms that evil counts against God's goodness. It just does not count *decisively*, since we do not know enough about God and his intentions. But we have no reason to go to the extreme contention that moral duties do not apply to God at all, for this moves the discussion even further away from human experience and rational discussion and understanding.

God's goodness contingently understood

The remaining option, which takes seriously the six criteria for ascribing goodness to persons, is to hold that God is not necessarily good. It is not that God is not perfectly good, but only that God is not necessarily so. The contingency view of divine goodness does not rely on the view that what is conceivable is possible. Rather, it rests on the contention that both God and humans must satisfy the same criteria, including criterion 6, for ascribing moral goodness. The logical possibility of doing evil is necessary for ascription of moral goodness. There is nothing morally praiseworthy about doing what one has to do.

A frequent objection that critics raise is that giving up God's necessary goodness carries "a rather high philosophical cost that we should not be willing to pay."[40] The cost is not only God's necessary impeccability but the possession of other essential properties like omnipotence, omniscience, and immutability.

Morris, for one, contends that the appeal to a contingent view of divine goodness will not meet criterion 6, for it would require giving up these essential properties of the divine. Even were God's goodness contingent, given God's other necessary and stable properties of omnipotence and omniscience, God's goodness would have to be a stable characteristic. For Morris, a characteristic is stable if whatever has it cannot either have acquired it

---

40. Baggett and Walls, *Good God*, 58

(it is immemorial) or lose it (it is enduring).[41] For example, God's existence is stable in that if God exists, God can neither come into nor pass out of existence. Morris's argument, in brief, is that, suppose the being is God. If this being that is God is to do evil, it must intend to do such, since all God's actions are intentional. If this being intended to do evil at t, then as omniscient, it knew before t (t-1) that it intended to do evil, and as omnipotent it would have the power at t to bring about its intention. If God intends to do evil, then at any prior moment God as stable intends and knows it. But intending to do evil is itself evil, and hence by intending at t-1 to do evil at t, the being that is God was blameworthy at t-1 and therefore not God. And the same holds for any prior moment of that being's intending such. Hence, since the being is God, in virtue of God's stability or immutability the being that is God cannot do or intend to do evil; and as omnipotent and omniscient this being would know about this and have the power to prevent its doing evil. If the being could do evil, the being was not God in the first place, contrary to what we supposed.

But this is precisely the point—with a modal modification. To merit the title of God, a being must be omnipotent, omniscient, and perfectly good. Hence, although it must be logically possible for the being who is God to do evil if it is to be morally good, to be God it must neither do evil nor intend to do evil. It must be morally perfect. So we need to modify Morris's conclusion. If a being actually is God, then by virtue of God's stability or immutability the being will not do evil. And if this being does evil, then it was not God in the first place, although one (mistakenly) might have thought it was God, that is, thought that it merited the title God.

It is important to properly distinguish between the use of "God" as a title and as a name. When we speak about "God" being used as a title, we affirm the characteristic that God is perfectly good. When we affirm that the being that is God must be good, we mean that being perfectly good is a necessary condition for any being to merit the title God. We cannot affirm that this being is good necessarily, for this, as we have seen, is problematic in that it fails to meet criterion 6 of what it is to ascribe moral goodness to something. When we affirm that God (as a particular being, such as Yahweh) is good, we understand that God can be and is morally perfect, just not necessarily so. It is true that we cannot "really conceive of [an essentially sinless] entity sinning";[42] that proposition is self-contradictory. But the issue is whether it is possible that a good being do evil. That it is logically possible is not to lose anything but rather gives meaning to the notion of the moral goodness of the being that is God.

---

41. Morris, *Anselmian Explorations*, 77.
42. Baggett and Walls, *Good God*, 62.

This distinction between name and title has significant biblical precedent. Yahweh affirms that other gods, though thought by some to be God, are not really God because they fail to have the requisite credentials. They are incapable of knowing the future (Isa 41:21–29; 44:6–8). People are misled into treating beings as gods when on closer inspection they are not. Israel is repeatedly warned not to be misled into making covenants with or worshiping false claimants to the title (Exod 23:32). Only Yahweh has legitimate claim to being God.

A being's omnipotence or, better, almightiness, is not affected by this contingency view of divine goodness. If being almighty is the ability to carry out what one wills or intends, then a being could be almighty and still not be perfectly good. In such a case it could carry out its intentions to do evil at some point. That is, it would manifest one necessary condition of being God but not another. We will say more about God's power in the following two chapters.

What then of impeccability? We have argued that no sense can be made of necessary moral goodness, but we still can understand impeccability. By differentiating "God" as a name from "God" as a title, we can see that "good" plays different roles in the two cases. If the being that is God (Yahweh) is to merit the title God, it must be morally perfect. That the being who is God is not good necessarily—that logically this being is able to do evil and that its choice in some cases will be between doing good and doing evil—does not imply or make is likely that it will do evil.

Although an established lineage exists for the belief that if something is conceivable (or inconceivable) it is possible (or impossible), the inference does not hold. Baggett and Walls develop the following argument. Consider any necessary truth, for example, Goldbach's conjecture—"Every even integer greater than 2 can be written as the sum of two primes." For many people who know little about mathematics this proposition could be either true or false, and even people who know a great deal about mathematics might once have conceived it to be false. However, the epistemic possibility of conceiving the conjecture to be false does not create the possibility of its being false. If the conjecture is true, it is necessarily true, and one could not have really conceived of it being false; it would be a pseudo-conceiving. But since we have no available criteria other than possibility itself to distinguish real- from pseudo-conceiving, we have to abandon the universality of the conceivability principle: conceivability is not an independent ground for determining possibility. One has to know whether something is in fact possible to determine whether the conceivability is genuine or not.[43]

---

43. Ibid., 59.

To say that the being that is God can do evil (God has the ability to choose to do evil given God's freedom, so that doing evil is logically conceivable) is compatible with saying that the being that is God cannot do evil, that given God's virtuous character and knowledge it is morally unthinkable or impossible that God would do evil. That the being that is God cannot do evil—impeccability—must not be understood as the "cannot" of logical force. Rather, it is the "cannot" of moral force, where God's character, knowledge, and virtues are such that doing evil is so totally repugnant to the being that is God that this being morally cannot do evil. The contingent nature of God's goodness does not jeopardize our trust that the being that is God is perfectly good.

It might appear problematic whether Yahweh knows that he is God. One might respond that Yahweh knows that he is God by virtue of his total knowledge, including foreknowledge; he knows that he never has nor will intend to do or actually do wrong or evil. He knows his own character. This would provide a basis for his certainty about his status, though not any nonmoral certainty for us since we don't have direct access to that knowledge. We still must rely on our moral, not logical, certainty. It might be objected further that on this scenario it is possible that, were Yahweh not God, we would live in a godless world. But this does not follow. Even if Yahweh or Jesus turned out not to be God, a being who is God could still exist. What we have done is misidentified the being who is God, as the Old Testament prophets noted about the surrounding nations and indeed as we might argue about worshippers of the gods of other religions and they about us.

One caveat remains. Suppose, as many believers in divine necessary goodness hold, that character does not merely predispose but necessitates. If, contrary to what we have argued, this is the case, then on their own grounds the view that it is morally impossible for the being that is God to do evil is greatly strengthened. If this being has the character of moral goodness and if character morally necessitates, then although it is *logically* possible that this being do evil, it clearly follows that morally it cannot.

Scriptural texts and logically necessary goodness

Earlier we noted two key passages to which those who see God's goodness as logically necessary appeal. What can be said about them? The first was from Job 34:10–12. "Far be it from God to do evil, from the Almighty to do wrong. . . . It is unthinkable that God would do wrong, that the Almighty would pervert justice." Does this show that it is impossible that God do wrong? It depends on how we understand "God" and "unthinkable." If what is referred to by "God" here is the title, then it is impossible for God to do wrong, since a defining characteristic of God is that God is perfectly good. But if we understand "God" as a name, then it is logically conceivable that God do wrong, though if he did (counterfactually), he would not be God but only mistakenly believed to be such. If by "unthinkable" is meant "logically impossible," then the passage is problematic. But if it means that it is unthinkable because of God's moral character, then this passage fits nicely into our argument. The author most probably never thought about this issue, so that the distinctions do not figure in the poetry. One meaningful hint, however, is that Elihu is intent on justifying God rather than Job (32:2). And justification is properly understood in terms of giving reasons in support or defense of persons and their actions.

Elihu focuses both on the greatness of God, which does not truck any complaint (33:12-13), and on the question of character. Through Elihu the author contrasts the goodness of the Almighty with the character of Job. Although Job affirms his innocence, Elihu treats him as a liar, an associate of evildoers, and as one who has abandoned the task of pleasing God. The "character assassination" that forms part of the contrast hints that the issue is treated not ontologically but morally. Exhibiting his just character God punishes evil impartially (which are not acts of supererogation) and responds to the cry of the needy (34:28), "gives the afflicted their rights" (36:6), and rewards repentance and obedience (36:11).

> The Almighty is beyond our reach and exalted in power;
> > in his justice and great righteousness he does not oppress
> Therefore, people revere him,
> > for does he not have regard for all the wise in heart? (Job 37:23-24)

This lends support to the latter interpretation of the passage, that God is seen not in his title role, but as the implementer of justice in his role as administrator over the earth.

The second passage was "God cannot be tempted by evil" (Jas 1:15). If God cannot be tempted by evil, then it would seem to be impossible for him to do evil, since the desire to do such cannot arise. But how does this square with the temptation of Jesus in Matthew 4:1-11 and the New Testament's comment that Jesus the Son of God was tempted as we were and did not sin (Heb 4:14-15). Jesus' temptation would not have been real or significant, nor would his empathy with us be significant, if it were not possible for him to have yielded to temptation and sinned. Of course, one might ascribe the reality of the temptation strictly to the human nature of the Son, as Oscar Cullman does. "The emphatic statement that he was 'tested' κατὰ πάντα καθ' ὁμοιότητα, 'in every respect, in quite the same way as we are,' implies that he was susceptible to all the temptations that are connected with the weaknesses inherent in the frailty of humanity."[44] But this fails to treat the incarnation holistically; more than Christ's humanity is in view in the Hebrews passage, since this high priest is designated the Son of God, the pre-incarnational being who in the beginning was the creator (Heb 1:2, 10).

To develop a resolution we can again employ the distinction between "God" used as a title and "God" used as a proper name. In fact, the first verse, where James mentions and distinguishes both God and the Lord Jesus Christ, provides the clue that this distinction is appropriately applied here. Verse 15 treats "God" as the title of the being who cannot be tempted. Since the divine being is necessarily good, he would not be capable of evil desires. When "God" is treated as a proper name, the being who is God can be tempted, as the Synoptic Gospels and Hebrews attest of Jesus. Attending to this important distinction helps us to properly address this passage.

In short, it is possible to read some scriptural passages as indicating God's logically necessary goodness. However, it is not necessary to interpret them in this fashion; indeed, we contend that it is more coherent and consistent with the overall context to interpret them as consistent with God's logically contingent but morally necessary goodness.

An empirical case

We began this chapter thinking about God's providential goodness, noting scriptural passages that by invoking human experience strongly affirm the providential goodness of God. Some people, however, introduce empirical evidence that they believe warrants a different conclusion.[45] In particular, how do we address divine acts or commands that *prima facie* appear to conflict with what we take to be recognized standards of goodness or justice? I will have more to say about the problem of reconciling divine providence with suffering and evil in chapter 9. Here I want to think about what some take to be a particularly telling example of voluntarily undertaken divine acts or divinely issued commands that appear to seriously jeopardize, if not contradict, our opening contention that God is good. Ironically, the very acts and commands in question occur in the context of divine providence. God, who on the basis of his creation claims all land as his own,[46] providentially chooses one group of people on whom to bestow a particular parcel

---

44. Cullmann, *Christology*, 95.

45. Bradley, "Moral Argument," 129–46; Morriston, "Divinely Mandated Genocide," 117–35.

46. Lev 25:23; Isa 27:4. See Reichenbach, "Genesis 1," 47–69.

of land, and at the same time, through the somewhat successful militarism of this group, kills or expels the traditional inhabitants of that parcel so that the chosen group can occupy it. God gives the Israelites the land of Canaan; the fertile land is neither their natural birthright nor theirs by their acts of conquest, although they forcefully occupy it by their military victories (Deut 6:23—7:2). Our issue relating to the question of God's goodness concerns not primarily the eviction of the inhabitants[47] but the way the land is cleansed; it worries about how the invading Israelites should treat the conquered people.

The Old Testament texts portray God as the one who gives victory over Israel's enemies. God, not great generals or large, moral armies (Judg 7:2), received the credit for subduing the Canaanites, although the conquest is accomplished through human armies. God delivers the enemy into their hand, but Israelite activity is not excluded. The ultimate success of the conquest depends on Israel's willingness and ability to expel or destroy the inhabitants. "I will establish your borders. . . . I will hand over to you the people who live in the land and you will drive them out before you" (Exod 23:31–32).[48] God is the victor but uses people to achieve his ends.[49] Unfortunately, Israel failed to remove the Canaanites (Ps 106:34–39), for which

---

47. The case for the justice of eviction goes back to the claim that God in virtue of creation owns the land he created and hence has the right to apportion it as he pleases. One might question whether once people have occupied or squatted on land for an extended period of time their removal would be just. They would have no reason to think that the land was not theirs by virtue of extended possession. But that would be a matter for ethical debate about the relation between original property claims and prolonged occupation rights, not easily settled however. Although this issue has considerable importance, we will focus on the more serious command of extermination.

48. "They fought against you, but I gave them into your hands. I destroyed them from before you. . . . You did not do it with your own sword and bow" (Josh 24:8, 12). "Be assured today that the Lord your God is the one who goes across ahead of you like a devouring fire. He will destroy them; he will subdue them before you. And you will drive them out and annihilate them quickly, as the Lord has promised you" (Deut 9:3). See Chapman, "Martial Memory," 53–56.

49. "The world view that understood gods as taking part in the events in the world and saw wars as wars between gods, was a view that the Ancient Israelites shared with their neighbors and with the superpowers of that day. . . . The biblical conquest account thus belongs to a standard repertoire for nations/empires in the Ancient Near East. It represents one common way of chronicling history. The Ancient Near Eastern understanding of war . . . is the common frame of understanding, and provides part of the context and rationale for understanding the text of Joshua 1–12." Thelle, "Biblical Conquest Account," 66, 70. Thelle goes on to summarize common themes, developed by Younger Jr., *Ancient Conquest Accounts*, including "a command by the deity that certain cities or kings be conquered," the god actively participates in the acts of war, the war includes supernatural phenomena, and most important for our purposes, the city is burned and all humans and/or living things are killed.

ultimately they paid dearly with their own expulsion from that very land for taking on Canaanite worship and ways (Jer 7).

God's ultimate goal for establishing his covenant people in the land was to bring worship and praise to himself through the obedience of his people. God

> gave them the lands of the nations,
> and they fell heir to what others had toiled for—
> that they might keep his precepts and observe his laws. (Ps 105:44–45)

The culture contemporary to the Old Testament accepted war as a means to achieve desired ends. God's desired end of the conquest was to establish a nation that by keeping the covenant would benefit all nations (Gen 12:3). Although Augustine's criteria for a just war (just intent, just cause, just authority, just conduct) had not yet been advanced, a case might be made that the first three of these conditions are met in the conquest narrative. The striking and ethically difficult piece relates to just conduct in the conquest narrative; it concerns the final Augustinian condition, namely, the treatment of persons and things devoted to destruction (ḥērem). In Deuteronomy 20, where the regulations for the conduct of war are laid out, the enemies of Israel outside of the inherited land are to be offered peace. If they accept, they are enslaved as forced laborers, but their lives are spared. If they refuse, all the men are to be killed and the women and children treated as plunder. But the enemies already living in the land promised to Israel are to be treated as ḥērem, to be completely destroyed—men, women, children, herds, and flocks (Deut 20:10–18).

Robert Boling notes that to understand ḥērem, i.e., being devoted to destruction, one has to understand the context. "[E]ven Holy War as an institution of early Israel cannot be separated from the larger conceptions of divine justice and the divine use of human agencies for his own purposes, without conferring righteousness on the agent or detracting from the righteousness of the Divine Warrior."[50] As part of a holy war the victors have to deal with the conquered people and booty, and these belong to God. Since they are not to be part of civil society, they are to be destroyed. But even so, the critic might respond, doesn't ḥērem contradict the concept of a righteous God or just Divine Warrior (Exod 15:3; Isa 42:13)? If one approaches the question of God's goodness empirically rather than *a priori*, how can

---

50. Boling, *Joshua*, 31. For criticism of the concept of "holy war" as being applicable to Israel's wars, and the use of the term "Yahweh's war," see the articles in Thomas et al., *Holy War*.

these war commands for genocidal treatment of the defeated be reconciled with the claim that God is good and merciful?

One response is to argue that these commands in Deuteronomy 7 and 20 are Mosaic or Deuteronomic commands and not those of Yahweh. Although the writers speak on behalf of God (Deut 20:17) or claim that the *ḥērem* command or ban came from the Lord through Moses (Josh 10:40; 11:12, 15, 20), no such divine command is actually recorded in these ancient texts. The fact that the narrative states that God gave such a command does not mean that it really is a divine command, only that the author took it to be such. The devoting of the items of the conquest, whether human or material, to a god, killing persons and destroying items, and setting some things aside for the god was a common ancient Near Eastern cultural practice replicated by Israel.[51] Hence, God is off the hook since the cultural practices were not instigated by him but are reported in a common cultural military genre.

This argument, however, cannot be sustained. One indication of the authenticity of the command is that when the ban was not kept, God took punitive action. In the next battle, because of Achan's disobedience, God gave Israel over to its enemies. "Israel has sinned; they have violated my covenant which I commanded them to keep. They have taken some of the devoted things; they have stolen, they have lied, they have put them with their own possessions" (Josh 7:11). Although the aggrieving act in Achan's case concerned only possessions and greed and not the part of the *ḥērem* regarding the violent treatment of persons, yet for violating the possessions part of the ban the Israelites suffered defeat at the hand of the soldiers of the Ruin (Ai). The author of 1 Samuel recounts a similar incident concerning King Saul and his warfare. This account clearly affirms that the *ḥērem* comes from God: "This is what the Lord Almighty says: 'I will punish the Amalekites for what they did to Israel when they waylaid them as they came up from Egypt. Now go, attack the Amalekites and totally destroy everything that belongs to them. Do not spare them; put to death men and women, children and infants, cattle and sheep, camels and donkeys'" (1 Sam 15:2–3). Saul ignored the instructions, and although he destroyed all the people, he spared the Amalekite king Agag and the best of the herds and flocks. "Then the word of the Lord came to Samuel: 'I am grieved that I have made Saul king, because he has turned away from me and has not carried out my instructions.... You have rejected the word of the Lord, and the Lord has rejected you as king over Israel!" (15:10–11, 26).

---

51. Chapman, "Martial Memory," 58; Thelle notes a similar justification is given in the Mesha inscription for Moab's king to annihilate the inhabitants of Israelite Nebo. Thelle, "Biblical Conquest Account," 64–66.

God and Goodness   111

A second version of the argument in defense of the view that *ḥērem* does not contradict the concept of a righteous God is that the books of Deuteronomy and Joshua are late and hence reflect either a mythical view of the conquest that was neither commanded nor carried out as described or else are hyperbolic presentations of a highly ritualized and stylized character.[52] "So if Joshua did just as Moses commanded and if Joshua's described destruction was really massive hyperbole common in Ancient Near East warfare language and familiar to Moses, then clearly Moses himself did not intend a literal, comprehensive Canaanite destruction. He, like Joshua, was merely following the literary convention of the day."[53] The scriptural authors followed a formalized symbolic tradition, reflected in the literatures of the surrounding cultures, in their treatment of the materials at hand. Hence, the injunctions to total destruction were never given or, if given, never meant to be taken literally. They are authorial constructions. Similarly, the genocidal events hyperbolically reported in Joshua and elsewhere never really took place. "Joshua did not conquer all the cities in the land nor did he slaughter all the inhabitants in the cities he did conquer."[54] The evidence is that the local peoples allegedly annihilated (Josh 11:16-23) reappear in significant strength in Judges (3:5).[55] And sometime after Saul allegedly destroyed the Amalekites they were raiding towns in Israel and David was pursuing them (1 Sam 15:30). One has to approach *ḥērem* (חרם) not literally but symbolically, as in "My team slaughtered their opponents last night."

> [T]he texts thus relat[e] to the character of God only opaquely and indirectly. . . . [O]ne cannot simply read the message of Scripture off the surface in what is apparently its "plain sense" to make deductions about the nature of God, the acts of God or what is morally acceptable or paradigmatic or historically accurate. . . . Thus the issue we face is not considering what a literal practice of חרם might say about the nature of God. This is simply not how חרם is functioning in Scripture.[56]

---

52. Wolterstorff, "Reading Joshua," 236-56.
53. Copan and Flannagan, "Ethics of 'Holy War,'" 219.
54. Ibid., 220.
55. The author's reasoning concerning their survival—that they were left to "teach warfare to the descendants of the Israelites who had not had previous battle experience" (Judg 3:2) and to test the Israelites obedience (Judg 3:4)—poses its own unique set of moral problems. It has echoes in the soul-building theodicy response to the problem of evil (see ch. 9).
56. Earl, "Holy War," 159-67, 172-73.

Interpreting the text as "hyperbolic, hagiographic, and figurative" handily removes the moral problem of conflict with God's goodness; the extinction command either was never given or else was not meant to be taken literally.

The problem, however, remains, for what then did God command, if anything? Some defenders of this view suggest that the Mosaic command, if given at all, was really the language of expulsion not genocide, and the military result of the Israelite tribal invasion by small bands over time yielded only a partial conquest and not genocide. The tribal bands militarily failed more than they succeeded, for the Canaanites remained, the Israelites intermarried with the inhabitants, and eventually the Israelites inherited their share of the Canaanite cities. But if the stories are thought to be hyperbolic and figurative, the points we made above return. Why was Achan punished so severely with capital punishment for a command that was figurative and hyperbolic? Why did God reject Saul and why cause him to lose his kingship if the command to kill all the Amalekites was only figurative and symbolic? Perhaps these events never occurred but are hyperbolic and figurative as well. The story is really a moral tale about the insider Achan's greed contrasting with the outsider Rahab's faith,[57] or about how Saul's impetuousness contrasts with David's devotion. Then again, maybe the description of the Canaanites' moral and religious practices is also hyperbole: they were not as bad as portrayed, or at least no worse than those groups that lived around them. After all, the Israelites were allowed to "use the women" as plunder (Deut 20:14), which might be figurative for marriage or concubinage. Hyperbole and figurative language is not restricted to Joshua; contrary to Wolterstorff's and Copan's thesis, it creeps into Judges as well (consider the Samson and Gideon stories) and into 1 Samuel (Benjamin's heroics). Indeed, one can readily claim that since it permeates Old Testament texts from Genesis to the prophets, it becomes ever more difficult, if not impossible, to determine what God did and did not command.

However, even if we attribute the description of the conquest events to being hyperbolic, hagiographic, and figurative, or attribute the particularly troubling account details to an ancient Near Eastern stylistic genre for reporting military victories, the problem remains. For the authors/editors of the Old Testament see God as bringing about devastating destruction as a punishment wholesale on peoples, cities, and kingdoms, including Israel itself, directly (as in the cases of Noah and Sodom and Gomorrah) or indirectly through conquering armies (Moab [Judg 3:12], Hazor [Judg 4:1–3], Assyria [2 Kgs 17], and Babylonia). In the cases of Israel and Judah, the LORD removed them or allowed their removal, accompanied by

---

57. Ibid., 164.

great destruction and loss of life. How could these writers and editors who believed in a good and just God figuratively and hyperbolically, or merely culturally, portray him in this fashion, as being like the gods they were to reject? Neither this hyperbolic approach nor one that attributes the account to cultural and stylistic motifs provides a sound justification for God's command or for the writers' belief that God issued or at least approved of the command, given the view that Yahweh differs morally from the other gods.

Suppose that, instead of taking the figurative or cultural way out of the difficulty posed, we assume that the instructions regarding how to treat the Canaanites are authentic, how are they to be justified morally? How are they consistent with a just and righteous God? The text justifies the practice of destruction on the grounds that God in his wisdom knows what will happen if the Israelites live in a religiously mixed society. Inevitably the Canaanites will lead them to sin against God by getting them to worship gods other than Yahweh in the high places and to engage in despicable practices (Exod 23:23, 32–33; Deut 7:1–6). These commands to destroy the inhabitants are proactive, attempting to nip in the bud what eventually comes to pass, where God has to punish his own people with the armies of others because of their sinful actions and their rejection of God by worshiping other gods in the high places in the land (Judg 3:6–7). "Because of all your detestable idols, and because you gave them your children's blood, . . . I will sentence you to the punishment of women who commit adultery and who shed blood. . . . They will bring a mob against you, who will stone you and hack you to pieces with their swords. . . . You not only walked in their ways and copied their detestable practices, but in all your ways you soon became more depraved than they" (Ezek 16:36, 38, 40, 57). The punishment of the Canaanites is meant as a *deterrent* to Israel. The ethical principle of punishment invoked here is, at the very least, utilitarian: to prevent future evils God commands that the seven people groups currently inhabiting the land must be punished by being totally destroyed without mercy.

Second, the command to give over to destruction is also *retributive punishment* for the wickedness of the inhabitants. The text makes this clear with respect to the Amalekites (1 Sam 15:2), who waylaid migrating Israel, and the Babylonians, who opposed the Lord and destroyed the temple (Jer 50:18, 21). The Canaanites were idolaters, worshiping other gods (Exod 34:15–17). They engaged in human sacrifice (Deut 12:31) and practiced divination, sorcery, and witchcraft (Deut 18:10–11). God's goodness is preserved by identifying this command as punishment brought to bear on those who refuse to acknowledge him, who choose to live in idolatry, who engage in detestable practices like child sacrifice (1 Kgs 11:4–8), and who attack his people. God's justice deontologically demanded the death penalty for idolatry and other detestable acts, whether they were done by the Canaanites or Israelites (Deut 13:12–17).

One might reply that surely God could have commanded the conquerors to be more discriminating and merciful. The punishment inflicted might have been more selective, affecting only the guilty parties and not the innocents. For example, Joshua and the conquering army spared some righteous (and maybe not so righteous); not only was the Canaanite prostitute Rahab from Jericho saved, but she plays a prominent role in Jesus' lineage. It is difficult to fathom that there were no other individuals of like or even better character who could have changed their ways had their lives been spared. An example of such can be found in the residents of Gibeon, who used subterfuge to save their lives and create a covenant with Joshua that allowed them to live (Josh 9:3–26). How, then, can a good God order the innocents—including women and children—to be slain along with the military?

An answer to the problem invokes the different way in which the ancients, including Israel, looked at moral accountability. Western ethics, derived from Greek thought, is very individualistic: each person is assigned responsibility for his or her own choices and actions. Punishment is allotted to the evil doers themselves, not to others innocent of the actions in question even though they are related, even intimately as in family, to the evil doers. But the ancient Hebrew notion of moral accountability was very different: it was not individualistic but corporate. Groups were considered holistically; they were not merely conglomerates of individuals that could easily be individuated into guilty and innocent. Considered holistically, the entire group was responsible for the decisions taken by their leaders. When the leaders of the group—family, city, nation, or tribe—took the correct or moral action, all were covered by it; similarly when the leaders took incorrect or immoral action (Lev 26). One can understand the plagues brought on Egypt in this fashion. Pharaoh's decisions affected all of Egypt, for he was *de facto* all of Egypt. The decisions made by each of the Israelite family leaders to smear their door frames with the blood of the lambs protected all who dwelt within the house (Exod 12). When Korah and certain Reubenites rebelled against Moses, God punished them by causing the earth to open and swallow them all up—families, followers, and possessions. The responsibility of the rebellion fell upon all because of their corporate family unity. Although Israel put all of Jericho to the sword, not Rahab (who took actions contrary to the community) alone, but she and her entire family, treated corporately, were rescued. Achan's theft of clothing, gold, and silver booty affected the entire military company, and Joshua and all Israel passed the death sentence upon his entire family, including sons, daughters, animals, and possessions (Josh 7:24–25). When David numbered his fighting force (for hubris?), because he stood as the identified leader/representative for the entire country his resultant sin led to the severe punishment of the entire nation (2 Sam 24). The sincere repentance of the king of Nineveh and his decree preserved all the inhabitants of the city from Jonah's prophesied cataclysmic judgment (Jonah 3:6–10). The same, in a more positive vein, is found in New Testament times. The belief of the Philippian jailor was enough for his entire family to be saved (Acts 16:34).

The ḥērem, then, must be seen in the light of a corporate ethic, where all are part of the corporate whole and hence responsible for the actions of the group leaders or representatives. When the behavior of the group leaders is moral and obedient to God, the entire group is blessed and prospers. When, on the other hand, the behavior of the group leaders is immoral and disobedient, the entire group suffers the punishment or consequences. Hence, the ban must be thought of corporately, not individually.[58] As inheritors of a Western ethic, we find this ethical approach unfamiliar, yet it still characterizes many non-Western cultures.[59]

The utilitarian, deterrent ethic for prevention of moral corruption, a deontological application of punishment for evil acts done, and corporate understanding of the ethics of responsibility and reward/punishment come together to provide a moral justification for God's command. God is concerned not only for punishment of current evildoers but also for the future wellbeing of the nation of Israel. Consorting with the native Canaanites and adopting their idolatrous worship and detestable practices will pollute the corporate Israelite community and lead them away from the God of the covenant. The nation, already with a historically-realized penchant to be rebellious, will become a covenant breaker and idol worshipper. Hence, not only does the ḥērem command reflect how God punishes the corporate Canaanite and Israelite communities for their sins, but it is one way that God attempts to preserve the corporate Israelite community, so that they will keep the covenant into which they have entered. The capital punishment

58. The beginning of a transition in Hebraic thought is found when the Lord speaks to Ezekiel, replacing corporate with individual accountability: "The one who sins is the one who will die" (Ezek 18:20).

59. For example, in response to two Palestinian youths killing four Israelis in Tel Aviv on June 8, 2016, the Israel military followed their established pattern of destroying the killers' parents' home and suspending the Israeli work permits for over 200 of their relatives. "'A village that has terrorists leaving from its midst will pay the price,' said deputy defense minister Eli Ben-Dahan" (Hjelmgaard, "Israel Revokes"). Although a utilitarian theory of deterrence might lie behind the additional actions taken against 70,000 Palestinian workers, Ben-Dehan's remarks clearly arise from a retributive theory of punishment.

commands can be seen to be consistent with God's goodness on these three counts.

Conclusion

We came into the discussion of God's goodness through the central doctrine of divine providence. Many have thought that the doctrine of divine providence invokes the view that God is necessarily good in a logical sense. But as we have seen, although it is meaningful to say that God is necessarily good in an ontological sense, we cannot provide meaning to the claim that the being that is God is necessarily good in a moral sense. To understand the doctrine of divine moral goodness, we need to distinguish between two meanings of the term "God." When used as a title, "God" applies to any being that is perfectly good, almighty, and omniscient. To be God is to be perfectly good. But from this is does not follow that the being that is God is logically necessarily active in the world in the loving and beneficial way that characterizes providence. It is when we talk about "God" as naming a particular being, a being that possesses and manifests all the traits of being God, that the doctrine of providence comes to life. God (as Yahweh) freely and actively manifests his goodness in the world.

Our distinction is important because God's providential goodness is not guaranteed by logic but flows richly from God's moral character. God's goodness is not a logical abstraction deriving from the title but is God's very character bearing fruit in action. God truly is praiseworthy.

> You turned my wailing into dancing,
>   you removed my sackcloth and clothed me with joy,
> that my heart may sing to you and not be silent.
> O Lord my God, I will give you thanks forever. (Ps 30:11–12)

Our account of God's providence, manifested in creation, in redemption, and most frequently in daily provision makes alive the ascription of goodness to God. Because God is loving and caring, which are central character traits, God acts on our behalf. Hence, we can say that this account of logically contingent divine goodness is not only best provisioned to accomplish the end of understanding what we mean by God's goodness; it also gives us the moral assurance that God will manifest his goodness unfailingly in creation and to us. And this, indeed, is the biblical view of God's praiseworthy goodness: we can gratefully trust the goodness of Yahweh.

> I trust in your unfailing love;

> my heart rejoices in your salvation.
> I will sing to the Lord,
> > for he has been good to me. (Ps 15:5–6)
>
> The Lord's unfailing love
> > surrounds those who trust in him. (Ps 32:10)
>
> Let them give thanks to the Lord for his unfailing love
> > and his wonderful deeds for humankind. (Ps 107:8)
>
> I will praise you forever for what you have done;
> > in your name I hope, for your name is good. (Ps 52:9)

Chapter 5

God as Omnipotent

THE DOCTRINE OF DIVINE providence connects God with the world and in turn the world with God. On the one hand, God's actions of creating, sustaining, and interacting with what God has created manifest his powerful intentions. Providential actions are not accidental; they are purposeful, reflecting God's desire to achieve some goal or objective. From our observation of these apparently providential and purposeful actions in history, nature, and human affairs, we can suggest that God is best understood to be a personal agent with desires, intentions, purposes, and the accompanying power to bring these about. On the other hand, the doctrine of divine providence directs us to daily rely on God's goodness, power, and knowledge. It encourages prayers of adoration, thanksgiving, and petition. Providence thus is a two-way street: it embraces God connecting to his world and especially to us; it encourages us to connect to the God who acts as a loving and caring agent. Providence is a central feature of the divine-human dance.

Since God's agency (ability to act) invokes power, any discussion of divine providence must address questions that people have raised about God's power. In particular, we must explore how that power is to be understood and, with respect to humans, how that power intersects and is consistent with significant human freedom. Bringing together what we have developed in chapter 2 with regard to freedom with divine power will be the topic of this chapter and the next.

Theologians and philosophers have conceived of God's power in diverse ways. Some note that the Scriptures often speak of God as almighty. Those who adopt an Anselmian perfectionist approach to God's properties describe God as being omnipotent. In this chapter we will consider God's power from the perspective of divine omnipotence and then evaluate the meaningfulness of the claim that God limits his power in his dealings with his creation.[1] In the next chapter we will turn from divine power under-

---

1. For discussions of omnipotence, see Urban and Walton, eds., *Power of God*; Kenny, *God of the Philosophers*; Hartshorne, *Omnipotence*; Hoffman, *Omnipotence*.

stood as omnipotence to consider what it means to say that God is almighty, a view we will suggest is more biblical in character.

God as powerful

Scripture portrays God as possessing power. "Two things have I heard: that you, O God, are strong, and that you, O Lord, are loving" (Ps 62:11–12). Scripture presents divine power in diverse ways. On the *one* hand, it is seen as God's might and strength. Scripture points to certain key events as definitive examples. God exercised his strength in creation: "God made the earth by his power; he founded the world by his wisdom" (Jer 10:12; 51:15). "The Lord is the everlasting God, the Creator of the ends of the earth. He will not grow tired or weary" (Isa 40:28). God also manifested his power in his providential and redemptive acts in the history of Israel, most notably their liberation from Egypt. By power God raised up Pharaoh to free the Israelite slaves (Exod 9:16); by his strength God brought those slaves out of Egypt and made a home for them by expelling the peoples already inhabiting the land (Deut 4:37–38). The psalmist appeals to the very power God used to deliver the inhabitants into the hands of Israel (Ps 111:6) when he requests God to deliver Israel from its enemies (Ps 68:28–30).

Biblical writers often describe God's strength and might that provide protection and deliverance metaphorically. God is our rock and fortress of refuge, our "shield and the horn of our salvation." God delivers by using the powerful and awesome elements of nature—thunder, lightning, storms—to frighten and scatter the enemy (1 Chr 22:1–20). Job 26 contains a similar, metaphorical description of God's cosmic powers.

"Yours, O Lord, is the greatness and the power" (1 Chr 29:11). From God's strength we derive our strength (1 Chr 29:12; Ps 68:35). "He gives strength to the weary and increases the power of the weak. . . . Those who hope in the Lord will renew their strength" (Isa 40:29, 31). It is clear from the above that God's providential power, as with God's goodness, is not an abstraction, but is manifested in concrete ways, from creating the universe to acts of providence, both for nations and individuals. This power exalts God, making him an adequate object of worship and praise (Job 36:22–24). "Praise him for his acts of power; praise him for his surpassing greatness" (Ps 150:2).

On the *other* hand, God's power is manifested in his ruling authority. "You are the ruler of all things. In your hands are strength and power" (1 Chr 29:12). "He rules forever by his power, his eyes watch the nations" (Ps 66:7). By invoking his overwhelming power and knowledge God answers Job, not to explain or justify his actions, but authoritatively to reject any attempt to contend with or question God (Job 38–42). (As we have seen, Paul uses a similar strategy in Romans, rejecting any questioning of God's deeds and appealing to God's power to carry out what he ordains [9:22]).

The New Testament likewise depicts God as powerful, continuing many of the same Old Testament motifs. God's providential power is the shield of protection (1 Pet 1:5). Its saving or delivering aspect comes through the gospel; Paul sees the gospel as God's power for salvation (Rom 1:16; 2 Cor 1:18). God's power is also the source of the disciples' power that is central to the spread of the gospel (Luke 24:49). Jesus promised that the disciples would "receive power when the Holy Spirit [came upon them]," and this power would enable them to become his witnesses throughout the world (Acts 1:8). Power is also associated with God's rule. "[Y]ou will see the Son of Man sitting at the right hand of the Mighty One and coming on the clouds of heaven" (Mark 14:62). This power is the authority that God gives to those who do his will (Rev 2:26).

The epitome of God's manifest power is shown in Jesus, from his earthly beginning to the resurrection ending. It plays a key role in the incarnation. Luke records that Jesus' conception occurred by "the power of the Most High" (Luke 1:15). It underlies Jesus' miracle ministry: Jesus has the authority (ἐξουσία) from God to heal the sick, give sight to the blind, allow the deaf to hear, raise the dead (Matt 9:6–8; 11:4–6), drive out demons (Mark 1:27), and judge (John 5:27). Jesus also bestows on his followers this authority to do much the same (Mark 3:15). The culmination of God's power is God's raising Jesus from the dead (Rom 1:4; 2 Cor 13:4). Ignorance of God's ability to manifest this particular power was the Sadducees' defect (Matt 22:29).

Even more notable is the fact that the New Testament adopts the trend begun in the intertestamental period to refer to God simply by the term "power." Power (Δυνάμεως) becomes one of God's names. "As the name of God retreats into the background in Judaism, being replaced by paraphrases, one of his descriptions is 'power.'"[2] This name Jesus uses to refer to God when he stood before the Sanhedrin (Matt 26:64; Mark 14:62).

However, not only is God powerful enough to act providentially in the world, Scripture goes on to portray God as all powerful. It is to the understanding of this that we turn next.

---

2. Grundmann, "δύναμαί, etc.," 297.

Scripture and omnipotence

That God can do all things has led theologians and philosophers to the doctrine of divine omnipotence. Believers who formulate God's power in terms of a being who can do anything have only a few biblical passages to which they can appeal directly. Three are from the Old Testament.

God announces to Abraham that Sarah would become pregnant, and Sarah, overhearing and disbelieving, laughs at something so seemingly absurd. Yahweh replies to Sarah that nothing is too hard for the Lord (Gen 18:14). What is in view is not the impossible, for it is not impossible that an older woman can become pregnant. Rather, the emphasis is that God has the power to carry out his intentions, here to continue Abraham's lineage, even though what God does for two elderly individuals would be too difficult to occur naturally.

God's disquisition that begins in Job 38 details diverse aspects of God's power. The passage moves from God's forceful assertion of his power to an affirmation that God is all powerful. God has the power of his justice, the power of splendor and majesty surpassing that of any monarch, and the power to control even the most violent and mighty of his creatures. In recognition of God's power and in the context of God's purposes, Job acknowledges, "I know that you can do all things; no purpose of yours can be thwarted" (42:2). As with Genesis, the power Job has in view is the power of God to carry out or implement his purposes. God's power is understood in the context of his will; whatever God intends or purposes he can do and cannot be thwarted.

Jeremiah 32:17 also addresses God's power, first in the context of creation: "Ah, Sovereign LORD, you have made the heavens and the earth by your great power and outstretched arm. Nothing is too hard for you." The passage continues, not with God doing the impossible, but with God administering just desserts, showing both great love and severe punishment, and performing signs and wonders in Israel's exodus from Egypt. The passage stresses the mighty power of God, the Lord of hosts. What would be too hard for humans is what God does. God, speaking to Jeremiah, repeats the theme: "I am the Lord, the God of the whole human race. Is anything too hard for me?" (32:27). God follows up by revealing his intention both to give Jerusalem to the Babylonians to conquer and set on fire and also later to restore his covenant people to the land. What Jeremiah ascribes to God's power is not the doing of the impossible but rather of God being able to carry out his intentions and plans. In short, all three OT passages emphasize God's ability to carry out his intentions, from creation to the exodus, from creating pregnancy in very unusual circumstances to bringing armies against Jerusalem and later restoring it from its devastation. None of these tasks is too difficult for God to accomplish.

New Testament passages more directly attend to the impossible, though they are rare. They affirm that all things are possible with God, even if they are impossible with humans. Luke 1:37 picks up on the theme that God can bring about pregnancy even under the most unusual circumstances. For Sarah, her old age militated against it; in Luke the problem is both Elizabeth's old age (a reiteration of Sarah's story, though this time the skeptic is her husband) and Mary's virginity (a reiteration of Sarah's story, though absence of sexual relations replaces age).[3] God can bring about pregnancy even if it appears impossible. It manifests God's power through the Spirit. Luke, echoing the Lord's statement to Sarah, states the general principle: "Nothing is impossible (ἀδυνατήσει) with God." Some may take it to be a stronger statement than what the three Old Testament passages affirm, claiming that whereas the Old Testament deals with the fact that nothing is too difficult or hard for God, Luke's birth account broadens the scope to include the impossibility of virginic pregnancy in the justifying statement. Yet Mary is not concerned with the impossibility, but with God doing according to what he willed and said.

Jesus invokes the same principle in Matthew 19:26 (and its parallels Mark 10:27 and Luke 18:27). Jesus assures his disciples, "With human beings this is impossible (ἀδύνατόν), but with God all things are possible (δυνατά)."[4] The Gospels set this saying in the context of the difficulty that entering the kingdom of heaven poses for the rich. The allure of possessions can prove much too great for the rich. The context includes the hyperbole of a camel going through the eye of a needle. It is noteworthy that the disciples do not pick up on the impossibility affirmed by a literal treatment of the hyperbole but rather on the difficulty of entering the kingdom, something that is not humanly possible but becomes possible by divine action.

The theme of the possible returns in Mark 14:36 (Matt 26:39, 44; 22:42). Praying in Gethsemane Jesus struggles with events he anticipates will be exceedingly difficult for him. He asks that, if possible, the cup of suffering be removed, on the grounds that "everything is possible (δυνατά) for you." Here the possible connects with the Father's will. The issue is not what God is capable of doing, for there is no doubt that the Father could

---

3. The detailed parallel language and textual structures between the announcement to Zachariah in Luke 1:11–20 and to Mary in Luke 1:28–38 intimately connect the two events.

4. This saying is probably taken from the Septuagint translation of Job 10:13: "you are able to do everything, and nothing is impossible for you" (πάντα δύνασαι, ἀδυνατεῖ δέ σοι οὐθέν). Hagner, *Matthew 14–28*, 562.

have successfully removed Jesus from the forthcoming scene (John 19:11). Rather, the possible connects with what accords with God's will. It is not what Jesus wills but what the Father wills.

Romans 4:21 also links God's power with his intentions. "God had power to do what he promised." Here the emphasis is not on impossibility, but on the connection between God's power and his word or intentions (his promises). What God promises God can do.

In short, with the possible but unlikely exception of two passages—Luke 1:37 and Matthew 19:26—God's over-arching power is presented in connection to God's intentions and will. The emphasis is not on God doing the impossible, but on doing what God wants, a doing that can supersede that of humans or anything else because nothing is too hard for God.

Philosophical basis for omnipotence

The scarcity of overt biblical statements that we can construe to affirm omnipotence has not removed its allure. The doctrine has had sustained life because of particular philosophical presuppositions that Christian theologians have entertained. While theologians like Origen and Augustine, whom we will consider later, seem to presume God's omnipotence, medieval theologians advance two related arguments for it.

Anselm does not rely on Scripture to establish God's omnipotence. Rather, for him it follows from his contention that God must be the greatest possible being. The greatest possible being must possess its properties perfectly. Hence, God must possess the property of power perfectly, else there could be something with greater power than that possessed by the greatest possible being. That there could be such a competitor would be contradictory; nothing can be greater than the greatest possible being. God, then, must be more powerful than any other possible being; the greatest possible being can do anything possible. The doctrine of divine omnipotence is established.[5]

Thomas Aquinas also appeals to God's nature to establish God's omnipotence. Whereas Anselm employs Neo-platonic/Augustinian concepts of degrees of being, Aquinas argues from an Aristotelian worldview. As we noted in the fourth chapter, Aquinas sees God as pure actuality, possessing nothing passive (which would signify deficiency and imperfection). Since God by definition is infinite, he possesses his actuality and properties to the

---

5. Anselm, *Prologium*, ch. 7.

highest or infinite degree and hence cannot possess any possible imperfection. Thus, God has infinite power, the greatest possible power to act.[6]

The appeal in both cases is to God's nature. God is perfect and cannot be exceeded by anything in any positive respect. It is impossible for there to be anything greater, that is, anything that would possess in a greater way great-making properties. Power is a great-making property, one that not only God possesses, but that he possesses in the greatest possible way.

The omnipotence paradox

Those who have advocated divine omnipotence have recognized that it faces serious problems. We will look at three issues that traditionally have been raised against divine omnipotence.

Suppose that we understand the power of God, a being than which none greater is possible, in terms of omnipotence. How are we to understand or define "omnipotence"? Literally, "omnipotent" means "all-powerful." Using this definition, one might be tempted to affirm that a being is omnipotent if and only if it is able to bring about *any* state of affairs. There is no action or task that an omnipotent being cannot perform. God as omnipotent can do all things.

There are good reasons, however, to be reluctant to define omnipotence in this fashion, that is, as the ability to do all things (δυνήσετια πάντα ὁ θεός).[7] As Origen noted, it is important to consider the "all" (πάντα) when asking what it is that an omnipotent being can do or bring about. Some things are impossible for God—or any—being to bring about. Yet this inability does not impugn God's omnipotence. For example, an omnipotent being cannot create a square circle, bring it about now that the past did not happen, or determinately cause another person to perform a free act (provided that one adopts an indeterminist or libertarian view of freedom). The former is impossible because being round is logically incompatible with being square; for something to possess both properties simultaneously is logically impossible. Likewise, the second case involves a contradiction; it is contradictory to claim that something that in fact happened in the past, like Barack Obama being elected the forty-fourth president of the United States, did not happen.[8] As to the third, an act cannot both be free in a libertarian sense and sufficiently caused by another. One agent cannot cause another agent freely to perform an action, for coercion is incompatible with

---

6. Thomas Aquinas, *Summa Theologica* I, Q 25, Arts. 1 & 2.
7. Origin, *Contra Celsum*, Bk 3, ch. 70.
8. Thomas Aquinas, *Summa Theologica* I, Q 25, Art. 4.

the freedom of the agent who is coerced. That an agent acts freely means (in part) that it has a choice to do one thing rather than another and no other agent causes it to do one thing rather than another. In short, whatever gives a self-contradictory description is impossible for an omnipotent being to bring about. However, these impossibilities do not count against God's omnipotence, for in fact these impossibilities cannot be done or brought about by anyone. No one can make a self-contradictory statement true. The inability is not due to any lack of power or ability on the part of the agent; it simply is logically impossible that any state of affairs obtain that would make such propositions true. In short, as Aquinas notes, not being able to do the logically contradictory is not a failure of being able to do something, for the logically contradictory is nothing.[9]

Following upon this discussion, we might redefine "omnipotence" as the ability to do anything that is logically possible. Put more technically, a being is omnipotent if and only if it is capable of bringing about any contingent state of affairs whose description does not contain or entail a contradiction.[10] Given this definition, statements about making round squares, making past events that happened not to have happened, or others causing another agent to act freely are excluded from those actions or states of affairs that an omnipotent being would be expected to be able to bring about.

This definition, however, runs into difficulties because there are logically possible states that finite humans can bring about that God cannot. The description of such a state of affairs is not self-contradictory. For example, I can create a wooden table bigger than I can lift. Making such an object is not logically inconsistent. But this would present a conundrum for an omnipotent being as defined here. An apparently inescapable dilemma results, both horns of which say that there is something an omnipotent being cannot do. If it creates a table bigger than it can lift, there is something it cannot do, namely, lift the table. If it cannot create a table bigger than it can lift, there still is something it cannot do, namely, create such a table. This commonly is referred to as the paradox of omnipotence.

George Mavrodes suggests a way out of this conundrum. He suggests that we define "omnipotence" more carefully. An omnipotent being can do any contingent thing (1) whose description is logically possible (does not contain or entail a contradiction) or (2) whose description does not exclude or entail the exclusion of an omnipotent being from doing it.[11] This addi-

9. Ibid., I, Q 25, Art. 3.

10. Omnipotent beings also cannot bring about states of affairs that are logically necessary. Since these obtain in all possible worlds, one cannot meaningfully say that someone brought them about.

11. Mavrodes, "Some Puzzles," 199–200.

tion seems reasonable; it would be unreasonable to formulate objections to omnipotence on the grounds that prohibiting an omnipotent being from being able to do something could count against it being omnipotent.

When we apply this analysis to the paradox of whether God as omnipotent can make something that God cannot lift, what it says in one of the horns of the dilemma is that an omnipotent being would create an object (here, a table) bigger than its maker (an omnipotent being) can lift. But since the maker referred to in the predicate is the omnipotent being mentioned in the subject, what is being asked of an omnipotent being is that it (as omnipotent) make something bigger than an omnipotent being can lift. It asks an omnipotent being to do something that it is excluded from doing. This way of phrasing it in effect excludes an omnipotent being from being able to make the object, and hence it fails to meet condition (2) of Mavrodes's definition. The paradox of omnipotence fails to impugn this characteristic of God.

Unfortunately, this way of escaping the paradox of omnipotence encounters a problem of its own, for if we use this definition of "omnipotence," any being that can do only what it can necessarily do is omnipotent. But this is unacceptable, for omnipotence could now apply to possible beings who, though extremely limited in what they can do, can do everything they are able to do. Suppose a being by its nature can only do three things and is excluded from or incapable of doing anything else. But then in virtue of doing all that it can do (the three things) such a being would be omnipotent. Aquinas clearly spots the problem. "If we say that God can do all things that are possible to His power, there would be a vicious circle in explaining the nature of His power. For this would be saying nothing else but that God is omnipotent because He can do all that He is able to do."[12]

To address this problem, we might attempt another definition of omnipotence. We will term this definition O. According to definition O, a being is omnipotent if and only if it meets three conditions: it can do any action or bring about any contingent state of affairs (1) whose description does not contain or entail a contradiction or absurdity, and (2) whose description does not exclude or entail the exclusion of any omnipotent agent from among those who may bring about that state of affairs, and (3) no being with greater power is possible. This definition has the virtue of eliminating from being omnipotent beings with limited powers but that can do whatever is described in those limited powers. Such beings would fail to be called omnipotent because they would fail to satisfy condition (3) of the definition.

---

12. Thomas Aquinas, *Summa Theologica*, I, Q 25, Art. 3.

Condition (3) of definition O involves a comparison between a being with power and a being that would have the greatest possible power. However, making condition (3) part of the definition creates the difficulty of specifying what it would mean for one being to be more powerful than another in general or overall. How does one determine the extent of power? We cannot say that it can do everything that anything else can do and more than anything else can do, for what something can do depends on its nature. We don't want to say that God is not omnipotent because he cannot eat or sleep, like his creatures can, since failing in this should not count against omnipotence. Timothy O'Connor suggests that the "extent of power seems to be a function of at least two variables: the amount of work that can be performed in a single task and the range of tasks one is able to perform in a given circumstance."[13] Regarding the latter, an omnipotent being would have a larger range of tasks it could perform because of its abilities; it would have more abilities than any other being, since all other beings are dependent upon it but it is not dependent on anything else. Regarding the former, it is not clear how one would determine the amount of work a being can perform. The threat here is of circularity: the amount of work a being can perform in a single task depends on the nature of the being (whether finite in power or omnipotent), and the nature of the being with regard to its power (whether finite in power or omnipotent) depends upon the amount of work it can perform. We don't want to say that it has to do with the number of events it can bring about. If it did, omnipotence might not be as much a matter of power as of duration; the longer an agent existed, the more states of affairs it could bring about. And if it were eternal, it could bring about an infinite number of contingent states of affairs, even if what it could bring about at any one time was limited. Specifying power, it seems, is a difficult business. Perhaps it is here that the concept of being almighty might assist us; we will turn to this in the next chapter.

The power to do evil

The second problem facing the doctrine of omnipotence concerns moral issues. It was raised by the second century non-Christian Celsus and responded to by the Christian theologian Origen.[14] Celsus expresses concern

---

13. O'Connor, *Theism*, 89.

14. To my knowledge, Origen is the first in the Christian tradition to philosophically address the doctrine of omnipotence. Since he is replying to Celsus, it can be argued that Celsus was the first to address the doctrine in the Christian era, though unfortunately what we know about Celsus's argument comes only through what Origin

with whether, if God is omnipotent and able to do anything, God can do evil. He appears to place the believer in omnipotence on the horns of a dilemma: if God can do anything and doing evil is possible, then if God cannot do evil he is not omnipotent. If God can do evil, then God is not morally perfect. Thus, either God is not omnipotent or not all-good. The problem here differs from the omnipotence paradox in that the conflict relevant to God's being omnipotent is not internal to the property of omnipotence. Rather, we have a conflict between two of God's essential properties, omnipotence and goodness.[15]

Origen replies to Celsus by stating that Celsus fails to analyze properly the two aspects of the definition, namely, "God's ability," (δύναται) and "what it is that God can do" (πάντα). Taking the first issue, Origen notes that God's ability is limited by God's nature. God can do only what is consistent with his nature; "God can do everything which it is possible for Him to do without ceasing to be God, and good, and wise."[16] Since God is by nature good and wise, God can only do what is consistent with his good and wise nature. With respect to what God can do (πάντα), Celsus's and hence Origen's concern is with whether God can do evil. The doing of evil is logically possible; as finite beings we are capable of such. If doing evil is logically possible, it would seem that it is among the "all" that God can do. But, Origen contends, what Celsus has missed is that God's nature makes it impossible for God to do evil. As essentially good by nature, God could not have evil inclinations and hence could not commit evil. That God's acts are good is not a matter of will but of his nature.

Hence, Celsus's argument generates a contradiction after all, a contradiction within God's nature. If God is essentially or necessarily good, then he cannot have the inclination to do evil and hence cannot do evil. So, when one says that God cannot lie because deceit is a shortcoming in power, in effect one says that a being who necessarily cannot have an inclination to lie should be able to have such an inclination. But this is contradictory. Hence, this analysis violates condition (1) of Mavrodes's and our definitions

---

reports. Origin discusses the topic of omnipotence by claiming that God is able to do all things (δυνήσεται πάντα ὁ θεός). Origen says that this is the view that Celsus considered. Origen suggests that Celsus at the very least accepted this definition of God's power and did not refer to or develop rational arguments against the definition. Origen's statement suggests that arguments against this definition were available to Celsus and that either Celsus did not know them or he thought they were not telling, that is, could be answered. What Celsus apparently does is to question the implications of the contention that God is able to do all things.

15. This same objection has been recast in the 20th century by Pike, "Omnipotence," 208–16.

16. Origin, Bk 3, *Contra Celsum*, ch. 70.

of "omnipotence." As such, the problem of reconciling omnipotence and divine goodness in God's nature disappears.

However, this solution runs into the problem Aquinas noted above, namely, that it means that God can do all that by his nature God can do, and since by nature God is necessarily good, God cannot do evil. And as Aquinas noted, this is circular and unacceptable.

As we argued in chapter 4, the view that God is necessarily all-good runs into difficulties. There we argued that God (as a particular being) cannot be necessarily good but is contingently good in a logical sense. God's goodness flows not from logical necessity, since the freedom to do either good or evil is a requisite for being morally praiseworthy (criterion 6 in chapter 4), but from his dispositions and virtue. That is, the being that is God cannot do evil, not in a logical sense, but in a moral sense. Because of God's character God cannot will to do evil. The point here is that if one does not root God's goodness in a necessity in God but rather in God's will and character, one can still reconcile divine goodness and divine omnipotence. If the being who is God possesses perfect virtue or character, God will act in accordance with that virtue. It is a moral, not a logical, point that reconciles divine goodness and omnipotence. This rules out the non-logical possibility of the being who is God doing anything that smacks of evil (the absence of the good) or impotence (the absence of power or ability).

The compatibility of omnipotence with human freedom

The final objection to omnipotence concerns whether, if we adopt the concept of omnipotence, any room for human freedom remains. If God is all powerful, so that there cannot be a being with greater power, and if God can do anything logically possible, can we reconcile God's power with human freedom? Freedom, both divine and human, forms an essential part of any doctrine of divine providence. Hence, we need to see whether omnipotence and human freedom can be compatible.

If we adopt a view of God as a personal being or agent, the claim that God can impose limits on his own actions becomes intelligible, for personal agents are just the sorts of beings that can voluntarily put limits on what they do. When I arm-wrestled with my son, I put limits on my power or strength, giving him the opportunity to win so as to encourage his competitive spirit. Such self-limitation did not negate my power; I still retained it, only I chose not to use it for a good reason. I could have exercised my power, but that would have negated the very purpose of stimulating competitiveness for which I limited it. Similarly, it is within God's power to limit his employment of his power. Some of the Old Testament epiphanies, where God reveals himself to people, provide instances where God limits himself (Exod 33:19–20). Most notably the Christian believes that God limits himself by his incarnation. For our purposes, God limits himself by his creation of human persons who possess free will, for if human persons truly are free, then as we argued in chapter 2, God cannot control them so that they are determined to choose or to act in a particular manner. For God to cause or manipulate free persons to do something is incompatible with their doing it freely. We are conscious beings for whom persuasion to freely live according to God's will and commands is appropriate. In effect, by creating persons who perform a very significant number of free acts God made something that he subsequently cannot control without overriding the conditions under which and for which he created those persons.

Some philosophers have questioned whether the notion of self-limitation is consistent with the doctrine of divine omnipotence. How can God limit himself without at the same time sacrificing his omnipotence? Self-limitation, they argue, conflicts with God's omnipotence. This can be shown, Mackie alleges, by constructing another version of the paradox of omnipotence.[17]

> 4. Either God can create things that he cannot subsequently control, or he cannot create things he cannot subsequently control.
>
> 5. If God can create things he cannot subsequently control, then it is possible that things exist that God cannot control, and hence God is not omnipotent.
>
> 6. If God cannot create things that he cannot subsequently control, then there is something God cannot do, and hence God is not omnipotent.
>
> 7. Therefore, God is not omnipotent.

Mackie contends that because God's self-limitation is incompatible with his omnipotence, we must sacrifice belief either in God's ability to limit himself or in God's omnipotence. Either God is not omnipotent but finite in power and there exist free beings, or God is omnipotent and cannot limit his power and free beings do not exist.

To discern whether the paradox succeeds, let us more closely examine premise 5. We might set out the argument in 5 more fully.

---

17. Mackie, "Evil and Omnipotence," 210.

8. If God can create things he cannot subsequently control, then it is possible that things exist that God cannot control.

9. If it is possible that things exist that God cannot control, then God is not omnipotent.

10. Therefore, if God can create things he cannot subsequently control, God is not omnipotent.

The crucial premise is 9. Why should we think that 9 is true? To answer this, we must first note that these are free creatures, beings whose choices and actions in a significant number of cases—and particularly in those cases that are morally significant—are not caused by anything other than the agents themselves when they are acting freely. Thus, we might reformulate the supporting argument for 5.

8*. If God can create free creatures that God cannot cause to do any free action A, then it is possible that there exist free creatures he cannot cause to do any free action A.

9*. If it is possible that there exist free creatures that he cannot cause to do any free action A, God is not omnipotent.

10*. Therefore, if God can create free creatures that he cannot cause to do any free action A, then God is not omnipotent.

But is 9* true? It claims that being unable to cause free beings to perform an action counts against one's omnipotence. But on the libertarian view of freedom presupposed here, freely performing an action is incompatible with being caused by another agent to freely perform that action. As such, being unable to cause persons to perform actions freely fails to meet condition (1) of definition O of omnipotence given above; there is no logically possible state of affairs which could make 9* true. As definition O affirms, being unable to bring about a logically impossible state of affairs does not count against anyone's claim to omnipotence. Therefore, since God's inability to determinately bring about or cause free agents to act in a certain way does not count against his omnipotence, 9* is false. And if 9* is false, no reason has been given to show that either 10* or 10, and thus 5, is true and this version of the paradox of omnipotence fails. In sum, we have no reason to think that being able to limit himself is inconsistent with God's omnipotence.[18]

This is not to say that God (or we, for that matter) should never compel or coerce others to act, that in the relations we have with others we can or

---

18. Reichenbach, *Evil*, 165–68.

should never limit, restrict, and even deny people their freedom. As with us, God at times does restrict human freedom. For example, God's rescue of Peter from prison restricted the freedom of the authorities who jailed him (Acts 6:18). Similarly, we restrict the freedom of others; by closing the cellar door I restrict the movement of my two-year-old nephew. But when persons must be manipulated or restricted (as, for example, when we must forcibly restrain one person from harming another by handcuffing the person), it must be recognized that in such circumstances the person is not a free agent with respect to the restricted action. Some restriction can be morally justified, but persistent overriding of the choices of free agents prevents them from being free agents. Repeated manipulation and interference will destroy the personhood of the individual. Thus, interference that restricts human freedom cannot be condoned without just cause or good reason. Interference that would totally remove morally significant freedom, where interference with the freedom to make our own moral choices would become the regular pattern of (divine) activity, is completely dehumanizing. Full humanization and moral growth occur when freedom is enabled and encouraged. It is not that God could not have intervened; but when he created free agents, to protect their morally significant freedom, God had to limit his action. But no conflict with God's power ensues; rather, God's power is manifested in his self-limitation.

Conclusion

We can conclude that God's power interpreted as omnipotence—the ability to do anything that is logically possible and does not exclude an omnipotent being from being able to do it, while being more powerful than any other being—is defensible. There is nothing logically inconsistent with understanding God as omnipotent. None of the paradoxes of omnipotence succeed against this notion. We also saw that this view of power is consistent with divine self-limitation and divine goodness. Indeed, quite apart from the philosophical arguments, Christians must feel somewhat comfortable with the concept of divine self-limitation. After all, it is central to the doctrine of incarnation, where out of love God limits himself in humility and becomes incarnate, "taking the very nature of a servant, being made in human likeness" (Phil 2:7). The limitation in this case is even more radical than the self-limitation that allows for human freedom.

We also noted that the roots of omnipotence are more philosophical than scriptural, which connects God's power to God's will. However, we also observed that defining "omnipotence" as we have done leaves us with some ambiguity with respect to condition (3)—no being with greater power is possible. With this difficulty in mind we turn in the next chapter to a slightly different conception of God's power, namely, the claim that God is almighty, a view we will contend is more biblically rooted.

Chapter 6

God as Almighty

IT IS TIME TO turn away from the notion of God as omnipotent, with its emphasis on omnicausality (ability to cause everything logically possible), to that of God as almighty. Whereas the first exhibits all the proper trappings of a philosophically-derived property, as the arguments presented for omnipotence evidence, the concept of being almighty roots firmly in the biblical tradition. We will contend that in speaking about God's power from a Christian perspective all that is necessary is that God be almighty. That is, to have an adequate concept of God we do not have to hold that God can do anything logically possible (which is omnipotence or omnicausality), but rather that God can bring about what he chooses (which is being almighty). God can do what he wills, whether in heaven or on earth. "What God cannot be said to do, he likewise cannot be said to will to do."[1]

We noted in the previous chapter that the definition of "omnipotence" as being able to do anything logically possible needed expanding because it is possible that something exists that can do everything in its power but would have very limited powers. Similarly with being almighty. It is possible that something exists that can do everything it wants but whose wants are extremely limited or qualitatively inferior. Hence, to our definition of being almighty as being able to do what one wills, we have to add that there can be no being with greater (in both a quantitative and qualitative sense) wants and hence that there is no being with greater power. That is, God is limited in what he can will only by who God is, in terms of both God's character and God's nature. We will see the implications of this when later we again look at the relationship of God's power to doing evil. Thus, we can say that as almighty "God is not just more powerful than any creature; no creature can compete with God in power, even unsuccessfully. For God is also the source of all power; any power a creature has comes from God and is maintained only for such time as God wills."[2] In effect, not only can there be no being

---

1. Geach, "Irrelevance of Omnipotence," 330.
2. Geach, "Omnipotence," 8.

The power of being almighty

What is meant by "power" when we describe God as being almighty? Here we must turn to Scripture for guidance. Scripture predicates three names of God, two Hebrew and one Greek, that traditionally have indicated God's power. The two Hebrew divine names often translated as "almighty" are *Shaddai* and *Sabaoth*.

Sabaoth, which the Old Testament uses 283 times, frequently refers to God from a military perspective. God is the Lord of Hosts/Armies (*Yahweh Sabaoth*), who comes with his own or coopted armies against Israel or the surrounding nations.

> Listen, a noise on the mountains,
>   like that of a great multitude!
> Listen, an uproar among the kingdoms,
>   like nations massing together!
> The Lord Almighty (*Yahweh sabaoth*) is mustering
>   an army for war.
> They come from faraway lands,
>   from the ends of the heavens—
> the Lord and the weapons of his wrath—
>   to destroy the whole country.
> Wail, for the day of the Lord is near;
>   it will come like destruction from the Almighty (*Shaddai*). (Isa 13:4–6)

Yahweh is supreme commander of national (1 Sam 17:45), foreign (Isa 13:4–5), and divine (1 Kgs 22:19) armies whom no one can withstand. Although use of the term *Yahweh Sabaoth* begins in the historical books (1 Sam 1:3), its frequency reaches its climax in the major and minor prophets, especially Isaiah, Jeremiah, Haggai, Zechariah, and Malachi.

At the same time, the Old Testament also uses *Sabaoth* in numerous contexts as an exalted title to portray Yahweh's authority and kingship. *Yahweh Sabaoth* is designated king and God (Ps 84:3); he is the King of Glory (Ps 24:9–10). Isaiah sees the Lord seated on a heavenly throne, "high and exalted" (Isa 6:5). *Yahweh Sabaoth* is not merely the king of Israel, but king of all nations (Isa 24:23; 37:4); in the end all nations will come yearly to worship him (Zech 8:20–22; 14:16). In short, both as the victorious commander of his hosts, heavenly and human, and as the sovereign king over all, God does what he wills and none can withstand him; God will be splendidly victorious.

The other word that is translated as almighty is *Shaddai*, which appears forty-eight times in the Old Testament. God reveals himself as *'El Shaddai* to Abraham in Genesis 17:1, promising Abraham future generations. The theme that the Almighty promises offspring continues with Jacob (Gen 28:3; 35:11; 49:25). Joseph asks the Almighty to show mercy (Gen 43:14). These Genesis usages emphasize the personal. In the act of promising, God uses his power personally and providentially for the patriarchs, especially in their role as progenitors of Israel. In Exodus 6:3 God identifies himself not only by the name *'El Shaddai*, by which the patriarchs recognized him, but with the new name *Yahweh*.[3] The most frequent appearance of *Shaddai* occurs in Job (thirty-one times). The author of Job writes, "I will teach you about the power of God; the ways of the Almighty I will not conceal" (Job 27:11). Even here, the name often emphasizes the personal relation between the individual and God. The Almighty gives Job life (33:4), is present to him (29:5), disciplines (5:17; 21:20), is aware of his pain (6:4), and can be petitioned (8:5; 13:3).[4]

There is significant debate over the root meaning of *Shaddai*. Some suggest that the word has Akkadian roots in the word *shadu* (mountain), so that God is "El, the One of the mountains," evincing considerable awe and power.[5] Others note that the term possibly derives from the Hebrew word for breast (*shad*), which indicates a mother's providential care of her child,

---

3. "El Shaddai is used almost exclusively in reference to the three great patriarchs: Abraham, Isaac, and Jacob, and (according to Exodus 6:2–3) was the primary name by which God was known to the founders of Israel (the Name YHVH given to Moses suggests God's absolute self-sufficiency). The word 'Shaddai' (by itself) was used later by the prophets (e.g., Num 24:4; Isa 13:6, Ezek 1:24) as well as in the books of Job, Ruth, and in the Psalms. In modern Judaism, Shaddai is also thought to be an acronym for the phrase *Shomer daltot Yisrael*—'Guardian of the doors of Israel'—abbreviated as the letter Shin on most mezuzot 'Guardian of the Doors of Israel.'" Parsons, "Hebrew Names of God."

4. It is of interest that the Septuagint translators generally do not translate *Shaddai* with the concept of power. In the seven instances in Genesis and Exodus, the concept of power is absent. Any hint of power is replaced with the personalization of God's relation of blessing with the worshipers/patriarchs; God is your God, his God, their God. Elsewhere in the Old Testament the translators give no consistent translation of *Shaddai*. In Job the Septuagint translation of the word takes many forms. It is translated as κύριος or Lord (6:4, 14; 8:3; 13:3, 21:20, etc.), as ἱκανός or mighty one (21:15), and as παντοκράτωρ, ruler over all (5:17; 8:5; 11:7; 15:25, etc.).

5. Martens, "God, Names of," 298.

nourishing it and supplying what it needs from her own resources.[6] If this latter derivation is correct, the name emphasizes that God is the nourisher and sustainer, a concept that accords well with a providential, personal God as evidenced in Genesis and Job, but one that does not require us to speak in the philosophical sense of omnipotence.[7]

The term Σαβαώθ is used in the New Testament in transliteration. In Romans 9:29 it transliterates *Sabaoth* from Isa 1:9. James 5:4 uses Κυρίου Σαβαώθ, which is the Greek rendering of the Old Testament name, to refer to God.

The New Testament generally translates "almighty," following the Septuagint, as *Pantokrator* (Παντόκράτωρ)—ruler over all. Second Corinthians 6:18 uses this term to translate *Sabaoth* in a quote from 2 Sam 7:4. Elsewhere *Pantokrator* appears nine times in Revelation.[8] Revelation 4:8 uses it to render the royal *Sabaoth* of Isaiah 6:3. This name emphasizes God's political position by focusing on his complete sovereignty (Rev 19:6), dominion (11:15–17), and power to judge (16:7), as well as his military role (16:14). "It has only a loose connection with the dogmatic concept of the divine omnipotence, which is usually linked with the omnicausality of God."[9]

In short, three divine names or ascriptions often translated as "almighty" in Scripture present diverse perspectives on God's power. *Shaddai* emphasizes God's ability providentially to bless individuals especially with offspring and to relate personally with his worshipers. *Sabaoth* introduces both the military and the kingly or authoritative perspectives, where God is the victorious commander of divine and human armies and the ruler not only of Israel but of all nations. And *Pantokrator* presents the vision of a sovereign God, in whose conquering might one encounters the ruler who has dominion over all to do as he wills.

None of this sounds like a God of omnicausality, who can do anything logically possible. Although the Vulgate translated *Shaddai* and *Pantokrator* as *omnipotens*, little in the original suggests such a strong rendering of these terms. Rather, we are presented here with a God whose might or power is clearly understood in God's relation to the world. God relates to

---

6. Some suggest a word parallel in Gen 29:25, where *'El Shaddai* blesses with "blessings of the breast and the womb."

7. "Most English translations render El Shaddai as 'God Almighty,' probably because the translators of the Septuagint . . . thought Shaddai came from a root verb (*shadad*) that means 'to overpower' or 'to destroy.' The Latin Vulgate likewise translated Shaddai as 'omnipotens,' from which we get 'omnipotent.' God is so overpowering that He is considered 'Almighty.'" Parsons, "Hebrew Names of God."

8. Rev 1:8; 4:8; 11:17; 15:3; 16:7, 14; 19:6, 15; 21:22.

9. Michaelis, "παντοκράτωρ," 915.

us, personally, as an awesome provider, one who can bring to bear armies, whether his own or those of others, to accomplish his will and purposes, who now is the ruler of all people, and who ultimately will be acknowledged as such in the eschaton.

Being almighty connects God's power with his will. God can do what he wills, the will being primary. This emerges clearly in relation to Christ. In Phil 3:23 Paul writes that Christ has the power to bring everything under his control. The control is determined by Christ's will; his power serves his will. That divine power serves the divine will carries over from the Old Testament. "The difference between the OT and the surrounding world is grounded in the distinctive relationship of the Godhead to history. . . . [T]he important and predominant feature is not force or power but the will which this power must execute and therefore serve. This is everywhere the decisive feature."[10] God's power is God's voluntary, willful acting in the world and in history. God is not an impersonal force but a personal being who acts intentionally in individual lives and in society according to what God purposes. This is evident in the archetypal Old Testament demonstrations of God's power in creation and in God's rescuing the people of Israel from Egypt, most notably at the Red Sea (Exod 15:6, 13).

Almighty God manifests his power in creation.

> Lift your eyes and look to the heavens:
>> Who created all these?
> He who brings out the starry host one by one,
>> and calls them each by name.
> Because of his great power and mighty strength,
>> not one of them is missing. (Isa 40:26)

More specifically, the power of creation is linked with God's creative will. As twenty-four elders sing in Revelation (4:11),

> You are worthy, our Lord and God,
>> to receive glory and honor and power,
> for you created all things,
>> and by your will they were created
>> and have their being.

God's creative power is not a mere artifact of the past, but a sign of what God Almighty will do. The God who "by his own hands stretched out

---

10. Grundmann, "δύναμαι, etc.," 291.

the heavens" and "marshaled their starry hosts . . . will raise up Cyrus," who "will rebuild my city and set my exiles free" (Isa 45:12–13).

The Scriptures discuss God's power not in terms of abstract possibilities or isolated events but especially as revealed in salvation history. "The LORD your God did to the Jordan what he had done to the Red Sea when he dried it up before us until we had crossed over. He did this so that all the peoples of the earth might know that the hand of the LORD is powerful and so that you might always fear the LORD your God" (Josh 4:23–24; see also Ps 77:14–20).

> Come and see what God has done,
>   how awesome his works in man's behalf!
> He turned the sea into dry land,
>   they passed through the waters on foot. . . .
> He rules forever by his power,
>   his eyes watch the nations. (Ps 66:5–7)

The power that implements God's will and that brought about awesome providence in the past is the same power we can expect working on our behalf in the future. Because of this redemptive power shown in the past, we can rely on God to again intervene mightily and providentially on our behalf (Neh 1:8–10).

This view has historical precedence in Augustine. In his *Enchiridion* Augustine emphasized this connection between power and will, contending that what God performs comes and only comes from God's will.[11] God's power or omnipotence is God's ability to carry out whatever God pleases. Power or ability is connected to willing. "He is not truly called Almighty if He cannot do whatsoever He pleases, or if the power of His almighty will is hindered by the will of any creature whatsoever."[12] Those who cannot do what they want are impotent; those who can do what they want are powerful.

In sum, in being almighty God can do what he wills to do, and there is no being with greater desires, quantitatively or qualitatively. Whereas other beings can be thwarted in carrying out what they will, it is not so with God. God's instrumental power implements God's providential will.

---

11. Augustine's view here differs from that of Origen. Whereas Origen builds on God's nature as necessitating what God can and cannot do, Augustine builds on God's will.

12. Augustine, *Enchiridion*, chapter 96. It is noteworthy that here the translator renders *omnipotentis* and its cognates as "almighty" rather than "omnipotent."

The possible and God's will

In the previous chapter we looked at instances where the justification given for God's miraculous actions was that nothing was too hard for God and that for God everything is possible. Although the Matthew passage allows one to interpret this in terms of God's causal omni-capability (omnipotence), we saw that the other passages connect the possible with God's will. In retelling Jesus' request that the cup of agony and death facing him be removed, Mark records that Jesus justifies his request on the grounds that "everything is possible for you" (Mark 14:36). But the "possible" in the text has little to do with God's causal capability; there was no question that God could have intervened in some way so that Jesus neither suffered nor died. God could have encouraged Pontius Pilate to have more backbone; God could have caused a severe earthquake that severely disrupted the legal proceedings or Judas to have suffered a deadly heart attack before his nocturnal betrayal of Jesus. Rather, as Jesus observes, the possible connects with what accords with God's will. Jesus wants not his own will, but the Father's will, to be done: "Yet not what I will, but what you will."

We noted this same linkage of God's power with God's intentions in Romans 4:21: "God had power to do what he promised." In speaking about possibility Paul emphasizes not God's causal power, but the connection between God's power and his word or intentions (his promises). What God promises he can do. In short, the New Testament discusses God's over-arching power in terms of how power connects to God's intentions and will. The emphasis is not on God's capability of doing or bringing about the logically impossible, but on God's doing what God wants. As Mary says in response to Gabriel's assertion about God's power: "Let it be done according to your word" (Luke 1:38). The word expresses God's intentions to have her conceive and bear the Son of the Most High. God's intentions and purposes dominate the discussion.

We might wonder whether, if we understand God's power in terms of being almighty rather than as being omnipotent, this enables us to better resolve the problems posed for omnipotence that we considered in the previous chapter. To answer this, let us return to those issues, beginning with the first omnipotence paradox.

The omnipotence paradox

When we speak about God as being almighty, as being able to do what he wills and that there is no being with greater power, the omnipotence paradox that we addressed in the previous chapter no longer confronts us. According to this paradox, if we understand God to be omnipotent, which emphasizes God's causal ability, there is something God cannot do in a causal sense: either God cannot lift an object that he can make, or he is unable to make such an object. The alleged impalement on the horns of a dilemma occurs because as omnipotent God must be able to do anything logically possible. But the posed description indicates two conflicting tasks, both of which are logically and physically possible in themselves for finite beings, whereas for God at least one of them purportedly is impossible. In the previous chapter we have shown that there are reasonable solutions to the problem, but the dispute over this paradox continues unabated nonetheless.

But if we understand God as almighty, God's power to bring something about is conditional upon and subsequent to his will. And God's will is not necessitated with respect to what contingent states of affairs God might or can bring about. God wills freely. Hence, God is under no necessity to will to bring about the contentious state of affairs of making something he cannot lift or destroy. Consequently, the omnipotence paradox disappears when we consider God as almighty. What matters is not what God *can* do but what God *wills* to do. As almighty, God can do what he wills to do. If God does not will to do something, then that he does not or even cannot do that thing is irrelevant to God's power.

The same reasoning applies to what God wills. God cannot will the logically impossible. Hence, any version of the omnipotence paradox that would require God to will to make such, like willing to make round squares, likewise founders. God can only will what is logically consistent. On the view of God as almighty, then, the omnipotence paradox does not arise.

God and the power to do evil

Considering God as almighty helps us to address the classical problem raised in the previous chapter concerning the relation of God to evil. If God can do anything that is logically possible, and if doing evil is logically possible, then how can one consistently say that God cannot do evil, lie, or break his promises?

If we consider God not as omnipotent but as almighty, we get two responses. From the logical point of view, the answer is, Yes, it is logically possible that the being who is God (for example, Yahweh) can do evil. However, from the point of view of God's (Yahweh's) character we also argued that a being who is God cannot do evil, and the reason has to do with God's character mediated through God's will. The "cannot" here is not a logical "cannot"; nothing self-contradictory lies in doing evil or in willing to do evil. The impossibility stems from the character of the being who is God; given that being's character or virtue, God cannot will to do evil.[13] As Heb 6:18 says, God cannot break his word. This is not because promises cannot be broken; breaking one's promise is a logical and factual possibility. But as morally virtuous, the being who is God cannot will to do so. This provides no limitation on the being who is God; as Anselm and Aquinas pointed out, to do evil would constitute an imperfection of God's moral character, indicating a serious defect in it.[14] In short, the question of the ability and inability to do evil by the being who is God has nothing to do with the causal power of omnipotence, but with character and will.

Of course, should the being who is God (for example, Yahweh) do evil, that being would no longer merit (and never would have merited) the title of God, for to be God the being would be morally perfect and not do evil. But this is an issue we already dealt with in chapter 4. There we distinguished between "God" as a name and "God" as a title. To merit the title God one has to be perfectly good. But the being that is God is not necessarily good in a logical sense, for a being that is necessarily good does not merit worship or praise on account of that goodness, for it would be impossible for the being to do otherwise than the good. But the being that is God is perfectly good because its goodness, manifest in its acts, derives from its virtue and will.

Self-limitation

Treating God as almighty also has implications for the question whether God's power is compatible with human freedom. In the previous chapter we inquired whether the idea of God's self-limitation was problematic and argued that we find no paradox in believing that God limits his power. But if we treat God as almighty, the concept of self-limitation makes even more sense. As almighty, God can carry out whatever he wills. God's actions follow upon his will. If by being almighty God can bring about what he chooses, then it makes sense to say that God can choose to limit his power if God so desires so that humans can have freedom of choice and action. Self-limitation poses no limit on God, for God himself wills limitation by

---

13. "A Christian must not believe that God can do everything: for he may not believe that God could possibly break his own word. Nor can a Christian even believe that God can do everything that is logically possible; for breaking one's word is certainly a logically possible feat." Geach, "Omnipotence," 9.

14. Anselm, *Proslogium* VII; Thomas Aquinas, *Summa Theologica* Ia, Q 25, Art. 3, Rep. Obj. 2.

allowing individuals to choose or do as they please, even where what they do does not please God. But then, if God wills not to take an action or to limit his involvement in human or cosmic affairs, there is no problem, for as free God can choose to will whatever lies in accord with his nature or character. God can will to limit the actualization of his power in order to grant humans morally significant freedom. In particular, God wills humans to be morally and spiritually responsive to him, to his gracious invitation to participate meaningfully in the covenant, to be part of God's expansive kingdom and church. He chooses not to determine human choices and actions but generally leaves choices and actions to humans. Our responsiveness cannot be coerced from us; if divinely coerced it would lack any saving moral value. Rather, God wills self-limitation as part of his loving invitation to humans to give a morally significant, personal, and willing response to God. That is, given the nature of what God desires and the requirements for attaining it, self-limitation of God's power is not self-contradictory but desirable; it is part of the total divine plan.

This means that we need to qualify what was said above that God can do whatever he wills, that God's will cannot be thwarted. God has chosen to create beings in his universe that can in fact thwart or frustrate God. Humans can and do frequently resist God's will. God wills that all be saved, but not all will be, not because of God's weakness or lack of love, but because of what is necessary to achieve what he desires. God desires that people freely love and serve him, but in granting humans this freedom God makes it possible that his persuasive will be resisted. The possibility of such thwarting, then, stems from God's desire that we willingly and freely return God's love and seek a meaningful, responsive relation with him. This requires that we have morally significant freedom, a freedom that allows human decision-making and divine risk.

This significantly departs from Augustine, who rejected divine risk but saw the attempted human thwarting of God's will as part of God's will. Ultimately, he believed, because of God's omnipotence God's actions cannot be hindered or resisted, for this would be tantamount to hindering God's will. What then of apparent counter-cases where people act against or resist God's will, especially to do evil? Augustine responds that sometimes God wills that people attempt to thwart his will, for out of this attempt comes the realization of God's will. Judas's betrayal of Jesus is a case in point. God purposed the sacrificial death of his Son, and Judas played a role in this not by doing good but by betrayal. Yet, in all of this God's will, which is always good, was accomplished. "It was through the wicked designs of the Jews, working out the good purpose of the Father, that Christ was slain; and this event was so truly good, that when the apostle Peter expressed his unwillingness that it should take place, he was designated Satan by Him who had come to be slain."[15] "Nothing, therefore, happens but by the will of the Omnipotent, He either is permitting it to be done, or Himself doing it."[16] Augustine realized that this created an apparent problem, for it seems to follow that God wills evil. If God wills or even permits evil, is God not evil? Not so, replies Augustine, for God's will is always just, and to be just is to be not evil, even when evil results. Although to us it is evil, and although considered in itself the event or effect may be evil, yet insofar as it follows from God's will and fits God's purposes it is good. The evil itself is not a good, it remains an evil, but it serves a greater good of God's purposes and therein is justified. For Augustine, then, there is no gratuitous evil; all evil serves a greater good of God's purposes. We will argue in chapter 9 that, contrary to Augustine, there is gratuitous evil, that not all evil directly leads to a good by which it can be morally justified. There we will argue that the problem of evil arising from human resistance to God is adequately resolved by God granting individuals freedom to act against his will, even though he does not want them to do so.

A second problem arises from Augustine's contention that God's will cannot be thwarted. Augustine notes that this raises a puzzle, for God "wants all persons to be saved" (1 Tim 2:4). But if nothing can thwart God's will, all should be saved. Yet clearly this is not the case: Judas's denial of Christ and his suffering perdition is a case in point of a lost person. So it seems that either God does not want all people to be saved or God's will actually can be resisted.[17] Augustine attempts to rescue both God's irresistible almightiness and the Timothy passage by rephrasing the Timothy claim as, "no man is saved unless God wills his salvation." If God does not will a person's salvation, that person won't be saved. "Therefore, we should pray Him to will our salvation, because if He will it, it must necessarily be accomplished."[18] In short, those saved are equivalent to those God wills to be saved. This interpretation, he claims, is consistent with other passages. God did miracles in the presence of those whom he knew would not repent; Pharaoh was not saved by God's mercy (Rom 9:18–20). Jesus chose not to do miracles for some whom he knew would repent if they had seen them (Matt 11:21), indicating that God does not will all to be saved.[19] In short, for Augustine Scripture does not claim straight out that God wants all to be saved (except

15. Augustine, *Enchiridion*, ch. 101.
16. Ibid., ch. 95.
17. Ibid., chs. 97 & 98.
18. Ibid., ch. 103.
19. Ibid., ch. 95.

God as Almighty   145

in the sense that some from all the various human races will be saved, a conclusion flowing from the great chain of being).[20]

This leaves us with several problems. First, Augustine's rephrasing of Timothy is not consistent with the obvious meaning of the text. The Timothy passage is not a conditional about what God might not will; it is about what God wills. It claims straightforwardly that God wills that all be saved— ὃς πάντας ἀνθρώπους θέλει σωθῆναι. Augustine's interpretation is actually a logically fallacious contrapositive. To say that God wills all to be saved is not logically equivalent to "if God does not will salvation, the person will not be saved."

Furthermore, Augustine's rephrasing creates its own problems. Is it just to show mercy to some but not to others? Augustine says it is just for two reasons. First, it is just because justice would be served even if none were saved. Justice requires that, since we are sinners at birth, we all are condemned. Salvation comes through the mercy of God "extended to the unworthy." Hence, God's mercy is served when some are saved. This connects with Morris's position that we discussed in chapter 4. According to Morris, God has axiological goodness, the goodness of supererogation but not of duty. God is good because God shows mercy; God has no obligation to show mercy to everyone or indeed to anyone. But then, we might object, on what grounds does God decide to whom to be merciful? If God were limited in his merciful resources, one might accept that God might grant mercy only to some, perhaps randomly. But God's mercy is an unlimited resource and hence could well be available to all at no additional cost to God, a point Augustine concedes. But then, we argue, given the criteria for a supererogatory action noted in chapter 4, restrictively given mercy is no longer a justifiable supererogatory action, for the good to be graciously done is not costly at all, the cost having been paid for to enable the first act of grace. The grace should be universally available (John 1:16; Titus 2:11), and

---

20. Augustine's emphasis on completion fulfilled in diversity reflects his inheritance from Plotinus of the principle of plenitude, according to which "the universe is a *plenum formarum* in which the range of conceivable diversity of *kinds* of things is exhaustively exemplified." Lovejoy, *Great Chain*, 52. "If all things were equal, all things would not be; for the multiplicity of kinds of things of which the universe is constituted—first and second and so on, down to the creatures of the lowest grades—would not exist." Augustine, *Contra adversarium* I, 4, 6. The saved should manifest the same plenitude. This principle is an important constitutive part of the historic idea of a great chain of being, which also finds residence (without the accompanying doctrine of emanation) in Augustine. "But from things earthly to things heavenly, from the visible to the invisible, there are some things better than others; and for this purpose are they unequal, in order that they might all exist." Augustine, *City*, XI, 22.

if not, on a moral notion of duty, God has failed. Selective axiological goodness is not enough.

We might construct an analogy. Our ship comes upon wreckage at sea, with survivors floating in the water. They were willfully negligent, were heavily intoxicated, wore no life vests, and ignored our offers of assistance, such that we could be justified in letting them all die based on their negligent behavior. We might claim that abandonment is what they deserve because of their willful negligence. But out of supererogation we decide to show mercy on some. So randomly we pull some from the water, leaving others to their fate. But, you might protest, you had room on your ship and time on your hands to rescue all of them. It is no longer a mere matter of supererogation. Surely, you have failed in your moral duty to do what you could to rescue all of the wrecked crew and passengers.

Augustine's second response in defending God's justice is to turn to foreknowledge and free choice. By means of his foreknowledge God knows that some will not will their salvation. God does not compel their will but gives them freedom. Thus, they freely choose to resist God, and hence God is just in not offering them saving mercy but in condemning them. They get what they deserve, but it is because of their will that they are not saved. It is as if the captain of the rescuing ship knows which persons floating in the sea will refuse the rescue, and these the captain makes no attempt to rescue.

Augustine's discussion raises serious questions about the nature of God's knowledge; can God's foreknowledge be used in the way that Augustine suggests, that is, to decide to whom to give mercy? This becomes especially difficult if, as Augustine holds, God foreknows his own actions. If God foreknows to whom he will show mercy, then this knowledge cannot be used to justify not showing mercy to these foreknown individuals, for his foreknowledge is based on God foreordination. That is, they are not rescued because God foreknows they don't want to be, and they don't want to be because God foreordained it. But then God does not truly want all to be saved, since he did not ordain it, and Paul in Timothy is mistaken about God's will. In sum, Augustine's attempts to limit God's desire that all be saved by saying that it is part of God's eternal plan does not succeed. We will say more about divine foreknowledge and its limited use in the next chapter.

In short, Augustine's account is deficient on several scores. For one thing, in trying to reconcile his assertion that God's will cannot be in vain with scriptural and empirical evidence that people do resist God, he has reinterpreted 1 Tim 2:4 in a way that is not equivalent to, and indeed distorts, its obvious meaning. The text is not about what God does not will, but about what God wills. Second, his account violates a clear understanding of God's goodness. God sent his Son into the world not for condemnation but to make it possible that all be saved (John 3:16). Selective distribution of grace violates God's universal love.

God's self-limitation in granting freedom makes it possible and reasonable that, although God actually desires all be saved, this will not occur. God could make it occur only by revoking his limitation on his almightiness. But this revocation would not yield the desired result. Coercion cannot compel love or willing obedience and service, and hence would not accomplish the desired end of a free response to God's invitation and the establishment of a meaningful covenant relationship. God calls, seduces, persuades, but does not compel.

Divine sovereignty

We have argued that there is good reason to consider God's power in terms of being almighty rather than being omnipotent. First, it is closer to the biblical concept of God as personally providential in individual lives, and of God being powerful both militarily and in authority in a larger national context. Second, it accords well with an understanding of providence in terms of what God makes available to us by his power according to his will. Third, understanding God's power in terms of will enables us to circumvent the omnipotence paradox. The issue is not what it is possible for God to do, cause, or make, but what God wills to do. Fourth, it makes better provision for reconciling God's goodness with his power. As we noted in chapter 4, the goodness of the being who is God cannot be necessary in a logical sense, though it is morally certain in virtue of God's character. Thus, the matter of not doing evil is not a matter of logic but of virtue, that is, a matter of disposition and will. Finally, being almighty better fits a God who, concerned for human moral and spiritual transformation and development, limits the exercise of what he wills. It is not that humans infringe on God's power, in the sense that God wants to control everything but cannot. Rather, since God wills human moral and spiritual change and growth, what God wills requires the possibility that what he creates can thwart aspects of what God wants. In the scheme of things, willing one thing has implications for what else one wills. The Bible records the contextual struggle between what God wills and the recalcitrant wills of those he creates. God could will to wipe humans off of the earth (Gen 6:7), but at the same time realizes that this conflicts with his will to have a covenantal relationship with those same humans (Gen 9:8–17). Thus, the Bible records a determined struggle within God's will: to abandon and pursue. It represents the conflict between justice and mercy. In short, being almighty is tempered with the reality of God's full creation of free beings with whom God desires a real, covenantal, loving relation.

What does being almighty have to do with divine providence? The answer is that divine power connects with God's provision for us through God's sovereignty. We have seen above that Scripture views God's power in terms of authority; authority is embodied in the use of both *Sabaoth* and *Pantokrator*. Sovereigns exercise authoritative power in the political relationship of governance. Governors or sovereigns have authority and power over the governed, but in that role they also have responsibility to seek the good of the governed. This is where sovereignty flows into providence. Authority over and responsibility for the governed travel hand-in-hand.

As we have just contended when thinking about God's self-limitation, to be sovereign does not mean that everything that happens accords with the sovereigns' will or that sovereigns can bring about anything they desire. The sovereign's ability to determine events depends, in part, on what freedom the sovereign grants to the governed. Where the governed are free moral agents, sovereigns cannot single-handedly achieve their desires without removing the freedom of the governed. Sovereigns can compel their subjects to perform ritual acts in their presence, but they cannot compel their subjects to perform them freely or out of love. An inverse relation exists between freedom granted and control maintained. The more freedom sovereigns grant their subjects, the less they can control their behavior without withdrawing the freedom that they granted. By granting their subjects significant freedom, sovereigns make it possible for their subjects to resist their authority or to give free, loving acknowledgement and obedience. If sovereigns command their subjects to perform some action and if the subjects are free, the subjects can refuse. But at the same time the subjects must bear the responsibility for and the consequences of their refusal.

As we noted earlier, in understanding divine sovereignty we must not confuse sovereigns with novelists. Whereas novelists create their story, with its characters, storyline, setting, and outcome, sovereigns have to deal with real people making choices and decisions. Whereas those created by the novelists do not exist apart from the authors, those over whom the sovereign rules exist apart from the sovereign, however dependent they are on and sustained by the sovereign. Whereas the novelist's storyline is unrolled by the author, the story of sovereigns and those they rule plays out as a complicated dance, each responding in one way or another to the moves of the other. God is sovereign, not determining everything, but standing in relation to everything. God is powerful to bring about what he wills, yet God limits his power so that what he wills is not always accomplished. Its realization depends on other wills that God has created. Yet that too is part of what God willed: he willed that all freely love him, and in willing this God had to will that those he created to love him be free. Thus, the very freedom used to resist God is willed by God so that God can realize the possibility of true love, obedience, and covenantal relation.

Since God is the sovereign creator, God bears responsibility for his creation. And since God is good, that responsibility will be borne out in actions that both benefit creation and seek its good in freely relating to him. And since God is almighty, he is able to carry out what he wills, while at the same time preserving the self-imposed conditions for covenant relations noted above. Hence, we can expect the manifestations of providential divine goodness celebrated by the psalmists. "Taste and see that the Lord is good" (Ps 34:8).

> The LORD is my shepherd, I lack nothing.
> > He makes me lie down in green pastures,
> he leads me beside quiet waters,
> > he refreshes my soul.
> He guides me along the right paths
> > for his name's sake.
> Even though I walk
> > through the darkest valley,
> I will fear no evil,
> > for you are with me;
> your rod and your staff,
> > they comfort me.
> You prepare a table before me
> > in the presence of my enemies.
> You anoint my head with oil;
> > my cup overflows.
> Surely your goodness and love will follow me
> > all the days of my life,
> and I will dwell in the house of the LORD
> > forever. (Ps 23)

This connection of sovereignty with providence raises two critical issues. First, did not God know that humans would attempt to rebelliously frustrate his providential will, and if so why would God create humans anyway? Second, if God is acting beneficially on our behalf, how can one explain the pain, suffering, and dysfunction that frequent our lives? These questions bring us to the important issue of whether God has foreknowledge, which we address in the next two chapters, and the problem of evil that we address in chapter 9.

Chapter 7

God's Knowledge

IN THE PREVIOUS CHAPTER we advanced hints that the doctrine of divine providence intrinsically invokes God's knowledge. "Providence," coming from Latin, literally means "fore-seeing." The meaning of the term has evolved to encompass much more than merely seeing. More broadly, it means that one anticipates what will happen and takes steps to plan and make sure that circumstances will be altered for the good or that relevant persons will get what they need. As we have already emphasized in this book, providence presupposes God's agency in the world on behalf of what God has created. God acts creatively, caringly, and intentionally. But God's agency requires that God know about his world. In particular, people argue that a robust view of divine providence affirms that God knows future events, for if God does not know the future it is difficult to understand how God could give us good advice and reliable guidance about the future, except in a most general sense. For a strong view of divine providence to work, propositions about the future have to be knowable true propositions, part of God's all-encompassing knowledge, to which somehow God has access. Divine foreknowledge has engendered great debate, and to this we now turn.

Divine knowledge

It is easier to say *that* God knows than *how* he knows. Manifestly, God knows in ways that differ from any of God's creatures. Since God has no body, God has no sensory experience; yet we want to say that in some sense he experiences, perceives, and knows what occurs in the physical, created world. God has no neurophysiology, yet we say that God has concepts, beliefs,[1] and knowledge that, were we to have them, we would have

---

1. William Hasker argues that insofar as God has knowledge, and insofar as knowledge is defined in terms of beliefs, God not only has beliefs but has both true beliefs because God cannot entertain falsehood and justified beliefs (insofar as God's beliefs are grounded either in the facts or in true general principles). See Hasker, "God Has

to process through our brain and central nervous system. God knows the past, at the very least insofar as he knows the truths about the past, possibly through his experience of it, and if God is timeless, knows it deeply in that the past is "ever before" him in an eternal present. God knows the present, a necessary feature if God is to interact meaningfully with his creation. God knows all possibilities that have truth values and whose truth values can be ascertained. Further, if God is to know all possibilities, it must be the case that God knows the future, for what is possible in the future depends on what will be the case. If it is now possible that thirty years from now my brother will travel to Indianapolis to visit his great-granddaughter, it must be the case that he had a great-granddaughter and that both are alive at that projected time. If she never existed or if neither is alive thirty years from now, that the visit will happen is impossible. Thus, for God to know that this is possible in the future he has to know something about what is actual in the future. God knows the future given the same conditions that God knows possibilities, namely, if propositions about the future have truth values and if those truth values can be ascertained. None of this, at this point, is usually denied—noting the very important "if" clauses.

Discussion of God's knowledge leads to the affirmation of the doctrine of omniscience. Since on an Anselmian view God in his nature possesses all perfections, not only does God know true propositions, but he knows all true propositions there are to know. Some—and I concur—make a parallel with omnipotence and claim that a logical limit should be placed on omniscience, namely, that God can know all true propositions that it is possible to know. The next chapter will address the possible significance of this qualification.

God's omniscience in Scripture

Some biblical support exists for a doctrine of omniscience. The Bible connects God's being almighty with God's knowing. "The Mighty One, God, the LORD! He knows!" (Josh 22:22). Hannah's poetical prayer repeats the theme of God's knowledge (1 Sam 2:3). God not only knows, his knowledge is unlimited (Ps 147:5). God's omniscience is beautifully portrayed in Psalm 139, where the psalmist writes that everything about him is known by God, from his physical being in his mother's womb to his very thoughts, even before expressed. He cannot hide from this knowledge—neither direction, darkness, nor death can interfere with it. "Such knowledge," he confesses, "is simply too wonderful for me." God's understanding is unlimited (Ps 147:5);

Beliefs!" 385–94.

from God nothing is hidden (Heb 4:13). God knowledge extends from the cosmos to the sparrows sold in the market and the number of hairs on our head (Matt 10:29–30), and this knowledge extends to the future. The Bible claims that God foreknew that Israel would become corrupt and disobey God's commandments (Deut 31:29), the rise of Cyrus (Isa 44:28—45:5) and the Messiah's coming in Bethlehem (Mic 5:2).

As with God's goodness and omnipotence, God's knowledge is not viewed as an abstraction. The interest of the scriptural texts is not in God's knowledge *per se* but in the ways it connects with God's providential care for us. For the psalmists, God's knowledge guides and protects; for Hannah it both warns the proud and comforts the oppressed; for Matthew, it assures that God values and cares for us.

It is not clear how God knows all these things. Part of the difficulty of answering the question "how?" arises from disputes about God's relation to time. If God is timeless, in what way can God know any current event happening now, for in the timeless world there is no now? It would seem necessary that God have temporal relations with the present in order to know it as now. Otherwise, God would have to know events as temporally indexed (I am eating watermelon in Oyibi, Ghana at 3:12 p.m. on February 24, 2016), which still leaves us with the question of how God knows temporally indexed propositions. How does God know the past? If God is timeless, the past is continually present to him so that it too must be known as temporally indexed (I finished my cool shower at 9:52 p.m. on January 2, 2016). But how does God know temporally indexed past events? If God relates to time (is temporal), does God know the past because God experienced it in his present? If we knew how God experienced the present this would reasonably explain how God obtains knowledge of the past and the present but would not apply to claims about how God obtains knowledge of future events, which have not occurred. How can God know future events, events that as of any given time have not yet occurred? The latter becomes particularly problematic when one claims that God knows future contingent facts about what we will or will not freely choose or do. If we have not yet chosen and if our choosing is not determined, how can anyone know such ahead of the time? I do not intend to attempt to answer the "how" question. I am unsure how we would even begin to deliberate about how God knows these things. And if we cannot understand how God knows, we cannot answer the question how God comes to know future events.

What we can say in the case of contingent truths about events, whether of the past, present, or future, is that the event itself is the ground or the basis for God's knowledge. It is not the cause of God's knowledge; that would throw us back into determining how it is that God knows. But the events are the basis of God's knowledge in that God would not know the event had the event not occurred in the past, is now occurring, or will occur. That God has knowledge about the past and present generally does not create logical problems. God's knowledge about the future, however, has led to persistent discussion, and to this we turn.

God's knowledge of the future

As we indicated, God's knowledge extends to the future provided that the future can be known. We might understand this in two ways. First, we might understand God's knowledge of the future in terms of his knowledge of all true propositions. If God is omniscient, God knows all true propositions, and if propositions about the future are true (that is, in virtue of what will or will not happen), they are known by God. On this view God's knowledge of all true propositions mediates God's knowledge of future events.

But we want to go beyond this to say that *the events themselves* provide the basis for God's knowledge of future events, for what makes the propositions true are the very events. It is not that the events cause God's knowledge, but they are the ground for God's knowledge: God believes and knows these events because in the future they occur. Propositions regarding those events are true because of those events, and God knows all true propositions that it is possible for God to know.

Since future events provide the ground for God's belief, it follows that whatever God believes will occur. It cannot be otherwise, else God, who believes only the truth, would have believed a different proposition. God's beliefs cannot be other than they are, for they are grounded on the events themselves.

This view makes prophecy possible. Because God knows what will happen in the future, God can reveal that to humans in advance, and humans can be assured that it will happen. Isaiah prophesies concerning Cyrus, who will restore Jerusalem (Isa 44:28; 45:1), Isaiah tells of Hezekiah's illness and life extension (2 Kgs 20:1–6; Isa 38:1–6), Daniel foretells events near and far (Dan 7–9) as well as the seventy years of exile (Dan 9:20–27), and Peter notes that the death of Christ was foreknown (1 Pet 1:19–20). Without foreknowledge prophecy about some future event becomes impossible, for prophecy requires knowledge of the actual historical players and their decisions.

Over the centuries the question whether God has foreknowledge has stimulated significant philosophical and theological debate.[2] Divine omni-

2. For discussions of omniscience and foreknowledge, see Kvanvig, *Possibility*;

science may be seen in a way to be parallel to divine omnipotence: God knows everything that it is possible to know. What cannot be known God cannot know. What cannot be known, some argue, are facts about future contingent events, especially events having to do with free choice and free action. God could know future events that result deterministically from the present, such as the location of the earth vis-à-vis the sun two thousand years from now, for God could know all the intervening causally determined events. But God cannot know events that are not the determined results of prior causal conditions, such as our future free choices and actions. The fundamental argument for this is that if God foreknew future contingent events, they would no longer be contingent (such that they either could or could not occur). What God foreknows must occur. Hence, God's foreknowledge is inconsistent with human freedom. God can know the past and present, but God can know only the future that follows deterministically from the present.

In what ensues we will investigate whether this philosophical argument for the incompatibilist view of God's knowledge is sound. We will contend that incompatibilists have failed to make their case against divine foreknowledge. God's knowledge of future contingent events is compatible with our freedom to choose and act.

Incompatibilism

Objectors to the possibility of foreknowledge contend that foreknowledge is incompatible with human freedom. Since at all times God knows all truths, if there are truths about our future free choices, God knows our decisions and actions before we make or do them. But if God knows what we will choose before we make the choices, the choice that occurs cannot be different from what God knows. Otherwise, God would hold a false belief. But because of God's omniscience God cannot hold false beliefs. Hence, if we cannot choose or do anything other than what God already knows, we are not free to choose or do otherwise. It is not that God's foreknowledge of events causes our choices or actions to occur and hence removes the possibility of those events being otherwise. God's foreknowledge does not cause the future event. As William Hasker writes, "foreknowledge can perfectly well *show* that an action [event] to be necessary even if it is not the foreknowledge that *makes* it necessary."[3] Rather, the problem is a logical one:

Molina, *On Divine Foreknowledge*; Fischer, *God, Foreknowledge*; Zagzebski, *The Dilemma*.

3. Hasker, *God*, 72. At the same time, if theological determinists (incompatibilists) are contending that foreknowledge is not the cause of the necessity, and if they are not

the fact that God has always known that someone would make particular choices is incompatible with those persons' being able to make the choice freely in a libertarian sense, that is, in the sense that they could have chosen otherwise.

The argument has been advanced in diverse contexts by both theologians and philosophers, including Nelson Pike[4] and Hasker. I will use Hasker's argument to explore the incompatibilist's position. Hasker puts the argument in terms of a person named Clarence choosing to eat a cheese omelet.

(1) Suppose it is now true that Clarence will have a cheese omelet for breakfast tomorrow.

(2) God can never believe what is false or not believe any true proposition that it is logically possible for God to know.

(3) God has always believed that Clarence will have a cheese omelet tomorrow.

(4) If God has always believed a certain thing, no one can bring it about that God has not always believed that thing. This follows from the unalterability of the past.

(5) "Therefore, it is not in Clarence's power to bring it about that God has not always believed that he would have a cheese omelet for breakfast."

(6) It is not possible that God has always believed that Clarence would have a cheese omelet for breakfast and that Clarence does not have one.

(7) Therefore, Clarence cannot refrain from having a cheese omelet for breakfast tomorrow. That is, Clarence's eating the omelet tomorrow is not an act of free choice.

(8) "Clarence will act freely when he eats the omelet for breakfast tomorrow."

(9) Therefore, God has not always believed that Clarence will have a cheese omelet for breakfast tomorrow.[5]

---

arguing for fatalism, then one would think it incumbent on them to give us some hint of *what* it is that makes, in a causal and not merely a logical sense, the choice or action determined.

4. Pike, "Divine Omniscience," 27–46.

5. Hasker, *God*, 73–74. In the ensuing discussion I will not use consecutive numbering, but employ Hasker's identification of propositions to facilitate the reader's checking

The argument is a *reductio ad absurdum:* if sound, it shows that foreknowledge of future human choices logically implies their not being free. As such, God's foreknowledge is incompatible with human freedom; were God to know future contingent choices or actions, they would not and could not be free.

Defense of compatibilism

Will this argument—or some of the many versions of it—succeed in showing that God's knowledge of the future is incompatible with human freedom? We grant premises 1 and 2 of Hasker's argument. 3 poses a bit more of a problem, for it claims that God "has always believed." "Always" is a temporal notion, which presupposes that God has always been in time; it presumes that we can apply temporal predicates to God. We will not dispute this premise, although that temporal predicates appropriately apply to God prior to creation is doubtful.[6]

The argument runs into real difficulties in 5 because 5 is ambiguous. Three interpretations are possible. We might interpret 5 to read

> (5a) It is not in Clarence's power to bring it about that God has always believed and simultaneously did not always believe that Clarence would have a cheese omelet for breakfast.

That is, Clarence cannot bring it about that God both believes and simultaneously does not believe that Clarence would choose a cheese omelet for breakfast. This, of course, is true, for Clarence cannot bring about something that would be contradictory. But such a claim is irrelevant to the incompatibilist argument, for 7 does not follow from 5a.

An alternative interpretation of 5 is

> (5b) It is not in Clarence's power to bring it about that it once was but no longer is the case that God believed that Clarence would have a cheese omelet for breakfast.

This likewise is true, for if Clarence had this power, either God changed his belief at some point or some fact about and intrinsic to his belief changed. Both are made impossible by God's omniscience and stability of beliefs, for it would mean that what God once believed God no longer

---

the source, although I will drop his use of C that precedes each number.

6. It should be noted that Hasker believes that the incompatibilist argument succeeds regardless of whether one thinks of God as atemporal or temporal.

believes. One cannot alter retroactively a fact about God's prior belief.[7] 7 likewise does not follow from 5b, so that although 5b is true it also is irrelevant to the argument against compatibilism.

The third possible interpretation is

> (5c) It is not in Clarence's power to bring it about that God has never believed that Clarence would have a cheese omelet for breakfast.

(5c) is relevant to the incompatibilist argument, for if it is true, Clarence's eating could not be the ground for one of God's beliefs, namely, that God believed that Clarence would not eat the omelet. However, (5c), although relevant, is false. Clarence could bring it about that God never believed that Clarence would have a cheese omelet for breakfast precisely by not having a cheese omelet for breakfast. Since Clarence's actions constitute the ground for God's belief or knowledge, it follows that God believes what in fact Clarence will do, and in this case, what Clarence will freely do. If Clarence eats the omelet, God believes so; if Clarence does not eat the omelet, God believes he won't eat it. Both cannot be true, but no matter; one is true in virtue of Clarence's action, and that is what God believes.[8]

In short, 5 fails as a premise in being either irrelevant or false. In either case, any argument, such as the above incompatibilist argument, that uses 5 or something similar fails. The result is that this or similar arguments gives us no reason to think that our freedom is incompatible with God's foreknowledge.

Since Hasker is aware of this objection, let us take up his replies. His first worry concerns the notion of the power to bring something about, especially as manifested in 5. Hasker notes that the compatibilist Alvin Plantinga referred to this power as a counterfactual power over the past. It is "our power to *do something, such that were we to do it, God would not have believed that thing.*"[9] Hasker then proceeds to wonder what this counterfactual power amounts to. Clearly this counterfactual power is not a causal power; causal powers have consequences whereas counterfactual powers do not necessarily have consequences.[10] Clarence does not cause God's beliefs

---

7. This finds its clearest expression in Hasker's proposition (19): "If at T1 God had always believed that [Clarence] would do X at T2 and it was in [Clarence's] power to refrain from doing X at T2, then it was in [Clarence's] power to bring it about that whereas it was true at T1 that God had always believed that [Clarence] would do X at T2, it was no longer true at T2 that God had always believed that [Clarence] would do X at T2." Hasker, "Foreknowledge and Necessity," 148.

8. Reichenbach, "Hasker on Omniscience," 92.

9. Hasker, *God*, 102.

10. Hasker notes that Plantinga also resists understanding this counterfactual

about what he eats. It seems, he argues, to be more of a relation of dependence than of a power. But what this relation of dependence amounts to Hasker is at a loss to know; "only if we see how little really is involved in counterfactual dependence will we feel the force of the motivation to go beyond counterfactual dependence to something more determinate."[11] That is, Hasker believes that the compatibilist, who believes that divine foreknowledge is compatible with human freedom, must affirm more than a counterfactual power, namely, that somehow one can bring something to pass. In particular, Hasker holds that if Clarence has this power, Clarence eating the omelet can actually, somehow, bring about a particular belief by God.

Now clearly this is true; when a person performs an action (in the future), it actually brings it about that God believes that the person performed the action. There is, in some sense or other, a bringing about. But in what sense or senses? What is this "bringing about?" We agree that a causal understanding is too strong. Clarence does not cause God's belief, just as my doing something does not actually cause you to believe that I do it. What is in view here is just this, namely, that God's knowledge is grounded in the states of affairs in the world, such that whatever states of affairs hold, God believes that they hold, and if they fail to hold, God does not believe that they hold. It is the power to bring about the past in the sense that what one does provides the ground for a belief, but it is not the power to cause the past. This is the case whether God believes a certain proposition about the future on the grounds that this proposition is true and it is true because it corresponds with a yet-to-be state of affairs, or whether God directly knows future events. Again, how God knows this yet-to-be state of affairs we do not know and is not our concern. Our interest is simply in the ground on which God's knowledge is based.

Hasker recognizes that this middle ground between causal and counterfactual understandings of bringing about is not an uncommon notion.[12] We might identify several types of bringing about. For example, I bring it about that my wife has a father-in-law by marrying her. That is, my having a father and marrying my wife are the grounds for ascribing to her the fact that she has a father-in-law, or that she is his daughter-in-law. But I don't say that in doing so I caused her to have a father-in-law or to be a daughter-in-law. The case of bringing about we have in mind with respect to God's beliefs or knowledge we might term bringing about in an epistemic sense:

---

power to bring about in any causal sense. Ibid., 106.

11. Ibid.

12. Hasker makes a similar point by invoking an example given by Jaegwon Kim of Xantippe's widowhood being brought about by the jailor giving poison to Socrates (Ibid., 107–8).

it provides the grounds for the truth claims, belief, or knowledge. Thus far, there is no problem with the notion of bringing something about in neither a causal nor a counterfactual sense.

Hasker, however, is not placated; he remains concerned with whether

> (51) God existed at T_1, and God believed at T_1 that [Clarence] would do X at T_2, and it was within [Clarence's] power to refrain from doing X at T_2

entails

> (53) It was within [Clarence's] power at T_2 to do something that would have brought it about that God did not hold the belief He did hold at T_2.[13]

"And this question is not answered by stating that (51) entails that Clarence has some *other* power, such as the one specified [in (53b) as a counterfactual power]. *That* is true enough, but what we really need to know is, *does (51) entail (53), or doesn't it?*"[14] But the point is—and this is what Hasker misses in his extensive discussion of this alleged entailment of (53) and of the various power entailment principles—that (53) is ambiguous in precisely the way we noted (5) was ambiguous (see 5a, 5b, and 5c above). It is ambiguous between an interpretation either that renders it relevant to the compatibilist's claim but is false, or that renders it true but irrelevant to the compatibilist's claim. So we cannot ask simply flat out whether (51) entails (53).[15]

Again, it is not that we can change or alter the past; the past is unalterable. It is not that we can cause the past, in the sense that we have backward causation. The relation found in foreknowledge is epistemic in character. God's beliefs or knowledge are grounded in the events themselves. They are true because they correspond with true states of affairs that hold regardless of the time dimension (which is precisely what *fore*knowledge affirms).

---

13. Ibid., 98.

14. Ibid., 102. 53b states that "It was within [Clarence's] power at T_2 to do something such that if he had done it, then God would not have held a belief that in fact he did hold." Ibid., 104.

15. One final point. Hasker thinks that, in applying his power entailment principles, God's belief that Clarence would act in a certain way is a necessary condition for Clarence having the power to act in that way (part of PEP4). And from this he concludes that (51) does entail (53). But God's belief is not a necessary condition at all, unless one holds that God's existence is logically necessary and hence necessary for all events. It is not that if God didn't believe Clarence would do *x* that Clarence couldn't do *x*. Rather, it is the other way around: Clarence's doing *x* is necessary for God to believe truly that Clarence does *x*. Ibid., 110–11.

Thus, in an epistemic sense, our future actions bring about God's beliefs in the sense that there is no difference between God having the belief and the belief being true, for all God's beliefs necessarily are true (in that as omniscient he cannot hold a false belief).

We might put our argument another way. What precludes God from having always believed that Clarence would not do X at T_2? It is that Clarence does X at T_2. That is, from God's perspective (that of *fore*knowledge) it is as if Clarence has already done X at T_2. But this relation—Clarence actually doing X at T_2 entailing that Clarence cannot refrain from doing X at T_2—does not remove Clarence's freedom regarding doing X at T_2. If it is now true that Clarence will do X at T_2, then there is a certain precluding condition—the truth of this claim—that necessitates that Clarence cannot refrain from doing X at T_2. But the truth of this claim about what Clarence will do is conditioned by what Clarence *actually does* at T_2. That is, what precludes Clarence from refraining from doing X at T_2 is that, given that the proposition about his future act is true, it is as if Clarence has done X at T_2. And his doing so was a free act: he had a choice of whether or not to do X.

One might be perplexed about the "as if" here invoked. Yet I do not think it is difficult to comprehend. Consider the following. Parsons has invented a special machine that allows him to go back in time. He enters the machine in 2016 and finds himself observing Robin in 1916. Parsons is an authority on Robin and knows immediately the situation Robin is in. Not only that, but Parsons remembers reading about the particular decision or act that Robin made in that situation. Thus, one might argue that from Parsons's perspective what Robin decides is as if already done. It is not already done, since Parsons is standing there waiting for Robin to do it. Parsons has gone back in time. Yet from Parsons's perspective, which is of one traveling back from the future, it is as if Robin already did it, since Parsons knows what Robin actually decides. Since Parsons believes in the unalterability of the past, it is not within Robin's power to do something other than what Robin in fact does in that situation. From Robin's perspective Robin's decision is not already made nor is the action taken, so that it is in Robin's power at that time to do either x or y. From Robin's perspective, that Robin will do x rather than y is indeterminate; it is not yet done, though at the same time Robin can grant that Parsons knows what Robin will do because for Parsons it is as if Robin has already done it.

What is the significance of introducing what we can call precluding conditions? It suggests (1) a basis for a difference between bringing about and altering the past, and (2) a basis for a difference between our inability to alter the past and our ability to act freely to bring about the future. Regarding (1), we are precluded from altering the past because the past has already occurred. Clarence cannot alter a prior belief because he is precluded from doing so by virtue of an omniscient God already having that belief. However, we are not precluded from bringing about the past when it is not future indifferent, for the future grounds the non-future-indifferent past. By eating an omelet Clarence can bring it about that God has a certain belief and that this belief is true, for Clarence's eating it is the ground of God's belief. The former case has precluding conditions, the latter not.

Regarding (2), a difference holds between the conditions that preclude our altering the past and those that give the *appearance* that we cannot act freely in bringing about the future. We cannot alter the past because the events have already occurred. And we cannot alter the future that God already believes (cannot do other than what God believes we will do) because from God's perspective of foreknowledge it is as if we have already done the event. That in the one case the act was done, and that in the other it is as if done, are both the precluding conditions for our not being able to alter the past or the future known by God, and at the same time are the conditions for God having the relevant beliefs. It is this latter that gives the (mistaken) appearance that we cannot in the future freely bring about events.

But note that neither case—our inability to alter the past nor our inability to alter the future known by God—speaks to the question of human freedom, for both the past action that was done and the action that we have yet to do can still have been free or be free respectively. That is, although we cannot alter the future that God foresees because for him it is as if already performed, we can freely act in the future, for the ground of God's foreknowing something is our very bringing it about. Hence, epistemologically freely bringing something about logically and epistemically precedes and determines God's foreseeing and believing it. That is, there is nothing for God to foresee or believe with respect to Clarence's eating the omelet except what Clarence does. Similarly with the past; there is nothing for God (or us) to know about the past except the past that has been brought about.

The epistemic nature of the discussion suggests that God's knowledge is analogous to my knowledge that arises from seeing you drop a ball. Does your dropping the ball cause me to believe that you dropped it? In one sense, no; there is no causal relation because you could drop the ball and I could disbelieve that you dropped it if I did not witness the event. And even if I had witnessed the event, I might still believe that you did not drop that ball, for I might think that my perceptual faculties were not functioning properly or that you were trying to deceive me by dropping something else. But surely your dropping the ball brings about my belief in that it is the ground for my belief that you dropped the ball being true. The belief would not be true had you not dropped it. The difference between this case and

God's believing is that my belief is contingently true, whereas God's belief is necessarily true. But the grounding relation holds.

In short, although we are unable to alter the past (because it is the past) and the future that God knows (for the reason that God has certain beliefs about it), the inability to alter these has no implications for our ability at one time to freely bring about what is now the past or in the future to freely bring about what is now in the future. We can freely bring about what is now in the future by our actions (because God's beliefs about our actions are grounded in our future actions), and with respect to God's beliefs about the future, we bring about those beliefs (because again God's beliefs about our actions are grounded in our actions). Consequently, compatibilists—those who think that divine foreknowledge is compatible with human freedom—are not impaled on either of the horns of Hasker's dilemma; there is no inconsistency in believing that we are free and that God knows our future free choices and actions.

Hard and soft facts

Recently Hasker has again considered the argument as phrased in terms of hard and soft facts.[16] Admittedly, this is not his favorite formulation of the issue, since as he well notes it is extremely difficult to give a precise definition of these two types of facts; the attempt to do so led to very complicated, if not esoteric, definitions.[17] Yet he has devoted substantial effort to this approach. Hasker believes that, properly and carefully formulated, the distinction may resolve the problem of logical determinism or fatalism, but adamantly affirms that it "*will fail to solve the problem of theological fatalism.*"[18] Roughly put, a proposition expressing a hard fact is totally about the past; whether or not there is time after the present, nothing can alter the truth of such a proposition; the fact is what it is. The truth of the proposition is indifferent to any time after the present.[19] Hasker, following Alfred Freddoso, terms the necessity involved here "accidental necessity." It is the necessity belonging to the past. Soft facts, on the other hand, are not totally about the past; they are partially about the future. In effect, they are not future indifferent. The

---

16. Hasker, "Divine Foreknowledge," 44. He addressed the problem earlier in "Hard Facts."

17. For a deep draught of the debate over hard and soft facts, see Hoffman and Rosenkrantz, "Hard and Soft Facts."

18. Hasker, "Hard Facts," 161.

19. "An elementary proposition is future-indifferent IFF [if and only if] it is consistent with there being no times after the present, and also consistent with there being times after the present." Hasker, "Foreknowledge and Necessity," 133.

truth of propositions expressing them depends in part on the future. Thus, for example, George Bush declared war on Saddam Hussein in March of 2003 would be a hard fact; if it is a fact, nothing in the future (after now) can affect the truth of the proposition that George Bush declared war on Saddam Hussein in March of 2003. It is future indifferent. A soft fact would be expressed by a proposition whose truth in part depends on future events or states of affairs. Such a proposition is not future indifferent. For example, the truth of the proposition, Martin Luther King delivered his "I Have a Dream" speech in Washington, D.C. eighty years before the members of the United Nations Security Council voted to declare a Palestinian state, depends on whether or not the members choose to declare a Palestinian state in 2043. The proposition that Martin Luther King delivered his speech in Washington, D.C. expresses a hard fact; nothing now can alter that fact or bring it about that it is not a fact. But that he delivered the speech before the Security Council voted for a Palestinian state expresses a soft fact. The members of the Council have the power to make the second proposition, although not the proposition about King delivering a speech, true by their voting. This is the type of power relevant to God's foreknowledge. What God knows about our free acts is relationally dependent on what we do. In this relational sense a person has the power to act so that the past, insofar as it is relationally dependent upon the person's future acts, is in part what it is. With regard to foreknowledge, what the person does or does not do makes it the case that God truly believes something about what the person does. Consequently, no contradiction exists between our human freedom and divine foreknowledge.

Hasker objects, however.

> However, a more fundamental difficulty attends efforts to avoid that Incompatibility Argument along these lines. . . . There remains the pressing question: why should we accept that facts about God's past beliefs are soft—i.e., that, unlike other truths about the past, these facts are such that it is possible for someone to bring it about that they are false. The transfer of necessity principle guarantees that [*God believes at T_1 that Clarence had an omelet at T_3*] and [*Clarence will have an omelet at T_3*] are either both hard or both soft [facts] prior to T_3. But why should we assume that it is the softness of the latter proposition that transfers to the former, and not vice versa?[20]

---

20. Hasker, "Divine Foreknowledge," 44. I substituted Hasker's old cases as used above for the different examples he employs in the quote.

First, Hasker is not careful here. Not all propositions about God's past beliefs express soft facts; this applies only to God's beliefs about the current future, and including and especially about our future free choices and actions (given that God holds his beliefs in time). But apart from this, why should one hold that God's belief about Clarence is a hard fact? For Hasker, it is such because it is parallel to or follows from other hard facts. The proposition "Yesterday Mary believed Clarence will have an omelet at tomorrow" expresses a hard fact about the past; it is future-indifferent. The only difference between the statements that yesterday Mary believed that Clarence will have an omelet at tomorrow and that yesterday God believed this is that "Mary" is replaced by "God."[21] This substitution, he claims, makes no appreciable difference with respect to the latter also expressing a hard fact. This is seen, he contends, in that we can replace "God" with "Yahweh," such that we have the proposition "Yesterday Yahweh believed Clarence will have an omelet at tomorrow." Paralleling the proposition about Mary, it expresses a hard fact about a past belief. But that Yahweh is God is metaphysically necessary. Hence, the propositions about Yahweh's belief and that Yahweh is God, as expressing hard facts, entail that God's belief about such is a hard fact, for what is entailed by hard facts must itself be a hard fact. And once this is granted, since God is essentially infallible and cannot hold a false belief, it follows that Clarence is not free. Clarence's future is determined. This, he notes, fits nicely with our intuition about the necessity of the past—the past is expressed by propositions recording hard facts, and this applies to God just as well as to us.

But can we so easily replace "Mary" with "Yahweh" or "God"? The latter two have the essential property of being omniscient, and if they are essentially omniscient at least some of their beliefs are about or contain references to the current future, such that propositions expressing beliefs about such facts express soft facts. That is, "Yesterday Yahweh (or God) believed that Clarence will have an omelet tomorrow" expresses a soft fact. Hence, though entailed by God's belief and the infallibility of God's beliefs, Clarence's actions are not theologically determined.

Hasker's reply to this is that if we allow essential properties to be considered in delineating hard and soft facts, then all the essential properties must be considered, in which case there will be no hard facts. If we say "Mary believes Clarence will have an omelet," a theist might affirm that "being created by God" is an essential property of Mary. But in referring to God who is eternal, one of Mary's essential properties is such that the proposition about Mary refers in part to the future, and hence any proposition

---

21. Hasker, "Hard Facts," 170.

about Mary, including those that are accidentally necessary (about the past), will express a soft fact. Instead, Hasker argues, "In classifying a proposition as a hard or a soft fact, only such essential properties of individuals are to be considered as are expressed in stating the proposition."[22]

We might grant that we cannot consider essential properties in all cases, else the distinction collapses. But a middle ground holds between considering all essential properties and considering only those explicitly expressed in stating the proposition. That is, we should consider essential properties that are *relevant* to the use of the proposition in the argument under consideration. In this case, the essential property of infallibility is relevant to God's belief being a soft fact. This critical feature distinguishes God from Mary in this case. This can be seen in that the incompatibilist argument trades on God's belief and the essential property of infallibility of God's beliefs, a property not had in Mary's case. It is not that God and Mary simply believe, but that Mary's belief is fallible and God's infallible. In virtue of this property God's beliefs about the future cannot be future-indifferent; they and their truth depend necessarily on the future. Hence, the alleged parallel between Mary's belief and that of God as being hard facts disappears.

Thus, returning to Hasker's question at the end of the above extended quote, the answer to the question Hasker poses is what we have contended all along: the reason that the softness of the latter proposition (Clarence will have an omelet at T_1) transfers to the former (God believes that Clarence will have an omelet at T_1) and not vice versa is that the former depends on the latter for its truth, and not vice versa. God has the particular belief as part of God's foreknowledge because in fact Clarence chooses one way or the other. Clarence's future choice is the ground for God's belief. Hence, the belief is soft because its truth depends upon something Clarence is yet to do.

Do statements about future facts have indeterminate truth value?

The doctrine of divine foreknowledge rests on the contention that propositions about the future, about what will happen, can be true or false before they happen. This applies not only to deterministic events that follow necessarily from their causes but also to indeterministic or causally open events. The latter are the events in which we have an interest, namely, choices and actions of free agents. Incompatibilists contend that statements about the future have no truth value either at all or unless they follow necessarily,

22. Ibid., 174.

either in a logical or causal sense, from truths about the present. That is, propositions about the future, such as, "Clarence will choose to eat an omelet for lunch tomorrow," or "Clarence will not eat an omelet for lunch tomorrow," have no truth value now, prior to his choosing or eating or not doing so.

This contention runs counter to our ordinary belief about future contingent propositions that are causally indeterminate. We normally think that contingent propositions about the future, such as "my wife will go to Curves to exercise tomorrow morning" are either true or false, true if she goes tomorrow and false if not. If these propositions have no truth value, then the proposition "either my wife will go to exercise tomorrow morning or she will not" also has no truth value. But according to the principle of excluded middle, one these disjuncts necessarily is true. Either she will or she will not go to Curves to exercise. One of these events will occur, and when it does we can determine which one of these future statements was true. The question is not whether or not we can now know or determine which disjunct or which future tense proposition is true. The point is that one of the future tense disjuncts and hence future tense propositions are true, regardless of our ignorance of which is true. In short, propositions about future events like my wife going to Curves are either true or false now, prior to the event.

Incompatibilists might respond that statements about future events cannot be true or false because nothing now makes them so. Since the future is not yet, nothing exists for these statements to correspond to to make them true. We cannot say that "Clarence will eat chicken for supper next Wednesday" is true because no current event makes it true; no state of affairs exists for it to correspond to now. But, we reply, with this reasoning, statements about the past suffer the same fate of being neither true nor false, for there is no current state of affairs for them to correspond to to make them true or false. On this incompatibilist view to say that Clarence ate chicken for supper last Wednesday would not have a truth value because Clarence is not now eating (or not eating) chicken. But then on this incompatibilist view the only statements that would be true would be present tense statements, since they would be the only statements with corresponding present events. Such a position would be absurd. If statements about the past have truth value because the event either did or did not occur, statements about the future can also have truth value because the event either will or will not occur. The tense simply informs us about the timing of the event with respect to now: when these states of affairs are to occur or did occur. A similar argument holds for universal statements, such as "all swans have feathers," since not all swans that ever have existed or will exist now exist to make this statement true. They can be true even though there is no current state of affairs to which they correspond in order to make them true. In short, denying truth value to future contingent propositions would unreasonably restrict truth values to present tense propositions.

In defense of this incompatibilist view, Alan Rhoda argues that assigning truth value to future contingent propositions depends upon how one assigns truth value. He suggests two possibilities. The first, which he refers to as Ockhamism, contends that "the truth value of a proposition about the future depends solely on what is the case at the future time (implicitly) referred to in the proposition."[23] Thus, the truth of the proposition, "Clarence will eat the omelet," depends only on what happens when Clarence either eats or does not eat it. If it is true at that time, since the truth of the proposition about what Clarence will do cannot change, it is always true. And if it is always true, is it true now, prior to the event occurring. And if it is true now, it is knowable, and knowable by an omniscient God (though not knowable by human beings)

The competing view, which he terms the Peircean view, "proposes that whether a proposition about the future is true at a given time depends on whether sufficient conditions for its truth obtain at that time."[24] Since the sufficient conditions for a future contingent event to occur are not now present (otherwise the future event would not now be contingent but causally determined), propositions about future contingent events are neither true nor false prior to their occurrence. And if they are not true now, they are not knowable, either by humans or by God.

In short, the truth of the claim that propositions about the future can be true and hence known depends upon which of these views one accepts. "If the Ockhamists are right, then the future can be both causally open and settled (with respect to their truth) in the same respects at the same time, whereas if the Peirceans are right then the future cannot be settled (with respect to their truth) in any respect in which it is causally open."[25] That is, in the former case, there can be (and are) true propositions about future contingent events; that I will choose to do x in the future is true or false. In the latter case there are no true propositions about future contingent events; that I will or will not do x has no truth value.

Rhoda's argument against the Ockhamist view is that "to predict that an event 'will' happen . . . is just to say that it 'does' happen in the future, nothing more. . . . Thus, to accommodate predictions that do carry significant

---

23. Rhoda, "Philosophical Case," 306.
24. Ibid.
25. Ibid.

causal force, Ockhamists have to append strengthening qualifiers, as in 'will *definitely occur.*'" But, Rhoda objects, the result is that there is no difference between *x* will occur and *x* definitely will occur, for both have to be stronger than *x* probably will occur. To say that *x* will occur is to treat the matter of its occurring as settled. But then does "definitely" add to this? There is in effect no linguistic space for a difference between will occur and definitely will occur, and this cannot be the case because we have added the qualifier "definitely," which should make a difference. This leads him to adopt the Piercean viewpoint.

But Rhoda makes a serious but not uncommon confusion. First, the claim that to predict that an event will happen is not just to say that it will happen; Rhoda should say that to *truly* predict that an event will happen is just to say that it will happen. Predictions, by their very nature, are either true or false; merely because it is a prediction does not mean that it is true. Second, following from this, the appended qualifiers to strengthen or weaken the case—it possibly will, probably will, definitely will—do not apply to future events *per se*, but *to the knowledge claim* about the truth of the prediction of those events. Thus, to say that *x* will definitely occur in the future is to claim that we know the proposition is true because, for example, we know the intervening causal conditions that make the event no longer contingent but definite. And to say that *x* probably will occur is to claim that we know some of the intervening causal conditions but not enough of them (even if there were enough of them) to be determinate about whether the proposition is true. One can see this because if someone said that *x* will occur, it is reasonable to ask why that person believes that. The appropriate response would be in terms of the (causal) conditions known to that person. If one says that it probably will be the case, then presumably that person has good evidence to support that belief. If it possibly will be the case, the person lacks reasonably persuasive evidence to support the belief. In short, the qualifiers have to do with my *knowledge* of the conditions affecting the future event, *not* the conditions or events themselves. Hence, there is no reason to reject the Ockhamist for the Peircean account. It is true that for finite humans there often are no present grounds for us to make an absolutely definitive claim that *x* will occur tomorrow, although we can say such with such a high degree of reliability that, in common language, it is certain. Although technically it is not absolutely certain that my wife will say something tomorrow, in fact for all intents and purposes she certainly will: I have absolutely no doubt about it. Presumably for a being with foreknowledge of all events making definitive claims about the future would not be a problem; no caveats qualifying its knowledge would be needed.

The Peircean account runs counter to our ordinary way of speaking about the future, in which we affirm that truly x will occur. The proposition that the sun will rise tomorrow is true because it happens; whether or not it is certain is a claim about my knowledge of the event, not about the event itself. That tomorrow I will teach introduction to philosophy to freshmen, that I will take my wife out for a special birthday dinner, and so on, I can also affirm to be true, even when uttered before the events, based on my knowledge of myself and my intentions. Note that I might have much more evidence for these statements being true than I would have for claiming that the earth revolves about the sun. Rhoda's confusion, therefore, is between the truth of the claim (determined by what happens) and the qualifiers of the truth, which deal with our confidence in our knowledge about the claim. There is good reason to adopt the Ockhamist view that is congenial to our ordinary way of speaking about the future, and this way is quite consistent with a compatibilist view of divine foreknowledge.

Conclusion

In short, the truth value of propositions about the future depends solely on what states of affairs obtain at the future time. Thus, propositions about the future can be known, certainly less assuredly by us, but assuredly by God. God's knowledge depends on and is grounded upon states of affairs in the world. This is true regardless of the time frame involved. That God knows future contingencies does not mean that their contingent status is removed. Human free choice is consistent with God's foreknowledge. Thus, omniscience includes not only knowledge of the past and the present, but also of the future, whether of determined events or contingent events involving free choice. Omniscience is compatible with human freedom. Establishing this removes much of the reasoning behind the view that God's knowledge of the future has to be limited to deterministically caused events; what remains is the question of this view's interpretation of and consistency with Scripture and whether foreknowledge can be useful. To this we turn in the next chapter.

Chapter 8

The Open View of God's Knowledge

IN THE LAST THREE decades philosophers and theologians have written extensively about the "open view of God." In this chapter we will examine this intriguing hypothesis regarding what God knows. According to the open view of God (which we will also term "open theism"), God has temporal relations with the world he created. These relations form the centerpiece of God's involvement with free persons. God loves and providentially cares for them, all the while inviting them back into a personal, covenantal relationship with him. God could have created robotic mannequins that he would have deterministically controlled, but these could not render the morally significant and personally satisfying free responses that God desires. Their responses would be instances neither of true love nor of willing obedience, but merely the results of prior, divinely-determined causal conditions. Rather, God granted humans morally significant freedom to make their own choices and pursue their own actions. The result is that humans can either willingly relate to God personally or resist being his covenant people; the choice is theirs, not without significant consequences. Despite frequent setbacks, God does not abandon humans, but continually endeavors to persuade them to return to the covenantal relationship he established with individuals and groups of individuals throughout history. Creating free creatures that can resist his advances was a risk God took. This risk was necessary for meaningful human responses, but at times it also led to God regretting that he had made such recalcitrant beings who, despite his pleadings, promises, and even the sacrifice of his Son, often refused to acknowledge God's sovereignty and accede to God's will. Yet, despite it all, God loves and forgives, and as a shepherd persistently seeks to bring sheep safely into his sheepfold.

For open theism, God has complete and comprehensive knowledge about all past and present events but little or no knowledge of the future contingent actions of free beings. God can form beliefs about what humans choose or do, but beliefs are not knowledge and can be mistaken. God might even be able to form and calculate probabilities about what might contingently happen, at least in the near future. But fore*knowledge* of future free actions is impossible. Not only would it conflict with human freedom, making all human choices necessary, but for some open theists such foreknowledge is impossible because propositions about future free acts are neither true nor false. Without foreknowledge God does not know, but only surmises, what his future creatures will do once they exercise their bequeathed freedom. God knows everything that can be known, but since the future is not yet, it cannot be known—at least the future that is not causally determined by or follows necessarily from present events. God might be able to infer causally determined future events from the information presently available to him, but he does not know the events themselves; any beliefs about future contingencies would be inferential at best.

This open theist's view of God and God's properties bears both similarities with and differences from the position we developed in the previous chapters. The open view affirms God's agency, power, and goodness, although not generally in the way we have developed these, that is, in terms of God's almightiness and logically contingent but morally necessary divine goodness. It affirms that God created humans with libertarian freedom to choose to relate in meaningful and obedient ways with the creator. It affirms that God's merciful love lies at the core of his divine sovereignty and that God's sovereignty is not meticulous, determining or covering every human action, but is an exercise in power consistent and cooperating with the freedom with which God endowed humans. God can but usually does not compel or coerce; rather, God persuades, invites, and solicits. Where open theism significantly departs from the view we espoused is in its view of divine knowledge. Open theists affirm, as we have done, God's omniscience, but they do so in a way that leaves God knowing the past and present but not the future free actions of human agents. It is possible that God can deduce what will happen in deterministic cases and can probabilistically surmise about soon-to-occur contingent events, but God has no knowledge of future free actions and their consequences. Whereas in the previous chapter we argued that propositions about future events, and especially future free actions, have a truth value and thus are knowable by God, many open theists deny this—at least for future free actions, if not for all future contingent events.

Open theists advance six fundamental arguments for their view. First, future decisions are not yet made and future actions have not occurred. Hence, there is nothing to know; no true propositions about future free choices or contingent events exist for there is nothing for such propositions with which to correlate. Second, foreknowledge is incompatible with human freedom. If God knows what someone will choose in the future, that person has no choice about the matter; the event already is determined. Third, Scripture contains evidence that stands in contrast to divine foreknowledge. Passages suggest that God is disappointed by unforeseen failures, repents, and changes his mind. These divine acts would be meaningless if God already knew the future. Fourth, open theists argue that divine tests of humans to assess their faith would be unnecessary if God had foreknowledge, for then God would already know whether or not those tested were faithful. Fifth, open theists advance particular understandings of prophecy that they believe do not require foreknowledge. Finally, knowledge of the future is useless to God, for God cannot make choices to change or alter events on the basis of this knowledge. If God altered the future on the basis of his foreknowledge, what he foreknew would not occur and hence God could not have known it. In the previous chapter we considered the first two arguments, and we will only briefly attend to them again here. We will more thoroughly address the third through sixth arguments in this chapter.

Knowledge of future free choices

Open theism's argument begins by affirming that at least some, if not many, events in the future are, as of now, causally open. Open theism invokes the free-will approach to theism. God granted humans the freedom to respond fully and freely to events, including God's own initiatives. What God wants is our free response in love to his gracious act inviting us into his life. God does not seek to manipulate us as robots, for such a relationship lacks genuine, meaningful fellowship; it establishes or maintains no real covenantal bond. In order to have such a personal fellowship relation, God had to grant humans morally significant freedom. This presupposes that future events involving human free choice are causally open, not determined either by nature or by God. This openness applies not only to the future free choices and actions of currently existing free persons and of free persons yet to exist, but also to events that are affected by the future free choices of present and future persons.

Since future free choices are as of now causally indeterminate, foreknowledge of future contingent events involving human free choices and acts is impossible. Open theists argue that a contradiction holds between foreknowledge and persons' ability to choose or act freely. If God foreknew human choices and actions, they would not be free. Hence, although God has comprehensive knowledge about the past and present, God has no knowledge of future human contingencies in that no one, not even God, can know what the choices and actions of free agents will be. The future is to a great extent epistemically open, not only to us, but also to God.

The bone of contention between traditional libertarians and open theists concerns whether or not God's knowledge is thereby limited. Open theists contend that God's knowledge is not limited because God knows all that can be known, and future contingencies cannot be known. Defenders of foreknowledge suggest that on the open view God's knowledge is limited because propositions about future free choices and acts are either true or false at a time prior to their occurrence and hence can be known to be true or false, maybe not by us, but by an omniscient being. It is now true (supposing that I go) or false (supposing that I do not go) that I will go to church tomorrow. Although I do not know now which proposition is true, a being with foreknowledge would know which of these is true, for it knows what will occur in the future. This analysis applies not only to future tense propositions about human free acts, but also to propositions about contingent events following from them. If God would lack foreknowledge, God would be barred from knowing the choices and actions of free agents, and if this is so, God also would be barred from knowing the many consequences of those choices (such as whether or not my car will add CO_2 to the environment tomorrow or whether or not my car will be damaged in an accident on the way to church next month, for these hinge on my choosing to drive it). This means that on open theism God cannot and hence does not know an *enormous* number of truths about our choices, actions, and what follows from them. From the foreknowledge defender's perspective, God's knowledge is greatly limited.

In the previous chapter we showed that we had reason to doubt the open theists' view that since propositions about future human free acts and their consequences are neither true nor false, they cannot be known by anyone. There we contended that propositions about the future—future tense propositions, whether about future free actions or future contingent events—are meaningful propositions and as assertions are either true or false. It is true that currently no events correspond to these propositions, but that is irrelevant. Future tense propositions are not about the present but about the future. It is not what occurs now but what occurs in the future that makes future tense propositions true or false. Thus, although we might not know now the truth value of future tense propositions, that is irrelevant to the question whether they have truth value now. There will be a state of affairs that will be relevant to their truth or falsity, and hence on the basis of that future event they are either true or false. And since God as omniscient knows all truths, God would know true future tense contingent propositions. Otherwise, God's knowledge is limited.

The second argument for open theism builds on the claim that foreknowledge is incompatible with human freedom. Preserving human freedom, open theists argue, requires jettisoning foreknowledge. In the previous chapter we responded to the incompatibility argument by showing that no *logical* incompatibility exists between God's foreknowledge and human free choices and actions. We will not repeat here the detailed and convincing arguments we advanced to show this is the case. Rather, we want to press the point that not only does no logical incompatibility exist, but there is no *causal* incompatibility either. No causal relation exists between God's foreknowledge and our future free actions. God's knowledge does not cause us to do anything. Since God's knowledge has no causal consequences with regard to our actions, the future remains causally indeterminate. Hence, from both a logical and a causal perspective, foreknowledge does not remove the causal openness of future free human choices and what follows from them.

In short, neither of these first two arguments that open theists commonly employ compels us to abandon the traditional view of divine foreknowledge for the view espoused by open theism. Future tense assertions are meaningful and either true or false, depending upon whether and how they correspond with future states of affairs. And there is no reason to believe that divine foreknowledge is incompatible with human freedom, for the very grounds of God's knowledge are the free choices and acts of persons in the future.

Knowledge of future likelihood

William Hasker holds that the open theist can rescue a significant amount of God's knowledge of future events because God has extensive knowledge of the future through knowledge of its possibilities. He writes, "God's knowledge concerning the future includes all of the future outcomes that are objectively possible, *as well as* knowledge of the objective likelihood that each outcome will occur, and in cases where one choice is overwhelmingly likely (though not as yet absolutely certain) to be made, God will know that also."[1] Put simply, God knows everything that is possible at this point and how likely it is to occur. Interestingly enough, Hasker does not defend this audacious thesis but merely advances it. But why should one think that God has "comprehensive and exact knowledge of the *possibilities* of the future . . . and of the gradually changing *likelihood* of each of those possibilities being realized"?[2] The key phrases here are "objectively possible" and "objective

1. Hasker, *God*, 188.
2. Ibid., 189.

likelihood." In his book Hasker does not define these terms, but in private correspondence he provided the following.

> Something is objectively possible at *t* if and only if it is possible, given the state of affairs that actually obtains at *t*. The notion of objective likelihood, or objective probability, rests on the idea that, of the things that are objectively possible in the future [given the state of affairs that actually obtains at *t*], some are more likely to occur than others. For instance, a person may have a free choice between several options, and yet be more likely to choose one than another.

The point here is that at every moment God knows what is possible in the future and the likelihood that it will occur, and this is constantly changing as the future moves into the present (with each new *t*). But since what is objectively possible in the future depends on the then-current state of affairs, and since that then-current state of affairs, insofar as it involves human choices and acts, is unknowable now, the reliability of discerning now both the possibility and the likelihood of what is possible occurring without foreknowledge is very much in doubt. The reason is that we might know now what is possible in the very near future given the present conditions, and given the conditions that currently hold we might even be able fallibly to determine particular likelihoods of events not too distant in the future. But as we move out to greater temporal distances, the contingencies of the intervening events are so great in terms of their occurrences that it becomes impossible even for God to know now what will actually be the case to make something possible and consequently how likely it is for the possible actually to occur in the future. To know what is possible and to establish its objective likelihood now (at *t*) requires that we know what actually occurred after *t* and what the conditions are of that distant event. That is, the objective likelihood of something in the future depends on what actually is the case both prior to it and at the time. For example, it is now (at *t*) possible that Chelsea will have a grandchild because she exists and has children. And suppose (although I am dubious) for sake of argument that the likelihood of having a grandchild can be calculated now. But suppose she now (at *t*) inquires whether it is possible (at t_{51}) that she will have a great grandchild and what the objective likelihood is that she will have a great grandchild. Both of these depend on whether she actually has a grandchild. If she never has grandchildren, then it is impossible now that she has any great grandchildren. But neither God nor Chelsea can know at *t* whether she actually will have grandchildren, only that it is possible. What we are left with is the possibility of a possibility at *t*, and if the second possibility does not become actual, an impossibility (about which she cannot know now at *t* since it results from future free actions). Only if God knows what is actual in the future, namely, that she actually has a grandchild, can God know that it is possible that she will have a great grandchild and perhaps (though unlikely) what its likelihood is. But without foreknowledge God cannot know that she has a grandchild (or even what if any sexual activities her grandchild will engage in to have or not have a great grandchild). Consequently, God cannot have knowledge now of the objective possibility or likelihood of Chelsea having a great grandchild. To know now (at *t*) what is possible or impossible, likely or unlikely, in the distant future depends on knowing what for the open theist is unknowable, namely, what is actual in the future.

This same argument applies to all the possible contingent properties of that possible great grandchild and the possible choices that that great grandchild might make. Chelsea might think now that it is possible that her future great grandchild will marry someone of French descent, choose to live in Boulder, Colorado, and like Brussels sprouts, but this might actually be impossible since she might not have a future grandchild and hence not have a future great grandchild, or her grandchild or great grandchild might die in infancy. In such cases there is no likelihood now that these events will occur, for none of the relevant states of affairs will obtain. And whether the required future states of affairs will occur cannot be known now without foreknowledge. Chelsea might now think it is possible when it is really impossible (she had no grandchild or none survived to maturity). Again, we cannot know now what the objective likelihood is without knowing a good deal about what actually exists or obtains in the future prior to and at the time of the event in question.

What happens or obtains in the future with respect to many contingencies and probabilities of events depends to no inconsiderable extent on the free choices and actions of human beings between now and then, and hence is very open. Both which persons exist to make free choices and what free choices and actions they make and take are, as one proceeds farther from the present moment, more and more undeterminable now, given the range of choices available to present and future free persons. The result is that the kind of calculation of objective likelihood now (at *t*) that Hasker envisions is not possible without foreknowledge. Which persons in the distant future exist depends on the intervening free choices of mates. The choice of a mate depends on which mates are available, and these depend on prior choices of prior persons in terms of with whom they choose to mate, where they choose to live, when they take actions to become pregnant, and so on. And what happens subsequently to the next generations of persons likewise depends on the same factors. Each of these countless reproductive choices rests not only on a great multitude of antecedent choices, but each has innumerable consequences for future agents and their free choices and actions. But without foreknowledge, even God cannot have knowledge of objective possibilities and the probabilities of future existents and their choices. Even with complete knowledge of everything at this present moment, without foreknowledge God cannot give any objective probabilities now that are connected with human free choices five, fifteen, fifty, or five hundred years hence, for God cannot know what the actual conditions will be at the time. The intervening number of choices and the consequences that flow from them make any kind of probabilistic judgments impossible, since all this is unknown to God. Whatever probabilities God knows now (at t) about how we might act in the coming days or weeks would diminish exponentially over the next years due to human choices, and would be impossible thereafter.[3]

Even the objective possibilities and likelihood of events involving nature are affected. Consider, for example, global warming. Since this is significantly affected and caused by human activity, the level of CO_2 in the atmosphere is a product of millions of human choices and actions that cannot be foreknown. And if this is not knowable, then all the events related to temperature rise, melting glaciers, sea levels, and superstorms likewise are not probabilistically determinable now. We can project what might happen if we keep key parameters the same, but if the parameters depend on human choice, calculations about the future cannot be "comprehensive and exact." In effect, God simply does not know even in a probabilistic sense much about the future on earth, and hence God cannot know what is objectively possible and what the objective likelihood is of any event occurring in the distant future given the present state.[4]

Hasker argues that objective likelihood can be determined by the probabilities based on people's character and circumstances. But this would be helpful only for those persons who already have established a character. For those who are young and have not developed their character, and for future persons there are no characters to rely on to make any kind of probabilistic calculation.

Hasker might reply that as time goes on, God knows more and more when the future becomes the present and then the past. What was

---

3. Ware, *God's Lesser Glory*, 124.

4. One can find excellent examples of this in the dire predictions of Robert Malthus (*An Essay on the Principle of Population*) and Paul Erlich (*The Population Bomb*) regarding the relationship between population increase and famine and disease. The predictions have not come true because of the revolutionary advancements we have made in food production.

unknowable for God yesterday is knowable today. And the probabilities that God will know what will happen will change as well. God learns about what happens as time progresses and more and more truths become available to God. God also learns about the increasing probabilities or improbabilities of events as the conditions become actual. Events whose probability was indeterminable fifty years ago God now knows are probable or improbable, based on the series of intervening free choices by agents and the conditions that now hold. In short, as events pass from the future to the present to the past, God's knowledge on which he can make predictions increases.

This would be true but fails to resolve the problem, for the future remains the result of an indefinite number of free choices, and without foreknowledge of what actually occurs in the future this knowledge is not now "comprehensive and exact"; there simply are too many intervening choices and acts that God without foreknowledge cannot know to make calculation of likelihood possible. The result is that little ground remains for trusting in the advice that one might want to garner now from God about the future: what to choose and how to act or live. Even God cannot determine the likelihood that my marriage will work out and that fifty years from now I will be happy. Too many unknown choices, each dependent upon the prior, intervene to create actual conditions at various times. Without foreknowledge, objective likelihood does not rescue providence.

With these first two commonly-advanced arguments behind us and the rejection of the view that knowledge of objective possibilities and probabilities will rescue providence for the open theist, let us turn to a third argument that open theists use to defend their view about God's foreknowledge.

God's disappointment, change of mind, and regret

Within Christian circles, much of the debate focuses on what Scripture has to say about God's knowledge. Open theists point to a variety of scriptural passages, largely from the Old Testament, that they believe suggest or imply that God in fact lacks knowledge of future contingent events. In these passages God is disappointed by events that happen in the future, expresses regret over decisions he has taken, relents, or changes his mind. We will note the most significant passages that open theists frequently present as evidence.[5]

---

5. For more detailed treatment of these and other passages from an open theist's perspective, see Sanders, *God Who Risks*; Boyd, *God of the Possible*; and Richard Rice, *God's Foreknowledge*. For a treatment of these same passages from the perspective of a traditional believer in divine foreknowledge, see Ware, *God's Lesser Glory*; Roy, *How Much?*; and Erickson, *What Does God Know?*

Several important passages suggest that the course of future events can frustrate or disappoint God. In Genesis 6:1–3 the behavior of those God created frustrates him. The sons of God[6] indiscriminately married human daughters and had offspring by them. It is unclear what specific infractions led to this frustration—was it the marriage itself, or their indiscriminate choice of women—but in any case God's frustration is quite clear, "'My spirit will not contend with human beings forever, for they are mortal; their days will be a hundred and twenty.'" As a result God changes his mind about the length of human life, shortening it significantly from the many years considered normal earlier.

The passage (Gen 6:6–8) proceeds with additional disappointment, leading to divine regret. What initially began as an auspicious creation, where God pronounced all to be good, deteriorated into a swamp of great wickedness, where "every inclination of the thoughts of the human heart was only evil all the time. The LORD regretted (*niḥam*) that he had made human beings on the earth, and his heart was deeply troubled." The Lord resolved to eliminate humans, along with all other living things, from the earth, but relented from total destruction when Noah found favor in his eyes. The expression of the Lord's regret signals that the created humans went a direction both undesired and unanticipated by God, and if unanticipated God must lack foreknowledge of the future.

Repeatedly God expresses disappointment with the disobedient responses of his chosen people. With mighty providential acts God rescued them out of slavery in Egypt and led them on a difficult migration to the land promised to their forefathers. After a prolonged discussion with their leader on Mount Sinai, God told him to descend and witness the Israelite degradation into idolatry and rejection of Yahweh as their deliverer. Yahweh conveyed his anger to Moses, deciding to abandon faithless Israel and start anew to build up a great nation from Moses and his lineage. It was Moses who talked the Lord out of his revised intent to destroy the Israelites. Moses councils the Lord, "'Turn from your fierce anger; relent and do not bring disaster on your people.' Then the LORD relented (*nāḥem*) and did not bring on his people the disaster he had threatened" (Exod 32:10–14). Disappointment led to a change in God's plans to abandon the old plan and rebuild with Moses, but at Moses's behest God again changed his mind, returning to the original plan to stick with bringing to Canaan those he rescued by his power from Egypt. Why would God change his mind and plans and make

---

6. On the one hand, these sons of God seem to be non-human beings (Job 1:6). On the other hand, the human life is what is limited, and the subject of the action is the sons of God, not the daughters of humans.

this astounding offer to Moses if God foreknew Moses's reaction and that God would eventually revert back to the original plan?

The Lord chose Saul to be king in perpetuity over Israel, but by his repeated disobedient, impetuous behavior Saul disappointed the Lord. Disobeying God's commands, Saul kept alive not only the Amelekite king Agag but the choicest of the sheep and cattle. The Lord then spoke to Samuel about his changed attitude. "I regret (*niḥam*) that I have made Saul king, because he has turned away from me and has not carried out my instructions" (1 Sam 15:11). The Lord, regretting his choice of Saul to be king, changed his mind about the perpetuity of his kingdom, tore away the kingdom from Saul, and gave it to David (15:28). Similarly, God promised Eli that his family would minister before him in perpetuity, but the sins of his sons in administering the sacrifices to God were so great that God changed his mind and said that the entire family would no longer serve as priests and would die in the prime of life (1 Sam 2:30–33). But if God knew the decisions Saul and Eli's sons would make, why did he promise them that their line would continue forever as Israel's ruler or priests and then in disappointment alter his mind?

In Jeremiah 3:6–7 the Lord expresses disappointment with his chosen people; he expected that after Israel had gone whoring after other gods and found them wanting, she would return to him. "Have you seen what faithless Israel has done? She has gone up on every high hill and under every spreading tree, and has committed adultery there. I thought that after she had done all this she would return to me but she did not." Despite the Lord's offer to providentially dispense offspring, a good land, and an inheritance, Israel turned out to be an unfaithful spouse (Jer 3:19–20).[7] It seems that God had not expected all of this, but even so God continued to hope for Israel's return (Jer 26:2–6). The Lord invites Israel to return to its "husband," to be faithful again so that God may restore them to Jerusalem. But, open theists argue, if God already knows Israel's faithlessness, why is God surprised? And why would God continue to hope that Israel would return? With his foreknowledge, God would know whether or not Israel would do as he wanted; surprise and hope require ignorance of what is to be.

Some Scriptures record God's apparent change of mind without the obvious aura of disappointment. God threatens nations with dire consequences but then indicates that if they repent God will remove the disasters he warned would happen to them. God likewise promises the opposite. To nations to which God promised blessings God warns that if they turn

---

7. Sanders notes that "at least thirty-five times God is said to repent or not repent." Sanders, *God Who Risks*, 72.

from doing right they will suffer judgment and punishment. "If at any time I announce that a nation or kingdom is to be uprooted, torn down and destroyed, and if that nation I warned repents of its evil, then I will relent and not inflict on it the disaster I had planned.... And if it does evil in my sight and does not obey me, then I will reconsider the good I had intended to do for it" (Jer 18:7–10). The story of Jonah exemplifies the first scenario. God promises to destroy Nineveh; "Forty more days and Nineveh will be overthrown," Jonah proclaims. However, the king and his court repent and order the city to do the same. To Jonah's chagrin—but consistent with his deeper understanding that God is compassionate—Nineveh is spared. The second scenario, where disaster replaces blessing, is repeated often in the history of Israel, first in the violent book of Judges and more dramatically in the capture and exile of Israel by Assyria and of Judah by Babylonia.

God not only changes his mind in response to behavior, God also apparently changes his mind in response to intercessory prayer. Most notably, the Lord responds to the petitionary prayer of ailing King Hezekiah. After the Lord through the prophet Isaiah announces to Hezekiah that he would not recover from his illness, Hezekiah prays, reminding God of Hezekiah's faithfulness and devotion and in effect asking for a life extension. As Isaiah leaves the palace the Lord comes to him and announces that he has changed his mind, that Hezekiah will rule for an additional fifteen years. God here seems to change his mind about Hezekiah's impending death and the length of his life span (2 Kgs 20:1–6).[8] If God foreknew that Hezekiah would live for fifteen more years,[9] why did he declare in the first place that Hezekiah would not recover from his illness? Of course, God does not always change his intent in response to petitionary prayer. God refuses to allow the infant Bathsheba conceived in adultery with David to live, despite David's fervent pleas (2 Sam 12:13–18). But that does not alter the fact that God responds to petitions, changing what seems to be God's original intent.

Sometimes it appears that God relents simply out of his sheer compassion. When the Lord viewed the slaughter of the 70,000 Israelites who died from the plague he brought as punishment for David's sin of numbering his fighting force, the Lord relented (*nāḥem*) and spared Jerusalem (2 Sam 24:16).

---

8. A similar successful petitionary intervention occurs in Amos; Amos is able to sway the sovereign Lord from inflicting the land with locusts and fire (7:1–6).

9. God specifies exactly how many years Hezekiah would survive; how does God know this? Believers in foreknowledge contend that foreknowledge is the only basis for making such a specific prediction. Open theists reply that this tells us God's intent to keep Hezekiah alive for fifteen years and then end his life.

Open theists argue that if God can change his mind or relent when people repent, repeatedly flaunt the divine commands, or petition God, then God could not have known what they would do. If God knows the future, how can he be disappointed? With foreknowledge God would know what will happen, so that his expectations would match reality. God would have no disappointment; one can be disappointed only if one anticipates that something will happen and it does not. If God had unlimited foreknowledge of all human choices, God would have known what the peers of Noah would have been up to, the construction of the golden calf by the rebellious Israelites, the hideous sins committed by Eli's sons, the frequent disobedient choices of Saul, the suffering caused by the plague that resulted from David's choice among the three options, and Solomon's being led astray by his numerous foreign wives. None of this would have surprised a foreknowing God, and he would not have regretted his actions of creation, choice of peoples, king establishment, and punishments. Yet God did appear surprised and regretted his prior actions that seemed not to turn out for the best.[10]

How, open theists ask, "can someone [sic] sincerely intend to do something they are certain they will never do? And how can they truly change their mind if their mind is eternally made up?"[11] If God knows that people will repent and he won't have to punish them, why intend that they suffer dire consequences in the first place? If God is going to grant a petition in

---

10. One should note that the very passage in 1 Samuel where God expresses regret and changes his mind continues with Saul pleading with Samuel to spare him the kingship. Samuel refuses this request, invoking a general principle, "He who is the Glory of Israel does not lie or change his mind; for he is not a human being that he should change his mind" (1 Sam 15:29; see Num 23:19). Yet in Hosea (11:8–9) Yahweh changes his mind regarding Ephraim.

> My heart is changed within me;
>   all my compassion is aroused.
> I will not carry out my fierce anger,
>   nor will I devastate Ephraim again.

The basis for this change is given: "For I am God, and not a human being." As a result we have two passages, one claiming that God does not change his mind like humans, the other that God is not human and can change his mind. One possible way of reconciling these is that God is not like humans who frequently or willy-nilly change their minds. God might change his mind for serious sins (in the case of Saul) or to bring people to follow the Lord (in the case of Ephraim), but not for every petition or event. Of course, this is an interpretation, although a reasonable one. At the very least, that these two apparently contradictory themes regarding change should appear in the same passage in 1 Samuel and that the same principle—God is not human—is used to justify both changing and not changing one's mind should give us pause about how much we can generalize from the Samuel story.

11. Boyd, *God of the Possible*, 77.

the end, why say that for certain something is going to happen that does not happen? God already knows what will happen. In effect, "the notion of change in God is problematic for the doctrine of foreknowledge."[12]

Believers in foreknowledge have several responses to this argument from Scripture. First, with regard to scriptural passages about disappointment, they respond that God can know what will happen and still be disappointed. It is true that often disappointment is connected with anticipation; disappointment occurs when the good that we anticipate fails to occur. But disappointment is not necessarily connected with a deviation from what we anticipate; rather, it can have to do with declined possibility. We might know that something is going to happen and still be disappointed in the people who bring it about, for we know what the possibilities were for those people. The disappointment is not in the event but in the people who bring about that event. The actual event reveals the person's true character, but we know what was possible for that person to have been different. For example, a woman might know that her husband is going to file for divorce because of what he has said and done to her, and yet when he actually files the papers she is disappointed in him and his instigating the divorce. His filing confirms that he was not the person with whom she took wedding vows of fidelity; he has changed, and this anticipated event is simply the final *experienced* confirmation in the drama confirming his character. She is disappointed, not because she does not know what will happen or even what he is like, but because he could have been a better husband or not have gone through with the proceedings. Scripture often portrays Israel's relation to God in this fashion: God is the jilted lover; Israel is the unfaithful wife. Although they had a covenant to begin with, Israel whored after other gods. Yahweh's disappointment is not that Yahweh did not anticipate Israel's infidelity or know what would happen; it was with experiencing what Israel did with the freedom and opportunities God gave them. They could have been a faithful wife. It was possible that those to whom God had shown his powerful redeeming and providential love remained faithful. The possibility contrasts with what happened and with what God knew would happen. He knew that Israel would reject him but still is disappointed that they did so because they could have done otherwise. They could have obeyed God's law and remained covenant faithful. Divine disappointment, therefore, does not mean that we have to reject divine foreknowledge.

Second, with regard to regret, one way of understanding these "regret" texts is to say that they concern God's emotional state, not God's knowledge. As with disappointment, we can have regrets even about what we know to have occurred. Regret can also address possibility, not knowledge. In our

---

12. Sanders, *God Who Risks*, 72.

own experience, we might know that something has happened and still express regret. We might regret taking an automobile trip that we know resulted in an accident. Or we might regret a marriage in the first place, or some words spoken or deeds done along the way, or something that was not done to save the marriage. That is, the regret describes one's emotions about what has happened or is happening. Since regret can apply to the past as well as the present, it has nothing to do with the epistemic question of whether one knew what would happen. With regard to God, although God knew what Israel would do, still he expressed his emotions about what might have been. God knew what was possible and, disappointingly, that the actual will depart from the possible.

With respect to changes of mind passages, defenders of foreknowledge contend that these likewise have nothing to do with foreknowledge. They do not presuppose or imply that God does not know the future. Rather, they concern the choices that are made available to us. The assertions that suggest that God alters his mind are really conditional statements, sometimes explicitly so, other times implicitly so. These statements inform about us what will happen if . . . . If we act one way, God will respond accordingly; if we act another way, God again will respond accordingly. The dire threat that God makes is intended to bring about change, and a change on the part of persons and nations is what God wants. God is not divorced from us, but relates to us as God solicits our love for and our obedience to him. Statements of this sort may be warnings not to abandon our covenant with God, for if we do—and the choice remains open to us—dire things will happen. But if we, like the Ninevites, repent and change our ways, then what God proposed will not come to pass. The statements express conditionals that tell us that the future is open, that if we repent and mend our ways what we were promised or warned would happen will not happen.

This is clear in the "relenting" passage of Jeremiah 26:2–6. God says that he will relent—if the people change their ways. The context is a message given to Jeremiah to proclaim to the people in the temple courtyard. God gives it to encourage the people to do what they should have done long before, to listen to God and to follow God's law. The relenting is really a conditional on the part of God: he will act one way if the people repent, another way if they do not. It is not a comment about what God knows but about what he wants people to do.

Change-of-mind statements are not incompatible with God foreknowing; God knows what we will do based upon what we do, and what we do might very well be affected by the threats that God makes. It is because the persons and nations actually responded or did not respond to God's threats (or promises) that God knows how they responded. It is not that

God changes his mind but that he responds to our actions. What happens is known by God based upon the choices we make, not apart from them. What we actually do is what God foreknows since it is the basis of his foreknowledge. And the choices we make might well be affected by the threats posed or rewards offered. In effect, it is not that God changes his mind. Rather, change of mind assertions remind us that our choices and actions affect God's responding intervention and the ultimate outcome.

Suppose, however, that the open theist is correct that God does not know what will happen and when encountering the new situation changes his mind and repents of his previous decisions and actions. The implications of this open theist view for providence are very significant. What is unclear is the basis upon which God made his earlier decisions—to create, to choose Israel as his covenant partner and Saul as king, to bring a serious plague on the kingdom of David, and to send Judah into captivity. Clearly these decisions were based on the information God had, given the past and the present. But for open theists they were not based on knowledge about the future, because there is no such knowledge about future contingents, which suggests that God's decisions were based on inadequate information. God lacked the necessary information to know that Eli's sons and Saul would turn out as they did. God's decisions might have been the best that God could have taken at the time, given the limited information God had about the future when he made the decision. God knew what the past and present conditions were but had no knowledge of the future. He had beliefs and possibly some idea of future possibilities but not knowledge of the future contingent events. Thus, God's decisions could be misguided. "[S]ince God does not necessarily know exactly what will happen in the future, it is always possible that even what God in his unparalleled wisdom believes to be the best course of action at any given time may not produce the anticipated results in the long run."[13] In effect, God can be, and probably often is, mistaken in his beliefs about what is to happen.

Contrary to the claims of open theists, this view provides little assurance to someone today seeking God's guidance, for this view of divine regret, change of mind, and mistaken beliefs leaves God significantly blind as to the future. Although God would have much more information than we do, given his comprehensive knowledge of the past and present, God still would have inadequate information about future persons' character, choices, and actions, and their consequences, let alone who exists in the future to have a character and to choose. This is particularly problematic when it is about persons who do not yet exist and have not developed any

---

13. Basinger, "Practical Implications," 165.

character. I might seek God's guidance on whether I should, for example, put my infant son into my will? How might he use that inheritance? Will he squander the money; will he use it to support terrorists or for a life of drug abuse? For open theists, God cannot now know what my son's future character will be and how he will use the money. How can we trust that God's advice or actions on our behalf is the best? His advice and actions might be the best he can give given what he knows at the time, but God might not be in much better position than we are to advise us on the choices we should make given the circumstances, especially when the decision complexly involves the future decision-making of other free persons. "Accordingly, we must acknowledge that divine guidance, from our perspective, cannot be considered a means of discovering exactly what will be best in the long run.... Divine guidance, rather, must be viewed primarily as a means of determining what is best for us now,"[14] that is, based on what God and we know now. God's guidance must be seen in a broader view of God guiding our character development and our making "godly" decisions, that is, about the kind of moral and spiritual person God wants us to become. God's risk-taking in giving any specific providential guidance about our taking particular actions becomes our risk as well.

Some open theists attempt to counter this and defend God's trustworthiness in that "God remains faithful to his overarching goals.... But God has different options available, and the one that he will choose is not a foregone conclusion.... God remains unchangeable in his commitment to this project of redemption but remains flexible regarding precisely when, where, and how it is carried out."[15] This might be reassuring for the achievement of overarching goals, though even here if God can change his mind, how are we assured that God will not change his mind about the overarching goals? After all, if God is reacting to circumstances, the very basic goals might themselves need adjusting. But furthermore, this view is not very comforting for any daily or more personal divine providence. How can God be trusted to give good guidance to an individual when at some future point he might change his mind? Had Saul known about God's change in plans, perhaps he would not have wanted to become king. The fact that God chose him and promised that his kingship would be perpetual (1 Sam 13:13) was no longer very comforting when he discovered that God changed his mind and rejected him, so that the perpetual kingship would perish along with his line. Indeed, Saul pleaded unsuccessfully with Samuel for God to change his

---

14. Ibid., 163.
15. Sanders, *God Who Risks*, 72.

mind. Perhaps overall Saul would have had a happier life staying a donkey herder. Providence, on an open view, is much less reliable.

Just as serious is the implication of the openness view for God's beliefs. In order to make decisions about the future consequences of God's decisions and acts, God must have beliefs. He must have beliefs about the adequacy of Saul to be king since he asked Samuel to find Saul and anoint him; he must have beliefs about Israel and their faithfulness, since God seeks to enter into covenantal relationship with them; he must have beliefs about Eli's competency and that of his offspring to administer the priesthood. But these beliefs turned out to be mistaken, which means that God can entertain false beliefs about the future. And not only a few false beliefs, but very many false beliefs. Some open theists admit as much and find biblical confirmation. For example, in Jeremiah 3:7 we find God speaking about Israel, "I thought that after she had done all this [committing spiritual adultery] she would return to me, but she did not." God's original belief about what Israel would do had to stand corrected.[16] Not only does this significantly reduce our confidence in God and in his ability to achieve his purposes, but it has serious doxastic consequences. Even if we grant that God cannot know the future, to say that God has false beliefs seriously damages our epistemic understanding of God and his perfection. Since God has the possibility of a greater range of beliefs than we do, more than likely on this view God has a greater number of false or mistaken beliefs.

Greg Boyd responds that God cannot be mistaken.

> If the future consists in part of possibilities, then God can infallibly think that a particular possibility has the greatest chance of occurring, even if it turns out that a less likely possibility actually occurs. Since God is omniscient, he always knew that it was remotely possible for his people to be this stubborn, for example. But he genuinely did not expect them to actualize this remote possibility. He authentically expected that they'd be won over by his grace. God wasn't caught off guard, but he was genuinely disappointed.[17]

If this isn't being mistaken, I don't know what is. If God *expected* Israel to respond and they didn't, regardless of whether he knew the possibility that they might not, God had a mistaken belief. Or to put it less charitably, God had a true belief that Israel might respond and a false belief that they actually would respond. False expectations involve false beliefs. John Sanders replies that God has unfathomable wisdom, is incredibly resourceful,

16. Boyd, *God of the Possible*, 60.
17. Ibid., 61.

and is omnicompetent.[18] All of this can be true and it is still the case that on open theism God holds false beliefs. Having unfathomable wisdom does not rescue God from having false beliefs.

In short, our point here is that the believer in foreknowledge can reasonably accommodate the evidence and passages that open theists suggest without having either to deny foreknowledge or to retreat into anthropomorphisms. That the Scriptures present us with a richness about God involving more than knowledge is consistent with a robust view of divine foreknowledge. Open theism leaves us with a God who, though wise, is woefully ignorant and entertains false beliefs, though great hopes.

God tests humans

For their fourth argument, open theists contend that if God knows future contingencies about human choices and actions, then reports of God testing humans make little sense. God already knows the outcome of the test. For example, Genesis records a most painful test that God conducts of Abraham. God tells Abraham to sacrifice his son Isaac and only at the last minute intervenes to prevent the horrible deed. In the end, God declares that now he knows that Abraham truly fears God (Gen 22:12). If God already knew this, open theists claim, a test would not have been necessary. The point of the test is for God to find out for sure about Abraham's faith. "It should be noted, however, that the only one in the text said to learn anything from the test is *God*. . . . Though Abraham has shown maturation, God has some lingering doubts. God tests Abraham because Abraham has some serious personal failings."[19]

But as Bruce Ware points out, this explanation of testing has implications not only for God's knowledge of the future but also for God's knowledge of the present.[20] For if God has to test Abraham to find out the state of his faith, God does not *now* know that state. Hence, God lacks full knowledge of the present. God can only learn the state of Abraham's present faith by testing him. This runs contrary to other passages that affirm God's intimate knowledge even of the present and of our inner state: "[T]he LORD searches every heart and understands every desire and every thought" (1 Chr 28:9; see Ps 139:1–2).

Open theists recognize that there are scriptural passages that suggest that predictions of test results, as with Peter and his denial of knowing Jesus,

18. Sanders, *God Who Risks*, 207.
19. Ibid., 51.
20. Ware, *God's Lesser Glory*, 45–46.

are known by God. The reason they are known, they suggest, is that "the person's character, combined with the Lord's perfect knowledge of all future variables, makes the person's future behavior certain. As we know, character becomes more predictable over time. The longer we persist in a chosen path, the more that path becomes part of who we are."[21] But for the open theist God only knows our past and present choices; he does not know our future choices, which at early stages of our lives may indeed compose a majority of our choices with regard to a particular character trait. The criticism here regarding character affirms, as we argued above, the need for more knowledge of what we will be like and our probable and possible future choices than is available to God under the view of the open theist. Further, how can God know all future variables when what those variables are depends upon our future choices and future circumstances? It would seem that some open theists want to have it both ways with regard to tests: God does not know the results because God cannot know our future free choices, and God knows the results because he intimately knows our character and that we will be constant in acting on it, no matter what the circumstances, so that what we do will be predictable.

But beyond all this, this argument regarding testing as an argument in favor of open theism is bogus, for God's foreknowledge is of the event itself. If God has used his foreknowledge to know that Abraham seriously trusted God and then removed the test, God would not have known that Abraham would have passed the test because the test would not have been conducted. God knows the result of the test only because Abraham actually took the test. When we speak of God's testing, what was an item of God's foreknowledge now becomes an item of God's *experience*, a view consistent with the Genesis usage of "knowing."[22]

Prophecy and prediction

Prophecy not only plays an important role in Scripture but is critical to the defense of divine foreknowledge. If there truly is prophecy that foretells the future, not only in general and not only conditionally but with some specificity, then foreknowledge is vouchsafed. Only if God actually knew what

---

21. Sanders, *God Who Risks*, 35.

22. Bruce Ware makes the interesting suggestion that "for now I know that you fear God" should be taken to "*express the idea that 'in the experience of this action, I (God) am witnessing Abraham demonstrate dramatically and afresh that he fears me, and I find this both pleasing and acceptable in my sight.*" Ware, *God's Lesser Glory*, 73–74. This accords well with the Genesis usage of "knowledge" in the sense of experiencing.

would happen could this be communicated to humans, not to change what God knows will happen, but as information to be revealed to people about what can happen so that people will change or about what will happen by people's and God's activity.

Scripture records specific predictions. The prophecy in Isaiah 45:1–7 concerns the actions of Cyrus, whom God summons by name so that he might act as liberator on behalf of captive Israel. God adds fifteen years to Hezekiah's life, while predicting the invasion of the king of Assyria (2 Kgs 20:1–6). Daniel 11 records prophecies about the free choices of future kings. Matthew 16:21 records Jesus' own predictions of what will happen to him, including the resurrection after three days. Likewise, Peter, as recorded in Acts 2:25–35, takes writings of David (Pss 16:8–11; 110:1) as being prophetic of God the Father's resurrection and glorification of Jesus. Messianic prophecies likewise support foreknowledge. Micah 5:2 records the birthplace, Bethlehem, of the "one who will be ruler over Israel." Matthew 2:6 makes use of this passage in the story of Herod and the visitors from the east. Indeed, the Gospel of Matthew is in part constructed around the concept of prophetic fulfillment. John 19:23–24 makes reference to the specific predictions found in Psalm 22:18. These predictions of free agent actions seem possible only with foreknowledge of those very choices.

Open theists take several attitudes toward prophecy.[23] First, they hold that many prophecies or predictions[24] are conditional; they indicate what God's response will be if people take or do not take certain actions.[25] This accounts for the fact that many so-called predictions do not come to pass. We considered this earlier, for example, with respect to Jonah and Nineveh. God tells Jonah to proclaim that Nineveh will be destroyed in forty days but relents when the city repents (Jonah 3:4–5). As we noted above, this feature of conditionality does not vitiate foreknowledge, for the conditionality is meant to encourage change of behavior in those to whom the conditional prediction is told. Nineveh repents. Had they not repented, God would have destroyed the city. In cases where what is "predicted" does not occur, the point of the prediction is to get people to change, not to say exactly what will happen. It says nothing about God lacking foreknowledge of the events in question.

Second, open theists see prophecy not as a foretelling of future human choices, but rather as stating God's *intentions* to act in a certain way in

23. Rice, *God's Foreknowledge*, 78–79.

24. Sanders distinguishes prophecies (which can be fulfilled repeatedly in diverse ways) from predictions (which are "specific forecasts of what is to occur," that "come about only once"). Sanders, *God Who Risks*, 134.

25. Ibid.

particular circumstances.[26] Open theists cite Isaiah 46:9–11 to support this interpretation; the prophecy announces that what the Lord proposes he will do; "I will do all that I please." A similar theme is reiterated in Isaiah 48:3: "I foretold the former things long ago, my mouth announced them and I made them known; then suddenly I acted, and they came to pass." "As I have done, so it will be done to them. They will go into exile as captives. . . . I will spread my net for him, and he will be caught in my snare; I will bring him to Babylonia, the land of the Chaldeans, but he will not see it, and there he will die. I will scatter to the winds all those around him . . . and I will pursue them with drawn sword" (Ezek 12:10–14).

Although many predictions record what God will or intends to do, many do not. Steven Roy notes the

> promise and fulfillment motif of 1–2 Kings. . . . A prominent motif of these books is Yahweh's covenant faithfulness as exhibited by the fulfillment of predictive promises uttered by his spokespersons. There are twenty different examples of this pattern in the two books, many of which utilize an explicit fulfillment formula (e.g., this particular event occurred "according to the word of Yahweh"). These fulfillment formulas call explicit attention to the fact that this particular event had formerly been predicted by God through his prophets.[27]

While some of these predictions specify what God will do (1 Kgs 11:34–37; 16:2–4; 17:9; 21:23) and fit the pattern open theists ascribe to prophecy, namely, of God intending to act, other prophecies do not fit this pattern but yet are specific. 1 Kings 13:2 prophesies that Josiah would be born in the royal linage and would sacrifice the priests of the high places on the very altars they used. 21:19 prophesies that dogs will lick up Ahab's blood where earlier they had licked up innocent Naboth's blood. 2 Kings 1:16–17 foretells the death of Ahaziah. The specificity of the prophecies in these cases strongly suggests divine foreknowledge.

Where prophecies record God's intentions to act, this feature actually strengthens foreknowledge rather than refutes it.[28] In order for God to tell us his intentions with regard to the future, God needs to know what the future free choices and actions of people will be so that he can declare his intentions. God needs to know the future states of affairs about which he makes intentions or which factor in his intentions. For example, when Isaiah 48 speaks of God foretelling first Judah's captivity and then vowing to

---

26. Ibid., 132; Hasker, *God*, 195.
27. Roy, *How Much?* 34–35.
28. Ware, *God's Lesser Glory*, 131–32.

bring Judah out of Babylonia, much had to be foreknown about thousands of human decisions leading up to this event: the decisions of people leading to the ascendancy of Nebuchadnezzar to the Babylonian throne, of Nebuchadnezzar to invade Judea, of Zedekiah to rebel and resist the invasion, of Nebuzaradan to burn Jerusalem and to deport its population, even to the choices and actions of the soldiers in the armies. God cannot simply disclose what he is going to do apart from the decisions future persons will make, because for open theists the divine plan unfolds in response to human choices. For open theists God changes his plans (there is no blueprint or script) according to our actions. But, we argue, since these actions are manifold and not known beforehand, God cannot simply say what he intends to do in the future, at least with the kind of specificity that characterizes biblical prophecies, without foreknowledge of the context of those intentions. That I tell you that I intend to do x next year requires that I know that the circumstances will obtain in which intending to do x can occur. Of course, God can make general statements that he will punish evil doers and forgive repenters, but that is not the kind of prophecy under discussion.

Third, for some open theists prophecy contains probabilistic forecasts about what will come about. Based on what God knows about the past and the present and about the character of individuals, God predicts that people will likely respond in a certain way. For example, in 1 Samuel 23:9–13 David enquires about the behavior of the citizens of Keilah with regard to the approach of Saul. God through the priest Abiathar tells David that the people would turn him over to Saul if he remained in the city, whereupon David flees and this does not happen. God, knowing the character or past behavior of these citizens, informs David what would probably happen should David remain.

> Given the depth and breadth of God's knowledge of the present situation, God forecasts what he thinks will happen. In this regard God is the consummate social scientist predicting what will happen. . . . For example, God says he expected Israel to put away her idols and return to him but they did not (Jer 3:7, 19–20). In this case God knew it was more likely that they would repent but he also knew the lesser possibility that they would not repent. God did not say that they would definitely repent. . . . God will not *definitely* believe that something will occur unless it is *certain* to occur. . . . When God expresses surprise it is evidence that the less likely event came to pass, but this is not a mistake.[29]

---

29. Sanders, *God Who Risks*, 133–34. See Hasker, *God*, 194.

But knowledge about the past and present and a person's present character does not allow us to predict even with probability what will occur fifty years down the road. To make such a prediction we need to know what happens in the interim and what conditions hold surrounding the event we want to predict.

Some open theists contend that sometimes things do not turn out as God apparently anticipated, such that that some prophecies are mistaken. If God has complete foreknowledge of future events, all prophecies or predictions should come to pass. God would not be mistaken in his prophecies. But, Pinnock argues, many prophecies did not come to pass, or they came to pass in a different way than the text would support. "We may not want to admit it but prophecies often go unfulfilled," and as examples he offers, "Joseph's parents never bowed to him (Gen 37:9–10); the Assyrians did not destroy Jerusalem in the eighth century (Mic 3:9–12); despite Isaiah, Israel's return from exile did not usher in a golden age (Isa 41:14–20). . . . Despite the Baptist, Jesus did not cast the wicked into the fire; contrary to Paul, the second coming was not just around the corner (1 Thess 4:17); despite Jesus, in the destruction of the temple, some stones were left one on the other (Matt 24:2)."[30] Even today foundation stones stand on each other marking the limits of the temple mount.[31] In the Moses story, "The elders (Exod 3:18) are never said to appear before Pharaoh. Instead, Aaron takes their place (Exod 5:1)."[32]

Pinnock also appeals to the cases of Tyre and of Memphis in Egypt, whose total destruction was prophesied by Ezekiel 26 and Jeremiah 46:25–26. The prophecies name Nebuchadnezzar as the destroyer and describes Tyre as forever uninhabited and Memphis burned to the ground. Yet although Nebuchadnezzar did attempt to destroy Tyre, he failed. Indeed, Tyre continued, such that the returning Jewish exiles hired men from Tyre to help rebuild the temple. Both Egypt and Memphis remained unconquered by Nebuchadnezzar.[33]

These examples, however, are rife with literalism. The examples of Joseph and his parents and Aaron and the elders ignores the representational nature of the culture, where the male represented the entire family (including the wife) and where one elder represented the others. When Jacob went to Egypt it is more than likely that he bowed before the royalty and in doing so represented his entire family, and Aaron represented the clans of

---

30. Pinnock, *Most Moved Mover*, 51, fn. 66.
31. Sanders, *God Who Risks*, 137.
32. Pinnock, *Most Moved Mover*, 55.
33. Ibid., 50.

the tribes of Israel before Pharaoh. Beyond this, the fact that these specific fulfillments are not stated in the Genesis and Exodus stories provides no evidence that the prophesied events did not occur. The fact that there is no statement either way provides no way of deciding whether or not the prophecy was fulfilled. Literalism is also applied to the stones of the temple. The phrase is a metaphor of complete destruction that makes the building unusable. Although foundation stones exist on each other below ground, the temple itself, as a visible place of worship, was so destroyed as to be unusable as a place of worship.

More seriously, if open theists are correct about mistaken prophecies, the implications for divine providence are dire indeed, for then we have little consolation that the extent of God's knowledge can provide a basis for his providential involvement in our affairs. God too might be mistaken in what he believes is best for us; God's advice is fallible. God thinks he knows what possibly might occur in the future, but God may get it wrong. Indeed, one open theist suggests that if what we took as God's will does not work out, we should go back to "discern his new specific will" for our lives.[34] This is not very comforting. God's specific will has to change as he and we discover his mistakes. What we took to be God's guidance is probably the best advice we can get, but nonetheless flawed for that.

Boyd is unwilling to say that God makes mistakes. To resolve this he argues that where what God prophesied would happen did not happen there is no mistake because God only says it is likely.[35] But although this is an interesting interpretation, textual evidence is lacking that God *thought* that any given prediction had the best *probability* of happening. Sanders says that strictly speaking this is not a mistake because God did not declare *definitely* that the said event would come to pass.[36] But not only would this be caviling that the prophets would not allow, it fails to address what God believes (rather than says), implying that God can hold false beliefs.

Finally, Sanders contends that what are proffered as prophecies in the New Testament are either general statements or backward-looking pronouncements. "It is in retrospect that the New Testament authors read the Old Testament for parallels or recapitulation between the life of Jesus and

---

34. Basinger, "Practical Implications," 166.

35. Boyd, *God of the Possible*, 60–61.

36. In his earlier edition (*God Who Risks*, 1998) Sanders allows that God makes mistakes. "[U]sing the term more loosely, we might say that God would be mistaken if he believed that X would happen . . . and, in fact, X does not come about. In this sense the Bible does attribute some mistakes to God." Sanders, *God Who Risks*, 132. But, Sanders continues, attributing mistakes to God is unusual. He omits this passage in his second edition, apparently changing his view that God can make mistakes.

Old Testament events."[37] Matthew 2:15 notes that the Holy Family's return from Egypt fulfilled Hosea 11:1, which really is not a prophecy but a recollection of God's redemption of Israel from Egypt. Similarly, Matthew 2:23 identifies Jesus's connection with Nazareth as a prophecy, though we have no source for it.

Treating prophetic pronouncements as retrospective provides one way to deal with the specific prophecies. One might date the authorship of the prophetic books after the so-called fulfillment, late enough so that the predictive prophecies are actually historical in nature (for example, Isaiah's predictions about Cyrus are really post-Cyrus accounts of a Second Isaiah). Or we can treat the New Testament fulfillments as reading back into the Old Testament texts what the New Testament authors wanted to find in them, not what the Old Testament authors really meant or intended. We cannot here turn aside to consider questions about the dating of these books or of hermeneutical methods. For our purposes it is sufficient to say that regardless of textual dating, the authors of these texts certainly *believed* and recorded their belief that God foreknew future events and the free choices and actions of future individuals, regardless of when they wrote and the relation of their writings to the actual events. They betray no hesitancy about divine foreknowledge of human contingencies.

This is nowhere clearer than in Isaiah, who emphasized that one feature or sign that distinguishes the authentic God from the spurious gods represented by the idols is the ability to foreknow and reveal to us the future. One might begin with Isaiah 41:22–29, where only the Lord was able to foretell the invasion from the north and the good news this would bring to Jerusalem. Isaiah consistently repeats the theme in 42:8–9; 43:8–13; 44:6–8; 45:18–25; 46:9–10; 48:3–8.[38] If one adopts the open view that denies divine foreknowledge, Yahweh would be unable to pass this critical test. Such a failure would have serious implications for Yahweh's position as the true God, for Yahweh would not differ from the score of false gods who cannot know the future. This theme of authenticity revealed through the ability to foretell the future is likewise found in John 13:19, when Jesus says, "From now on I am telling you before it happens, so that when it does happen, you may believe that I am who I am." This leads into Jesus' prediction that Peter would deny him. What is striking about this prediction is that a specific individual is identified, along with the time of the denial (the crowing of the rooster) and the number of times Peter will choose to deny him (three

---

37. Ibid., 136.

38. For an extensive treatment, see Roy, *How Much?* 43–55. He suggests that Isaiah 40–48 has a structure of a trial, where the gods are called to account. Yahweh functions as the prosecutor and the judge who renders the verdict.

times). Clearly, this passage indicates not the resolve of Jesus to act but rather his foreknowledge of specific free choices of another person. It can be escaped only by attributing the prophecy to a post-denial construction. In short, the very reliability of the claim to being divine and having divine authority rests on having foreknowledge, a feature open theists cannot deny away.

Impracticality of foreknowledge

A sixth and final major argument for the open view of God focuses on the contention that simple divine foreknowledge does not get God (or us) very far in terms of providentially controlling or sovereignly directing our world.[39] Foreknowledge is not useful providentially, for it cannot be used to alter prospective events. It lacks teeth for exercising sovereignty. The argument for this is fairly straightforward. God can only foreknow what actually will occur. (Even though God might know all possibilities, this knowledge is not germane to the discussion here, and as we argued above, this knowledge requires foreknowledge of what will be.) But if God foreknows what will occur, God cannot in turn use that knowledge to alter the future so that what God foreknew does not occur. For if God altered the future, he would not have known the original future event but rather the event that resulted from his intervention, and alteration of what would have happened had God not acted. But then either God would have known something that was false because it did not occur due to divine alteration (what God was taking action to avoid), which is impossible for God. Or else God would have known something that was true, namely, that which resulted from his action. But then God's action itself could not have been based on God's foreknowledge, for what God would foreknow is what resulted from God's action, not what was changed or avoided by his action (since it never really occurred). What God foreknew was thus the result of, not the basis for, God's action, and thus was not available to use providentially. In effect, God cannot use his foreknowledge to providentially alter the future.

Suppose that God foreknows that President Kennedy is going to be assassinated. But in answer to prayer, God providentially so works that Lee Harvey Oswald's rifle jams and the presidential motorcade passes by the Texas book depot without incident. But then God did not have foreknowledge of JFK's assassination, for JFK was not assassinated. That terrible Dallas event never occurred. God can only foreknow what actually happens. What God would foreknow is Oswald's rifle jamming and a smiling President

39. Hasker, *God*, 55–58.

Kennedy passing by to the cheers of the waving crowds. But this scenario would not need divine intervention, for the undesirable shot did not occur. Hence, God's foreknowledge of the assassination (which actually occurred) could not have been used to prevent that event. In short, foreknowledge will not provide a basis for God's future sovereign actions. If God sovereignly alters the future based on his alleged knowledge of what will occur, what God supposedly knew he really did not know since it did not come about.[40]

Consider the biblical case of Judas Iscariot. Suppose that God foreknew that Judas would betray Jesus at Passover. That is, suppose that "Judas will betray Jesus at Passover" is a true proposition, known by God. According to the doctrine of foreknowledge, God knows this because in fact Judas does betray Jesus in the garden. As we suggested in the previous chapter, God knows what happens in the future either because it is expressed in true propositions and God knows all true propositions or, more likely, because God knows the event itself as occurring in the future. (Of course, the event occurring in the future is what makes the proposition about the future true.) Suppose that God did not want Judas to betray Jesus at Passover. To accomplish this end, he had Judas die of a stomach ailment prior to the Passover. Now the proposition, "Judas does not betray Jesus" is true, and the proposition "Judas betrays Jesus at Passover" is false. Judas simply did not betray his Lord. But since God can know only true propositions, in this scenario God could not have known that Judas betrayed Jesus because it never happened. And if God did not know this, he could not have used this information to decide to cause Judas to die of a stomach ailment prior to the event. In short, God's foreknowledge cannot be the basis for God's future providential action.

Ironically, this point cuts two ways: not only does it show that God cannot use foreknowledge to alter decisions, but it makes moot objections raised by open theists against divine foreknowledge. Making his case, John Sanders writes concerning God's test of Abraham on Mount Moriah, "If one presupposes that God already 'knew' the results of the test beforehand, then there was, in fact, no test and God put Abraham through unnecessary suffering." Again, with regard to the children of Israel, "Why test them if God eternally knew with certainty exactly how the people would respond?" And again, "How can a conditional promise, say to Saul (1 Sam 13:13), be

---

40. Even knowledge of possibilities does not help. If it is possible that Oswald would try to assassinate Kennedy, God would know it. Knowing this possibility and attempting to eliminate the possibility, God makes it impossible for Oswald to make the attempt. But then, God would not have known that the attempt was possible, for had he believed it was possible he would have had a false belief about a possibility that in fact was impossible.

genuine if God already foreknows the human response and so foreknows that God will in fact, never fulfill his promise?"[41] But the objection Sanders and others similarly raise is based on a misunderstanding. They fail to see that God's knowledge of the future is based on the future event itself. Thus, as we argued earlier in this chapter, God can perfectly well issue conditionals and conduct tests of individuals, for God cannot use his foreknowledge of how the conditionals or tests work out to structure a policy where the tests do not happen in the first place. It is only because the individuals actually pass or fail the tests or respond to the conditionals that God knows this.

This provides a very neat answer to the common question that arises from the story in Genesis 3: why did God create humans, place them in the Garden, and give them a command when he knew perfectly well that humans would fail to keep the command? Couldn't God in the story have avoided giving the command or conducting the test, made the fruit not delectable, or prevented the tempter from gaining access to the Garden? The answer is that God knew that Adam would sin because in fact Adam sinned. Eve and Adam's actual rejection (in the future) of the primacy of God provides the basis for God's knowledge of their act. But God's knowledge that the rejection would happen cannot be used by God to develop a different scenario where Adam and Eve did not fall. This other scenario would alter the course of events, there would be no fall of disobedience, and God would not have known that Adam and Eve would succumb to the temptation to disobey. One might reply that God knew that this was a pretty good possibility, given the nature of human beings. But on what grounds could God know that it was a pretty good possibility rather than a mere possibility or a possibility at all? He would have to know about the choices that Adam and Eve made prior to the fall, choices that established their character. But prior to the fall they had not sinned, so there is no indication yet in their character on which to calculate this probability. But even more significantly, if the fall was a possibility and he wanted to prevent it from happening (by making it impossible), he would not have known the fall was possible because in fact it was not (because of God's actions). In short, God could not have used any alleged knowledge of the fall or a propensity to displace God (or their possibility) to change the order of events, for then what God allegedly knew he could not have known since it did not (and could not) happen and propositions describing it would not have been true.

The objection that foreknowledge has no practical value is telling against the traditional view of omniscience not only in a practical sense

---

41. Sanders, *God Who Risks*, 51, 81, 133. See also Sanders's discussion of kings Zedekiah and Ahab on p. 80.

but also in a theological sense. Divine providence is an essential part of a theistic, as over against a deistic, view of God. On a deistic view God created the world perfectly and then, for all intents and purposes, abandoned it, since a perfect being would not need to tinker with its perfect creation. But for theism, God is intrinsically involved in the world providentially. This means that God will be looking to the future in order to bring about his purposes for himself, nature, and created humans. "But divine control will be hamstrung and God's purposes jeopardized if events can ever catch Him by *surprise*, or find Him *unprepared*, or force Him to *react* after the fact to patch things up. This means that God must have the ability to anticipate where events are headed."[42] Divine providential intervention is possible in a meaningful way only under the thesis that God knows future contingent events and can do something about them. God can alter or change what would have happened to avoid harm and benefit only if he knows what will occur if he does not intervene. But this is precisely what is problematic for the doctrine of divine foreknowledge where God's knowledge of the future is based on the events themselves, either directly or indirectly through the true propositions that record them.

Although this objection does not vitiate divine foreknowledge by making it a logically contradictory doctrine, it does indicate that foreknowledge as traditionally understood is not of great, useful value. It simply cannot serve the purposes to which many believers in omniscience put it, which is a significant negative implication. To give just one example, the impracticality of foreknowledge puts in jeopardy the possibility of God responding to petitionary prayer to bring about the changes we desire. How can God respond to our petitionary prayers to change the future if he cannot know what he is to alter, since as a result of his positive response to our prayer the event to be altered never happens and hence is not known? In this regard believers in foreknowledge are not any worse off than open theists, who likewise cannot rely on God to structure the future providentially. But this provides little consolation if foreknowledge cannot be usefully employed by God to bring about changes by divine action. Thus, the denial of the practical applicability of foreknowledge poses a very serious problem for traditional believers in the doctrine, for it affects every dimension of divine providence.

God limits his knowledge

David Hunt rejects this criticism that foreknowledge necessarily militates against providence. His argument invokes the contention that God can

---

42. Hunt, "Divine Providence," 395.

limit his own knowledge.[43] He notes that knowledge of the future is, in some sense, not all that different from knowledge of the present and past. We can block out or ignore pieces of information about the past and present, such that they no longer factor in our decision making. If God can ignore present and past information in making providential decisions, God can ignore pieces of his foreknowledge in making decisions about the future, especially when it comes to making providential decisions such as in response to human repentance or prayer.

Hunt's point is that God's knowing something (or everything) does not entail that this information must be used in decision making. For example, in testing Abraham God might choose not to foreknow how Abraham reacts to the command to sacrifice his son Isaac. In bracketing this foreknowledge, God really would be testing Abraham regarding his faith to find out whether Abraham was true in his faith. If what is foreknown is not that on which God takes action, then God's foreknowledge does not conflict with God's ability to act providentially or sovereignly. Since what is foreknown but bracketed is unchanged by God's action, it still actually results and foreknowledge does not conflict with it.[44]

Hunt suggests a scenario where persons might foreknow a particular event and then use this information to channel their actions so that a possible outcome of that event does not occur. He gives the example of someone, say Peter, who knows that an arrest warrant will be issued for him next Thursday. Armed with that information, Peter leaves the country and avoids the arrest. Here the foreknowledge of the warrant does not conflict with the possibility of Peter doing a free action, since what is foreknown is not the escape itself but the issuing of the warrant, which is not affected by Peter's action. Limited foreknowledge does not present an immediate problem to human free agency so long as the decision taken does not depend on a belief that itself depends on a future event that depends on the original decision. Again, this scenario presupposes attending to selected foreknowledge and ignoring other aspects.

If this is to help us in preserving divine freedom to act, it has to apply to God who knows all truths, including those describing his own free agency and that of others. Hunt replies that there is no problem with regard to the extent or scope of divine knowledge. It is not how much God knows that is problematic but only the use of what he foreknows. If what he foreknows is not used to bring about an event, there is no problem. But, we reply, if God

---

43. To my knowledge, this possibility was first briefly suggested but left undeveloped by Swinburne, *Coherence of Theism*, 176.

44. Hunt, "Divine Providence," 400–402.

knows everything, then the extent does matter, for God would have to limit the extent of his knowledge to exclude not only that about which God is taking action but *also* what else is causally connected with it.

Hunt's suggestion presupposes that God can limit his knowledge only to features that are not affected by a particular free decision on God's part. It might be asked how it is possible for God not to attend to what God knows. For us as finite beings it is possible not to attend to what we know. I might know that I intend to go to the dentist today, but when I get to the intersection I take my usual route, ignoring the knowledge that I need to take a different direction to visit the dentist. I might be distracted or on "automatic-pilot," subconsciously resisting the dental visit—various explanations might be given for my ignoring what I know. But if God knows everything, how could he bracket some of his knowledge in order to deliberate and act providentially?

Up front, it does seem paradoxical: how would God know what to ignore? Does he first look at the future and then decide what to ignore and to what to attend? This leads to a paradoxical result that God has to attend to what he knows in order to ignore it; God would have to know what he wants to ignore. For another, can God selectively choose what he wants to ignore? Events are causally interconnected, so that for God to ignore some pieces of information would require him to ignore a great deal else.

One possible explanation of how God might ignore future truths or events would be that knowledge involves true belief. Belief can be both an active conscious state (what is called an occurrent belief) and a disposition or tendency. We can actively entertain a belief right now (that I am drinking a glass of skim milk), but we also might believe something about which we are not currently thinking or not considering (that Cuzco was an important center of Incan civilization). The latter is dispositional in that if I were asked whether I believed Cuzco was such a center, I could answer affirmatively even if I am not currently considering it.[45] This belief is a dispositional, not an occurrent, belief. If belief were only an active conscious state, there would be very little we would believe because it is not possible for us to consciously attend to many things. But we want to say that we believe a great many things, that multiple beliefs are part of our belief structure, even if they are not part of our current consciousness. A dispositional approach to belief allows us to do so. Applied to God, if God's beliefs were active states only, God would consciously know everything at once. As such, God could not bracket what he knows or set aside individual beliefs that function in his

---

45. For a much more detailed treatment of belief, see Reichenbach, *Epistemic Obligations*, ch. 6.

knowledge. But if belief is also a disposition for God, then there is much that he knows and believes that he is not currently affirming and that he could ignore or not attend to. If God's knowledge involves belief, and if some of that belief can be dispositional, then it is possible for God to ignore or not attend to items of his foreknowledge that are dispositional in making providential decisions. With this explanation, God does not so much self-limit his knowledge as not actualize his disposition to know certain things. While some of his knowledge is occurrent, it is the dispositional knowledge that makes providence possible.

That God's knowledge might be self-limited or, better, dispositional is an intriguing suggestion, similar to the suggestion that God as almighty can limit his power in order to grant freedom. God has the power to do what he wills but intentionally limits that power. Here God limits his foreknowledge, putting some of his knowledge into or allowing it to remain in a dispositional mode, in order to be free to act providentially. Self-limitation of knowledge might seem parallel to self-limitation of power, but there is a critical difference. The latter is done to allow human persons freedom of choice; it is to allow for a meaningful free response on our part. But self-limitation of knowledge is only indirectly for our benefit; it is to allow God to act providentially. God limits his knowledge so that he can deliberate and act on our behalf.

This creative suggestion runs up against some very serious problems. First, to what kind of evidence could we appeal to show that at least some if not all of God's beliefs are at some time dispositional rather than active states? Holding all of his beliefs actively would not pose a problem for an infinite God in the same way that it would be problematic for a finite human being. Our conscious states are limited; not so with God. So there is no reason to think that holding all his beliefs occurrently would be something God could not do. The concept of a God who puts or allows some of his knowledge to be dispositional presupposes a God who has a relation to time. But even here, God's infinity allows, if not requires, that all knowledge be simultaneously present with God. And indeed, holding all events continually before his understanding is a feature of views that hold that God is essentially timeless.

Second, it might be questioned whether God occurrently knowing only some of his knowledge is the wisest tack to take to resolve the practicality difficulty. Is it not better to use all one's knowledge in planning how to act providentially? We employ knowledge, not ignorance, to make wise decisions. But in a scenario where God limits his knowledge or does not activate his dispositions to know in order to act providentially, God abstains from the use of knowledge of what is useful. But this is the contradictory puzzle: lack of conscious or used (fore)knowledge is what makes providence possible, whereas we ordinarily think that God's guidance is furthered by his complete knowledge. That the less God uses his foreknowledge, the better God is able to deliberate and act providentially surely is puzzling. That foreknowledge cannot be used in God's providential actions and that it must therefore be restricted does not show that the doctrine of foreknowledge is false. But having less conscious foreknowledge of future contingent events does not increase the usefulness of God's knowledge or our confidence in God's wise providence. This is the practical paradox of divine epistemological limitation.

At the same time, open theism's restriction of God's knowledge to the past and present and God's enhanced beliefs regarding the near future provides no advantage for providence. God's knowing less, in that God does not know true propositions about future contingents, does not assist God in making wise, providential actions. Ignorance fails to provide a sound basis for giving good advice. Ascribing to God unfathomable wisdom, incredible resourcefulness, and omnicompetence[46] is no substitute for a God who actually knows true propositions about the future.

Both views encounter serious issues regarding the relation of foreknowledge to providence. For those adhering to foreknowledge, limiting God's knowledge means that God cannot give as good advice as might be expected to providentially alter the future; self-limiting foreknowledge allows for providence but conflicts with divine wisdom. For open theists, abandoning foreknowledge puts in jeopardy any appeal to divine wisdom in guiding more future providence. Both restraining and denying knowledge to allow for providence or freedom respectively are weak bargains.

Theological and practical implications of the open view

Denial of foreknowledge has theological and practical implications. Clark Pinnock writes that when God created free creatures, he "accepted a degree of risk with the possibility, not certainty, of sin and evil occurring."[47] John Sanders affirms that not only did God not foreknow that the first humans would sin, but God must have believed that its occurrence was "implausible."[48] But 1 Peter 1:10 affirms that the prophets themselves were "trying to find out the time and circumstances to which the Spirit of Christ in them was pointing when he predicted the sufferings of Christ and the

---

46. Sanders, *God Who Risks*, 207.
47. Pinnock, *Most Moved Mover*, 42.
48. Sanders, *God Who Risks*, 45–46.

glories that would follow." Verse 20 affirms that "Christ was chosen before the creation of the world" to deal with the entrance of sin. If, as open theists claim, God did not know that sin would enter into the world, why was Christ's redemption planned so far in advance, indeed, even to the detail of an incarnate human sacrifice?[49] Will ascribing his redemption to a general plan suffice to satisfy these Scriptures?

The biblical writers portray the redemptive scenario as planned by God in advance. The Lamb was slain before the world was created (Rev 13:8). That God would hand Jesus over to the authorities was fore-planned and foreknown (Acts 2:23; 4:27–28); yet it was accomplished by the free acts of the Jewish and Roman authorities. God knew beforehand that Jesus would go through the excruciatingly painful ordeal that awaited him, even though as a free agent, Jesus could have called the whole thing off. If Jesus had chosen, he could have invoked an entire legion of angels to rescue him from the authorities (Matt 26:53). Even the justification of the Old Testament saints is made possible by God's foreknowledge of Christ's future death.

It might be replied that this is an intended divine action, and hence God's overlooking of sins in the Old Testament was a conscious act based on his determination to act in a particular way in the future. But this determination depends on the free actions of innumerable people, from the ancestors of Jesus who made possible his birth, to the religious and civil authorities in Palestine who chose to proceed with the crucifixion of Jesus over Barabbas, to the acquiescence of Jesus himself to his death. God's predetermination to act in a specific way, "through the redemption that came by Christ Jesus" (Rom 3:25–26), is fully dependent on the foreknowledge of acts of free agents.[50]

The open theists' view leaves the question of the nature and extent of divine providence in doubt. As Bruce Ware puts it, "It leaves us with a *God who lacks massive knowledge of future human affairs, who possesses innumerable false beliefs about that future, whose wisdom is less than perfect, whose plans can prove faulty, whose actions might be regrettable, whose word may be mistaken, whose self-claim to deity is undermined, a view of*

---

49. Open theists' attempts to get around this passage are weak. Sanders writes, "First Peter 1:20 says that God foreknew Christ and thus can be understood as affirming that the cross was foreknown from eternity. But this verse does not necessitate such an interpretation, and so there is no problem for the relational model. All that is required is that the incarnation of the Son was decided on from the beginning as part of the divine project." Ibid., 102–3. But surely there would have been no divine project of this incarnational and atoning sort if God did not foreknow that humans would become so sinful that they needed atonement. The number of other ways the divine "project" could have developed is endless.

50. Ware, *God's Lesser Glory*, 27.

God whose inability to declare future free human actions renders him strikingly similar to the pretender deities denounced by God himself."[51] How can we be assured that "God works for the good of those who love him" (Rom 8:28); it might be that God *intends* to do good, but there is no assurance that the result will be good at all.

But perhaps, as open theists claim, this doubt about providence is what we in fact have. Where were God's providential actions in twentieth-century China, Poland, Cambodia, Rwanda, present-day Syria, and thousands of other places? Yet, if we adopt an open view where God is surprised, where God can regret his decisions, where God has mistaken beliefs, can we have confidence that God not only has at least some control of the universe, but also can direct us in our lives? If what God knows about the future is limited by his lack of foreknowledge of future contingencies, and if this is significant—as indeed it must be, especially when it comes to providential actions on behalf of humans—then we can have little confidence that God's purposes for us will be fulfilled. One might grant that God's knowledge of the past and present increase the likelihood that God can intervene wisely in the short run, but "seeing" into the distance is another matter. Our confidence in God's guiding wisdom for the more distant future would be shaken.

If God can be mistaken about his decisions, wrong about predictions, only can think that events will probabilistically happen, then we must rethink God's superiority. God is in a position of learning along with us, of discovering contingent truths as time moves on, and of finding out that his beliefs about the future were sometimes wrong. Since God has no or little knowledge of distant future contingencies, his ignorance of the future is prodigious, especially when it comes to human choices and actions. It is true that on this view God can know all that it is possible to know, but that praise gives us little consolation about God's knowledge that underlies his wisdom.

At the same time, whether and to what extent divine foreknowledge can be of practical use to God remains highly problematic. It is true that the more God limits his foreknowledge, turning it into dispositions, the greater ability God has to act providentially. God can alter what might be without running afoul of his foreknowledge. But then the paradox remains: the greater the knowledge, the better the guidance; the less the foreknowledge, the more but less well God can providentially guide. These tensions indicate the difficulty of understanding God's foreknowledge and provide reasons why the matter has and remains under serious scrutiny and extended debate.

---

51. Ibid., 33–34.

Chapter 9

When Providence Seems Absent

THE DOCTRINE OF DIVINE providence faces two very significant concerns. First, if God loves and cares for us, how can we explain not only the existence of pain or suffering in the world (that there is suffering at all), but also the great amount of pain and suffering humans and other living creatures experience. Second, if God loves us, why does it seem that so many prayers for things that seem reasonable and *prima facie* consistent with the good fail to be answered or responded to? We will address the problem of suffering in this chapter and the issue of prayer in the next.

I revised this chapter while residing temporarily in Eastern Europe. Visiting the memorials at Auschwitz, seeing its barbed-wire enclosures, the inhumane and unheated housing with crowded bunks, the remains of the furnaces where unknowing people were gassed and the courtyard for the execution of resisters, and the rooms filled with shoes, suitcases, eyeglasses, dolls, and the items of everyday life that belonged to real people who passed through or temporarily stayed in these houses of horror, there is a sense in which no chapter of explanation, no morally sufficient reason, can seem plausible. As I stood as the end of the rail line at Birkenau and looked at the platforms where families were separated and lives determined with a nod of the head or a simple wave of the hand, the awful feeling of deep, unfathomable injustice prevailed. The place exudes evil, such that no visitors can converse louder than in a solemn whisper. Even photography seems out of place, except to serve to recall the adage that it should never happen again, an adage rarely followed even today. This theme of unrepentant cruelty, displayed in the individual country museums at Auschwitz and in poignant Jewish museums in Vienna, Bratislava, and Krakow, at times is tempered with the bravery of those few non-Jews who, at great risk to their own lives, acted courageously to preserve the lives of the threatened. Good plants grow among the thorns and the uncaring weeds. Yet it is difficult for us to judge those who did nothing, for what would we have done in such circumstances facing threats of death to self and family?

This past weekend I visited the seaside stone and brick castles in Ghana that served as holding pens for African prisoners who were shackled and placed unwillingly on slave ships to the New World. Kept for many months in dark, damp, crowded dungeons, underfed, without toilet facilities so that the feces simply hardened under their feet on the floor, the prospective slaves languished and died, while the Dutch and British slave traders worshiped in glory to God in their churches built directly over the dungeons. Failure in any attempt at escape meant dying in a dark room without water, food, or the removal of the corpses of those who starved to death before them. Women were selectively chosen and raped by the white officers who leeringly watched them bathe. Words cannot do justice to the anguish, evil, and untimely deaths those captured and traded for faced.

Conditions of extreme and undeserved suffering—and of the sacrificial care of people who are the ministering hands of God—continue today, and we cannot avoid the intellectually demanding question of how to reconcile divine providence with pervasive evil: past, present, and future.

Pain and suffering

We do not need to spend much time providing convincing evidence that both humans and other sentient creatures continue to experience significant amounts of pain and suffer greatly. Pain, suffering, and dysfunction, which philosophers and theologians term evils, figure as part of our own daily experience and of the experiences of others vividly transmitted to us by the media. A parent suffers the debilitating effects of Alzheimer's disease; a young child is born with serious internal organ defects requiring multiple surgeries; a friend skis into a pine tree and is paralyzed by the impact; an active football coach no longer can function because of Parkinson's disease; a mother suffers because a heart attack claims the life of her young daughter; people drown as their homes are washed away by an advancing hurricane; a lion devours a photographing tourist while other tourists look on helplessly; a malnourished child dies in her mother's arms in the desert; a pregnant woman contracts the zita virus and gives birth to a child with microcephaly. These, and innumerable evils like them, are instances of what we will term *natural evil*. Natural evils are instances of pain, suffering, and states significantly disadvantageous to consciously aware beings that are caused by actions for which human persons cannot be held morally blameworthy. The causes of natural evils are numerous: cancerous cells, viruses, defective genes, flood waters, drought, famine, tornadoes, falling rocks, and creatures such as mosquitoes, parasites, and carnivores. Natural evil also includes pain and suffering caused by humans but for which humans, though responsible, are not morally to blame. For example, two persons might be lifting a heavy piano when one trips and falls, causing the piano to fall on the partner and painfully pin him to the ground. Events such as a driver accidentally injuring a child who dashes into the street between parked cars or a batter hitting a line drive that strikes the opposing pitcher in the eye are also examples of humanly caused natural evils.

Pain and suffering also result from human actions for which persons can be held morally responsible. Children writhe in pain from sarin gas contained in exploding shells; a newly wedded spouse pushes her husband over the edge of a cliff on their honeymoon; a male nurse injects deadly toxins into elderly patients in a nursing home; a young man guns down two dozen children and teachers in an elementary school; a purse snatcher shoves an elderly woman to the ground and breaks her arm; trusted stock brokers deceive their clients and steal their life savings in Ponzi schemes; over social media teenagers bully another into committing suicide; a stranger abducts a child from her bedroom in the middle of the night; a middle-aged man imprisons and physically abuses three young women in a house for ten years; members of a white secret society lynch a black man; a young woman is dragged off a bus and gang raped until she dies; a pilot intentionally steers an airliner filled with people into a French mountain; and so much more. We will term these instances of *moral evil:* instances of pain and suffering and states significantly disadvantageous to consciously aware beings for which human persons can be held morally blameworthy. As noted in the previous paragraph, we do not classify as moral evil all pain, suffering, and dysfunction caused by human agents, but restrict "moral evil" to evils for which humans can be held morally culpable. We understand the categories of moral and natural evils to be mutually exclusive and totally exhaustive of the possibilities.

We do not classify pain, suffering, and dysfunction by reference to any inherent or derived quality that the effects might manifest. Such a classification would be impossible to implement. Rather, we classify instances of pain, suffering, and dysfunction with respect to their causes, and more especially with reference to the moral culpability of the agents. It is true that in practice we cannot always tell into which category we are to place an experienced evil, for we may not know persons' intentions and whether and to what degree persons are morally responsible for actions and effects. But this categorization provides at least a *prima facie* way to satisfactorily address intellectually the problem of pain and suffering and divine providence. In what follows we want to see whether a doctrine of divine providence can be consistent with each of these two kinds of evil. In particular, we are interested in what reasons God, as good, almighty, and all-knowing, might have for allowing and even causing moral and natural evils. We will term these morally sufficient reasons: reasons that render blame inappropriate.[1] Since God has all three properties, why is there suffering? Such suffering and dysfunction initially appear to be inconsistent with a God who providentially cares for his creation. Since God is good, one would expect God both to will and to remove or prevent such evils from occurring. Good, loving parents, it is argued, would not tolerate such effects if the parent knew about and could do something about these evils. Since God is almighty, God should be able to prevent or eliminate evil, if not all evil, at least most evils or the worst ones. God is capable of doing miracles, and such divine intervention could remove or eliminate all evil, or at least the more serious evils. Since God is omniscient, God surely knows about the pain and suffering that sentient creatures experience or will experience. God cannot plead ignorance. How, then, can we reconcile the existence of God who has these properties with the tremendous amount of pain, suffering, and dysfunction that exists in the world? The evils in the world seem to point not to a providential God who loves and cares for this creation, but rather to the absence of God or to a being who lacks key properties that we have considered part of our understanding of what it is to be God.

The question—why does a loving, providential God cause or allow this to happen—is not novel. The Psalmist wondered why the wicked prosper while the good suffer.

> But for me, my feet had almost slipped;
>   I had nearly lost my foothold.
> For I envied the arrogant
>   when I saw the prosperity of the wicked.
> They have no struggles;
>   their bodies are healthy and strong.
> They are free from common human burdens;
>   they are not plagued by human ills. . . .
> Surely in vain I have kept my heart pure
>   and have washed my hands in innocence.
> All day long I have been afflicted,
>   and every morning brings new punishments. . . .

---

1. For example, a surgeon operating to remove a cancerous tumor has a morally sufficient reason for causing pain and suffering in the patient. The pain and suffering remain real and undesirable, but no moral blame attaches to the surgeon causing the suffering. The surgeon is morally justified in performing surgery.

> When I tried to understand all this,
>> it troubled me deeply
> till I entered the sanctuary of God;
>> then I understood their final destiny. (Ps 73:2–5, 13–14, 16–17)

The psalmist finds the answer in his trust in the providential God who holds him by his right hand, guides him with his counsel, and takes him into glory, while the wicked are ruined and destroyed (vv. 18–24). His confidence in the sovereign Lord who adjusts the balance of justice in the end brings him through this existential struggle.

Although this answer might satisfy in terms of future outcomes, it does not answer the question as to why God allows or causes these afflictions in the first place. To this we now turn, and as we shall see, the response is complex. Typically philosophers and theologians have looked for a single, all-sufficient answer, but there is reason to believe that the morally sufficient reasons that reconcile divine providence with suffering are many. Actually, we should expect this since we often have many, varied, and complex reasons for our actions, depending on the circumstances. Similarly, we would expect that God would have many, varied, and complex reasons for causing or allowing suffering. Even the morally sufficient reasons we will consider are probably too few and not complex enough to address the myriad instances of evil. As the writer of Job notes, it is pretentious to think that we can circumscribe completely the mind and reasoning of God (Job 40:6–8). At the same time, we cannot abandon searching for and understanding possible morally sufficient reasons for evil, if we are to comprehend anything of God's dealings with his creation. We will consider a general schema, but it should be acknowledged that this comes with the understanding that in any particular case of suffering God's reasons might include not only some of what we address below, individually or in conjunction, but other morally sufficient reasons as well about which we have no idea. This means that the degree to which what we say helps individuals deal with particular cases of suffering will vary. We will provide a general schema (theodicies) to reconcile divine providence with suffering, but the application to particular instances will vary with the individual cases, without our being able to say exactly what the reasoning would be that would reconcile that case of suffering with God's providential goodness.[2]

---

2. Since the literature on the problem of suffering or evil is enormous, we can give only a very small sample of relevant books. Lewis, *Problem of Pain*; Hick, *Evil*; Plantinga, *God, Freedom*; Reichenbach, *Evil*; Howard-Snyder, ed., *Evidential Argument*; Swinburne, *Providence and Evil*; Adams, *Horrendous Evils*; Peterson, *God and Evil*; Davis, ed., *Encountering Evil*; Hasker, *Triumph of God*; and Keller, *Problems of Evil*.

Initial presuppositions

Some might think that since good beings would prevent evil whenever and wherever they could, providence necessitates absence of pain or suffering. Indeed, a version of this lies at the heart of one of the more formidable critiques of divine goodness. J. L. Mackie writes that a good being is opposed to evil in such a way that it always eliminates evil as far as it can. And since this being is omnipotent, it should be able to eliminate evil completely.

But even in our ordinary experience this claim about eliminating evil completely is mistaken. The parents who step in and prevent the child from ever experiencing pain, suffering, or frustration will have a helpless child on their hands. The child will not be able to walk, since learning to walk is accompanied by falling. It will not be able to know when to eat, since it will never know what it is to be hungry. It will never be properly potty-trained. It will not know how to read and write, since suffering and frustration accompany learning. Such a child would be far worse off than a child who has faced the painful challenges of life. Pain, suffering, frustration play such important roles in our lives that it is unrealistic, if not unwanted, to think that a good being would see to it that we avoid all pain and suffering.

We noted above that being almighty has to do with what God wills, not with the issue of what God can do. We also saw in chapter 2 that God's desire to have moral agents with whom to communicate meant that God would create creatures capable of making free choices. They would be significantly free, such that on a given occasion they could either choose to perform or to refrain from performing an action that is morally significant for them. It is not that freedom in itself is the greatest good; rather, freedom is a requirement for being able to achieve the greater goods such as entering into relationships with God and others. Put another way, a world that contains significantly free persons capable of making choices between moral good and moral evil and who choose a significant amount of moral good is superior to a world that lacks significantly free persons and in turn lacks agents and actions that are morally good. We have already seen that to achieve this end God limits his power in order to grant human autonomy. This does not mean that God does not act or intervene in nature or in human affairs, but as we will see below it means that God cannot run or operate the world populated by free beings by miracle. Such would ultimately remove the very freedom necessary for attaining moral good and the kind of personal, interresponsive relationships that God apparently desires when God endeavors to enter into covenant relations with his created people. If God limits his power to grant freedom, then it is reasonable to believe that a good person will not eliminate all instances of pain and suffering, for some of these instances arise from human free actions.

Providence and discipline

We begin our understanding of the relation between providence and suffering with the concept of discipline. In order to achieve goals, whether physical, mental, behavioral, or spiritual, we need to discipline ourselves. And since discipline requires facing adversity of some sort, suffering, frustration, and sometimes even pain will be involved. Achieving discipline involves a cost.

Consider, first of all, the development of our physical bodies. Several years ago I was on my way to the racquetball court when I passed the college weight room. Looking in I saw two young men, one laying on his back lifting a barbell loaded with heavy weights on each end; the other student stood over him, spotting lest the bar slip. I heard the latter say to the lifter, "Make it hurt; make it hurt!" A famous athletic proverb—no pain, no gain—captures the point. If the young weightlifter is to develop his physical muscles, strain and pain will have to accompany training.

To develop strong muscles, a robust heart, lung capacity, and a healthy blood flow we must exercise physically. We cannot achieve physical health without it. Indeed, lack of exercise leads to more physical problems and suffering in the end than engaging in regular exercise. But as anyone who exercises knows, exercise is a strenuous, usually somewhat painful, activity. For our muscles to develop and strengthen, they must encounter resistance.

Natural evils can also be necessary means to goods in that they are nature's way of informing us that we need to rectify our behavior. Pain and suffering are biological and psychological warning signals, without which we would not know that something is amiss with our physical or psychological state and needs to be corrected. The toothache tells us that bacteria are destroying our teeth and that we need dental care; headaches remind us to relax our frantic, stressful pace. Sunburn warns us against the dangers of overexposure to the sun, while other burning sensations get us to avoid dangerously hot objects. The pains caused are means to greater goods.

Similar things can be said about behavioral discipline. The parent who tolerates everything that the child does is not doing the child a favor but rather preparing the child for a life of difficulty and trouble. Discipline involves training that often incorporates pain and suffering as well as reward and praise.

The principle applies not only to physical and behavioral strengthening but to moral strengthening as well. We develop our moral character in the face of both of natural and moral adversity or evil. Our virtues develop only as we face hardships, temptation, frustration, fear, need, and difficulty. In the book of Job, Elihu contends,

> He may speak in their ears
> > and terrify them with warnings,
> to turn them from wrongdoing
> > and keep them from pride,
> to preserve them from the pit,
> > their lives from perishing by the sword.
> Or they may be chastened on a bed of pain
> > with constant distress in their bones,
> so that their bodies find food repulsive
> > and their souls loathe the choicest meal. . . .
> Yet if there is an angel at their side,
> > a messenger, one out of a thousand,
> > sent to tell them how to be upright,
> and he is gracious to them and says to God,
> > Spare them from going down to the pit. . . .
> God does all these things to people—
> > twice, even three times—
> to turn them back from the pit
> > that the light of life may shine on them. (Job 33:16–20, 23–24, 29–30)[3]

The writer of Hebrews sees discipline not as counting against divine love, but rather manifesting it (Heb 12:5–11). That we are to "endure hardship" as a measure of God's discipline is a "word of encouragement," demonstrating that God treats us as his children. God's discipline of us shows his concern that we develop the qualities of character and "share in his holiness." The writer begins by quoting the Septuagint version of Proverbs 3:11–12.

> My son, do not make light of the Lord's discipline,
> > and do not lose heart when he rebukes you;
> because the Lord disciplines those he loves,
> > and he chastens everyone he accepts as his child.

---

3. The Lord says that he is angry with Eliphaz and his two friends, Bildad and Zophar, for their unwise counsel, but does not extend this anger to Elihu (Job 42:5).

The writer of Hebrews continues: "If you are not disciplined—and everyone undergoes discipline—then you are not legitimate children at all" (Heb 12:8). For the writer God's disciplining has its human analogy in the disciplining that all good, caring parents do with their children. The fact that parents correct us shows they love us, and in turn they ask us to respect them.

> Moreover, we have all had parents who disciplined us and we respected them for it. How much more should we submit to the Father of spirits and live! Our parents disciplined us for a little while as they thought best; but God disciplines us for our good, that we may share in his holiness. (Heb 12:9–10)

It is not that this discipline is pleasant, but it is for a greater, future good.

> No discipline seems pleasant at the time, but painful. Later on, however, it produces a harvest of righteousness and peace for those who have been trained by it. (Heb 12:11)

John Hick writes, "The divine purpose behind the world is one of soul-making.... [T]he kind of goodness which ... God desires in his creatures could not in fact be created except through a long process of creaturely experience in response to challenges and disciplines of various kinds."[4] Aristotle noted that courage is not fearlessness, but incorporates fear: knowing what to fear at the right time, in the right place, in the right way, for the right reason. We cultivate courage when we face danger; without danger there would be no fear and no courage. We develop perseverance when we are confronted with difficulty; in such situations we foster the disposition to carry on despite adverse circumstances. We develop the virtue of honesty when we defy the temptation to be dishonest, to take or claim what is not ours. We become charitable when we are confronted with the privation and needs of others; seeing others in dire circumstances calls us to empathize with them and to find ways to assist them to escape their situation. We develop the virtue of self-sacrifice in the context of struggle, self-esteem in the face of challenges from circumstances and the skepticism or denial of others, confidence in the context of uncertainty, and love where obstacles abound. We become compassionate when we see others suffering. James echoes this character-building view. "Consider it pure joy, my brothers, whenever you face trials of many kinds, because you know that the testing of your faith produces perseverance" (Jas 1:2–3). In effect, the very notion of virtue or quality of character links its development and realization with adversity. If

---

4. Hick, *Evil*, 344.

Hick is correct that God wants us to be people who have a character of a particular sort, then we can expect that we will confront difficulty and adversity that result in pain and suffering. Thus, it is reasonable to expect that God would allow and even cause suffering for our spiritual and moral development.

It is important to note that this way of connecting or reconciling divine providence with the fact that we suffer is neither universal nor definitive. It is not universal for several reasons. First, it does not explain or account for the pain and suffering experienced by higher-level but non-human sentient beings. Since they lack the ability to develop moral character, we cannot appeal to character-building as a reason why God would allow them to suffer. If we are to understand how a good God can allow animals to suffer, a different morally sufficient reason must be found.

Second, it is sometimes the case that pain and suffering do not work very effectively in character-building. It is true that some people develop character and discover God in times of crisis and disaster. Yet the opposite also occurs; the apparent randomness and unjustified calamity of natural and moral evils, their prevalence and intensity, can turn people away from God and cause them to give up. "How can a good God allow my child to suffer from spina bifida or leukemia, or allow thousands to suffer homelessness and starvation from the monsoons in Bangladesh?" they query, with diminishing faith. Rather than inspiring reverence, awe, and repentance, natural calamities and moral wrongdoings can bring defection from faith, which is the opposite of what God might have intended. The outcome of discipline is not guaranteed.

The hardships and difficulties people face can become so overwhelming that they destroy rather than build up their virtues. Temptations prove too strong so that persons compromise their honesty. Privation is so great that people simply are overwhelmed by appeals to their charity. As John Hick writes, critiquing his own position,

> It is true that sometimes ... there are sown or there come to flower even in the direst calamity graces of character that seem to make even that calamity itself worthwhile. A selfish spirit may be moved to compassion, a thoughtless person discover life's depths and be deepened thereby, a proud spirit learn patience and humility, a soft, self-indulgent character be made strong in the face of adversity. All this may happen, and has happened. But it may also fail to happen, and instead of gain there may be

sheer loss. Instead of ennobling, affliction may crush the character and wrest from it whatever virtues it possesses.[5]

So it is that in the face of adversity people can develop character and find God, or they can succumb to doubt and despair and lose their faith and spiritual endurance.

Not only can excessive suffering destroy character, it sometimes happens that death intrudes before the sufferer can develop or exhibit the qualities of character. Indeed, some with dysfunctions from birth such as mental deficiencies never achieve a level where they can learn and fashion their virtues. Even in the case of natural evils of diseases, sometimes pain comes too late to be a warning; it appears after the disease is well-established and the prospects are terminal, and it comes with an intensity disproportionate to character-building. A colleague of mine dies a month after she first learns that she has pancreatic cancer. Thus, instead of functioning as an early-warning signal leading to people taking appropriate action to rectify the problem, pain becomes an excruciating companion through the final stages of life. We must not view our pain control only from the perspective of our modern society where medicines can alleviate significant pain; pain management is a relatively recent development that until the advent of modern medicine was unavailable to us (and still is unavailable to much of the world's population). In cases where pain comes too late or is too intense, it is difficult to see how character development could be the reason for why God allows or causes suffering and pain. It would seem, rather, that a providential God would design a painful warning system where the warning occurred in the earliest stages when corrective action would benefit, or at least which, after warning for so long, could be turned off so the doomed arthritic could live with her affliction in peace.

In short, the appeal to character-building as a reason why God allows or causes suffering is not universal; it is one reason amid many reasons, so that it is a mistake to expect that character-building will explain all instances of pain and suffering. Clearly it cannot, but it does provide in *some* cases a way to reconcile divine providence with human suffering. God desires us not to remain moral children, but to develop into mature persons manifesting the traits of a good moral and spiritual character. Discipline can flow from a being of love where love goes beyond a life free from pain and suffering to helping develop a meaningful moral existence.

This account is not definitive either in that we cannot tell in most cases whether this is the reason that we are suffering. We can infer from discipline that there will be pain, but we cannot infer from pain that we are

5. Ibid., 366–67.

undergoing discipline. But seeing the suffering situation as an opportunity for character development is one response we can make to evil, and might even be seen as being providential.

Providence and punishment

Discipline also displays another dimension, namely, the administration of justice. Pain and suffering might arise as the consequences of our actions—I slice my finger while sharpening my pocket knife—and in this sense are not really punishments but the natural consequences of what we do. But pain and suffering might be intentionally imposed on persons who have performed morally evil acts and hence deserve punishment. It is warranted by their wrong-doing.

A loving parent not only develops discipline in the offspring; the parent also administers justice. The parent not only allows suffering but brings it about not only as deserved but to reform. The first is a deontological notion of punishment; we are punished because we deserve it. People justly administer punishment not to the innocent but to the guilty. It is because we have done wrong that we are punished. The second is a utilitarian concept of punishment; we are punished either as an example to create a deterrent to others in society or else to reform us. In both cases punishment brings pain and suffering.

This view of providence also has ancient roots in the book of Job. Elihu, in reviewing the natural calamities of windstorms, fire, marauders, death, and boils that came upon his friend Job, puts the argument this way.

> . . . far be it from God to do evil,
> from the Almighty to do wrong.
> He repays everyone for what they have done;
> he brings on them what their conduct deserves.
> It is unthinkable that God would do wrong,
> that the Almighty would pervert justice. (Job 34:10–12)

God is a god of justice who punishes wrongdoers, who are morally responsible for their actions and hence deserve punishment. God would be unjust if he gave pleasure in place of pain as punishment; punishment by its very nature is painful.

Pain and suffering resulting from punishment are not signs of the absence of love but of both justice and love. When punishment is viewed deontologically, it is a sign of justice. Punishment follows upon wrong-doing as just deserts. It is warranted by the wrongdoer's action. Were punishment not administered, we would properly question the justice of those in authority. The pain and suffering of punishment is not a sign of weakness but of goodness. We do not dispense just punishment willy-nilly; rather it is conditioned and structured by the person's wrong actions. We are not to punish the innocent, and when this does occur, we term it an unfortunate miscarriage of justice.

Punishment also has another side that reveals the love behind it. When punishment is viewed from a utilitarian perspective, the goal is to improve the person. We administer punishment to better people, as a form of discipline.

Although we focus on God's justice, the providential God is also a god of mercy. Providence invokes both. Hence, God's punishments are almost always accompanied by merciful acts of providence. From the very beginning God spares the lives of Adam and Eve; the death they suffer is not an immediate physical death, but a death of removal from a place of blessing from undue toil. God shows his mercy to the murderer Cain by placing on him an undeserved mark of protection. And so on through countless examples in Scripture. "Brothers, as an example of patience in the face of suffering, take the prophets who spoke in the name of the Lord. As you know, we count as blessed those who have persevered. You have heard of Job's perseverance and have seen what the Lord finally brought about. The Lord is full of compassion and mercy" (Jas 5:10–11).

As we saw with the character-building, connecting providence with the fact that we suffer as punishment for what we have done is neither universal nor definitive. It is not universal because many instances of suffering are neither directly nor indirectly connected as punishment with evildoing or sin. For one thing, this view cannot account for the pain, suffering, and dysfunction experienced by animals, for as noted above it is generally believed that animals have no moral consciousness and hence cannot be held morally accountable for their actions. "Punishment" of animals can alter their behavior by stimulus-response training but it does not develop their moral character; hence, it is difficult to see that pain and suffering would have a punishment role here.

For another, no clear or apparent connection exists between the pain and suffering that people experience and the state of their moral character. Both moral and natural evils strike in ways that often bear little resemblance to persons' virtues or lack thereof. Floods, tornadoes, diseases, shootings, beatings, rape, and other pain-causing events appear to strike individuals randomly, without reference to what the victims have done or their moral character. Several years ago a tornado went through my community, and

I toured the devastated area. The standing houses were affected to varying degrees, but at the center was one house where only an interior closet remained. It would be totally inappropriate to judge the moral character of those whose houses were affected by the degree of damage. As to the house completely destroyed, the owners were away on vacation and had sealed the house; it is this action, rather than their character, that resulted in the total devastation. Floods are no respecters of persons. The devastation wrought by hurricanes Katrina and Sandy was no respecter of the persons whose homes were destroyed or lives lost. Good and bad people both suffered loss and drowning; the water did not select the non-virtuous to be drowned or suffer loss while protecting the virtuous. When the Colorado floods and fires swept through the narrow canyons, the devastating effects were morally neutral.

I have lived in Africa and seen the effects of malaria first hand. Malarial mosquitoes do not first assess the moral qualities of their potential victims before they bite. Similarly with cancer and Parkinson's disease; they do not correlate with moral character. Physicians do not differentiate benign from malignant breast tumors by discovering the moral virtues or lack thereof of their female patients. Although at times a causal relation exists between moral behavior and disease, no necessary connection holds. Likewise with respect to moral evils; they can be inflicted equally upon the just and unjust.

This explanation in terms of sin is not definitive either because in any given case we cannot tell whether for sure the suffering is a divine punishment. It is clear that sin results in suffering; what is not clear is the converse of this, namely, that any given case of suffering is punishment for sin. The matter of the connection between sin and suffering is difficult and complex. On the one hand, there is a strong biblical tradition that connects sin and suffering, both through natural consequences and through divine punishment. The Old Testament is filled with instances where divine punishment for disobedience brings pain and suffering. The punishment affects individuals (Adam and Eve); families and groups are punished for individual and collective sins (Korah, Achan, Israel suffers for David's numbering of his army). Nations likewise feel the wrath of God against sin; this is particularly the case with Israel, which persistently breaks its covenant with the Lord. But God also applies it to the surrounding nations of Egypt, Assyria, and Babylonia. The Bible leaves little doubt: sin brings punishment, involving pain and suffering. In the New Testament James makes this connection clear: "And the prayer offered in faith will make them well: the Lord will raise them up. If they have sinned, they will be forgiven. Therefore, confess your sins to each other and pray for each other so that you may be healed" (Jas 5:15-16).

On the other hand, some biblical passages reveal a skepticism that this reasoning can be applied universally. John 9, where Jesus encounters a man born blind, poignantly raises the issue. Jesus' disciples query, "Rabbi, who sinned, this man or his parents, that he was born blind?" The disciples suggest two possibilities: either the blind man had a prior life and is now paying for the sins he committed in that life, or else the sins of his "father" are being visited on him. The first accords with the Hellenistic view introduced into Palestine that the soul lives on after death and is reincarnated, perhaps to experience the results of actions done in the previous life. The second accords with ancient Jewish traditions that children are affected by the sins of their parents. Jewish law and rabbinic opinion were divided over whether the child might be punished for the wrongdoing of parents. Some canonical passages (Exod 20:5; 37:7; Num 14:18; Deut 5:9; Ps 79:8; Isa 65:6–7) stated that the sins of the father could be visited on his children. Others, fewer in number (Deut 24:26; Ezek 18:20), opted for punishment meted out on the basis of individual wrongdoing. Each involves a particular view of how society accounts for moral acts. The former, where the children can be punished for their parents' actions, makes sense where a communal or lineage approach is applied to the analysis of moral actions. We are intrinsically bound up with society. We are not individuals divorced from those around us but assume corporate responsibility for individual moral actions. Hence, the actions taken not only affect the entire society, but the responsibility for the actions falls on the entire society, community, or family. In our current culture, we might see this as an ethic that applies to corporations, where the group has to take responsibility for what is done, even though particular individuals might not have participated in the actions. The ethic of personal responsibility represents our more individual approach to society and actions. Each person is responsible for her or his own actions and can be held accountable; but the moral responsibility does not spread to those who had no role in the decision making or the willful carrying out of the actions.

In the story of the man born blind, Jesus rejects both options, attributing the situation of the man's blindness to an anticipation of God revealing his glory in Jesus' miraculous healing. In doing so Jesus gives a morally sufficient reason more in line with the final chapters of Job than the intervening ones. At the same time, we cannot simply generalize from this one instance to a general statement about the relation of suffering and sin. In Mark 2 Jesus hints at this very connection when in healing the paralyzed man he uses not words of physical healing but the spiritual healing of sins forgiven (Mark 2:3–12). Jesus does not flat out say that the paralysis resulted from sin, but his discussion of how language might be used to address this case— "'Which is easier: to say to the paralytic, 'Your sins are forgiven,' or to say,

'Get up, take your mat and walk?'" (2:9)—implies that there *can* be a connection between suffering and sin, and that healing can apply to both.[6] The apostle Paul likewise affirms the connection between sin (here, unworthily partaking of the bread and cup) and sickness and death (1 Cor 11:27–30).

In effect, we can reasonably conclude from Scripture and experience that sin results in suffering, both as a natural result and in the form of intentionally-applied punishment. But experience also teaches us that *not all* suffering, especially with respect to natural evil, and probably not most suffering, is occasioned by sin. Pain and suffering arise from diverse causes; that sin is the cause is neither universal nor definitive in every case.

Moral evil and human freedom

So far we have seen that allowing or even causing pain and suffering might well be part of God's providential actions. God allows or administers pain and suffering for the good of the individuals who suffer. Hence, although the experience involves suffering and is undesirable in itself, it works for a greater good. As surgeons cause pain when they remove the cancerous uterus to save the woman's life, so God sometimes uses divine surgery to discipline us by sharpening our moral character or by punishing us for the wrongs that we have committed. The pain and suffering are not turned into good and pleasure, but they are justified by the prospect of the greater good brought by discipline.

But as we have seen not every instance of pain and suffering can be accounted for by appeal to a greater good. Many, many instances of pain, suffering, and particularly dysfunction do not appear to serve such a purpose. That a Kenyan woman is shot in a Nairobi shopping mall and bleeds to death waiting for help seems to serve no good for her. Moviegoers are shot randomly in a Colorado theater and concertgoers are gunned down in a Paris auditorium by deranged or fanatic young men; families watching a basketball game in a Chicago park are shot by passing gunmen clothed in black; young women are kidnapped from a city street or their bedroom and sexually assaulted; terrorists attack a Kenyan university and after separating the Christians from the Muslims execute the former because they adhere to the "wrong" faith—none of these seems to be covered by the above reasons that God might have in showing his disciplining love for us. Reasons other than serving a greater good must be sought for these abundant instances of moral evil that affect our daily lives.

---

6. For further development of the connection between sin, healing, and the atonement, see Reichenbach, "Healing View," 117–42.

These and innumerable similar cases are instances of moral evil, where people who can be held morally accountable for their actions bring about the pain and suffering. The spectrum of such evils is immense. Those who endured the genocidal killings in Germany and Eastern Europe, Russia, Rwanda, Cambodia, Congo, Bosnia, Nanking, and elsewhere have a right to ask, "Where was God when this happened?" But we would be short sighted if we limited moral evils to the great slaughters. The mother who loses her son to a Chicago gang killing, the young boys who were molested by trusted coaches and priests, the children who were raped by family members, the trusting clients who were cheated by lawyers, the people who lost their homes because of dishonest mortgage companies, the spouses whose lives were destroyed by adulterous partners—these individual cases likewise provide fertile ground for wondering where the sovereign, loving God was. If God loves us, why is God not more active in such cases to prevent the suffering of the innocent?

We have noted that God desires that we enter into meaningful relationship with him. This relationship is covenantal, moral, and responsive. God calls us to love him as he loves us. But for such a relationship to be possible, when we espouse this love or enter into this relationship we must be free; the response of automatons is neither truly love nor moral obedience but merely trained stimulus-response. As we argued in chapter 2, to be free we must have been able to do otherwise than we did given the causal conditions present. And we must be free in a morally significantly sense, that is, we must be free with respect to doing actions that are morally significant for us, such that doing a particular action at a particular time is morally right or refraining from doing an action at a particular time is morally wrong, or vice versa. God's choice to create beings that are free in a morally significant sense shows the kind of world God values. It is a world that contains morally significantly free persons who make moral choices between moral good and moral evil and who choose a significant amount of moral good; this is better than a world that lacks such free persons and moral good and moral evil.

In such a world inhabited by free persons, whether or not there are moral evils depends upon the choices and actions of those free persons. It is up to them whether they will choose to do right or wrong. And not only are they free to *choose* such, but as moral agents they are capable of *doing* right or wrong actions in morally significant situations. If they choose to do wrong, God cannot prevent them from doing that wrong or even choosing it without removing their significant freedom. It is possible and probable that God at times intervenes to prevent worse evils than occur, but God cannot consistently intervene, such that God runs the world by miracle, without removing their significant freedom. If God ran the world by miracle, then our presupposition that God values significantly free persons making moral choices and choosing a significant amount of good is violated. Accordingly, to bring about God's desires with regard to people, we must be morally significantly free, which means it is *possible* that we engage in or experience moral evils. Moral evils are thus consistent with a providential God.

It is important to note that we are not claiming that individual moral evils always lead to greater goods. That is highly improbable. To affirm this leads people to ask, when they suffer, for what specific good their suffering is a means. If we are correct, there is no divine reason designating a greater good for every evil. God does not allow or bring about evil in every case to prosper some specific greater good. Rather, much evil is gratuitous, that is, it does not serve directly as a means to a greater good; it arises from the larger cosmic story about what God desires and what is necessary to realize that desire. While specific evils may, but often do not, lead to a specific greater good, their *possibility* results from the freedom that is necessary for us to achieve the greater good of becoming moral beings and relating to God. The evil itself is not desired, but the possibility is necessary to realize the greater good.

Some have objected that God should have made only those persons who would act freely but always choose the right. This way, moral evil would not occur, but its prevention would not impinge on either divine or human freedom. But such a scenario is impossible for two reasons. First, it presupposes a view of God's knowledge that we rejected in the previous chapters. It assumes that God knows the future and can adjust his actions accordingly. But what God knows about the future is what actually occurs. Hence, God does not have a list of persons whom he knows do evil or wrong and a list of persons whom he knows do right and then chooses the first to exist. God simply is not a divine novelist; he creates people and in that creation takes a risk regarding how they will use their freedom, since what God knows about them depends upon how they act.

There is a view of God's knowledge according to which God knows all the actions that people would freely choose under all circumstances and then uses this information to decide whom to create. On this view God has what is called middle knowledge: knowledge of all counterfactuals of free will. This means that God knows states of affairs that not only never will occur but are the alleged results of free choices that never were or will be made. But in what sense can it be said that these possible choices would be part of God's knowledge? To be such, counterfactual conditionals of free will must be true. But on what basis are they true? Not by correspondence with any actual occurrence or state of affairs, for since they are counterfactuals no actual occurrence or state of affairs is described. Neither are they true in that they are logically necessary, for they are contingent propositions. Neither are they true because they are causally necessary, for they are conditionals of free choice. Neither are they true in that they correspond with or follow from the possible persons' character or intentions, for persons' characters are not necessarily determinative of their action. In sum, counterfactual conditionals about free acts of actual or possible agents have *no* grounds for being true and hence cannot be part of God's knowledge. They cannot provide a basis for God's creating particular persons and not others.

Second, God cannot guarantee that all the people he creates will do only right without removing or violating their morally significant freedom. It is possible that all those created by God do only the right and good; unfortunately, history has not worked out this way. People have chosen and undoubtedly will continue to choose to do wrong or evil; God has given them the option, hoping that he can lure them into doing the right and entering into the divine covenant. It is we who reject doing the right and entering into the covenant. God offers; we refuse. The result of this refusal accounts for the tremendous amount of moral evils that we see around us.

Natural evil and natural laws

As we just noted, many, many individual instances of pain, suffering, and dysfunction serve no specific greater good. The freedom required to realize the greater good of moral and spiritual development makes moral evils possible, for it allows us to choose to do evil as well as to choose to do good. But the evils experienced in moral development are not themselves necessarily or always means to that greater good of moral and spiritual development. The same applies to natural evils. As I write this, a friend is rehabilitating, working her way back from a fall and spinal injury. We might want to ask why God allowed her to black out and fall. My aunt, her daughter, a friend at church, and the former president of my college all contracted Alzheimer's disease and died after years of memory loss. A friend discovers she has breast cancer and undergoes a radical mastectomy and painful chemotherapy. My colleague's daughter contracted leukemia and died after several months of suffering. A pastor friend was hit by a vehicle while riding a bicycle and suffered serious brain injury. A colleague gave birth to a young boy who was deaf and blind and suffered frequent epileptic seizures. I am sure that all of us can add to this list of natural evils—instances of pain, suffering, and dysfunction for which humans cannot be held morally accountable.

Many, if not most, natural evils are gratuitous: there is no apparent specific good that they serve. Hence, to understand how they might fit into

God's providence, we have to consider broader reasons that allow them to be possible. In the previous section we suggested that there are moral evils that are not desired or willed by God but are made possible by the freedom necessary for us to enter into personal relationships that God desires. This same reasoning applies here. Natural evils *per se* are not desired by God but are the outworking upon sentient creatures of the stuff of the universe and the natural laws according to which our universe operates. In order to make it possible for moral agents to exist and function, creation had to be made of something and be ordered, and this ordering requires some set of natural laws that govern our physical existence. As a result, the possibility arises that sentient creatures, including ourselves, can and undoubtedly will be negatively affected at times by how these laws play out in nature. Generally the combinations of laws and matter work out for good; without these laws and matter we could not build buildings, sail ships, fly airplanes, grow crops, eat food, see, breathe, swim, walk, talk, and so much more. In effect, without these laws and the structured matter of the universe we simply could not live and function. But what makes for our good also produces our pain, suffering, and dysfunctions. It both enables and thwarts the realization of our desires. The natural evils we experience are simply the consequences of the natural system of which we are a part, by-products made possible by what is necessary for the greater good. God could have avoided making sentient beings, but then God would have failed to realize his desire to have beings in the kind of relationships he wants. A world with free persons making choices between moral good and moral evil and choosing a significant amount of moral good is better than a world without free persons and moral good and moral evil. Hence, God had a reason to create a world that operated according to natural laws. His creation of a natural world order, along with its concomitant pain and suffering, is consistent with his overall providential plan.

Miracles

Lurking behind this discussion lies the question whether God could miraculously intervene to prevent at least some moral and natural evils. Miracles are an important part of God's providential arsenal, for in miracles God introduces into nature new causal conditions that affect the outcome. So if God can perform miracles, is there not a middle ground between the two options we just considered, namely, that God operates the world by miraculous intervention and that God operates by natural laws? Or again, is there not a middle ground between God granting humans freedom and

God operating the world of human affairs by miraculously intervening in every case to bring good out of human evil? If God is good, powerful, and all knowing, is there not a possible world where God intervenes miraculously to prevent evils, but where the remaining events are governed by natural laws? In such a world God would intervene to prevent moral and natural evils, but where no pain or suffering are involved or where events would not negatively affect sentient creatures God would take a hands-off approach, allowing events to follow a regular pattern or course. In such a hands-on/hands-off scenario, sometimes causal conditions a and b would result in a particular effect e, while at other times the very same causal conditions would be followed by an effect of a different sort because God intervened to change the causes to protect humans and other sentient creatures. For example, heavy snowfall in the mountains and the collapse of snow walls would normally cause an avalanche to proceed down the mountain slope according to the relevant natural laws when no sentient creature lies in its path. But should a skier be present, either God will see to it that the conditions that cause avalanches under normal circumstances will not produce this effect this time, or God will maneuver the avalanche in such a way that it misses the skier. In effect, God uses his power and knowledge to meticulously alter the course of nature each time sentient creatures are affected so that good always results, but at other times when pain and suffering is not involved God allows nature to proceed in its regular fashion.

The problem here is that natural laws such as the law of gravity assert universal and necessary connections or regularity between phenomena. If God allowed events sometimes to follow a regular pattern and sometimes not, there would be no natural laws regarding such particular events. Without natural laws, the appeal to regular patterns of nature would be specious, for regular patterns presuppose normative natural laws that describe or govern the course of events. Without regular patterns we cannot distinguish what is regular from what is irregular. "Regular pattern" has meaning only within the context of natural laws. Furthermore, should this absence of universal and necessary connections be widespread, as would be required in order to prevent all moral and natural evils, God would have to constantly perform many miracles, with the result that the world would have few if any natural laws. The world would, in effect, be governed by miraculous intervention—the "extreme" we were trying to avoid. Thus, although this so-called middle ground might remove instances of pain and suffering, it would make rational prediction and rational action impossible, and hence make moral action impossible.[7]

---

7. This solution faces other serious problems as well. Even invoking miraculous

Someone might object that we don't really need natural laws to make rational predictions so that we can act. All we need is statistical probability. As long as events happen generally in a particular way, this coupled with God's regular non-intervention in instances involving the absence of evil are enough to allow us to predict probabilities and make rational choices. General regularity is enough to enable us to consider, rationally plan, and carry out actions, and hence to be moral beings.

This objection is suspect in that it attempts to correlate two unknowns. It assumes both that we have some knowledge of the grounds of rational action in a world not governed by universal natural laws and that predictability is possible where only some pattern of events is present. It is true that we entertain rational expectations, make predictions, and calculate rational action on the basis of statistical probability. We do not experience uniformity and necessity. But this probability is itself based on the assumption that the universe is governed by natural laws, that there really is uniformity, at least above the sub-atomic particle level. It is a function of the fact that causes a and b always do result in e (either a specific state of affairs on the macro-atomic level or one within a set range of limits on the subatomic level). But given a situation where the world contains no regular, necessary connections between specific causes and specific effects, in calculating action one would then have a statistical probability of a probability.

But, it might be argued, could not God intervene in a miraculous fashion in human events at least to remove the worst moral and natural evils and therefore providentially show us his love and concern? Failure to intervene in a miraculous fashion seems inconsistent with God's goodness; a good being acts to remove evils wherever possible without removing a greater good. Two replies are in order. First, it is very possible that God already intervenes to remove the worst of the evils. If God did not exist and act in this world, we would be much worse off. A good God is restraining the worst of evils as part of God's providential plan. The story is similar to that of the child who does not see how her parents provide for her; she is not hungry because they give her food, not cold because they clothe her, not lonely because they accompany her. Not knowing anything different these parental activities are not recognized. But were the parents absent or not caring, she would have a far different set of life experiences.

Second, when the principle is advanced that a good God would remove the worst evils, it must be recognized that the term "worst evils" is a comparative notion. Suppose that God removed all worst evils in the world,

---

intervention, events might not be resolvable in ways that please everyone. While the park groundskeeper wants it to rain on the park, the picnickers want sunshine and dry weather.

say those of 10^7 magnitude. There would still be instances of "the worst evils" in our world, namely, evils of 10^6 magnitude. Were these removed, by the same reasoning about God's obligations God would have to remove the now-worst evils (those of 10^5 magnitude), and so on. In short, by consistently applying the principle that a good God is obliged to intervene to remove the worst evils, we derive the consequence that God as providential is required to remove all evils, moral and natural. But this would be to remove our significant freedom and to operate the world by miracle, against which we argued above.

It is no reply to this argument to suggest that there is a point where the worst evils are not so bad (say, at 10^3 magnitude) and thus could be allowed by a good God. For an individual who knows only these evils, evils of 10^3 are the worst and would seem to argue forcefully against God's goodness or existence in the same way that the critic appeals to the worst evils humans experience today. The critic would not countenance the argument that since greatly worse evils are conceivable, say 10^{12}, which a good God prevents, the present evils of 10^3 magnitude are not so bad after all and thus would not count against God's goodness.

In short, it is not that God does not perform miracles to help us avoid pain and suffering or to eliminate it. Indeed, the story of Jesus is of a miracle worker who ministered repeatedly, even to the point of exhaustion, to relieve human suffering. More than 25 percent of the text of the Synoptic Gospels is devoted to recording his healing ministry. We are questioning the power or ability of God to work miracles. And it is not that God does not respond to petitionary prayer, our topic in the next chapter. What we argue is that running the world by miracle would be contrary to God's objective of having beings capable of moral action and developing moral character, with whom God can enter into a personal relationship. Miracles fit well into God's providential actions; running the world by miracles does not, for it disallows the rational calculation of what we could do that is necessary for our development as moral beings.

Concluding considerations

We have argued that it is possible to reconcile God's providence with human suffering. To this end we presented several morally sufficient reasons why a providential God might allow and at times even cause suffering. No single morally sufficient reason applies to all instances of pain and suffering. Further, God may have reasons for allowing suffering of which we are unaware.

It is just that our experience suggests that the reasons we considered reasonably may be counted among those reasons.

We also contended that these reasons are not definitive. Why we or other individuals suffer in a given instance may be more complex than exemplified in one reason. We might never know in any particular case what reason God has for allowing suffering. This uncertainty may leave us existentially unsatisfied. But from not knowing why we are suffering we should not jump to the other extreme to suggest that God has a purpose in all our suffering, that the evil we experience will always lead to a greater good. As we argued above, gratuitous evil is made *possible* by a greater good, but the gratuitous evil experienced need not itself lead directly to a greater good. And it need not do so to be consistent with the goodness of God. What is required is that the possibility of evil be necessary for some greater good, not that each instance of evil itself leads to a greater good.

God too suffers; that is the story of the incarnational death. Jesus suffered empathetically for others (John 11:35) and himself underwent excruciating torment on the cross. For both, reasons are given—so that others can see God's glory (John 11:40) and to free us from death (Heb 2:9). God is no stranger to suffering; it results from God's providential involvement in the world and engagement with free creatures.

But divine suffering does not license us to interpret individual instances of human suffering as emulating that of the divine. A kind of perniciousness occurs when people use evil to suggest to others that this evil fits in with God's providential plan for them, that God wills this evil for their good. Sometimes this may be the case, as in the cases of discipline or punishment, but it is not clear that this always or even frequently occurs and that we can identify such cases. Gratuitous evil remains evil not leading to a greater good; God allows it even though the specific evil does not lead to any specific greater good. Of course, evil might lead to a greater good insofar as we deal with our pain and suffering in wholesome ways that lead to development of our character or empathetically help others address their pain, suffering, and dysfunction. These evils call for loving and caring responses, but God does not inflict these evils on one person to call forth loving responses on the part of others. To torture one person—say a child—so that another person—a parent—develops character is malicious.

Some might think that in attempting to provide reasons why God might allow or even cause pain and suffering we do not fully appreciate the extent, force, and severity of pain and suffering. It might appear that, in holding that God has morally sufficient reasons we are trying to turn evil into good or are denying the reality and depth of evil, that we have no genuine concern for the victims of suffering. This definitely is *not* the case.

That God has morally sufficient reasons for evil does not alter the character of the evils: evil remains evil, horrendous evils horrendous. That a physician has a justifiable reason for administering anti-rabies medicine does not make the injections and the effects of the drug any less painful. What the reason does is show that the physician takes seriously the potential pain and suffering from rabies itself, and calculates that the injected medicine will ameliorate the pain and suffering. Similarly, the fact that we consider reasons that God might have for allowing or causing pain, suffering, and dysfunction shows that we take seriously both their existence and the belief that God is providential. We acknowledge the awfulness of inhumane human actions; we empathize with those who struggle with natural evils and take meaningful steps to ameliorate the suffering.

Further, that we suggested reasons for allowing suffering does not mean that we should not act in the world to relieve whatever pain and suffering we encounter. We should not stand by passively while others suffer, saying that it is God's will. One way that God acts providentially is through our own actions to prevent or alleviate suffering. We are God's hands and feet on earth. That God has morally sufficient reasons for allowing suffering is consistent with our working to ameliorate suffering.

It must be admitted, however, that after all is said and done, after we look at how providence can be reconciled with suffering, and that God himself suffered, we may feel unsatisfied with the results of this chapter. We may want more, for in any particular case we want to understand the reasons why God allows us to suffer.

> The problem of pain is not one you can neatly solve, then file away. It roars to life every time a tornado touches down, every time a neighbor learns bad news about a disabled child, every time someone in my family hears the ugly diagnosis of cancer, every time a physical symptom forces me to the doctor. We are born slathered in blood and bodily fluids, amid tears and cries of pain; we die in like manner; and in between birth and death we ask, *Why?*[8]

If God is a god of miracles, why does not God intervene more frequently on the behalf of others and us? We look for answers and, indeed, pray for God's intervention. If we were satisfied with our state, we simply would accept the evils that happen to us and others. But we are not satisfied, and the evidence for this is our use of petitionary prayers. We ask God to intervene on our behalf and on the behalf of others, to work miracles to remove the results of moral and natural evils or to prevent them in the

---

8. Yancey, *Bible Jesus Read*, 46.

first place. We ask God to heal, change the weather, calm the storms, rectify economic conditions, change people's character and behavior, rescue friends from terrorists or mine cave-ins, bring people to acknowledge and love God, and many other things. Petitionary prayer is an essential aspect of the believer's life. So we need to turn in the next chapter to the question of the relation of divine providence to petitionary prayer.

Chapter 10

Providence and Petitionary Prayer

SINCE GOD IS INVOLVED providentially in the world and in our individual lives, and since God seeks our response to him, we find a natural connection between providence and prayer. Paul writes that we should "pray in the Spirit on all occasions with all kinds of prayers and requests. With this in mind, be alert and always keep on praying for all the Lord's people" (Eph 6:18). Christians identify four types of prayers: adoration, confession, thanksgiving, and petition. In prayers of adoration, we praise God for who God is in terms of his greatness, goodness, power, wisdom, love, and eternity, properties we addressed previously and that play such a critical role in divine providential acts. In prayers of confession we acknowledge our moral and spiritual short-comings and request divine providential mercy and forgiveness. We acknowledge that although we do not deserve grace, we may request it because we are in covenant relationship with God. In prayers of thanksgiving we express our deep gratitude for God's daily provision for us and for others.[1] In prayers of petition we ask God to be involved providentially in the world and in our individual lives. We want God to change the future to benefit us and others, to address our suffering and the difficult situations we and others face. In this chapter our interest is in petitionary prayer, where we request that God take action because we believe that God knows about our situation and can effectively intervene in the world, our lives, and the lives of others. Petitionary prayers provide one way for the Christian to be in constant contact with God. "In everything, by prayer and petition, with thanksgiving, present your requests to God" (Phil 4:7).

But noting the importance of petitionary prayer in our lives also introduces several serious problems. First, why should we make petitionary prayers? If a good, loving, almighty God already knows our situation and

---

1. "The OT has no independent concept of 'thanks' as distinguished from 'praise.' ... [T]he hiphil of *yādâ* often occurs in parallelism with other terms for praise, e.g., the piel of *hālal* and the piel of *zāmar*.... Moreover, it never has a human being as its object." Dillman and Opperwall. "Thank," *International Standard Bible Encyclopedia* 4: 822.

seeks our good, why should we have to petition God to act on our behalf? A perfectly good God already will be acting for our benefit. Second, should we petition God once or should we continue our supplication when we do not receive a response or the response we desire is not granted? If God knows what we and others truly need and we pray for it, why do we need to pray repetitively about the same matter. Once should be enough; God will hear it. Third, how should we pray? Should we petition God in the same way that we ask other people, that is, for specific things that we believe we need or that we think would benefit us or others? Or should we pray that God's will be done in each case, so that prayer is not so much directed at God as it is directed toward our willingness to submit to whatever God wills for us? And finally, why is it that seemingly so little for which we make prayers of petition occurs, especially in light of Scriptures that assure us that God will give us that for which we ask in faith, believing it will be done? This chapter will consider these four very difficult questions. A fifth question, How does God bring about change in our circumstances, we will address in the next chapter.

Purposes of petitionary prayer

Before we address these questions, we need first to consider the purposes of petitionary prayer. Two primary reasons are suggested. First, in petitionary prayer we request divine providential action in the world. From our vantage point we see things that need addressing: people are sick, injured, dying, hungry, poor, jobless, and so on. People are not living the way they should: nations are at war, co-workers cannot get along, children rebel, people seek happiness or escape in serious drug abuse, scammers cheat vulnerable people, spouses abuse each other or are unfaithful, gangs roam our streets, and thieves empty our stores. Or we think that nature needs to be altered: a tornado bears down on us, a cyclone pounds our town, someone is drowning, and dangerous animals confront us in the backcountry. People have spiritual needs to which we want God to attend. Our petitionary prayers ask God to intervene on behalf of the requesters in their own lives, in the lives of others, or in the natural world. "God, please . . . ." We will term this the *objective* purpose of prayer. Prayer asks God to do something that, if God does not act in response, will not get done. "Is anyone of you sick? He should call the elders of the church to pray over him and anoint him with oil in the name of the Lord. And the prayer offered in faith will make the sick person well; the Lord will raise him up" (Jas 5:14–15).

Providence and Petitionary Prayer

Second, we engage in petitionary prayer to alter or manifest the condition of the requester. Petitionary prayer discloses our true desires, showing God what we really consider important and significant. It demonstrates our ferventness about particular issues. It reveals an attitude of dependence on God; we are willing to have God involve himself in our lives. We recognize that we cannot resolve the issues or negative situations ourselves; they are too big or we lack the necessary resources. We trust that God in his grace will assist us. We will term this the *subjective* purpose of prayer. Prayer asks us to reveal something about ourselves that, more than likely, we would keep hidden, or it asks us to change in ways we would not do otherwise.

A critical question concerns which of these functions of petitionary prayer is primary. Some say that if God already knows what we need, want, or desire and understands our ferventness, then the objective piece seems unnecessary. God does what God does. Prayer fundamentally has a subjective purpose, preparing our own hearts for what lies ahead. Thus, they reduce petitionary prayer to the subjective. But this appears to be inadequate, for the very nature of the prayer as a request indicates that the objective purpose is primary. We do not usually pray, "God, change me," but rather ask for things to happen because we want real change in the world. Other dimensions of prayer—adoration of God, confession of our sins, and thanksgiving for past intervention—suffice to change our hearts and open us to God's intervention. Making petitions introduces volition into the mix: we want God to act to bring about change and believe that God can do so. The point of our making a petitionary prayer is precisely the petition.

This is not to deny the subjective dimension of petitionary prayer. As recorded in Matthew 6:5–7, attention is to be paid to the subjective. Jesus rails against those who pray for the wrong reason. They pray to attract the attention and praise of others around them rather than to carry on a meaningful conversation with God. Form and context replace substance and piety. Jesus also rejects the repetition of meaningless ritualistic words. Rather, we should pray in secret, with meaningful content. The only reward that matters is that which God gives us (and it is not clear whether the reward refers to a positive response to the petition). Thus, petitionary prayer reveals something about our motives; we are not to pray to be heard and seen by others so as to elevate our religiosity, but rather to engage in intimate conversation with the Father. The goal is not to receive a reward even from God, although Jesus promises such for those who seek this kind of intimate relationship. It is to seek conversation with God in the secret place. At its base, prayer is a conversational practice

Yet in the very same larger context of the Sermon on the Mount, we are commanded to ask in ways that indicate that petitionary prayer trades on its objective purpose. "Ask and it will be given to you; seek and you will find; knock and the door will be open to you. For everyone who asks receives; those who seek find; and to those who knock the door will be opened" (Matt 7:7–8). God, we are assured, "gives good gifts to those who ask him" (7:11). The asking is followed by receiving; good gifts result from the very asking. James writes that if we lack something (here, wisdom), we are to ask God to give it to us. Elsewhere, even more strongly, James affirms that we do not have because we do not ask (Jas 4:2). Asking is both sufficient and necessary for us to receive what we need. It is not that petitionary prayers simply help us to subjectively recognize our need or discern our motives; we recognize our need, pray to God in faith to meet that need, and God gives it to us. Yes, prayer has a subjective dimension; it is possible to ask without receiving when we ask from the wrong motives (Jas 4:3). Thus, we need to attend to our motives when we pray. But more than the subjective is emphasized; the objective part is important, indeed, necessary, if we are to receive what we need. We cannot reduce petitionary prayer simply to the subjective on the grounds that God knows ahead of time what we will ask. Petitionary prayer has an objective purpose, namely, to invoke God's will and power to bring about something in the world that we think might not occur had we had not prayed. We do not know whether or not it will happen without our prayer, but we believe that if we ask and God acts, God can bring it about.

These purposes are consistent with each other. When we pray we can be thinking about our own motives and willingness to submit to God and about changing features in the world. The issue concerns how these get deployed in prayer. As we will see, the difficulty will be to maintain both purposes as we consider the four critical questions we posed. It is non-controversial to believe that prayer effects a subjective purpose; the problems arising from the subjective are practical: how can we avoid making prayer merely a show of our religiosity, articulateness, religious learnings, piety, or spiritual fervor? Prayer in the public arena is often *pro forma* or a medium for preaching to the audience. The intellectual problems challenge us regarding not only how to make room for the objective dimension of petitionary prayer, but what happens when we emphasize the biblical assured response to this objective dimension. The problems of petitionary prayer, we might contend, lurk in the objective function.

Why pray if a good God already knows?

Jesus says, "Your Father knows what you need before you ask him" (Matt 6:8). This striking verse, which invokes God's omniscience, establishes that the purpose of petitionary prayer is not to inform God about our situation or that of others. God already knows what we and others need and desire.

Further, since God is loving and perfectly good, presumably God already desires and seeks to benefit us. God is not out to harm us, but acts for our good. According to what might be called a *principle of goodness and beneficence*, a perfectly good being would do what it can to maximize the true goods for each person while not precluding providing equal or greater goods granted to others.[2] God, as a perfectly good being, would want to maximize our quality of life without lessening the goods for others.[3]

Praying with the realization of both of these facts is illustrated by Catherine of Genoa. "As I think about you, my spiritual children, I see that God's pure love is attentive to all of your needs. It is because of this tender love that I need not ask anything of God for you. All I need to do is lift you up before his face."[4] But if God knows what is good and already seeks our good, why do we pray? What is the objective purpose? It would appear that we are trying to change God's mind about something, so that God would bring to pass what would or might not otherwise happen. But this creates a puzzle. On the one hand, if we are trying to change God's mind or purposes, this should be the very last thing we would want to do since God already intends our good. We don't want to alter that good intent but rather simply trust that God seeks and will deliver our good. On the other hand, if we are not trying to alter God's mind or purpose, what is the objective purpose of petitionary prayer? Is there any objective reason to make petitionary prayers at all? Objectively speaking, it would appear that petitionary prayers are otiose, since such prayers ask God to intervene to meet needs or wants for ourselves or others about which God already knows, and to resolve such God presumably will act. In short, it is difficult to see any objective purpose of petitionary prayer to an omniscient, omnibenevolent, and almighty God.

If we are to address and attempt to resolve this puzzle we need to understand and assess the presupposed principle of goodness noted above: a perfectly good being would do what it can to maximize the true goods for each person without lessening the goods for others. In particular, should we assent to this principle? As we noted in chapter 4, Morris and Davies might agree that this principle could apply to humans but would strongly object to applying it to God. Since God's goodness has nothing to do with moral duties, God has no moral obligations. Although this would provide a neat way

---

2. Murray, "God Responds," 243.
3. Basinger, "God Does Not," 260.
4. Catherine of Genoa, in Foster and Smith, eds., *Devotional Classics*, 183. The editors attribute this to her *Life and Doctrine*, although I have been unable to substantiate the attribution.

out of the problem, we affirmed in that chapter that moral obligations are necessary to understand God's goodness. Hence, denying that this principle applies to God is not an option for us.

So do we have to assent to this principle of goodness? First, even on the human scale, it is not obvious that persons must satisfy this obligation in order to be morally good. We can introduce cases where good persons will reduce the goods available to some people in order to benefit others. This is the heart of a communitarian approach to social goods. A good government might pass a progressive income tax, such that those with higher incomes are taxed more heavily in order to benefit those at the bottom of the income scale. Those at the higher economic level will have less money and consequently their goods reduced so that those at the lower economic level will have increased resources to purchase necessary goods. Redistribution of wealth is justified by its provision of a greater overall good; indeed, in some cases it might be justified even if the overall good is reduced. Or consider the Affordable Care Act, in which young, healthy adults are coerced by penalties to purchase health insurance they might not want so that their premiums will help subsidize those who cannot afford the health care coverage or who have high health care costs. Even the practice of eminent domain, where land and property is taken from someone (whether or not at a fair price) to benefit the public. These are just three examples of what are held to be morally justifiable actions, where a person who is good does not necessarily benefit all other persons equally and might even reduce goods for some people in order that others might benefit. The policy of selective benefit is justified in that it leads to an overall greater good while not eliminating goods available to those affected, since, for example, healthy young people still receive medical insurance from which they may benefit should anything happen to them, or those whose land is confiscated receive some compensation for their loss. Or it may be justified in that the worst off are better off under this particular policy than they would be under any alternative policy and the total amount of good in the world is not significantly reduced.[5] Hence, because intuitively we would not call the goodness of those who create or implement such programs into question, the principle of goodness as stated above is suspect.

It might be responded that this communitarian approach to social goods applies to humans because of their limited resources. Since humans

---

5. One might think here somewhat of John Rawls' principle of difference, where policies of distributive justice are to be implemented in ways that benefit everyone, but that especially benefit the least well-off, even though they do not maximize the good of those most well-off. The question of overall good differentiates the utilitarian from the communitarian at this point.

have a limited pool of goods, one has to distribute these goods in ways that benefit the most people or at least the neediest people, even if some are either disadvantaged or their goods are not maximized. But God has unlimited resources, and hence God would not have to deprive anyone of their maximal goods in order to make goods available to others. All persons' goods could be maximized from God's storehouse of goods.

But even with unlimited divine resources it is not true that everyone's goods can be maximized. The reason for this is that we are involved in social interactions which require certain limiting conditions in order to function. Suppose that God maximized the financial resources of every person. Economic order would disappear because of the resulting gross inflation. We could not conduct financial transactions for goods because every item could have competing bidders with infinite resources. It might be replied that this is only because the goods themselves are limited. But it is not clear that God could make unlimited goods available in this finite world. Again, the economic consequences would militate against it. Further, one can only imagine the environmental catastrophe that would result from each person having unlimited, maximized resources. Consider a similar situation regarding death. Suppose that God to be good had to maximize the goods of infinite life extension and continuing birth. In a world in which no one would perish but births would continue, overpopulation would result and social ills would multiply dramatically. It is true that God and his resources are infinite, but the world God created is finite, such that maximization of goods for individuals would wreak economic, social, and environmental havoc.

Second, does a good person have an obligation to maximize the goods or quality of life of others? Again, it is not obvious what justification could be given for such a claim. Bill Gates has tremendous resources, which he has not used to maximize my quality of life or that of my veteran neighbor who needs money for a hip replacement. There are many sorts of things Bill Gates could do to improve my circumstances or those of others, and even after his recent outstanding and commendable benevolence with regard to addressing malaria and Ebola, he still has the resources to benefit my neighbor. It does not follow that he is not a good person for failing to maximize my good or that of my neighbor—or the particular good of anyone. Indeed, were he so obligated, the category of supererogatory actions (actions that are especially morally praiseworthy but not obligatory) would be severely limited, for one would be obligated to maximally better the lives of others, including the least fortunate, at possibly great personal cost. Supererogatory acts that now stem from mercy and generosity would become part of our obligations. It is neither that Gates has an obligation to share his justly earned wealth, nor that if he shares it we have a right to determine whom he benefits, but his sharing of it as he intends is his prerogative. When he does share, we praise him for it, but his goodness does not rest entirely on his supererogatory actions, although those actions manifest his goodness.

We often think of God's actions in terms of mercy and grace. Mercy and grace are free gifts that God bestows, not because God is required to do so but because of his love and concern for us. But affirming the truth of the goodness principle as applicable to God makes mercy and grace obligatory, such that they no longer function in a supererogatory way.

To defend the principle of goodness, David Basinger gives the analogy of parents who as good are obligated to maximize the quality of life for their children. But even this special relationship between parent and child does not require this kind of maximization. My son would have been especially pleased—and he believes his quality of life would have been better—had I responded to his request and bought him a jet ski while he was in high school. Suppose he is correct that his life quality would have been improved, and suppose that I agree that he could have had even more fun during those years so that his quality of life or happiness was improved by driving his jet ski on our neighborhood lake. From the fact that I did not purchase one for him it does not follow that I was not a good father. If I had purchased one it would have been a nice gift, but I doubt whether purchasing it was an obligation, regardless of how much money I had. It might have been a supererogatory action, but certainly not a duty. My goodness will be shown in keeping my duties, in showing my love, in my mercy and justice, but not in maximizing my children's and other people's goods.

Basinger says that the principle *might* be weakened, so that a good person has the obligation to meet the *basic* needs of others (although he prefers the stronger version). For example, good parents have an obligation to satisfy the basic needs of their children. They should provide food, shelter, clothing, education, and other things for their children. Failure to do so reflects on the moral character or goodness of the parents. This, of course, is true so long as they are my children and the children are unable to fend for themselves. But as they get older, it becomes less of an obligation because greater goods can be achieved by facilitating both their independence by getting them to act on their own and a realization of their dependence on others in life (that they belong to a community) by not automatically meeting every need. That is, maximizing their quality of life goes beyond supplying them with goods; it includes affecting their character and understanding.

In sum, the objection to petitionary prayer from God's knowledge and benevolence rests significantly on this principle of goodness, and as we have seen, the formulation given above is unsatisfactory. We have not seen any compelling reason to understand personal goodness in terms of maximizing benefits to others. We addressed personal goodness in a much more thorough way in chapter 4. There we argued that a good person has a good character, possesses relevant knowledge and wisdom, has good motives or intentions, does right acts, acts freely, and has a meaningful choice with respect to the rightness or wrongness of the action. This way of understanding the goodness of a person circumvents the benevolence problem, for it does not require that a good person maximize benefits to others. It is not that good persons will not do this, but rather that this does not constitute one of their obligations. We indeed leave room for mercy, grace, and generosity: manifestations of supererogation (acts that are not obligatory but morally praiseworthy).

It might be said that we have not resolved the tension, only shown that the above formulation of the problem is inadequate because it relies on a particular and mistaken duty—the formulation of the principle of goodness. One might still wonder why petitionary prayer is needed if God knows about and cares for us. To resolve the tension, we need to ask what greater goods are made possible by petitionary prayer. We will take this up later in this chapter.

Why pray repeatedly about the same thing?

When we pray, we often pray repeatedly for the same thing in the same prayer, using different words. If the request is not granted with the first prayer, we make subsequent prayers to God for the same thing. We might petition God for the same thing over hours, days, even years. We make it such that our prayers, often for the same thing, are ever before him. Scripture suggests precedence for this practice.

Jesus tells a parable about a persistent widow who repeatedly came to the judge in her town pleading for justice (Luke 18:1–7). The judge steadfastly refused to hear her case but finally relented because of her persistence. It might be thought that the text draws a parallel with God, who will bring justice to those to cry out to him day and night.

Several things need to be made clear initially. First, the judge and God are not parallel; the judge does not fear God. Second, the judge apparently cares little about justice, whereas God centrally cares about justice. Third, the judge delays, putting off the widow and repeatedly refusing to grant her justice, whereas God responds speedily to the cries of the chosen. Finally, the judge relents out of self-interest; no reason is given for God's dispensing of justice, but even a quick perusal of Scripture reveals God's great concern for dispensing justice to the poor, widows, orphans, and oppressed. Hence, the two cases are not parallel or analogies, but rather present great contrasts. The reluctant judge is not in the likeness of God.

At the same time there is one important similarity. In both cases the supplicants are persistent in their requests: the widow is persistent in her plea for justice, and God's "chosen ones cry out to him day and night" (Luke 18:7–8). So although this text does not require the repeated pleas of petitioners, it certainly presupposes them in the discussion; Jesus says that God will answer repeated pleas quickly and not put them off.

Other texts reinforce that prayer may involve repeated requests. Hannah keeps on praying to the Lord, requesting that God end her childlessness (1 Sam 1:12). Nehemiah confirms that he prays "before you day and night for your servants, the people of Israel" (Neh 1:6). Similarly with the psalmist, "[M]y God, I cry out by day, but you do not answer, by night, but I find no rest" (Ps 22:2); "Lord, you are the God who saves me; day and night I cry out to you" (Ps 88:1). Jesus tells us to be continually both watching (present imperative) and praying (present participle) that we will escape the terror to come (Luke 21:36). Paul writes that we should pray continually (present imperative; 1 Thess 5:17). We are to continually make requests of God in all seasons or occasions (Eph 6:18). In fact, Paul says that he prayed day and night, petitioning that he would again visit with the Thessalonians, and asks them to do the same for him (1 Thess 3:10; 5:25). These texts do not say explicitly that in order to receive the answer to our petitions we should pray repeatedly about the same thing, but they model repeated, persistent, continual prayer, which strongly suggests that praying for something over and over is recommended, if not the norm. Yet, as Matthew 6:7 notes, the repetition is not to be a meaningless babel or ritualistic recitation, but a meaningful communication.

But why should one have to keep petitioning God to respond to our prayer? Knowing everything, God hears our prayers the first time and knows the situations about which we are concerned. Why then should we have to reiterate the prayer? It makes sense to pray for different things and hence continually be in an attitude of prayer. But repeated petitionary prayer for the *same* thing or desired event seems less like requesting a good God to act than begging God to act, at least until God tires of our supplication. God does not forget what we have prayed for. Hence, from the objective point of view, there seems little point to repeatedly praying for the same thing.

If repeated prayer makes any sense, it will have to be part of a practice or institution of petitionary prayer. There must be a good that the practice of repeated, fervent prayer accomplishes. One possible good is that it reveals our sincerity, demonstrating that we really want what we have prayed for to happen. But this runs into God's omniscience, for as we noted above we do not pray to inform God either about our request or our sincerity. If God knows everything about us at this moment, he would know that we are sincere. If repeated prayer revealed to anyone his or her sincerity, it would be to the persons making the prayer. They would disclose to themselves how important the issue about which they prayed was to them. This establishes a subjective reason for this aspect of the practice of petitionary prayer, but the objective dimension remains unaddressed.

A second response is that repeated prayer shows our continued dependence upon God. We wait, patiently or often impatiently, for God to act. We continue to realize that without God we cannot obtain that for which we ask, just as the widow cannot obtain justice without the judge's action; we need divine assistance. But again this reinforces a subjective view of petitionary prayer. Prayer is for our benefit. If there is to be an objective dimension for the practice, it would have to be introduced to keep us "at our prayers." That is, God must be seen as wanting us to continue petitioning but at some point answering our repeated prayers "quickly" in order to motivate us to continue to pray. Otherwise, we would become discouraged and abandon continued pleading with the divine. The objective dimension is necessary to give us hope that eventually our petition will be answered. But even this justification is subjective in that it is directed to maintaining our hope and persistence and is not directed to the content of the prayer.

The need for repeated prayer creates additional problems for the contention that petitionary prayer enables us to more clearly discern God's will. Where our petition is not granted the question arises whether the negative response reveals God's will or whether we should continue to plead our case. If the former, then we have little reason to continue to pray for that thing, for God has denied it. If the latter, then the question arises when we should stop petitioning God and take the "No" as expressing God's will. When does continued pleading without a response become a "No"? In effect, we get little guidance about God's will when we incorporate repeated petitioning into the practice of petitionary prayer.

In sum, while repeated prayer serves a subjective function, it is difficult to discover an objective reason for requiring continued petitions even when made part of a practice or institution of petitionary prayer. The good it serves in the practice is a subjective good; it functions to further our realization of our dependence on God. And even the possible objective dimension serves the subjective dimension of giving us hope.

How should we pray?

How should we make our petitionary prayers? Christians often use the Lord's Prayer as an effective model for our prayers. Interestingly, it contains two different patterns of petition. *On the one hand*, Jesus taught that we should pray for God's will to be effected. "Your kingdom come, your will be done, on earth as it is in heaven" (Matt 6:10). We are to accede to what God desires, to mesh our wills with God's will. Jesus' prayer in the garden models this when he puts aside what he wants and his request that he not undergo the suffering involved in what is about to happen in favor of what the Father wills (Luke 22:42). We will follow C. S. Lewis in identifying this as pattern A, where we make petitionary prayers conditionally. We ask God for a specific thing, but then qualify our request by saying, "If it is your will." Our petition involves both acknowledged submission to the will of God (the subjective feature) as well as a "voice of joyful desire."[6] In this case there is no certainty that what we ask for God will grant because any response depends entirely on God's desires and will and the consonance of what we ask for with his will. To be implemented our request must fit into and be consistent with God's plan or purposes. "This is the confidence we have in approaching God: that if we ask anything according to his will, he hears us. And if we know that he hears us—whatever we ask—we know that we have what we asked of him" (1 John 5:14–15).

Thomas à Kempis provides a moving example of this type of prayer.

> O Lord, You know what is the better way, let this or that be done, as You please. Give what You will, and how much You will, and when You will. Deal with me as You know, and as best pleases You, and is most for Your honor. Set me where You will, and deal with me in all things just as You will. I am in Your hand: turn me round, and turn me back again, even as a wheel. Behold, I am Your servant, prepared for all things; for I desire not to live unto myself, but unto You; and oh that I could do it worthily and perfectly.[7]

On the other hand, the Lord's Prayer models petitioning God for specific items that we need or desire. "Give us today our daily bread. And forgive us our debts, . . . and lead us not into temptation, but deliver us from the evil one" (Matt 6:11–13). We are to ask for our daily needs (food) and for our spiritual needs (forgiveness and deliverance) to be met. Lewis terms this pattern B, which involves asking God for specific things, and then in

---

6. Lewis, "Petitionary Prayer," 143.
7. Thomas à Kempis, *Imitation of Christ*, III, 15, 2.

faith trusting confidently that God will respond affirmatively to our request. We are to ask in faith: "When you ask, you must believe and not doubt. . . . Those who doubt should not think they will receive anything from the Lord; they are double-minded and unstable in all they do" (Jas 1:6–8).

Besides the Lord's Prayer, the Bible contains numerous instances of specific requests. A frequent Old Testament request is for children. Abram (Gen 15:3), Isaac (Gen 25:21), Leah and Rachel (Gen 30:17, 22), and Hannah (1 Sam 1:10–11) provide poignant examples. But the Old Testament also records requests for protection (Pss 64:1; 140:1), deliverance (Pss 17:13; 143:9), healing (Gen 20:17; Num 12:13), and continuance of Davidic rule (2 Chr 6:17), among many other things. Requests made of Jesus are also specific. Martha asks Jesus to act on behalf of her ill brother Lazarus (John 11:25). Jesus' mother Mary (in a roundabout way) asks Jesus to intervene at the wine shortage at the wedding in Cana (John 2:3–5). All sorts of people in need—blind, very ill servants and daughters, those with skin and blood diseases, paralysis, and demon possession—specifically petition Jesus for healing (Matt 9:27; 20:30; Luke 5:12; 5:18–20; 7:3–5; 8:41–48; 9:37–40). What is noteworthy about these requests is that they are not proffered as conditional on divine will.[8] This is consistent with Jesus' promise that whatever we ask in his name, if we have faith, will be given to us (Matt 21:21–23). The example given of a mountain thrown into the sea may be a metaphorical hyperbole, but the point is that even great requests will be answered affirmatively. James concurs that it is appropriate to make specific requests: "You do not have because you do not ask God" (Jas 4:2).

So the question arises: Should we ask for specific things but qualify our request with the statement that the Lord's will be done, or even more generally simply ask that the Lord's will be done, or should we pray for specific things or events, trusting on God's promises that he will respond positively to our requests?

On a view that invokes meticulous providence, following pattern A—to ask that God's will be done—can only have a subjective purpose. After all, God has planned every event and has the power needed to bring about everything that God desires. Hence, it would be self-defeating for God, having this power and knowledge, not to bring about what God desires and plans. If God desires something and can bring it about, asking that God's will be done does not seem to be the sort of request that we need to make or would be making. There is nothing for us to request; God is in control of

---

8. It might be thought that Matthew 8:2–3 is an exception, "Lord, if you are willing, you can make me clean." The emphasis is not so much on Jesus' plan or will, but on his power to do whatever Jesus wants. The man thus wants Jesus to want that the man be healed.

everything and does what God wills. On meticulous providence, a prayer for God to do his will is not for God but for us. It reflects a subjective attitude toward prayer, showing our submissiveness to God, our willingness to accept whatever God has in store for us and others. We realize that whatever happens accords with God's will and we consent to it.

In chapter 2 we rejected meticulous divine providence, arguing instead for a cooperative approach between God and humans in bringing about events in the world. There is no evidence that God has laid out for us a detailed, meticulous life plan that we are to accept or to which we are to adapt. God gives us wisdom and direction, but not a blueprint for our lives. We are to seek to do what God desires of us (Matt 7:21). But this passage does not support a blueprint scenario. We are to do good and not evil, to bear good and not bad fruit, to respond to God's initiatives. It is true that God might lead us to do particular things as we go through life. God told Gideon to tear down the altar built to Baal (Judg 6:25). God led Peter to the Roman Cornelius, and at Troas God called Paul to bring his church-planting mission across the Aegean Sea into Macedonia (Acts 10; 16:10). But we get no follow-up that God called Paul to each of the cities that he visited or that God had a definite Mediterranean itinerary for Paul to follow. That God makes specific callings or guidances cannot be denied, but neither can it be generalized to preclude us from making critical decisions about what we think is good and the accompanying appropriateness of making specific requests to God from our own understanding of our needs. We might be mistaken about what we need, but that provides no reason not to make a particular request. God treats us as free persons, not as automatons, so that in seeking God's guidance we make decisions about our life journey.[9]

We agree that God has desires, a will, and purposes. But God incorporates us into these in order to realize his goal to have meaningful relationships with us. God's purposes include our responsive return of his love and willing cooperation in administering his world as stewards on his behalf. Since God gives us freedom with respect to his desires and purposes, it is possible, and Scripture indicates that it is the case, that God's will often is not done. We use our freedom to counteract what God desires. Indeed, we have so frequently rebelled that God took the radical step of becoming incarnate and dying a sacrificial and healing death in order to correct the direction that we were going. Yet even here, people reject the proffered gospel. In such an understanding, it makes sense to pray that God's will be accomplished. The prayer for God to exercise his will requests that God bring about what he desires while incorporating us as his hands and feet into his actions in

---

9. Sanders, *God Who Risks*, 285–86.

the world. It not only expresses our willingness to accede to God's desires but also our desire to cooperate with God in achieving his ends. It requests that God reveal his will to us, use his power to accomplish it, and give us the strength, wisdom, and courage to participate in that accomplishment, all the while respecting the freedom necessary for us to be moral agents who want to engage with God. On this view, praying that God's will be done merges the subjective and objective, for the petition is that God, in carrying out his will, bring about what we ask, as well as bring us and others by persuasion and enlightenment to know, love, understand, judge according to, and implement his will.

Both pattern A and pattern B are consistent with a providential God who includes our decision making as an important feature in what he does. In both cases the petitioner believes that God can act in response. The tension has to do with the expectations of the petitioner. On model A the petitioner relinquishes the certainty that the petition will be fulfilled, since whether or not it will be fulfilled depends on its concordance with God's will. As Lewis notes, the petitioner must be prepared for denial. On model B, the petitioner expects, indeed, is told to expect in faith that God will grant the petition. The petitioner would be disappointed with denial, since God promised that we would receive whatever we asked in faith, believing.

So can we relieve the tension about how we should pray: with petitions conditional upon God's will or with petitions unconditionally based on our trust that God will respond affirmatively? Before we work toward a solution, let us advance the final difficulty.

Why are so few requests answered?

We have seen that the problems we have posed regarding petitionary prayer often leave unscathed the subjective benefits of petitionary prayer. But as we noted from the outset, we want if possible to protect the objective dimension of petitionary prayer, and much of the debate comes down to understanding the way the objective dimension runs through Scripture. As we have noted repeatedly, the difficulty is created by the assurances given us that if we ask, it will be given; if we seek, we will find; if we knock, doors will be opened to us (Matt 7:7–8). We are promised that if we have faith, whatever we ask in Jesus' name God will give us (Matt 21:21–23). "I will do whatever you ask in my name, so that the Father may be glorified in the Son. You may ask me for anything in my name, and I will do it" (John 14:13–14; see also 1 John 3:22). We are to ask and not doubt; not wavering, but trusting (Jas 1:6). "Anything" indicates a very broad promise. These passages commit to strong promises, full of hope and assurance. On this hope, many of our prayers are answered, for which we are to thank God.

With the exception of James 1:6–8, which puts faith as a necessary condition, these passages place no necessary conditions on our requests. In Jesus' teaching not even faith or asking in Jesus' name are given as necessary conditions. Rather, both are given as a sufficient condition: if we have faith, if we ask in Jesus name, God will do it. The passage does not say that if we don't have faith or don't ask in Jesus' name, God won't do it. This point is important, for it shows that prayer is not about us and what we do but about God.

"Again, I tell you that if two of you on earth agree about anything you ask for, it will be done for you by my Father in heaven" (Matt 18:19). All things considered—I am sure I can find another person who will pray with me—this presents a very powerful, providential promise. It leaves little room for ambiguity: God will grant the petitions we make of him, including and especially in a corporate setting.

But if no necessary conditions are placed on what we pray for, and if faith and asking in Jesus' name are two sufficient conditions (and there may be others), why are so many of our requests apparently not granted? As we noted in the previous section, if the necessary condition were to ask in accord with God's will, we could more easily understand not receiving what we asked. But these strong Matthew passages do not speak of necessary conditions and hence raise the issue of unanswered requests. I ask in faith for healing of Janice's back, for Tim to get the meaningful job he desperately needs, for creating stability for the troubled marriage of Wendy and Dan, for the end to the civil war and killing in Syria, Darfor, and the Central African Republic, for resolution of the Israeli–Palestinian conflict, for tuition for Jonathan so that he can complete his education—and yet months and years drag on for pain, for unemployment, for war and conflict, and educational postponement. We must admit that after long seasons of praying in faith, we begin to waver.

It might be suggested that other statements in Matthew 7 qualify the obvious "getting for asking." God knows what is good for us and others, and so our requests and their answers have to be understood in that light. "Which of you, if his son asks for bread, will give him a stone. Or if he asks for a fish, will give him a snake? If you, then, though you are evil, know how to give good gifts to your children, how much more will your Father in heaven give good gifts to those who ask him!" (Matt 7:9–11). The qualification here might be that although Jesus promises that God will grant all requests, what God in fact gives is only the good. (It should be noted that it does not say that God only gives the good that we *ask for*; God gives us good, even including things like discipline that we might not consider as good.) But if God gives us only what is good, it might be that when our prayers are not answered, it is because what we request is not good, either for us or for others. God knows what is good for us and others, and so our requests and their answers have to be understood in that light. Requests that God take another's life or injure them in retaliation for what they have done to us are prayers for which we should not expect a positive response (yet on this account many Old Testament prayers of petition seem out of bounds—Pss 3:7; 17:13–14). This is an easy case, but the same might not hold with more difficult cases, for example, with respect to a dying parent or friend. We might pray that someone not die, but God cannot consistently respond affirmatively to prayers for healing that denies death, for this is contrary to the natural system that governs our world. Should none of us (and whatever else we pray for—our pets, plants, or lawn) not die, serious population and environmental issues would encumber our planet. If our children requested something that we deemed not good for them, even though they thought it was good and we promised to answer their requests, we might justifiably refuse their request—on the grounds that parents know best. In short, perhaps we should read Matt 7:7–8 (and all other similar passages) in light of vv. 9–11, for although it is not clearly stated that the latter provides a condition on the former, in fact it does so.

But then other conditions might be introduced as well. Our requests might go unanswered because what we request would require God's removing someone's significant freedom. Petitions that request that God change the will and choices of others must be tempered with the condition that God generally respects human freedom. Hence, prayers requesting that God bring particular persons to love and serve him must be prayed with the realization that God wants their free, not coerced, response. This is a difficult dimension, especially when it comes to asking God to bring other people into relationship with him. We want God to act to bring our children, our parents, our siblings, and our friends into divine communion. We might request, for example, that God convict our children of their sin and return them to an intimate relationship with himself. Such a request, although proper and necessary, would require that God interfere with, if not remove, their freedom, so that the love the children return would not be freely given. We believe that reconciliation would be desirable. At the same time, we must remember that God wants persons' free, uncoerced love and obedience. It would be proper to pray that God use maximal persuasive power; this runs consistent with our emphasis on our free choices to enter into loving relationships with God. We can appropriately request that God through the Holy Spirit convict people and attempt to persuade them to come into a loving relationship with God, but to pray for compulsion goes counter to the scriptural scheme. Thus, there are self-imposed limits on what God can do and on what we should ask for. It is appropriate to ask God to persuade but not to coerce others to acknowledge Jesus as their lord.

However, with both of these conditions—asking in accord with what God knows is good for us and respecting human freedom—it must be recognized that we must abandon what might be taken as the *prima facie* meaning of the Scriptures noted in the first paragraph of this section. The unconditional will have to be qualified, and whatever qualifications we envision, as we will see, have to do with the structure and purposes of petitionary prayer.

Greater goods of petitionary prayer

To address the difficult problems this chapter poses we need to think more seriously and carefully about the nature and functions of petitionary prayer. The first thing to note is that petitionary prayer is a form of *conversation* between us and God. Where God does not automatically and unrequested satisfy all our desires, petitionary prayer becomes not only possible but exceedingly meaningful because it is a form of deep communication. Our very engagement in prayer is a great good in itself. Since God desires a personal, covenant relationship with us, having us regularly engage in petitionary prayer is one way to encourage a conversational relationship. If all goods are automatically supplied, conversation between God and us is unnecessary; expectation rather than petition and thanksgiving would dominate.

Second, God not only encourages conversational petitionary prayer, he has established it as a particular *practice*, an exercise that God desires that we do regularly. God wants it to be part of our routine, to be done "without ceasing." Petitionary prayer is a practice that achieves several desirable goods that justify the practice. That is, the very practice of petitionary prayer has significant value that outweighs the absence of the practice. The value is found not only in the goods achieved by petitionary prayer, but especially in the goods made possible by the practice itself. These goods provide the reason why God instituted and sanctioned the practice of petitionary prayer. We need to identify and inquire into the benefits that arise and that God desires from being in a conversational mode.

Michael Murray suggests that *one significant good* of the institution or practice of petitionary prayer is that it *keeps petitioners from idolatry*, which biblically is always a sin. Idolatry comes in many forms, but Murray has in mind the idolatry that comes from the belief in our own self-sufficiency.[10] As the story of Adam and Eve suggests, we believe that we do not need God, that we can accomplish what we want to do and get what we need on our own. We become like gods when we replace God at the center of our lives with our self. We are our own idols. Being a petitioner changes all that, for when we are put in the position of petitioners we quickly realize that we depend on God for many things, including our basic daily physical needs, our spiritual needs, and our discretionary wants. If we were self-sufficient, we would not need to ask for divine (or any other kind of) assistance. In the practice of petitionary prayer "the creature is kept from that sort of idolatry that leads her to look only to nature or her neighbor for her daily bread rather than [to] God. In this way, the creature remains humble in the face of the recognition that God is the ultimate source of all goods and thankful for this sustained provision."[11] Every time we ask for something we are reminded of our true position in the divine economy; we are the created, not the creator and sustainer. "Every good and perfect gift is from above" (Jas 1:17), not from ourselves. Since idolatry is a sin, and since sin is a serious offense against God, the conversational practice achieves a significant good in revealing and emphasizing this.

Deuteronomy captures this theme of (in)dependence and idolatry.

> When you have eaten and are satisfied, praise the LORD your God for the good land he has given you. . . . You may say to yourself, "My power and the strength of my hands have produced this wealth for me." But remember the LORD your God, for it is he who gives you the ability to produce wealth, and so confirms his covenant, which he swore to your ancestors. . . . If you ever forget the LORD your God and follow other gods and worship and bow down to them, I testify against you today that you will surely be destroyed. (Deut 8:10, 17–19)

Three serious objections to this justification of the practice of petitionary prayer arise. First, this feature of creating a practice to avoid idolatry is not unique to petitionary prayers. Other spiritual practices like prayers of thanksgiving also remove idolatry. Thanksgiving reveals our dependence upon God and thereby instructs us in the practice of gratitude.

Murray replies that petitionary prayer works differently than thanksgiving, for it "harnesses the appetites of the believer's physical body and forces those appetites to serve the needs of her spirit."[12] It physically and

---

10. Murray and Meyers, "Ask," 314.
11. Ibid.
12. Ibid., 315.

emotionally encourages perseverance, which would fade from an emphasis merely on thanksgiving. After a while we might tire of offering thanks for what God provides and begin simply to take for granted what is provided. Thanksgiving becomes something either rote or non-existent. But our needs and wants that form the topics of our petitionary prayers do not cease; they are persistently present and almost always individualized. As such, they push us to do more petitioning and hence further enforce our understanding of being dependent, which in turn leads to more genuine thanksgiving. In effect, petitionary prayer does not replace but enhances prayers of thanksgiving.

A second serious objection is that this emphasis on curbing idolatry reduces petitionary prayer to the subjective, where the practice of petitionary prayer serves our benefit. Murray attempts to correct this by noting that "[o]ne important consequence of reading the practice of petitionary prayer in this way is that its benefit cannot be realized if the petition is not efficacious. In fact, one might go so far as to say that, on this account, provision for daily needs must, to some extent, hang directly on believers' petitions."[13] If petitionary prayers become non-efficacious, despite our or others' pressing physical, emotional, and mental needs, we will despair and abandon the practice. The fact that our prayers are at least sometimes answered spurs us on. The practice must be accompanied with the condition that God established an "economy of blessings such that on some occasions he makes provision of goods dependent on petitions."[14] That is, if the practice is to have objective content, then the practice must be coupled with the view that some goods will depend on the petitions. This does not mean that all petitionary prayers will be successful or efficacious all the time; some things that we think are good and petition for God does not grant. What is necessary is that occasions of fulfillment be frequent enough to keep us persistently engaging in the practice. But again, this justification reduces the practice to a primarily subjective intent. Periodic fulfillment ultimately serves the subjective purpose to keep us in conversational engagement and is not an end in itself.

A third objection, noted by Murray, to prayer having the purpose of keeping us from idolatry is that if this constitutes an adequate justification for the institution of petitionary prayer, one should find that believers would be in a much better economic or social position because of their petitionary prayers than nonbelievers. Since petitionary prayers are at least sometimes successful and nonbelievers don't make petitions to God at all

13. Ibid., 316.
14. Ibid., 317.

or at least don't believe on faith or ask in Jesus' name, the believer should be distinctively better positioned in this world. Believers' needs, wants, and even desires should show a greater percentage of being met than unbelievers. However, this is not the case. "The fat pagans, who have all they want of caviar, much less bread, are ample in number as well as girth. They seem to be living, corpulent proof that prayer is just not efficacious, at least in the sense that it is a necessary condition for provision."[15] The psalmist similarly notes that it is often the case that the wicked have it good while the good suffer.

> For I envied the arrogant
> > when I saw the prosperity of the wicked.
> They have no struggles;
> > their bodies are healthy and strong.
> They are free from the burdens common to man;
> > they are not plagued by human ills. . . .
> This is what the wicked are like—
> > always carefree, they increase in wealth. (Ps 73:4–5, 12)

Murray responds that the institution of petitionary prayer is meant only for believers.

> [B]eliever and nonbeliever live under different economies of blessing. While the unbeliever does not need to pray for her daily bread, the believer must. The reason for this is that God has different aims for each and thus holds them accountable to different standards. The believer already recognizes God as Creator, Sustainer and Provider, and has the further responsibility of maintaining and growing in this faith. One way for God to cultivate this deeper faith is by establishing the relationship of petition-and-provision outlined above. For the unbeliever, on the other hand, such expectations on God's part would be in vain. The first order of business with the unbeliever is to bring her to faith—cultivation of that faith must come later.[16]

God out of his goodness simply supplies the wants and needs of nonbelievers. It would be cruel, Murray says, to impose this practice on nonbelievers and thus deprive them of goods when they are denied participation in the conversational practice because they have not entered into a position of faith.

15. Ibid.
16. Ibid., 318.

But this discussion is skewed by the shadow of the goodness principle. If we do not require God to be maximizing the good for everyone and if we reject meticulous providence, as we did in chapter 2, then there is no need to worry about discrepancies. God can shower his mercy on whomever he wishes, whether a believer or not. God has an obligation to be just, but justice is not equality. Indeed, the assumption that nonbelievers do not petition God and that God would not hear them if they did is undoubtedly presumptuous, if not mistaken. If God causes it to rain on both the just and unjust, God can also hear and respond to their prayers, perhaps for the very reason Murray suggests—that through this nonbelievers may find faith in God. As we noted above, faith and asking in Jesus' name are not necessary but sufficient conditions for obtaining responses from God. It is a mistake to say that God has no relation to nonbelievers, although that relationship may be different from that with believers.

Furthermore, if one reads further in Psalm 73 we get the hint of an answer to this question, namely, that the good that we should be attending to and worrying about is not wealth and health, for in the end we all lose that (73:18-20).

> I am always with you;
> you hold me by my right hand.
> You guide me with your counsel,
> and afterward you will take me into glory. . . .
> Earth has nothing I desire besides you.
> My flesh and my heart may fail,
> but God is the strength of my heart
> and my portion forever. (73:23-26)

Our lives are, as it were, a short dream, at the end of which all of this is stripped away. What is of value is being connected with God, and this is what happens in the conversational practice of petitionary prayer. The comparison between the well-being of believers and nonbelievers is ultimately not about material goods but about God, for we are made to be in relation to God. The practice of petitionary prayer fosters that relationship, so that ultimately, if the comparison is correctly done, the believer comes out "ahead" because of the overwhelming advantage of being known by and in a deep relationship with God. We recognize and seek God's counsel and find our strength not in ourselves but in God, who is our strength and guide.

Murray suggests a *second good* realized by the institution of petitionary prayer, namely, that through it *we can understand God's will*. If we ask that God's will be done (and even if we don't) we can discern God's will by noting which petitions God answers and which not. Those petitions granted accord with God's will; those not granted do not. "Through this process, her desires and her prayers become increasingly aligned with God's, and the more closely her prayers are aligned with His will, the more likely they are to be granted.... By learning which prayers are effective and which are not, the believer may in turn learn to become more righteous, and thus better conformed to the image of God."[17]

But this justification also faces serious problems, not the least because it is difficult to discern whether what happened occurred because God favorably responded to the petition or it did not happen because God denied the petition. Suppose that Janice is healed from severe back pain; does it mean that God healed her and that it was God's will that she be healed? Or was it one of the goods that God supplies independently of our asking: God did not take action but simply allowed the processes of nature to work their way. Or suppose that she is not healed from severe back pain; does that tell us that asking for her healing was not in God's will? Discerning God's will is quite an ambiguous undertaking. It is true that the Bible presents cases where God's will is given directly, and Murray appeals to these examples. But these events and the accompanying revelations, I suggest, are outliers. It is no easy task to discern God's will, and the response to petitions, whether positive or negative, does not clearly provide an accurate discernment method. How do we know whether the event is really an answer or not to prayer? Hindsight may prove helpful, and hence may be employed, but it is not a fully reliable guide. It tells us what happened but not the cause of or why it happened.

Further, this view runs counter to the strong promises that our prayers asked in faith will be answered. "Ask and it will be given to you; seek and you will find; knock and the door will be open to you. For everyone who asks receives; those who seek find; and to those who know the door will be opened" (Matt 7:7–8). Receiving, we are assured, follows the asking. If we take this seriously, there would be no denying our requests.

Further, if we grant that God allows for human freedom, this affects our petitionary prayers that involve the choices and actions of others. If persons are free, it is perfectly possible that they act against or frustrate God's will. In such cases the failure of our petitions to be answered has less to do with God and discerning God's will and more to do with the free actions of others who thwart God's and our wills. God's granting of freedom makes responding to petitionary prayer extremely more complex, for through his self-limitation God no longer has a monopoly on power (a point we made

---

17. Ibid., 319.

in chapters 5 and 6). God works through others who themselves have God-derived freedom and power to act according to their wills.

In short, it is not clear that discerning God's will is a justifying good for instituting the conversational practice of petitionary prayer. The responses we receive to such prayers are not only very ambiguous but subject to competing reasonable interpretations. This does not mean that we cannot infer from the effects that God played a causal role, but it is to acknowledge the difficulty of going from effect to cause when that involves persons and intentions. We will say more about God's intentional intervention in the next chapter.

Third, the practice of petitionary prayer allows God to grant us the good of *freedom in response to God*.[18] If God simply provided out of his benevolence for our good, we would lose our independence. We would simply rely on God to take the initiatives that result in our good rather than being active participants in the world. We all know people who love to be waited on hand and foot. They might be relatives, husbands, or wives for whom we make their bed, clean, cook and serve their meals, wash their dishes and laundry, do their shopping, take them to the doctor's office—all the while they sit and watch TV, sleep, or read. They are couch potatoes—or worse. In attempting to make life good for them we really have harmed them. They no longer request things with a "please" or express their gratitude; they simply live lives of expectation of being served. A first step in their rehabilitation is to move them from a position of passivity to having them at least make polite requests for assistance and express their gratefulness. A second step is to get them as far as possible to take responsibility for their own welfare as independent beings, even if in some cases their physical condition makes them to varying degrees dependent upon others.

The same holds true for children. Initially we must care for the every need of infants and young children. We feed them, change their diapers, bathe them, carry them around, and soothe them: all because they cannot do these things for themselves. But if this continues, so that everything is provided for them without their requesting it or participating in the household program, they do not develop their own initiative, responsibility, and independence. To shake them loose from indolence and dependence we must get them to engage in the practice of asking and, indeed, of doing things for themselves and on their own initiative.

The same argument can be developed for the practice of petitionary prayer. We have already contended in chapter 2 that God created human beings with the freedom to be in meaningful relation to him. God created

---

18. See Stump, "Petitionary Prayer," 81–91.

us to be both dependent on his sustaining power and also independent to freely and willingly return love to him in a covenant relationship. If God simply provided for our good at every turn without our participation we would become not only completely dependent upon him but also ungrateful. Our expectations would wash out our appreciation of what God does for us. The practice of petitionary prayer gets us back into the game. We become aware of our need, realize our dependency, order our desires, and request God's assistance, with the result that in the end we freely render thanksgiving to God. Grace is balanced with labor. In short, the goods realized by the practice of petitionary prayer are double-edged: it makes us realize our dependence on God and encourages thanksgiving for what is provided, and it encourages our independence to freely ask and participate in divine providence for ourselves and others.

In sum, the practice of conversational petitionary prayer might be justified, not without questions, by appealing to its double, almost paradoxical good: it encourages the recognition of dependence on God for our goods, and it encourages independent and meaningful participation in God's providential action in the world. In both cases, however, it is essential that the prayers be answered frequently enough to encourage maintenance of the practice. But here is the major rub: this caveat puts the objective dimension of petitionary prayer at the behest of the subjective dimension. The objective dimension is not a primary end but rather functions to encourage the subjective ends of avoiding idolatry and of creating responsible independence. Putting the objective dimension in service to the subjective dimension creates a significant worry about petitionary prayer. It reverses the roles of the objectives we noted earlier in this chapter.

Addressing the problems

This worry, however, can be addressed by taking a broader look at the practice. We suggested that petitionary prayer is located in the context of a conversational practice. Prayer is conversation between us and God, and as in many conversations the conversants may have differing agendas while they engage in a common meeting point. In petitionary prayer the petitioners focus on asking favors that grow out of their personal understanding of their own and others' needs and wants. This accounts for the focus of the petitioner on the objective dimension of petitionary prayer and for the observation that the objective dimension is primary. Petitioners want their prayers to be answered; they want change to occur that will address their requests. Hence, from our human perspective as petitioners, the objective purpose is primary; we are interested in obtaining positive responses when we engage in the practice. And it is this that is frustratingly thwarted when we have to make repeated petitions for the same item day in and day out, when we have to ask according to God's will, and when we discover that many of our petitions go unanswered affirmatively. The biblical verses about asking and receiving noted above derive from a focus on the petitioner's viewpoint and concerns.

The petitioned stands in a position to grant the petitions (within the limits that we have already noted, for example, with the self-imposed restriction respecting human freedom or achieving some greater good). But the petitioned focuses on what he desires to arise or result from the conversation. The focus may be less on the requested favor (although that is not negated) than on the conversational relationship itself and the purposes for which the practice of engaging in the conversation was instituted. For God as the petitioned, the goals include engaging the petitioner in such a way as to bring the petitioner into a relationship with God, to the extent that the petitioner takes on the very image of God. The change sought is not primarily a change in the world, for God can accomplish this even without the petitioner's request. The change wanted is in the petitioners themselves, that they freely choose to become like God, seek what God desires, merge their will and intentions with those of God, and become God's instrument of change on earth. So, whereas for *us* the objective function is primary, for *God* the subjective is primary. In effect, the two are in both tension and perfect balance in the petitionary prayer, a situation revealed by both the tension and consonance of patterns A and B.

On a libertarian view of freedom we must couch our requests for God's actions in the context that God is likewise a free agent and thus is free to respond however he chooses to our request. God can respond affirmatively or negatively, according as God wills. The point here is that petitionary prayer is part of a conversation, and just as we often ask others to do something and we get mixed responses that do not always come with clear reasoning, so our petitioning God is a conversation. We want to conform to God's will, but we also request that God act in various ways. The tension reflects a double want: I want what you, God, want *and* what I want. It is bringing these two together in dynamic tension that can be seen as a goal of petitionary prayer.

No one put this better than Thomas à Kempis in another of his prayers.

> Grant me, O Lord, to know what I ought to know, to love what I ought to love, to praise what is most pleasing to Thee, to esteem what appears precious to Thee, to abhor what is offensive to thee. Do not suffer me to judge according to the sight of my

bodily eyes, nor to pass sentence according to the hearing of the ears of ignorant men; but to discern with a true judgment between things visible and spiritual, and above all, always to seek Thy good will and pleasure.[19]

It is not that God does not want us to make requests that he can answer; surely the passages that we noted above that assure us of God's positive response to our petitions encourage such request making. God has room for the objective, for God desires our good. Just as we want the good for us, so does God. But God's primary concern is with the goods that we have termed subjective, with the changes in the petitioners themselves, that meld their desires and wills with the good of God, so that they fully achieve becoming in the image of God.

It might be suggested that this is the point of asking in Jesus' name (John 14:13–14). Jesus' name is not to be thought of as a magical formula or incantation, where by invoking it the objective dimension of our prayers is achieved. Rather, the "name" here stands for the whole person.[20] When we pray in Jesus' name, we seek to align our desires with those of Jesus, such that our petition dovetails seamlessly with who Jesus is and with his desires for what happens on earth, in our lives, and in the lives of others. This is, in part, the heart of the Christian message: that we put God and his mission at the center of our lives, rather than putting ourselves there. The purpose of the practice is not only removing idolatry, as we noted above, but it is primarily Christian conformity to being in the image of Christ. Here we can locate one of the biblical meanings of the *imago Dei*. We are "to put off your old self, which is being corrupted by its deceitful desires; to be made new in the attitude of your minds; and to put on the new self, created to be like God in true righteousness and holiness" (Eph 4:22–24). God wants us to adopt a "new self, which is being renewed in knowledge in the image of its Creator" (Col 3:10). The *imago Dei* also has a functional dimension. The second creation story emphasizes that humans are given dominion over the earth, to take care of the garden God planted (Gen 2:15). Because God is the one who delegates power to humans, our dominion over the earth reflects God's ultimate lordship. We are to act—and accordingly pray—on behalf of God. God takes our self out into the world to act as the hands and feet of God's providence.

19. Thomas à Kempis, *Imitation of Christ*, III, 50, 7.

20. As Leon Morris writes, "This does not mean simply using the name as a formula. It means that prayer is to be in accordance with all that the name stands for. It is prayer proceeding from faith in Christ, prayer that gives expression to a unity with all that Christ stands for, prayer which seeks to set forward Christ himself. And the purpose of it all is the glory of God." Morris, *John*, 646.

To make this interpretation work, we have to abandon one-sided interpretations of these petitionary passages as complete in themselves and instead view them as one aspect of a two-dimensional practice of petitionary prayer. It is a practice where two persons engage in a conversation sometimes with differing agendas. We might struggle with the fact that aligning our will with that of God comes up against the declarations made by Jesus that asking is sufficient for God to respond affirmatively to our request. Focusing solely on this assurance drives a wedge between asking what is in accord with God's free will and asking for what we want with the assurance that asking in faith is sufficient to receive it. Only if we interpret these passages in the broader scope of an alignment of wills that is found in the deepest conversation can we resolve the tension.

It is only when we appreciate the bi-functionality of petitionary prayer—that as a practice it serves different functions for the petitioner and petitioned, but that God desires that these functions be united in harmonious relation—that we will be willing to compromise on our desire for the primacy of the objective dimension of prayer. He does not desire that we dispense with our objective concerns, but that we locate these within the greater purpose that God has for us and the world. So long as we see the practice only from our viewpoint of changing the world we will be dissatisfied with the lack of positive response to our prayers and with aligning our will with God's will. But when we see that the practice brings together the mutual interests of our desires to realize the objective of changing the world and God's desires to realize changes in the petitioners can we see that to demand fulfillment of every request misunderstands the purpose of petitionary prayer. We must first see its depth in the alignment of wills and purposes.

The story of David, Bathsheba, and their first son is instructive in this regard. Through the prophet Nathan, David learns that as punishment for his sin, the child born in adultery will die. "The Lord struck the child that Uriah's wife had born to David, and he became ill. David pleaded with God for the child. He fasted and went into his house and spent the nights lying on the ground." David's fervent petitions, however, God did not answer affirmatively; the change in the condition of the child for which he repeatedly prayed did not come about, and after seven days David noticed the servants whispering and asked whether the child had died. Upon learning that the child was dead, "David got up from the ground. After he had washed, put on lotions and changed into his clothes, he went into the house of the Lord and worshiped." Later his servants asked about his change of behavior, fasting while the child was dying and eating when the child had died. David answered, "While the child was still alive, I fasted and wept. I thought, 'Who knows? The Lord may be gracious to me and let the child live.' But now that he is dead, why should I fast? Can I bring him back again? I will go to him, but he will not return to me" (2 Sam 12:16–23). David realizes that nothing more can be done about the son; God did not grant his petition. But he realizes that more can be done about himself. His request having gone unanswered, he must continue in worship and communication with God. David does not get the affirmative answer he sought, but he persisted in his prayer. Once his situation with his son was resolved, he moved on. But he still maintained an attitude of trust and worship of the God whom he petitioned.

Chapter 11

Providence and Miracles

To COMPLETE AND CONCLUDE our treatment of divine providence, we need to discuss how God interacts with the world. One way to understand God's intervention is that God acts in the world by miracle. Miracles are providential, although they might serve other purposes. For example, the Gospel of John treats miracles not primarily as providential but as signs that authenticate the claims made by Jesus with regard to his relationship to the Father (John 20:31). Our interest in miracles is in their role as significant providential divine interventions. Earlier, in addressing pain and suffering as counterevidence to divine providence, we made the negative point that God cannot operate the world solely by miracle. But much more needs to be said about the nature and role of miracles. To more adequately understand miracles as *sign*ificant divine interventions, we will consider three interrelated questions.

First, how can we show that miracles really occur, that they are actual events? To establish that they occur we need to be able to recognize a miracle we personally experienced or witnessed or else authenticate a miracle account given by others. How are miracles recognized, especially if, as we shall argue, part of the definition of a miracle is that miracle events result from an act of God? Since we have access to the wondrous effect but not the imperceptible cause—that is, to God initiating the action to bring about the effect—it would seem that to identify an event as a miracle we need to be able to determine from the effects alone that God was the cause, which, given our finitude, appears *prima facie* to be very difficult.

Authenticating miracles occurs in two contexts. For one, how do persons who themselves witness what they take to be a miracle establish that what they witnessed was truly an event wrought by God and not merely a happenstance, a piece of luck, a coincidence, or simply an unusual natural event? After all, unusual or wonderful events occur with some frequency. As I look out my window a distinctive pattern of frost, produced by a -21 degree F temperature, creates a unique magical garden of ice ferns and frilly flowers across the bottom of the glass pane, never to be repeated exactly. For another, how can we credit the accounts of others who claim that a miracle occurred that either they witnessed or that they have learned about from evidence or other witnesses? That is, how can we show that the eyewitness or transmitted accounts of others are reliable? What makes witness accounts trustworthy? We must address both of these questions in thinking about the occurrence of miracles.

Second, to ask whether miracles really occur presupposes that miracles are possible. If miracles are impossible, then we do not have to inquire whether what we observed or what others reported was a miracle or not. If from the outset we know that miracles cannot be actual because they are impossible, other explanations of the unusual event must be sought. Some philosophers suggest that advancements in and the sophistication of science establish that miracles just are not possible. Not only are we becoming more knowledgeable about natural laws, but we are gaining a better understanding of what natural laws are. We recognize that natural laws are descriptive of the regularity of events rather than normative. Any denial of natural laws or affirmation that natural laws are violated is absurd. It would be denying what actually occurred, for what actually occurs is described in terms of natural laws.

Third, the second question regarding the possibility of miracles presupposes that we have a clear understanding of what a miracle is. How one defines "miracle" goes a long what toward helping us to clarify whether miracles are possible. As we shall see, miracles become impossible when we define them in a way that, in effect, makes them to be impossible.[1]

Defining "miracle"

Since questions about the actuality and possibility of miracles hinge on our definition of "miracle," let us begin with our first, underlying issue, defining "miracle," and then explore the relation of our definitions to the question whether miracles are possible. Some people understand anything unusual, extraordinary, wondrous, propitious, and naturally inexplicable to be a miracle. So it is that people speak about a miracle finish to a basketball game, where a player launches a desperation shot from the opponent's end and it goes through the net. Or persons will speak of their miraculous winning of the Powerball lottery or the passing of an exam for which they did not study. These characteristics feature in miracles, but our definition has to be more

---

1. Helpful treatments of miracles can be found in Swinburne, *Concept of Miracle*; Swinburne, *Miracles*; Brown, *Miracles*; Basinger and Basinger, *Philosophy and Miracle*; Twelftree, *Miracles*.

precise. Perhaps the most influential definition of miracle, still in vogue philosophically and theologically today, was advanced in the eighteenth century by David Hume. He argued that "a miracle is a violation of the laws of nature."[2] This definition afforded him a powerful tool whereby he could then proceed to show *a priori* that miracles are impossible. He structured his argument in this way.

1. "A miracle is a violation of the laws of nature."
2. Laws of nature are established by unalterable or uniform experience.
3. Therefore, uniform experience stands opposed to any miracle.
4. Therefore, miracles are impossible.

For Hume, this amounts to a "direct and full proof" that any account of a miracle must be false; no witness testimony could possibly establish any event as miraculous. At best we have an argumentative wash if the falsity of the witness account would be more miraculous than the event itself.

Granting that 3 and 4 follow from the previous statements, we need to address 1 and 2. Let us begin with 2. Statement 2 appeals to our uniform and necessary experience. However, on Hume's own account expressed elsewhere in the same book, experience cannot yield the universality and necessity needed to call something a law of nature. According to Hume, we cannot experience necessity; hence, we have no good reason to believe it is a property of things. Rather, the necessity that we speak about derives from a feeling we get from our experience of the constant conjunction between things. Our repetition of similar experience creates in us a propensity to believe that things or events are connected or connected necessarily.[3] Neither can we ever experience the universality of any causal relation. We have had many experiences where we observe that, for example, unsupported objects fall. But from this it does not follow that we have good rational evidence to show that unsupported objects *always* fall, for we have not experienced all or even the majority of falling objects. Our experience of falling objects is greatly limited. An indefinite number of such objects in the past we did not experience, we are not experiencing in the present all unsupported objects, and the future is yet to happen. What this shows is that, given our very limited experience, we cannot rationally claim that it is even probably the case that there is a natural law about gravity that shows that all unsupported objects necessarily fall. We may believe this, but beliefs arise from our sentiments. So, using Hume's own arguments, we have no reason to think that 2 is true.

2. Hume, *Enquiry*, 122.
3. Ibid., 85–86.

One might reply that at least we can use induction to establish that unsupported objects fall. That is, from our limited experience of unsupported falling objects we can inductively generalize to all such objects. Hume responds that this appeal to induction presupposes the principle of uniformity, namely, that all events with the same causes will have the same effects. But this very principle is based on induction and hence is not certain; we believe that the future will be like the past because the future we experienced when it became present was like the past. But then we have argued, Hume claims, in a circle. We have used experience to establish inductively the principle that the future is like the past, and have used this principle to ground the rationality of induction itself.[4] Since induction is founded on circular reasoning, rationally we cannot use induction to ground conclusions about universal laws of nature. In short, since the only grounds we have for establishing the rationality of universal and necessary natural laws are inductive and since the basis for induction is circular, we have no rational grounds to establish universal laws of nature. It is not that there are no natural laws; it is just that we have no good, rational reason to believe in such and no way to properly analyze as objective the conditions of necessity and universality that are required for there to be such. Hence, on Hume's very own grounds, 2 is false. Uniform experience fails to establish universal and necessary laws of nature, and his argument to the impossibility of miracles collapses.

Not only is 2 troublesome for Hume, so is 1, for in defining miracles as violations of laws of nature he has begged the question. Miracles do not dispense with laws of nature; the laws of nature are operative before, during, and after the miracle. Miracles do not violate natural laws but rather introduce a new causal element, namely God, into the event structure. With a different cause we get a different effect. In nature, when we introduce new causal elements we obtain new and different effects. If I make a pie with apples, I get apple pie. But if I substitute peaches, I no longer have apple but peach pie. The laws of nature regarding pie-making are not violated but operate this time with new causal conditions. Similarly, unsupported objects fall, we say, because of gravity. But if someone drops a ball and I intervene and suddenly reach out and catch it, it no longer falls because it is now supported. The laws of nature regarding unsupported objects still obtain; if unsupported it would continue its descent. It is just that new causal conditions—my hand—that support the object in question have been introduced. The object now is physically supported and does not fall. Change the causal conditions and you alter the effect. That is precisely what happens in cases of miracles; miracles involve changing the causal conditions. Adding God

4. Ibid., 49–51.

to the mix alters the outcome. As J. L. Mackie notes, "The laws of nature . . . describe the ways in which the world . . . works when left to itself, when not interfered with. A miracle occurs when the world is not left to itself."[5] This applies not simply to the world but to any event that is not "left alone." C. S. Lewis notes that a more adequate definition of miracle is "an interference with nature by a supernatural power. . . . A miracle is emphatically not an event without cause or without results. Its cause is the activity of God: its results follow according to Natural Law. In the forward direction . . . it is interlocked with all Nature just like any other event. Its peculiarity is that it is not in that way interlocked backwards, interlocked with the previous history of Nature."[6] Miracles do not break or violate the laws of nature; rather, with a new cause they feed new causal conditions into the natural pattern, after which nature takes over and things proceed apace. The sick persons Jesus healed got sick again; the dead he raised breathed and lived but later died; the food he multiplied nourished just like any other food; the water turned to wine obeyed the rules of liquidity throughout, tasted like wine in the end, and inebriated. It is just that in these relevant instances we cannot trace the causal conditions back to only natural conditions; a non-natural being intervenes. In sum, there is no reason to adopt the definition of miracles that Hume suggested. Other, more satisfactory definitions of miracles than that advanced by Hume are available. Hence, his *a priori* argument against the possibility of miracles fails. The presence and operation of natural laws, whether deterministic (universal) or probabilistic (statistical), do not make miracles impossible.[7] On either understanding of natural laws, new caused events are possible when the causal conditions are altered.

Miracles would be impossible only where no God exists to intervene in nature or where God is incapable of intervening or unwilling to intervene in nature. The latter is unworthy of consideration if we concede that God created the universe. If God can create, God can certainly intervene, and if God acts providentially, God is willing. Both hypotheticals are relevant to our considerations, since we are assuming that a powerful, providential God exists. One might search for adequate evidence for both of these contentions,

---

5. Mackie, *Miracle of Theism*, 19–20. Despite this, Mackie persists in defining miracles as violations of natural law, for this enables him to create a dilemma for the theist that allegedly disproves the actuality of miracles. Ibid., 26.

6. Lewis, *Miracles*, 5, 60. One might say it is interlocked backwards, but not done so completely.

7. Statistical probability applies where, in Quantum Theory, one cannot say specifically what will happen with respect to an individual fundamental particle, but one can probabilistically identify how a group of them will behave.

but that is not the point of this book.[8] Given the theistic framework of the topic of providence with which we are dealing, Hume's discussion gives us no *a priori* reason to think that miracles are impossible, although, as we argued in chapter 9, a world run by miracles is inconsistent with there being rational, moral beings.

The possibility of miracles

Since we cannot establish the impossibility of miracles *a priori* by definition, others have taken alternate routes to achieve the same end. Some adduce scientific advancements as providing compelling evidence that miracles are impossible. In the twenty-first century we know so much more about the expanding universe and its natural laws, with the result that miracles are just not possible. People in ancient times accepted them because they were ignorant of natural laws and hence took unusual events as wonders to be explained in terms of powerful divine activity. As Hume writes, "It forms a strong presumption against all supernatural and miraculous relations that they are observed chiefly to abound among ignorant and barbarous nations; or if a civilized people has ever given admission to any of them, that people will be found to have received them from ignorant and barbarous ancestors."[9] But now we are so much more scientifically sophisticated as not to be easily misled.

A close look at the argument reveals that the conclusion that miracles are impossible fails to follow from the premise that believers in miracles are ignorant of natural laws, for people's ignorance of relevant causal conditions does not imply that naturalism is true or that their reports are false. As a parallel, I might not know the natural laws of digestion, but it does not thereby follow that digestion of food when I eat does not occur or that my reports of it occurring are not to be trusted. What we look to is confirming evidence, a point to which we will return shortly. That I do not know natural laws implies nothing about whether God can intervene in human affairs and in natural events or whether my testimony reports are true. God's intervention is quite independent of my knowledge or ignorance. Further, not only does the conclusion not follow, the premises of this argument are themselves suspect. The reason people interpret events as miracles is precisely because they have some idea of the relevant laws governing events similar to those they witnessed and realize that the different effects must have resulted from

---

8. For arguments for theism, see Swinburne, *Existence of God*; Swinburne, *Is There a God?*; Craig and Smith, *Theism, Atheism*.

9. Hume, *Enquiry*, 126.

different causal conditions. They realize that what happened ran contrary to their normal expectations and past experience of regular phenomena. We might take biblical miracle accounts as examples. When Jesus healed the paralytic man who was lowered into a house through the roof by his persistent friends, those in the house already knew that paralyzed people do not normally get up from their bed and walk out the door when requested to do so (Mark 2:1–12). Paralysis removes these powers. They quickly realized, from the words Jesus uttered, that by his divine causal powers Jesus was able to bring it about that the paralyzed man walked. A new causal condition had altered the situation for this afflicted man. Had the people in the house been unaware of the normal course of events, they would not have thought that anything unusual had happened when he arose from his mat. Similarly, when through God Elijah extended the dwindling flour and oil supply of the widow of Zarephath (1 Kgs 17:15–16), this was recognized as a miracle only because people had an understanding about the laws that apply to using up supplies of flour and oil. When they are used, they do not replenish by themselves. What God did through Elijah introduced a new causal condition into the situation, and people were able to recognize it because of their regular experience. In short, rather than feasting on ignorance of nature and its laws, our understanding of miracles presupposes knowledge of relevant regularities and uniform conditions.[10]

The critic might reply that these ancients did not know all of the relevant causal conditions, but if they had they would have recognized that what they witnessed was merely a different kind of natural event. What made the event wondrous or unusual—a miracle in their eyes—was their ignorance of the relevant causal conditions. We might concede that this may be so in some and even in many cases. But for one thing this is not characteristic simply of the ancients; it applies in present day scenarios where even physicians may be stumped as to why a particular person is healed. There is nothing about ignorance of causes that is time-oriented; even with our modern sophistication we are often ignorant of the relevant or critical causal conditions. For another, this ignorance might affect whether we term a particular event a miracle or not, but ignorance of causes has nothing to do with establishing that miracles are impossible. We may look for natural explanations, but we are not guaranteed that we will always find them, a requirement if miracles are impossible.

Some suggest that advancements in and the sophistication of science with regard to understanding its natural laws establish that miracles are not possible. Not only are we becoming more knowledgeable about natural

---

10. Lewis, *Miracles*, 46–47.

laws, but we are gaining a better understanding of what natural laws are. We understand that they are descriptive of regularity rather than normative, and because of this we can have a more flexible interpretation of events. Natural laws are simply descriptions of how things actually happen. "Someone who insisted on describing an event as a miracle would be in the rather odd position of claiming that its occurrence was contrary to the actual course of events."[11] Hence, accounts purporting to be about miracles are not about the supernatural; they do not introduce anything into the scenario other than the natural. They simply give alternative descriptions of natural events, possibly suggesting that current descriptions are inadequate and need adjustment.

This argument raises questions concerning what natural laws are: are they normative or are they descriptive? Fortunately, we do not have to decide this matter, for neither makes miracles impossible. We have already seen, in examining Hume's argument earlier in this chapter, that the former does not establish the impossibility of miracles. And neither does the second view, for a descriptive account leaves open the possibility that new causal conditions will result in different effects. If natural laws describe what normally occurs, we have no reason to rule out events occurring that are abnormal or unusual because the causal conditions are abnormal or unusual. Further, natural laws are descriptions not merely of what occurs but are descriptions of regularities. "Natural laws describe what happens in a regular and predictable way," not just what happens.[12] As such, they allow for and do not rule out descriptions of alternative individual scenarios where regularity appears to be absent. In such cases we attempt to account for the absence of what is expected—the anomaly. Scientists look for repeatable anomalies that will allow them to extend old or devise new natural laws to cover them. However, where we have no repeatability and hence no basis for prediction, it makes little sense to develop descriptive accounts of unique, non-repeatable instances and term these natural laws. To do so blurs the line between natural law and mere event description. Hence, nothing in this view suggests that miracles are impossible. The affirmation of natural laws is not incompatible with and hence does not rule out the possibility that there are non-repeatable but individual, unique events of divine intervention about which we can give descriptions but do not presume the descriptions constitute natural laws describing regularity and predictability.

The parallel to divine activity is not regularity in nature but human intentional action. Just as human intervention as irregularly responsive

---

11. McKinnon, "Miracle," 50.
12. Swinburne, *Concept of Miracle*, 26.

to existing conditions does not accommodate formulation of natural laws regarding intentional behavior, likewise divine intervention cannot be subsumed under descriptions promising regularity. As with humans, we cannot predict exactly how God will act or respond to a request. This is why personal explanations, either of human or of divine action, differ significantly from natural explanations. "A scientific explanation of an event or state cites two things—some previous event or state of the world, and a law or laws of nature (or other true generalizations about what always or usually happens) of which it is a consequence that the latter state is followed by a former."[13] In personal explanation, we explain the occurrence of the event by appealing to some person or agent who brought it about intentionally. In the two cases, *why* something happened differs. Natural laws and prior natural conditions provide the reason why, given the cause, the effect occurred; in personal explanation we appeal to persons' intentions and their abilities to bring it about. We cannot reduce the latter to the former. Since we have differing types of explanations it would beg the question to require that descriptions of events that do not fit under current descriptions of regularities be descriptions that only invoke natural conditions. Personal explanations can be given that do not invoke natural laws alone as sufficiently explanatory.

Others have contended that now that we have a more sophisticated understanding of world literary genres, we can see that certain people in particular eras had a penchant for interpreting events witnessed by themselves or others as miracles. Such genres fit well with mythological understandings of the world but not with carefully researched historical or scientific accounts. We now know that we should not understand such literary accounts as the equivalent of modern-day history but as symbolic and mythological representations of some deeper truths or as superstitious imaginations and creations.

We readily grant that we can find a plethora of examples of literature that can be described in this fashion, but there is no reason to think that those who wrote the accounts or read them understood the descriptions as providing the type of accounts that we treat with scientific or historical intent and rigor. We face a danger of reading our literary categories back into the past and dismissing what the ancients wrote as somehow failing to describe or account for reality in the same scientifically critical and literal ways we do today. It is quite possible that the literary categories we employ are themselves insufficient to fully understand and appreciate world literature. But even if this critical description of ancient literature were accurate

---

13. Swinburne, *Coherence of Theism*, 131–32. See also Swinburne, *Concept of Miracle*, 53–57.

(which is greatly suspect), this does not show that miracles are impossible, only that some people in the past employed diverse ways to understand their experiences. They did indeed appeal to superstition, myth, and magic. But we have enough contemporary accounts in current literature of divine miraculous intervention to forestall the attempt to relegate miracles simply to past mythological and magic genres. Miracles have been reported in all eras, including the present, in diverse literatures, many with historical or factual intent. The attempt to show they are impossible by corralling them under a particular literary genre and then disposing of what is in that genre as unhistorical or scientifically untrustworthy is not only a gross oversimplification that ignores many contemporary accounts but also begs the question. It assumes from the outset that miracle accounts cannot be historical, factual, or trustworthy, and it is precisely this that has to be shown, not by a blanket dismissal of the reporting literature, but by a careful analysis of the literary type of the account, the claims to historicity by the accounts, and an assessment of the reliability of the witnesses.[14] We must attend not only to the literary composition but also to what other evidence that might be relevant and obtainable. We shall return to this later in this chapter.

In short, we have no *a priori* reason to think that miracles are impossible. Neither a scientific understanding of the world nor a literary analysis of miracle accounts serves to achieve this goal. As we have already noted, miracles are understood to occur within a theistic context. But unless the existence of God is impossible or there is good reason to believe that God does not exist, is lacking the power to intervene, or is unwilling to act upon nature and in our experience, we can continue to justifiably believe that miracles are possible. The affirmation or denial of the possibility of miracles truly is an issue of the paradigm we adopt: rigorist metaphysical naturalists cannot see them; theists look expectantly for them.

A deeper understanding of miracles

Granted, then, that miracles are to be understood as divine interventions in nature and that miracles are possible for a providentially-acting God, the remaining issue concerns whether we can establish that a miracle has or miracles have taken place. Rather than militating against miracles, natural laws are necessary for miracles to be recognized. Natural laws tell us what to expect given the presence of certain causal conditions. They help us identify

---

14. I would be remiss if I did not express my own bias. My mother reported the miraculous disappearance of an untreatable spot on her lung six months after its diagnosis, its inexplicable disappearance attested to by her attending physician.

both regularity and anomalies. Where normal causal conditions are present and operative and we get a different result (an anomaly), it may be the case that a miracle occurred. That it was a miracle is not certain. Upon witnessing an anomaly, scientists want to know whether the event is repeatable. It is possible that we simply are unaware of certain natural causal conditions or that we have a mistaken notion of the natural laws involved, or that what we think we witnessed was not what we thought it was. But natural laws and witnessing anomalies have the virtue of helping us to think that experiencing deviation from normal results just might put us in the presence of a miracle, although it may be difficult to confirm this.

If we are more specific about miracles, the issue draws into sharper focus. Although miracles are events of an extraordinary kind, given their causal origin, we should not classify every unusual, strange, fortuitous, or inexplicable event as a miracle. When we think about miracles as acts of God, we think that they occur as part of God's purposive activity in the world. They are intentional: they occur for a reason or a purpose, not willy-nilly. This suggests that a "miracle" may be defined as a special act of God that, according to a divine program, for a moral or spiritual purpose, produces in nature a new being or mode of being either directly by divine action or indirectly by means of natural processes according to natural laws. We can point out several significant things about this definition. First, miracles are divine acts. Humans might in some way function as the mediums for miracles; for example, they might occur at the request of humans. But technically miracles are brought about by God, not by us. Peter did not heal; in the name of Jesus, *God* healed and was praised (Acts 3:6, 8).[15] "God did extraordinary miracles through Paul" (Acts 19:11). Second, miracles are part of a divine program or plan; they have a religious significance.[16] Lewis notes that we should be reluctant to call Mother Egarée Louisa's discovery of her second best thimble with the help of St. Anthony as a miracle.[17] We must be careful not to judge how critical Mother Louisa's discovery was to her life, but the point is that miracles are not side texts, exceptions, or irrelevancies. They lie at the heart of the story of divine interaction with and

---

15. Thomas Aquinas notes miracles are unqualifiedly wondrous events whose cause is completely hidden from us. He identifies three degrees or types of miracles: those done by God that nature could never do, such as the sun reversing its course; those that nature could do, but not in a given order, such as someone seeing after being blind; and those that both God and nature can do, but that God does without using nature, such as curing illness. All of these, Thomas notes, point to the contention that "God alone can work miracles." *Summa Contra Gentiles* III, ch. 102, 1.

16. "To be a miracle an event must contribute significantly towards a holy divine purpose for the world." Swinburne, *Concept of Miracle*, 8.

17. Lewis, *Miracles*, 107.

providential concern for us. Divine involvement with us in and through nature is what the story of God's providential concern for us is all about, although our responsive return of glory to God is the ultimate purpose of the divine initiative.[18] This does not mean that miracles cannot be misused. Frequently, attempts have been made to turn miracles into magic (Acts 8:18) or to turn the miracle event or the medium of a miracle into something to be worshiped itself, as a relic, rather than worshiping the God who does the miracle. When the relics receive more attention than God, and when they are treated magically, manipulation and idolatry replace God's grace as the central feature of the story. The adoration of magical relics creates more harm than mere suspicion about miracle accounts; it leads people to think that they can manipulate the objects for their purpose.

Third, we can identify two kinds of miracles, one I would term miracles of production and the other miracles of timing. *Miracles of production* are usually what we think about when we hear of miracles and what we have largely addressed in this chapter. The introduction of a new cause produces a new, unexpected (in terms of natural sequences) effect. Biblical readers will immediately think of Aaron's staff becoming a serpent; Elijah and the unending supply of flour and oil; Jesus' turning water to wine at Cana; his enlargement of five loaves and two fish to feed five thousand people; Jesus' healing of the paralytic, the blind, the lame, and the woman who bled; his raising of Lazarus and other deceased people from the dead; and God's raising of Jesus himself. The effect cannot be traced back in a series to precedent natural causes; a new, non-natural cause is needed to produce a new effect, which might be either a new being or a new mode of being.

Miracles of timing are somewhat different. Here the effect might indeed be traced back in a series to precedent natural causes. What is miraculous is the timing of the causal conditions, namely, that they occurred when they did. The emphasis is not on the production of a new being or mode of being. R. F. Holland gives the example of a little boy riding his tricycle on the railroad tracks.[19] His wheel gets stuck in the rail at the same time that a train is approaching. The train engineer cannot see the child around the curve in the tracks, and the speeding train is about to strike him. But it happens that the engineer faints, his grip on the throttle is relaxed, and the engine's brakes are applied automatically, stopping the train just in time before it hits the little boy who is engrossed in extricating his bike wheel from the track. His mother, who anxiously observed the whole event unfold, credits her son's survival to a miracle. She is correct, but what is miraculous is not the

---

18. Ibid., 98.
19. Holland, "The Miraculous," 43.

event *per se*, for what happened can be traced back to natural causes. The miracle is the *timing* of the event; the engineer fainted and the brakes were applied with barely enough time to save the child. The miraculous is found in that God somehow brought it about that the engineer fainted and the brakes were applied at just the right time. A possible and tantalizing biblical example can be found with the plagues in Egypt. Some conjecture that many of the plagues (in whole or in part) can be explained naturally by a series of eruptions from the exploding volcano in Thera (Santorini), a Greek island in the Aegean. Geologists have confirmed that enormous clouds of emitted ash blew south on prevailing winds and were deposited over Egypt. The ash of successive eruptions created a series of circumstances where the resulting plagues led one to the other. The first plague occurred when dark red volcanic ash from the volcano filled the river and other water sources, causing the Nile to turn blood red and making it undrinkable. The second plague, where the frogs left the river and died on the river banks, resulted from the pollution of the water. The fourth plague of flies occurred when the dead fish and amphibians attracted hordes of insects. And so on through the litany of misery. Even the passing through the Reed Sea might have been made possible by a tremendous tsunami. Regardless of whether or not this explains the plagues, and whether or not the timing of the eruption fits the timing of Israel's exodus, it aptly illustrates miracles of timing.[20] The events can be traced to and explained by natural causes. What is miraculous is the timing; they occurred at the time Moses, at the behest of God, said they would, constituting an incentive for the Egyptians to release the Israelite slaves and for Israel to escape from the trailing army. In the timing of the eruption and Moses' presentation to the Pharaoh God had a hand.

Some have raised doubts about the second category of miracles. If the event is explicable by natural laws and if the causes can be traced back to precedent causes, then it seems possible that every fortuitous event might be designated a miracle. Absent from miracles of timing is the apparent impossibility of a tracing to naturalistic causes and natural laws found in and characteristic of miracles of production. We seem to lack criteria to differentiate miracles of timing from propitious events. Consider the case of nineteen-year-old Katie Lentz, who in 2013 was trapped in her crushed Mercedes for forty-five minutes after a horrific crash with an intoxicated driver near Hannibal, Missouri. Near death, and with the first responders experiencing great difficulty extracting her from the wreckage, she asked them to pray

---

20. The theory is intriguing but faces difficulties. For one thing, many scientists hold that the eruption occurred in the late seventeenth or early sixteenth century BCE, too early to affect the exodus. For another, it may be difficult to account for all the plagues in this fashion. For a detailed analysis, see Trevisanato, *Plagues of Egypt*.

for her as her chances of survival from her many serious injuries dimmed. Then a Catholic priest, Patrick Dowling, coming upon the scene, walked to her car, prayed over her, and anointed her with oil. After he finished praying and left, a larger fire department rescue crew arrived with better equipment to get her out of the car and to life-saving medical treatment.

Both Ms. Lentz and the first responders viewed the priest's sudden appearance (and disappearance) as a miracle, for he was at the scene at just the right time to anoint her and give encouragement. "'I can't be for certain how it was said, but myself and another firefighter, we very plainly heard that we should remain calm, that our tools would now work and that we would get her out of that vehicle," New London Fire Chief Raymond Reed told Quincy's KHQA-TV. Lentz's rescue, he said, "was nothing more than sheer faith and nothing short of a miracle.'"[21]

That one could explain the priest's presence at the accident scene simply by the fact that he had just concluded substituting for a sick colleague at Mass and was now returning home by this route, and that as a priest he would be concerned for the injured and seek to assist them spiritually, did not remove Ms. Lentz's and the responders' perception of the event being a miracle. To those present the timing of his presence made all the difference in her rescue and survival. What this suggests is that miracles of timing, more than miracles of production, require a particular perspective that allows for God to work in accord with natural laws and personal choices for a moral and spiritual purpose. In such cases, it is not a question of the role of natural law and natural causes, but the apparent consistency of the event with divine goodness and the timing of the events. But this is consistent with the admission that any certainty regarding the accuracy of any categorization of the event as a miracle cannot be expected.

This leads us to the question of how we determine the actuality of miracles. Supposing these features are essential to miracles, several problems arise. First, how do we know that the event actually was a miracle, a divine intervention in the natural course of things? Second, how do we know that God did it, and third, how do we know that what happened was done for a purpose?

The actuality of miracles

What constitutes evidence for accepting that miracles actually occur? To properly claim that miracles happen in our world, they have to be witnessed or experienced either by ourselves or by others. But how would we recognize

---

21. Townsend, "'Miracle Priest.'"

a miracle? What would it require for us or someone to experience a miracle? We also learn about miracles from miracle accounts that are transmitted from one person to another, by either verbal or written testimony. If we want to treat these as having veracity, we need to be able to accredit the testimony of others regarding their transmission of witness miracle accounts. Clearly, the second—accrediting miracle accounts based on transmitting testimony—depends upon the first—someone actually experiencing a miracle, for initiating the transmission of witness accounts requires that someone experience the miracle event. Someone had to witness or experience the miracles if true witness accounts are to commence. Accordingly, two questions present themselves. First, how can persons know that what they have observed or experienced is a miracle? And second, how can we accredit reports from others that miracles have occurred?

The experience of miracles

Addressing the first, how do we know that what we have experienced is a special act of God, done according to a divine program, for a moral or spiritual purpose? With respect to miracles of production, how do we know that the particular event is not ultimately explicable by natural laws with which we are unfamiliar? If we knew more either about the event witnessed or about nature in general might we be able to trace the relevant natural causes that sufficiently produced the witnessed effect? With respect to miracles of timing, how do we know that the particular event was not merely serendipity? Consider, for example, the report of a young skier waiting in the tow line who suddenly collapsed from a potentially fatal heart attack. Standing near him in the line was a former fireman with EMT training. The fireman was at just the right place at just the right time to administer CPR to restart the young man's heart and save his life. The young man's family thanked both God and the fireman for saving their son. But was it God's timing or sheer good fortune that both stood at the same place when tragedy almost struck?

Miracles are unusual events, for they have a key causal condition lying outside the natural norm. We have good evidence that we are not very accurate observers of normal events, let alone of abnormal or extraordinary events like miracles. Our witnessing capabilities are limited and flawed, so that we make many and serious mistakes in our observation. In a meta-analysis of known wrongful felony convictions, 52 percent of the cases were attributable to false or misidentification by an eyewitness of the person convicted. Observers are not passive recorders of information but active in structuring and recalling the setting. We are perceptively selective and do not observe many of the details of the scene; we remember things in confused orders; our memories and imagination can fool us by filling information into the gaps in what we remember about our experiences; our past experiences and present psychological state condition what we experience and how we experience it by selecting and using interpretative categories; the length of observation, which frequently is very short, gives us only glimpses of what occurred whereas our accounts are usually continuous narratives; we conform our reporting to social expectations of us. We are often inattentive, or if attentive our focus is selective, and capping all of this we have fallible memories, affected by the passage of time, for the details of what occurred.[22] If our observational skills are so imperfect in even normal instances of observation, how can they be relied upon to determine what really occurred in the case of miracles, which are not normal circumstances? This issue is exacerbated when miracles of production cannot be explained simply by invoking natural laws, that is, where natural laws that trace events back to natural causes do not or cannot provide an adequate or complete account of what we experienced. In these cases our ordinary explanatory categories fail us. It is a normal reaction to be skeptical about what actually occurred when what we witnessed was unusual, wondrous, and not readily explicable by natural laws. Often it is easier to believe that our experience, our perceptual faculties, or our memories were deficient than that what we experienced was miraculous.

To substantiate what we have experienced, our own experience might be supplemented with witness accounts from others who were present at the event and with relevant physical evidence. Confirmation both by others and by physical evidence can help substantiate our *description* of what we experienced. They give us more confidence that although we cannot subsume what we experienced under natural laws, what we experienced really happened. This additional evidence is relevant to our critical judgment about the actuality of the event. But does this confirmation help support our *interpretation* of what we experience? It helps establish that something happened as (or, better, approximately as) we describe it, but it does not establish that the event is a miracle. It might confirm that what we experienced was unusual, but it does not tell us that *God* did it, that it fits into a divine program, or that it has a moral or spiritual purpose. How, then, can we be justified in moving from the contention that the event is significantly unusual and not readily explicable in terms of natural laws to the contention that what we experienced was a divinely-occasioned miracle?

22. Buckhout, "Eyewitness Testimony," 23–31. See also Rattner, "Convicted," 289.

One suggestion derives from paying attention to the context in which we experienced the extraordinary. Let us consider a parallel case of experiencing the wondrous. We are properly incredulous in the presence of a performing magician. When we studiously observe some feat of prestidigitation, we believe, given the context, that what the magician did could be explained by natural laws provided we had enough relevant information. This accounts for why we want magicians to explain how they performed the feat. The magician's reluctance to do so might add to our wonder but it does not remove our skepticism that we are being misled about the unnaturalness of what we observed. We are willing to abandon the view that what we witnessed really happened in the way we observed it because of the context in which we find ourselves. Since they call themselves magicians and perform in such a publicized setting, we know that we should expect things not to be as we perceive them, although they are wondrous nonetheless and we do not know and cannot explain how they are done.

We might suggest something similar with respect to miracles. Many times, although not always, miracles occur in a context of anticipation. If in our daily lives we witness an unusual event, we may be reluctant to term it a miracle because the event simply occurred "out of the blue." We might simply consider it to be serendipitous, inexplicable, or lucky. And if the event yielded negative results, we say that we were unlucky. At this time and place we were not expecting such an event. But if, as with the case of the magician, if we find ourselves in a context where certain anticipatory features are present, we may be more willing to term what we observed as a miracle. What might those features be? One feature involves the person through whom the miracle is performed, the person who occasions the miracle. God can work through anyone, but one would expect that those through whom God would work would be persons who have a high moral character, are reliable and trustworthy, and who proclaim and demonstrate some spiritual connection with God. This helps explain the Pharisees' failure to appreciate the works of Jesus, for they could not understand his character and hence had a difficult time believing that what he did could be the works of God and not of the evil one (Matt 12:22–24).

Second, if what is observed is the appropriate response to a particular petitionary prayer or request of God, it easier to term what occurs as a miracle. In our discussion of petitionary prayer in the previous chapter we noted that we make petitions for God's providential intervention in our lives. If we believe that God can and does intervene in human affairs, then we have some reason to think that an event was caused by God when it is a positive response to a petition we or others have made to God. If we write a friend and ask for money and sometime shortly thereafter receive an anonymous cashier's check in the mail for the exact amount we requested, we have good reason to think that our friend sent it to us. Although we did not see it mailed or written, the circumstances of the amount sent and the timeliness are enough to warrant such a conclusion. Similarly, if we make a request to God and the request is answered positively, we have reason to think that God brought it about in response to our petition. It is true that we lack certainty; the check we received for the requested amount could have been a fortuitous coincidence. But if we ask for the best explanation of the event, serendipity would not be the best explanation of the check's arrival. Rather, we would appeal to the account that our friend positively responded to our request. Similarly, we lack certainty that God responded to our prayer, but the best explanation of the event is that God responded positively to our request. If we pray for a specific healing and are healed, we have at least some good reason to hold that God did it in response to the prayer. Since the request made of God *prima facie* fits into some purposive structure created by our petition, it is at least somewhat likely that the event is an act of God who responds to the request and not merely a random event. Connecting the event with the deep providential structure of petitionary prayer helps us to interpret the event as a miracle; the event fits with our theological understanding of our actions and of God and his actions on our behalf.

At the same time, these anticipatory and petitionary contexts are not necessary conditions for attributing the unusual event to divine causation. Moses did not expect to encounter the Lord's angel in the midst of the burning bush while he was tending his father-in-law's sheep in the desert (Exod 3:1–3). Mary, the mother of Jesus, did not anticipate her angelic visitation and the shocking announcement that as a virgin she would bear a child (Luke 1:26–29). Her prayer came after the announcement, not before. Just as we as persons can intervene in contexts without advance warning, so God as a person can likewise intervene however and whenever he desires and chooses. But from our perspective, it is easier to accredit an event as miraculous if it occurs within a purposive or teleological structure like petitionary prayer.

Experiencing God

One might still wonder how we know that the event that we call a miracle was caused by God, for according to our definition if an event is to be a miracle God must be causally involved. Even if we are correct in our description, what we have experienced is the effect. We don't experience God causally bringing about the effect. Rather, from these effects we must make a judgment regarding God as the cause of the effects. This situation is not unique. In much of our experience we have to make the inductive move from the effect that we witness, observe, or experience to the cause that we have not experienced producing the effect. We do this when the thermostat for our furnace suddenly goes blank and no longer registers a temperature, when our new tire goes flat, when our apple cake does not rise in the oven, when we hear a strange noise coming from the ceiling above our bed. We are not left helpless. From our experience, our knowledge, our research, and at times with some fancy guesswork we attempt probabilistically to ferret out the causes, which we can often confirm through physical evidence: the thermostat batteries went dead, we find the culprit nail, we forgot to add baking powder, or we catch a mouse in an attic trap.

However, with miracles we might be more skeptical about invoking induction since the cause is empirically non-observable. How might we sharpen our understanding of the experience of causes to address this? In discussing scientific experience, Dudley Shapere notes that "the body of physical science includes assertions about the existence of entities and processes which are not accessible to the human senses"[23] To understand how we might access observational information about such he distinguishes between observability in the sense of perceptibility and observability in the sense of yielding knowledge or evidence. This important and helpful distinction helps shed profitable light on how we can understand our experience of miracles as events caused by God. Shapere contends that philosophers use "observation" in a significantly different way than scientists do. Whereas empirical philosophers traditionally treat being observable as what humans can experience with their given bodily sensory equipment if it is possible for humans to be present,[24] scientists speak of being able to directly observe things or events even where humans cannot be present. For example, scientists speak about observing electrons in a cloud chamber or the central core of the Sun, despite the fact that electrons cannot be sensed and the Sun's core lies 400,000 inhospitable miles beneath its surface. The Sun's interior is a nuclear furnace emitting both neutrinos and photons that scientists can use to observe the core. In the case of photons, "a packet of electromagnetic energy produced in the central core will take over 100,000 years to reach the surface. In that journey, it will be absorbed and re-radiated or scattered many times, and the original character of the radiation, and therefore of the information carried by it, will be drastically altered (it won't even be

---

23. Shapere, "Concept of Observation," 505.
24. van Fraassen, *Scientific Image*, 16.

the same photon)."[25] The information about the Sun's core from photons is not directly but indirectly observational; it results from inferences scientists make from received photons. But scientists also receive information about the Sun's core by means of neutrinos that reach them rather directly, with little if any interference. Since the information neutrinos carry is only very rarely altered by interactions with other atomic material, Shapere argues, scientists can say that they directly observe the interior of the Sun's core. They do not infer information about the Sun's core from the neutrinos, just as we don't infer the characteristics of the rabbits running through our yard from the light rays reflected from their bodies to our eyes. As we directly observe the rabbits by means of the reflected light rays, the scientists directly observe the Sun's core by means of the neutrinos, despite the fact that neither the core nor the neutrinos are palpable to human senses. Thus, Shapere generalizes, for something to be directly observed or observable, information about it must be received or receivable by an appropriate receptor without interference.[26] We need not sense or be aware of the medium for the experience to count as an observation so long as the information conveyed is not significantly distorted in the process.

Shapere identifies several items of interest in regard to observation. One is that direct observation need not require that the information from what is observed be transmitted to the receptor sensorially, only that it can be "read." The core of the Sun and the neutrinos that transmit the information transcend human sensory ability. Hence, although human senses form part of a larger group of information receptors that are relevant to direct observation, what is directly observed is not restricted to what humans are capable of sensing. Carefully crafted recording instruments, from which we can derive the information, likewise count as appropriate receptors. Second,

25. Shapere, *Reason and the Search*, 342–43.

26. Ibid., 492. Toby Linden objects to this account of direct observation on the grounds that it is phrased in terms that allow no possible interference if the observation is to be direct, whereas Shapere discusses the observation of the Sun's core by means of neutrinos in terms of the likelihood of being interfered with. But, Linden argues, "the likelihood of the interference (alteration) is not relevant to whether an observation has taken place on a particular occasion. . . . Since a determination of whether a direct observation has taken place is not made until several readings have been taken, it is hard for Shapere to claim that the lack of interference on a given occasion is crucial in permitting the conclusion that a direct observation has taken place to be drawn" ("Shapere on Observation," 293–99). Hence, the probabilistic account Shapere gives conflicts with the no interference requirement. However, what Shapere is arguing is that the likelihood is relevant, not to whether or not one has a direct observation, but rather to its directness. If it is unlikely that it has been interfered with, it is likely that it is a direct perception. Whether or not we know this at the time is quite another matter; I might think that an observation is direct when in fact it is not, and vice versa.

the neutrinos from the Sun are recorded by instruments on earth placed in underground caves or mine tunnels to avoid interference. Scientists need not be present to witness their actual impact to say that they have directly observed the core of the Sun; they can read the recorded neutrino data (gather the information from the neutrinos) at some later date. This differs from how philosophers normally treat the receptor of an observation; for them the observer or sense perceiver must be present and active for one to say that the person has made an observation. Third, neutrinos are imperceptible although sophisticated technological instrumentation records their presence. Thus, the medium of transmission from the observed object might itself be insensible. In short, Shapere claims that for the scientist it makes sense to say that sensorially imperceptible things and processes can be directly observed and that observation occurs when information is conveyed undistorted from the observed to the observer.

Shapere's point is that "observation" as used by scientists involves much more than mere sense perceptibility of the object and information transmission; scientists are interested in observability in the sense of being evidential or providing grounding for belief in a way that leads to knowledge. As he notes, "observation" has at least two aspects: the *perceptual* or sensory aspect (what we will call the *perceptible*) that has attracted and absorbed empirical philosophers' attention and has led to worries about deception and malfunctioning sensory apparatus, and an *epistemic* aspect. The latter concerns "the *evidential* role that observation is supposed to play in leading to knowledge or well-grounded belief or in supporting beliefs already attained."[27] He notes that scientists are particularly interested in the evidential role since they are concerned with data as evidence to understand, explain, or justify. Indeed, "*science has come more and more to exclude sense-perception as much as possible from playing a role in the acquisition of observational evidence;* that is, it relies more and more on other appropriate, but dependable, receptors. It has broken, or at least severely attenuated, the connection between the perceptual and epistemic aspects of 'observation' and focused on the latter."[28] It is not that sense-perception is abandoned; it plays a role at some stages in that, for example, the information gathered by the technical receptors has to be humanly read. Rather, perception or direct observation has been broadened beyond the mere sensory to include an observation through which scientists obtain information. For something to be directly observed or observable, information about it must be received by

---

27. Shapere, *Reason and the Search*, 508.
28. Ibid.

an appropriate receptor without interference or distortion.[29] In this case, it makes sense for the scientist to say that imperceptible things can be directly observed and can provide information and evidential grounding for a specific scientific theory.

Moreover, the fact that observation—including what counts as information and how it is transmitted and received—is theory-structured does not militate against the use of the practice to justify beliefs. The existence of neutrinos, how they are produced and travel, their speed, how their presence is registered, and what information they are capable of bearing are all part of a background nuclear theory. Observation of the Sun's core is couched in background theories about the solar system and its structures, the mass and chemical composition of the Sun, its surface, its age, and so on, so that the received data are understood and interpreted within the context of a robust scientific theory about nuclear fusion. Scientists also use both theoretical and particular background information about the transmission, the receptor, and its location conditions. But although the very information neutrinos carry, what counts as information, and the conditions of transmission and reception are theory-structured, the experience is not rejected as being perceptually unreliable because of this. "*It is precisely the assimilation of observation to the general category of 'interactions', and not its use by us, that constitutes the important point in understanding the role of observation in the search for knowledge and the testing of beliefs*; for that assimilation reflects the fact that 'observation' has been ... integrated with the larger body of our best-warranted beliefs about nature. It is that process of integration that frees observation from the subjectivity of its philosophical associations."[30]

Background information in science plays a significant role in shaping observation. It is necessary to reliable perceptual practice. Shapere argues that "what science uses as background information is the *best* information available, ... but nevertheless appropriately, information which has shown itself highly successful in the past, and regarding which there exists no specific and compelling reason for doubt."[31] Scientists have no good reason not to use this background information to understand the information obtained via observation since they consider the background information to have been shown to be reliable (though not certain) by past experience.

---

29. Although Shapere defines direct observation in terms of no interference, it might be more apropos to talk about no *significant* interference, that is, not changing the essential information or qualities that is transmitted so that the information is reliably transmitted—the emphasis being on reliability (Linden, "Shapere on Observation," 299).

30. Shapere, *Reason and the Search*, 510.

31. Ibid., 514.

Indeed, background information is essential if they are to understand the acquired information, since what is observed is encoded in a web of scientific theories. Without the background theoretical information, they could not make sense of the observations, use the information to obtain further information, establish the reliability of the information, and so on. Far from theories effectively constructing the informative data, theories make data acquisition and determining data significance possible. Neither does the presence of background theoretical information reduce the observation to subjectivity (in the sense of strict relativity), for the scientist in a given context assumes that it is the best and most appropriate information extant, and it is stronger when it is couched in theories that are independent of the theory under consideration.[32] Perceptual or observational practice in science as used in an epistemic role has nothing to fear from the fact that our data are theory- or assumption-laden and that theories have a subjective component. Rather, we are encouraged by the success of the theories to make claims about the *observability*—content, properties, events—of what philosophers have treated as imperceptible or unobservable.

Experiences of miracles

Much of what Shapere has said about the distinction between observability in the sense of perceptibility and observability in the sense of yielding knowledge or evidence applies to our experience of miracles as events caused by God. First, if we free ourselves from the requirement that the imperceptible must reveal its causal activity in our sensory experience, we no longer have *a priori* reasons for rejecting our ability to experience miracles. We do not have to locate our experience in any original or particular sensory experience or identify particular phenomenal qualia in order to claim we have experienced a miracle. Treating observations as epistemic (knowledge-producing or evidential) rather than sense-perceptual (in a philosophical sense), we might directly observe or experience the miracle as a God-event just in case we have reason to believe that the event is from God. The person who experiences the miracle is rather less interested in the sensory perceptual aspects of experiencing God producing the effect than in the epistemic aspect of the event, that is, in the evidential role that the experience plays in the person's life in leading to well-grounded knowledge or belief about God and God's actions or properties. That is why the Gospel of John treats miracles as signs or revelations. It is true that for believers the focus of the experience of miracles is not primarily on justifying religious

---

32. Kosso, *Reading*, 161.

belief. When a miracle occurs in the context we noted above, for example, of petitionary prayer, the person is especially interested in the objective effects of the event. But in terming the event a miracle, the experiencer is claiming that God had a hand in producing the effect. The experience is epistemic in that the experiencer is interested in the miracle as part of the larger context of understanding God's providence in the world and in the person's life. The miracle is a *sign*ificant revelatory event.

Features parallel to what Shapere noted with respect to scientific observation play a role in understanding and justifying the experience of miracles. First, as with our experience of the core of the Sun via neutrinos, the fact that experience of God in a causal role lies beyond human sensory ability does not mean that we cannot experience God as causing the miracle in an epistemic sense. Although our senses are involved in the experience of miracles, for example, in witnessing physical changes, direct observation does not require that we actually experience in some *sensory* way God causing the miracle event. Our senses need not play a role specifically in experiencing that God is the causal agent. Second, we need not be present to affirm epistemically that the event was a miracle. We can "read" the data generated by the event at some later date to give us understanding that God intervened in nature. With miracles of production, the inexplicability of the event by natural laws provides probabilistic support for the contention that it was an act of God. Third, the fact that the process of God's involvement is in-principle unobservable in a sensory sense does not mean that we cannot experience God as the cause of the event. Direct observation of miracles need not require a phenomenal qualia aspect of which we are or could be aware in normal circumstances to be able to claim that we have had a direct experience of a miracle. In short, the unobservability of the cause itself and the causing are not reasons to hold that we have not experienced a miracle as a God-caused event when we treat the event epistemically, that is, as helping us to probabilistically understand the *sign*ificant acts of a providential God.

As with scientific observation, in the experience of miracles the experience itself is theory-structured. It is contextual, lying within appropriate background knowledge. The existence of God, his properties, and how he interacts with the world are all part of a theology of miracles. The data in terms of which we understand events believed to be miracles is structured by and interpreted through the background of a robust theology of a good, mighty, knowing, caring, and loving God who is active in the world. But although our experience of the event as a miracle is theory-structured, it should not be rejected as being unable to function epistemically because of this. This is perfectly consistent with the epistemic practices of obtaining knowledge in other areas such as science. Indeed, without this context it would be as difficult to make sense of the miracle experiences as it would of any other experiences, since at least with miracles of production we cannot resort to natural explanations to fully account for the effect. Placing miracle experiences in this background context allows us to establish not only the probable reliability of the claim of providential intervention, but to understand its significance for our lives.

In short, using Shapere's insight about the difference between philosophers' conception of sensory perceptual observation and the epistemic observation meaningful to scientists, we can make sense of the claim that we can experience miracles as God-caused events. Both scientific experience of unobservables and the experience of miracles caused by an unobservable God can be meaningfully spoken of in terms of observation, even when the cause itself is sensorially unobservable and the means by which it causes the effects is sensorially imperceptible. What this shows is that we can meaningfully speak about experiencing miracles as a truly *epistemic* observational practice without requiring it to be swallowed up with the kinds of questions that have plagued traditional empiricist analyses of perceptual practice.

Plans and fit

We might say similar things about intentions and plans. Determining the place of someone's actions in their functioning life plan is fraught with great difficulty and ambiguity. We see people do things, but unless we can interview the persons themselves (and even here they might not be telling the truth about their intentions or might not be fully aware of them), we must surmise or construct what their intentions and reasonings are or might be. To assign intentions we put our past experiences, our previous intention-action combinations, previous communications with the persons, the context, and other clues together to form a reasonable ensemble explaining why they performed their actions. We attempt to make the actions we observe cohere with a reasonable, intentional story that brings together what we know about the agent, agents in general, and the context.

As we noted above, our past experiences, divine revelation, research into the ways events ordinarily proceed, and discovery of physical evidence all help establish that attributing an event to God is a reasonable explanation. But what about the "God plan" part? We do not have direct access to God's activities, purposes, or plans. We can make reasonable claims about these from Scripture, but even here we must note that Scripture purportedly derives from miraculous intervention insofar it is God-originated or inspired.

Revelation itself is a miracle. If we are to take some experience to be connected with a divine program, we will have to see how it connects with what we and others understand about the entire theistic paradigm: that God has a certain nature and character and is interested in and acts providentially in the world. We look for clues, patterns, and *sig*nificance in the events, to see how what we have experienced coheres with various aspects or dimensions of this paradigm. C. S. Lewis builds on this to provide a criterion by which we might identify an event as a miracle. He terms it "fitness."[33] For Lewis, miracles "are not exceptions (however rarely they occur) nor irrelevancies."[34] Rather, they are the heart of the plot, the centerpiece of the story, the hub on which events turn. It is when events that we take as miracles fit in with our deepest needs, knowledge of divine purposes revealed to us, an affirmation of God's providential concern for us, and an understanding of the patterns of life and nature in which we might discover the hand of God that we can begin to think that although we cannot see God do the work, God is at work according to his plans and purposes. The miracle accounts most likely to be true are those that fit or accord with the overall understanding of God's working with humans. Miracles write in small letters what is written in large across the canvas of history and nature. For example, one might wonder how God can select one person on whom to bestow a healing miracle but not another. Lewis notes that selectivity is a persistent theme of created nature, but selectivity is neither meant to be cruel nor based on merit but rather occurs for the sake of the unchosen.[35]

Lewis refuses to give an analysis of "fitness."[36] In effect, he says that you will know it when you see it. God's work has a certain coherence, and when one penetrates that coherence one can see what does and does not fit at the center or core. Those who fail to acknowledge that God is at work will miss not only the overall patterns but also the deep structures of the universe, and hence fail to see, recognize, and comprehend what is the core of God's providential work. Those for whom this paradigm is a genuine option—live, forced, and momentous, as William James might say—find that fitting with the greater story illuminates the events they experience.

Lewis admits that fitness has an unabashed aesthetic dimension, and this is appropriate, for often how we decide that a particular piece of artwork has been produced by a particular painter invokes the same criterion of fitness. Often we have a good idea of how the artist worked, either from

---

33. Lewis, *Miracles*, 104.
34. Ibid., 98.
35. Ibid., 116–18.
36. Ibid., 107.

contemporary descriptions of his or her work or else from a careful analysis of works that already have been accredited to that artist. Color, style, use of particular paints, brush strokes, subject matter, and setting, among other features, are used to make the inference from an effect (the unsigned painting we have in front of us) to the cause (the artist). Even if none of the comparison pieces have a signature, from descriptions and employment of the above conditions we can reasonably conclude that they are the careful works of a given artist. The reason is that the questioned work of art aesthetically fits into the larger corpus. The assignment of a recently discovered, unsigned landscape painting entitled "Sunset at Montmajour" is a case in point. The van Gogh Museum's director Axel Ruger said that "the museum attributed the painting to van Gogh after 'extensive research into style, technique, paint, canvas, the depiction, van Gogh's letters and the provenance.'"[37] In short, it fit aesthetically and materially into the works van Gogh painted at the apex of his artistic career and now, after years of being thought to be a forgery, critics accredit it as one of van Gogh's masterpieces. From the effect inference is made to the cause by means of how the discovered painting fits into the corpus of van Gogh's accepted works.

Similar arguments can be made for written or published pieces. The dispute over the authenticity of Shakespeare's plays illustrates this. Some scholars question whether Shakespeare was really the author of the plays attributed to him. They contend that his background and perhaps lack of education (of which we have no record) would not have prepared him to have the detailed knowledge of the activities of the aristocratic society of his day that he expertly portrays, of English politics, and of foreign cultures exhibited in his plays. He simply could not have been properly prepared to be such an illustrious playwright. But most scholars point beyond contemporary testimony, official records, and title pages, to a stylistic fitness about the plays attributed to him. His use of hyphens and less frequent relative clauses are just some of the coherence indicators. Scholars find in his works a harmony of style, character portrayal, plot development, and use of language that, despite their different settings, present an aesthetic and literary continuity.

God too is an artist, and although we do not have direct access to him causing the events, we can look at the pattern of events that people have attributed to him to suggest that God is at work in a pattern consistent with his nature and with other works central to the theistic paradigm. This pattern fits our theological affirmations that God acts providentially on our behalf.

---

37. Mullen, "New van Gogh." For the employment of fit, along with other criteria, to reject widely accepted works of van Gogh as authentic, see Born and Lanais, *Schuffenecker's Sunflowers*.

His actions take the lead in the providential dance, guiding our steps, bringing us into relationship with him. The fitness is not merely logical, rational, and theological but aesthetic as well. When we experience the wondrous in the appropriate setting, we can see that this is how a loving God apparently has acted and would respond toward his creation.

Lewis thinks that although miracles are the heart of the plot, they are rare. He writes,

> God does not shake miracles into Nature at random as if from a pepper-caster. They come on great occasions: they are found at the great ganglions of history—not of political or social history, but of that spiritual history which cannot be fully known by men. If your own life does not happen to be near one of those great ganglions, how should you expect to see one? If we were heroic missionaries, apostles, or martyrs, it would be a different matter. But why you or I?[38]

But, we might ask, why should not you or I also experience miracles? If God acts providentially in human history and if God acts providentially in each of our lives, there is good reason to think that we will, if we have not already, experienced his miraculous action. This fits intrinsically into the kind of God about which we have thought. We have contended that divine love is the center of the theological web and that divine providence extends out from it. Love manifested in providence is indeed the heart of the plot. Out of goodness and graciousness God can intervene miraculously for his own purposes and for our own good. Lewis sees miracles only writ large in the incarnational and transformational events. These too are manifestations of God's providential intervention, but miracles are also written in our daily lives. Here God is incarnational and transformational; his real presence seeks our good for his glory as he seeks to transform us into the likeness of himself. The intervention need not be anything that we deserve but flows from God's love and mercy, for the moral and spiritual purpose of bringing us to him and glory to himself. We have already characterized these as the supererogatory actions of God.

We might think that we have understood the plot, but God is also master of surprises. It is true that some features of God's actions can be anticipated: he is incarnational and transformational, to be sure. He acts out of love and concern for justice on behalf of the poor and oppressed. Hence, events that we might consider to be miracles that have this agenda

---

38. Lewis, *Miracles*, 167. Although, paradoxically, Lewis considered and believed in petitionary prayer and called the healing of his wife "an almost miraculous recovery." Kilby, *Christian World*, 22.

in view are consistent with our vision of God. But like artists who having mastered their technique stretch out in new and unpredicted ways, God also at times acts out of character. God brings goodness that we do not anticipate and merit, so that through these events he might be glorified. A god who is restricted to our box of anticipatory interventions is surely a god who is too small; God acts surprisingly not only at the great ganglions of history and of our lives, but in the small and ordinary dimensions of our lives in ways that can amaze us and yet might be so invisible that we fail to notice them. Just as a great donor might contribute anonymously, the Secret Santa of the universe comes in among us at times without a whisper or without leaving his footprints. We might not have recognized God's intervention or known that it occurred, but that failure is inconsequential to the question of actuality of miracles. What matters is that God can and does take both consistent and surprising providential actions in our lives to bring us to himself. God's acts often may be hidden, as they probably frequently are, and only rarely are openly manifest in the great stage of history. It is these latter that Lewis recognizes. But if we believe that God responds to petitionary prayer, as the Scriptures teach, and if we believe that God is merciful and loving, even to those who may reject him, then we have to be prepared for God's more frequent intervention. We will recognize it when it fits into providential contexts, often occasioned by petitionary prayer, and coheres with the litany of divine acts that others have reported experiencing.

Yet our experience of divine intervention need not be the same as others. How his parishioners experienced my pastor father was very different from the way I experienced him. His caring actions toward them differed in many significant ways from his loving actions toward his family. Yet a uniformity and coherence lay about and behind both sets of experiences, so that a careful observer could recognize a common hand and heart behind the deeds done. This is the consonance and fit that is at the heart of the plot.

Accrediting testimony about past events

Most miracle accounts that we deal with are transmitted to us by others. People who transmit the stories provide us with testimony on the basis of which we affirm or deny the reality of what they or others experienced sometime in the distant or very recent past. A woman recounts to a group how she was diagnosed with a virulent form of rectal cancer encased in a tumor that was immediately life-threatening. The exploratory surgery revealed that the tumor was so large that the doctors told her to immediately take radiation therapy to reduce it to operable size. After the therapy she returned to the hospital for the surgery, which when the surgeon opened her up turned out to be unnecessary since the surgeon discovered that the tumor had unexpectedly completely disappeared without a trace. Her prayers and those of others for her healing had apparently been answered. Having experienced this miracle and keeping the promise she made to God while undergoing therapy, she now recounts to others her healing miracle.

As noted above, since miracles authenticated by testimony presuppose that someone somewhere at sometime observed and affirmed that a miracle has occurred, this discussion of testimony presupposes a positive resolution of the issues raised in the previous section. That the woman healed of rectal cancer can recount her healing miracle story presumes that she experienced the event and now authentically can relay her account to others. Granted that people can at times reliably affirm a miracle experience, we now need to inquire under what circumstances we can trust testimonies or reports from others. This is especially significant since we (in the cultural West) are generally very suspicious of accounts that extend the causes of events beyond appeals to natural laws and natural causes. In the above story, we probably would accept what is factually verifiable about her account but may be more reluctant than she was to attribute her healing to a special act of God. We might suggest that probably the radiation had been even more successful than the surgeon anticipated. Her story was believable because we have had experiences with or known of healing by radiation. But if she said that she never underwent any radiation treatments or took any drug therapy but was healed through prayer alone, we might be more skeptical that either she had the tumor in the first place or that it had disappeared, let alone about her explanation. Her testimony in this case, both about the facts and about the cause of the healing, might be more difficult for scientifically-minded Westerners to believe.[39]

We are not strangers to testimony in our daily lives. Much of what we know and learn comes to us through testimony. The auto mechanic tells us that our car needs new ball joints, the doctor conveys his diagnosis to us of a hernia, a teacher lectures about the history of the Civil War or the meaning of the Periodic Table, a friend tells us that someone is critically ill or has died suddenly. Since there is no way we can experience everything, indeed, since our experience, skills, and knowledge are so greatly limited, we must rely on testimony to know about the world and even about ourselves. Consequently,

---

39. I don't have space to address it here, but the very raising of this question reveals a distinct cultural bias. The kind of skepticism that scientifically-minded Westerners would express over witness accounts of miracles or even of miracles themselves would not be thinkable in, for example, a traditional African setting.

it is essential that we think about how we proceed to accredit the bearers of testimony, not only with respect to miracles, but in general.

Hume suggested that we ought to proportion our belief in testimony to the reliability of the evidence, and in the case of testimony certain features should immediately give us pause. How then would we go about assessing the reliability of witness testimony? Richard Swinburne suggests four conditions that affect our accepting as evidence reports of the past: (1) our own apparent memories of past experiences; (2) the testimony of others about their past; (3) physical traces; (4) an understanding of what is physically impossible or improbable. Swinburne takes (4) as a corrective to or check on the first three conditions. Where the evidence conflicts, we have to use our considered judgment in weighing individually and jointly the relevant pieces of evidence; we invoke the basic principle to "accept as many pieces of evidence as possible" in forming a coherent judgment about the claims being made. Our goal is to use this information to form a coherent picture consistent with the evidence—where things best fit together.[40]

With regard to Swinburne's first condition, his claim is that not all testimony should be given comparable weight. Where the testimony involves features connected to me, then generally or at least *prima facie*, I should rely on my own memories to test the reports of others. At the same time, while I am justified in giving priority to my own experience and remembrance, this criterion depends on the degree of confidence I have in my own memory of events related to the events in question. The stronger my confidence in my observations, the more I am justified in relying on it, recognizing at the same time the very fallibility of my powers of observation that we highlighted above. My own memories form one piece of evidence that has to be addressed in assessing the testimony of others.

As to Swinburne's second condition, we might consider relevant characteristics of the persons giving the testimony. Hume lists four factors that we use to evaluate testimony: the availability of contrary testimony, the character and number of witnesses, the way the witnesses deliver their testimony, and lack of bias or personal interest in the event.[41] To this Mackie adds that the witnesses should give independent testimony.[42]

Hume is undoubtedly correct in pointing to these factors, but he is all too ready to abandon testimony when there is conflict. The presence of conflict does not mean we should reject any or all of the reports. Since observation is perspectival and fragmentary, we must remain vigilant about

---

40. Swinburne, *Concept of Miracle*, 33–34.
41. Hume, *Enquiry*, 120–21.
42. Mackie, *Miracles of Theism*, 25.

conflicts without petulantly declaring falsehood. Each witness will have a varying perspective on the observed event, so that any full and final account really embodies material from all the diverse witnesses. The character of the witnesses is important, since truth-telling is a prime requisite of being a reliable witness. A history of personal integrity and veracity does much for accrediting the testimony of a witness. Likewise, a plurality of witnesses present a stronger case than that of a lone individual, although we would be a fool to reject the testimony of a lone person coming to tell us that our house is on fire because only one person, and a person with a sullied reputation at that, was the bearer of the distressingly bad news. Further, it is not clear that one should expect persons who witness what they take to be a miracle to be "calm, cool, and collected." The Enlightenment conditions of rationality and suppression of emotion impose too severe a constriction on how we think and act. Indeed, one might even allow the observer or experiencer of a miracle to exhibit the exuberance of a Minnesota Viking's wide receiver on scoring a touchdown. After all, if the event is truly a miracle one has participated in the providence of God. Similarly with Hume's bias factor. On the one hand, he is correct that we should be suspicious of people's reporting when they use the event to enhance their own position, enrich themselves, or put themselves in a position of power or authority over others. Testimony apparently directed toward personal economic, social, political, or religious gain should be treated with suspicion. At the same time, if persons truly experience a miracle, they would have a bias in that regard. One would not expect atheists to be reporters of miracles. The general point is that each of these factors will be weighed in accrediting the testimony and will play a role in the final evidential assessment of the testimony presented.

 About Swinburne's third kind of evidence we do not have to say much. Surely physical evidence, especially of changed conditions, constitutes important evidence. In the case we noted above, if we had physical evidence that the woman had cancer in the form of x-ray results from various tests and now can show by the same or related physical evidence no indication of cancer, this provides strong evidence of a change. But what does this evidence show? It shows that there has been a change and indicates that an explanation for the change is called for. What it does not establish is the cause of or purposes for the change. To ascertain the cause or purpose involves inductive reasoning: we infer the nature of the causes from the changed condition. If we invoke the principle of uniformity, we look for causes similar to previous events. But where the events do not follow previous patterns, where normally radiation shrinks the tumor but does not eliminate it as in this case, we no longer have the principle of uniformity to guide us as to the proximate cause and now have to consider divergent causes as providing the best explanation for the occurrence. The naturalist will grant the primacy of physical evidence of change; what the theist must not concede is the inference that physical change can result only from natural causes.

Swinburne's fourth consideration concerns impossibility and improbability. We have already argued that miracles are possible in a world in which God intervenes. But whether they are likely or probable is another matter. Undoubtedly they are unusual or extraordinary, otherwise we could formulate natural laws to cover their occurrence. Yet any given confluence of events is unlikely. That you are sitting reading this with the specific clothes you have on, while at the same time other persons in your city are doing exactly what they are doing wearing exactly what they are wearing in their own circumstances is extremely unlikely, given all the possible things you and the others could have chosen to do and to wear. The odds of it occurring cumulatively and simultaneously are exponentially low—yet the sum total of all the events *did* occur simultaneously and will never be repeated. But, it might be replied, miracles are unlikely in a different way, namely, in that miracles are contrary to events for which we can provide a completely natural explanation. They are physically unlikely, given what we know about natural conditions. The tension between the first three conditions and the fourth is what accounts for the skepticism shown by Hume and many others when they hear about reports of miracles. We have a penchant for accepting testimony about events that can have natural explanations and for being dubious about testimony regarding events that do not have natural, ordinary explanations.

Antony Flew suggests that one reason for relying more heavily on the fourth condition, which invokes physical improbability in preference to testimony, is that scientific evidence provides sounder, more reliable, and more predictable evidence than does testimony.[43] For one thing, there is the matter of numbers. Scientific evidence allegedly presents us with universally uniform experience, whereas testimony relies on the reports of a few. Even where the witnesses are numerous, it is difficult for them to compete with contrary, naturalistic scientific accounts, for it would not be a natural law if universality or at least significant statistical probability were not behind it. We bank on this uniformity in calling it a natural law.

For another, Flew notes that scientific evidence presents us with repeatable events. It reports events that have testability, so that natural laws function to give us predictability in instances of similar causal conditions, whereas testimony about miracles concerns what is not repeatable and hence subject to testing. We do accept testimony, but we are much more

---

43. Flew, *Hume's Philosophy*, 207–8.

congenial to testimony about events that are repeatable than to testimony about events that are not. In particular, we are more apt to believe testimony about natural events than about events arising from human free actions, for the latter events often are not repeatable.

But if miracles are acts of God mediated through human persons, they are more like events arising from free human actions than like events following natural laws. Lack of repeatability, although it may count against reports of merely natural events, often does not count against witness reports regarding events requiring personal agents. That Babe Ruth hit sixty home runs in 1927 tells us nothing about how many home runs he will hit in 1928; indeed, he was never able to repeat that feat. And he may not have wanted to if he had decided to take retirement in 1928. Similarly, there are feats that you and I have done that we simply cannot or do not want to repeat. I may have entered a hot-dog-eating contest and barely lived to so regret it that I would never do so again. Thus, although repeatability of an event is an important piece for accrediting testimony about natural events, it does not follow that testimony about unrepeatable or unrepeated events should be dismissed out of hand, especially when they report intentional actions of persons. We need to ask what provides the best explanation, not only for the testimony itself, but also for what the testimony is about. Testimonies that invoke personal causation will be rife with unrepeatable causal conditions.

Repeatability is important where the causes are impersonal. That is why scientific reports must detail not only the results obtained but also the methods used to obtain them. These methodological descriptions allow others to test whether what is reported is accurate. But repeatability is not a requisite where causes are personal, for cause and effect in such cases are not wholly connected by natural laws. But what about reports of unusual events or anomalies? These are the bread and butter of scientists, who are always on the alert for the exceptional, unusual, and inexplicable by means of current theories.[44] In dealing with anomalies, human testimony is taken as a basis for questioning and sometimes overturning currently accepted understandings of the natural law and in-vogue paradigms. In dealing with reports of anomalies, scientific-law accounts should not always take precedence over historical accounts (or witness experiences), especially if those witness accounts are well-grounded in evidence. The fourth criterion provides a check on witness accounts; on this Flew is correct. But that it provides a check does not mean that we simply grant absolute veto power over witness reports to scientific accounts based on natural law. Witness accounts of anomalies can and do overthrow reports of accepted natural laws.

44. Kuhn, *Scientific Revolutions*, chs. 6–8.

Flew thinks that we can just expand natural laws to account for anomalies. In effect, for him there are no permanently unrepeatable events; we simply need to hang in there and look for natural explanations of the anomalies. If the anomaly is repeatable, this approach is generally reasonable. But there are instances of anomalies, such as healings or resurrections, where it is better to keep the governing law as is and accept miracles than to change the law. To change the law would more likely throw the natural explanations out of kilter than would the acceptance that the event is miraculous. Since the natural law works just fine in all or most other explanations, it would be disruptive and destructive in an explanatory sense to attempt to amend the natural law to cover this one anomaly. Amending the natural law to cover a singular past event will not necessarily lead to predictability of future events. In general, amendments are not a satisfactory approach to the deliverance of laws. Only if the amendment makes progress toward explaining repeatable anomalies will this approach be preferable to accepting the extraordinary as a possible instance of a miracle.[45] Indeed, as Swinburne argues, even if the event is repeatable, our explanatory consistency and power in some rare cases might be better served if we keep the law as it is and accept the testimony of a miracle than change the law.

In short, scientific laws and testimony are established in the same way: connecting observed data coherently. Hence, scientific law accounts should not always take precedence over historical accounts (or witness experiences), especially if those witnesses accounts are well-grounded. What is required, as Swinburne points out, is a careful and coherent evaluation of all the evidence, including that given by witnesses, to provide the best explanation. We should weigh all the evidence "to obtain as coherent a picture as possible of the past as consistent as possible with the evidence."[46] Not all the evidence will have the same weight in every case; we possess no algorithm to resolve witness conflict. Yet, we accomplish this in everyday life; by using a multitude of evidences, we can construct an indirect assessment of testimony we receive. We assess witness testimony on the grounds that it does or does not best fit the evidence.

Conclusion

In many respects it does not ultimately matter whether or not we can identify a particular event as a miracle. The case of miracles bears resemblances to cases of donation. For the donees it does not ultimately matter whether

---

45. Swinburne, *Concept of Miracle*, 27–32.
46. Ibid., 37.

there was an actual donor, whether the donees know the donor, whether they can establish that the donor was a person, group, or organization, that the donor really cares for them, or that some purpose lies behind the donation. It is nice to know whether these are the case so that we can thank our donors for their graciousness and generosity and perhaps even establish a relationship with the donor. But even without this knowledge we simply can be grateful for what has happened to us and, if appropriate, for the love and mercy shown to us in the provision. When we are benefited, whether we believe we are graced depends upon our outlook. If we believe that we are beneficiaries of someone who truly cares for us and who acts for the good on our behalf, then we can interpret good things happening to us not as serendipity but as the conscious, personal activity of those who intentionally have our best interests at heart. Our own outlook will influence how we interpret our experiences.

This is the context in which we have viewed miracles. Miracles are how God intervenes in the world and in our lives. They are God's means, God's actions of providence, God's implementation of his desires and intentions. Whether we experience a particular, unusual event, a series of events, or a pattern, when we understand that God is good, almighty, knows, and cares about us, when we understand that God listens to our prayers and desires that we be in covenant relationship with him, we can begin to interpret this pattern as divine activity in our lives. It is like looking at a richly woven oriental carpet. If we presume that the carpet is the random result of an unguided machine, we will not believe in an intentional maker. The person who made it is lost to us. If we take a myopic view of one corner, we can see lines and colors but no overall arrangement of design. No plan or pattern emerges, simply lines, marks, and colors. But as we look at the carpet pattern over all, as we peruse the interconnected lines, delicate structures, intricate patterns, and colors shading into each other, we begin to see the ways the weaver has decided to create, where the weaver intervened to introduce novelty, where the weaver appears to have wanted to communicate and create. We don't understand all that the weaver did; much lies still hidden in the intricacies and subtleties of the designs, for we only have the effect and no direct access to the intent and plans of the designer. Yet through careful analysis we can begin to see how all the patterns, lines, and figures fit together. And if the old carpet is missing a part and a piece is presented to us, we can assess whether it is an authentic piece from the old carpet by studying how what it bears in color, style, and structure fits with the pattern of the larger carpet.

Similarly with the carpets of our lives. The Weaver acts providentially according to his own plan. This plan is unique, both in scope and individuality, in that it involves interacting with living carpets. The carpets are not made merely to settle on themselves but to return the glory they exhibit to the weaver. As we move through our carpet life, we begin to see events that fit into patterns. The relationships and structures may be created by us, existing only in our minds. We may not know how the events occurred or why. But in one sense that does not matter, for we deeply understand that a Weaver exists who has intents and purposes, who communicates and reveals his desires to have us in relationship. Although we cannot perceive in a sensory way the Weaver bringing about the providential actions, as we can with human agents, we can perceive in an epistemic way and know that what happens often is the sort of thing that the Weaver would create and do, for we have a long history of witnesses to his creating and providing power. A multitude of stories recount interventions. What happens to us and others, the effects we witness and to which others give testimony, fit into the divine patterns to which we are given unclear reflections. We, at this juncture, see things through clouded, frosted glass, but the physical and spiritual events and their fit are seen nonetheless.

Some might never "see" the Weaver. The carpet, they say, is an accidental production of nature and nurture, woven with our genetic fabrics entirely by us, or progenitors, and by those whom we encounter. They find no space for miracles because their paradigm will not allow it. For those who acknowledge the activity of an intentional, providential Weaver, marks and designs in the carpet are signs of his activity. They call us to note a different order, signal to us that more is involved than natural causes and effects. We are given no guarantee of assurance, but the best explanation of the presence of the designs in our lives is the loving activity of Another.

Since miracles are divine interventions in nature and in our lives, and since they are possible because a new cause produces new effects, we can rest assured that God is active, even though we cannot always or even often determine when and where. We may not know which events are truly miracles, but we can justifiably believe that some are and in everything give thanks. Where we cannot explain the event by natural causes, it does not follow that there are none, but it might be a place where God has providentially intervened on our behalf. Where we can explain the event by natural causes, but the timing is so incredulous and the event carries spiritual meaning and significance, we might find the hand of the Master of Timing. If we look at the events and attempt to determine whether or not individually they are miracles, we have engaged philosophically and theologically. But if we look along them to see something about their cause, meaning, and significance, then we might see the hand of God in our lives and begin to appreciate the marvels of divine providence. The writer of the Gospel of John was correct after all: as providential signs, miracles point beyond themselves by calling attention to God and by calling us to respond to God. The dualistic points of view we noted in the previous chapter reappear. In our daily lives we are concerned with the objective dimension of miracles, for what they can do for us and others. We look out at the surprising and wonder, gratefully, how it came to be. God is concerned with the subjective dimension, with our seeing him and his providential love through the miracles. We don't infer him through the miracles; we can actually experience him in an epistemic way that leads us to action. "If the miracles [δυνάμεις, works of power] that were performed in you had been performed in Tyre and Sidon, they would have repented long ago in sackcloth and ashes. . . . [They] would have remained to this day" (Matt 11:21, 23).

Chapter 12

Enjoying the Provider

I HAVE COME TO the end of crafting diverse pieces and fitting them into our divine providence puzzle. Other interesting and controversial pieces remain that eventually will need to be placed,[1] but my reconstruction gives the fundamental structure of the puzzle. I have assembled the frame and interlocked the pieces that constitute the major theological and philosophical pictures internal to the puzzle. You will undoubtedly agree that putting together what we have of the puzzle was neither easy, uncomplicated, nor noncontroversial. If only, you might say, we had the picture of the finished project with which to check our results. But alas, this we lack, and for that we can be both grateful and disappointed. Grateful because God has given us minds to use: to consider, think, ponder, surmise, analyze, argue, imagine, synthesize, and creatively construct. Disappointed because we long to understand and know. Interestingly enough, the latter feeds upon the former.

A case for humility

What have we learned from our endeavors? Hopefully at the very least, humility, along with a good dose of perseverance. It is clear that not all the pieces seem to fit smoothly into place. How to fit, for example, God's foreknowledge into the puzzle is problematic. We have good and persuasive reasons to believe that God has foreknowledge. Not only is this position biblical, but it is essential to divine providence, for without knowledge of the future God's guidance is greatly compromised by any number of future contingences. If anything, God is held to be trustworthy. At the same time, foreknowledge presents almost insuperable difficulties of a practical kind,

---

1. For example, if God is primarily interested in humans and their moral response to him, given God's power and creativity, why did God allow billions of years to pass after creation or the Big Bang before humans came to be? Or again, how are we to best understand God's relation to time and temporal events? Interestingly, these two questions may be connected.

for without violating his own knowledge God cannot use this knowledge either to direct us to change what it is that he already knows or to make the changes himself. These implications have consequences for how we fit the pieces about petitionary prayer and miracles into the puzzle. We make petitionary prayers to bring about change, and God encourages us with his definite promises to do so. Yet seemingly the only way God can knowingly participate in this process is for him to limit his knowledge of the future, which in turn puts the matter of his guidance into difficulty. Miracles are one means of God's involvement in the world, but that participation has to be informed by what God knows not only about the past and the present but also about the future. Since God works miracles for moral and spiritual purposes, they are part of divine teleology, and this employment involves knowledge. We may adjust these pieces we have considered, noting and experimenting with the diverse ways they interconnect with and affect each other and other pieces, some of which we may not have considered. Nonetheless, they make the puzzle challenging to assemble.

We have seen that the only way we can put the pieces of human freedom and divine power into the puzzle is for God to self-limit his power. This seems less problematic than God self-limiting his knowledge, but for some it may prove a troublesome mis-ordering of the puzzle pieces. It may appear that we placed the pieces in the wrong order, with human freedom being situated first, forcing the piece about divine power to conform to it. What assures us of God's priority in self-limitation is that it is intrinsically connected to creation (where he first creates the other), to reconciliation (where he enters the created through the incarnation), and healing (where he takes on our infirmities in restoration). Only when it is observed that creation on earth reaches its apex when God brings about humans, that the incarnation is strategic to the divine-human story, and that God undertakes healing to address the brokenness of our fallen condition, can the ordering be understood and can we see freedom playing its proper role reconciling us back to God. Within the Christian context, self-limitation should not be all that problematic, especially when we consider that the Christian story centers on divine self-limitation. The incarnation epitomizes self-limitation so that God can bring about his purposes of healing, reconciliation, and free acknowledgement of Christ's lordship (Phil 2:6–11). Hence, we should not be surprised that self-limitation plays a significant role rather than being a disordering factor in the total divine economy.

We might be queasy about how the pieces that address dysteleology or disorder in nature and in our moral experience can be put into place. Again, this connects with the pieces of God self-limiting his power and miracles. And these in turn connect with the piece that makes evil possible. The real problem, however, is not the presence of evil but its plenitude. Perhaps we might like, if possible, more divine intervention. At the same time, in our daily lives, we cherish our freedom from intervention and the ability to make our own choices and decisions. This connects to the piece that addresses how we intersect our wills with God's will, with being formed in the image of God, and how we realize the fullness of the image (2 Cor 3:18). In the face of evil and dysteleology we "do not lose heart," but realize that "we have this treasure in earthen vessels" for a purpose. Out of that which is "desolate and empty" (*tohu wābohu*, Gen 1:2) we bring care, courage, and beauty.

Looking at the pieces in the larger context we can understand the rationale that lies behind their positioning. Yet, when we focus on the individual pieces themselves, particularly on their ambiguous shadings and indefinite lines, what looked to be a reasonable fit at times may appear forced to some. The possibility of obtaining the greater good connects with the pieces of the divine program, God's gracious and free reconciliation of us, and the freedom on our part that this requires. Yet some might argue that the cost of placing these pieces as we have is too great; too much divine knowledge and sovereignty must be sacrificed to achieve it. But sovereignty without participation or consent of the governed is not sovereignty at all; it is only manipulation. To not see this is to miss the God who creates in his image stewards of the earth and its inhabitants[2] and who covenants in a way that asks for reciprocity.

Even divine goodness may seem fragilely placed. A contingent divine goodness might seem a piece less than we bargained for. We searched the pieces for something stronger, something that gave us the assurance of logical necessity. But no such piece was found; it simply did not fit into the puzzle. Often what we want to be the case turns out not to be the case, and at times it is difficult to realize that this is a plus and an advance rather than a negative feature. We don't have the freedom to make God's puzzle what we would like or want it to be. And in this case, we have a God who not only desires righteousness and justice, but exemplifies it.

As we make our construction, we may turn these pieces round and round, enriching and affecting how we will place others. My hope is that contemplation of how we constructed and pieced together the puzzle leaves us thoughtful, hopeful, and excited about carrying the work forward. This is perfectly consistent with some dissatisfaction. Looking at and analyzing the pieces, we want more: we want the entire puzzle completed, with each

---

2. For a more detailed treatment of stewardship, see Reichenbach and Anderson, *On Behalf*, ch. 1.

piece fitting and seamlessly hooked into the others. If this would happen, we could sit back and relax with theological gratification (and bravado) for a completed work. All is well, we can say. We can retire from theology with our puzzle finished and our trophies won. After all, completing the puzzle has been a long time coming—as with Fermat's last theorem.

Realizing and admitting the difficulties and ambiguities is not a sign of defeat or lack of confidence in our arguments and conclusions, but an indication of the honesty and humility we must have as we stand confronted not only by what we have accomplished but by the enormity of the task of trying to understand God both as transcendent and as immanently at work in the world. Realizing that not all can be smoothly fitted does not mean that we have labored in vain. To the contrary, I believe that what I have argued to this point is true, but at the same time I must admit that others will disagree and that I may be mistaken about some of the pieces and their relationship. Philosophers and theologians, like others, can profitably use a bit of humility when they speak about their craft, and even more so when they speak about God. As the apostle Paul noted, "we see through a glass darkly." But at least we see, and much can be said for seeing—and thinking, reasoning, imagining, and understanding—even imperfectly.

Looking at and looking along

Michael Ward, in his extremely insightful book on the planetary themes in C. S. Lewis's *Chronicles of Narnia*, points to a distinction, to which we have already hinted, that Lewis borrowed from the English philosopher Samuel Alexander. What Lewis terms an "indispensable tool of thought" is the distinction between contemplation and enjoyment.[3] Contemplation is analysis, "abstract, external, impersonal, uninvolved knowledge." It is looking at the themes of providence as we have done, to define our terms, argue for true propositions, see relationships, critically interact with ours and others' ideas, and all in all come to reasonable, analytical, synthetically defensible positions on divine providence. This has been our major task in this study. There is nothing amiss with seriously contemplating the pieces and making inferences to the best explanation. Indeed, doing theology, philosophy, or puzzle-solving is a notable and respectable endeavor, well worth the steep price of academic admission. It can bring unimaginable enlightenment.

But Lewis suggested that we need not only analyze the pieces by the light of reason and experience, but we need "to look along them." Lewis, following Alexander, called this enjoyment. We need to have the pieces we

3. Ward, *Planet Narnia*, 16–17.

analyzed lead us to their maker, to show us not the completed picture but the creator of the picture, the one who not only makes the picture and its pieces but is its very subject. Lewis provocatively and creatively puts the distinction this way.

> I was standing today in the dark toolshed. The sun was shining outside and through the crack at the top of the door there came a sunbeam. From where I stood that beam of light, with the specks of dust floating in it, was the most striking thing in the place. Everything else was almost pitch-black. I was seeing the beam, not seeing things by it.
>
> Then I moved, so that the beam fell on my eyes. Instantly the whole previous picture vanished. I saw no toolshed, and (above all) no beam. Instead I saw, framed in the irregular cranny at the top of the door, green leaves moving on the branches of a tree outside and beyond that, nine-odd million miles away, the sun. Looking along the beam, and looking at the beam, are very different experiences.[4]

When we look along the pieces we experience enjoyment as we see divine goodness revealed in the freedom God providentially has bestowed on us. Without this freedom we would be bereft of the glory of entering into a meaningful and significant covenant relationship with God. We would be conditioned to "love" and "respond," but our love and response would not proceed from our own desires and motives. When we look along the puzzle pieces, rather than merely contemplate them, we see divine goodness, not as necessary, but as freely flowing towards us from the infinite character of God. It is a goodness full of free providential grace, leading to our bounty from God's goodness. The blessing comes accompanied by pain and suffering, dysfunction and disability. Yet it is all possible because God desires of us not only that we freely love him but also that our person and character are sharpened, at times by passing through the refiners' fires. We can revel in divine goodness.

When we look along the pieces we experience enjoyment as we see that divine power implements God's goodness. God can do what he wills, and yet at the same time he cannot, for God's loving providence is directed to the subjective. We focus on the objective dimension of God's power, wanting God to exercise it to bring us good while, with the Psalmist, calling down fire on our enemies. We want to see power exercised unequivocally and beneficently in the world for the poor and distressed, for the widows and orphans, for those who have been unjustly deprived. And we want to

---

4. Lewis, "Meditation," 607.

see it applied for ourselves, for our benefit: good exercised; evil exorcised. To that end we petition. Yet if we look along the piece of divine power we begin to see God's unwavering concern, not only with the other, the poor and oppressed, but also with the subjective. God wants us to return to the covenant relationship with him; that is his primary concern, to the end of which the Father sent the Son. God's power is perfected in the weakness of becoming human, in the act of self-limitation and sacrifice, so that ultimately God's mercy can reclaim our own freely returned love (2 Cor 12:9). For both God and us divine power serves our good, but we often entertain differing concepts of the good. For God, the good is not primarily our happiness or our own self-fulfillment; it is found in becoming like God himself, continually being obediently formed in God's image—this time not of our own making, but of the remaking designs of the gracious creator. Power serves love. Looking along in enjoyment we see God's love coming to us in providential power.

When we look along the pieces we experience enjoyment when grace erupts in guidance, and the quality of guidance is assured by God's knowledge of us and the future. He sees the road ahead. Contemplating God's foreknowledge leads to intellectual struggle with realizing the arguments on both sides of the debate regarding the extent to which God knows the future; enjoying it leads to the assurance that God guides us with his all-knowing eye (Deut 11:12). In God we have one we can trust, who can help us wisely address our approaching future.

When we contemplate the pieces we see the struggle between good and evil, the prevalence and oppressively destructive power of pain and suffering, and the reign of injustice. When we look along them we hear—without fully understanding—the assurance that things work together for good when we return the love God has shared with us. This assurance does not provide a justification for pain and suffering; finding that justification is the role of contemplation. Rather, we look to God's assuring love and care for us. Even what is evil and bad—and it still is evil and can be horrendous evil—cannot hide or separate us from God's abundant love. In this we find comfort, even though this fact does not diminish the pain and suffering, the hurt of sin, and the healing of forgiveness. Arching over all is God's love, stemming from his character of goodness and his providential presence. God's love for us and our love for God can be in union, shaped around suffering experienced deeply on both sides.

As we look along the pieces we experience enjoyment when we see God responding to our prayers, not necessarily in the ways we want but in the way God desires, for he desires both our free return of his love and our maturation. We see a God who weeps for those who reject him, who continually desires to respond to their confession with forgiveness, who even before they pray provides for their needs (Matt 6:8). God is interested in the petitioner, and so in his establishment of the practice of petitionary prayer God desires intimate, heartfelt communication regarding our deepest needs and desires. To bring these before God is to open to him, as the morning flower invites the pollinating bee, and invite him into the ongoing conversation. In this we not only realize our dependence upon him, but even more deeply we long to be remade in his image, so that God's will is our will, with the result that our will is God's will, to which he can say the affirmative "Yes, it is done." Petitionary prayer is a remaking of us so that we—with God's assistance and yet being God's hands—can remake the world.

As we look along the pieces we experience enjoyment when we see God miraculously involved in our world and in our lives. God intervenes not only at the great crossroads of life and in its astounding events, but also in the little things that give our life meaning and significance. We may not see God's hand, but if we listen and feel perhaps we can sense his Breath and taste his Fire, which providentially ministers to us. We begin to look not for the miracle but for the one who works the miracles, who through them signals and reveals to us his concern and winged coverage.

The dance of enjoyment

Early on we introduced another metaphor. Providence is a kind of dance, a dance of enjoyment. God took the lead by creating the universe to reflect his glory. God also created us and invites us to partner with him, to learn from him, to participate meaningfully in the dance that moves the world. God guides our steps, teaches us his ways, invites us to emulate him and others who reflect him. We may contemplate the moves of the dance, but in carefully watching and analyzing the placement of our hands and feet we take our eyes off our partner, the dance-master. We do not learn to dance by watching our feet. Dancers do more than contemplate moves; in the dance they enjoy the partner. To follow in the dance of life is to look for, appreciate, be thankful for, and pray for God's love, mercies, and providence. We may not know which events are truly miracles, displaying God's providence. But we can justifiably believe that even the unlikeliest rocky event may turn out to be a treasured jewel, that some events are miracles, that through them we can see along and encounter God, and in everything give joyful thanks (1 Thess 5:16–18).

Bibliography

Adams, Marilyn McCord. *Horrendous Evils and the Goodness of God.* Ithaca, NY: Cornell University Press, 1999.

Adams, Robert M. "Middle Knowledge and the Problem of Evil." *American Philosophical Quarterly* 14 (1977) 109–14.

Árnadöttir, Steinvör Thöll, and Tim Crane. "There is No Exclusion Problem." In *Mental Causation and Ontology*, edited by edited by Sophie C. Gibb, et al., 248–66. New York: Oxford University Press, 2013.

Audi, Robert. "Mental Causation: Sustaining and Dynamic." In *Mental Causation*, edited by John Heil and Alfred Mele, 53–74. Oxford: Clarendon, 1995.

Anselm. *Proslogium*. Translated by Sidney Norton Deane. Chicago: Open Court, 1939.

Aristotle, *Nichomachean Ethics*. Translated by Roger Crisp. Cambridge: Cambridge University Press, 2000.

Augustine. *City of God*. Basic Writings of Saint Augustine. Edited by Whitney J. Oates. Grand Rapids: Baker, 1980.

———. *Contra adversarium legis et prophetarum*. Turnhout, Belgium: Brepols, 1985.

———. *The Enchiridion on Faith, Hope, and Love*. Translated by Thomas S. Hibbs. Washington, DC: Regnery, 1996.

Averill, Edward, and B. F. Keating. "Is Interactionism a Law of Classical Physics?" *Mind* 90 (1981) 102–7.

Baggett, David, and Jerry Walls. *Good God*. New York: Oxford University Press, 2011.

Baker, Lynn Rudder. "Metaphysics and Mental Causation." In *Mental Causation*, edited by Heil and Mele, 75–95. Oxford: Clarendon, 1995.

———. *Persons and Bodies: A Constitution View*. Cambridge: Cambridge University Press, 2000.

Basinger, David. "God Does Not Necessarily Respond to Prayer." In *Contemporary Debates in Philosophy of Religion*, edited by Michael L. Peterson and Raymond J. Van Arragon, 255–63. Oxford: Blackwell, 2004.

———. "Practical Implications." In *The Openness of God*, edited by Clark Pinnock et al., 155–76. Downers Grove, IL: IVP, 1994.

Basinger, David, and Randall Basinger. *Philosophy and Miracle*. Lewiston, ME: Mellen, 1986.

———, eds. *Predestination and Free Will*. Downers Grove, IL: IVP, 1986.

Behm, Johannes. "Καρδία." *Theological Dictionary of the New Testament*, edited by G. Kittel et al., 3: 605–13. Reprint. Grand Rapids: Eerdmans, 2006.

Beilby, James, and Paul R. Eddy, eds. *The Nature of the Atonement: Four Views*. Downers Grove, IL: IVP, 2006.

Bergmann, Michael, and J. A. Cover. "Divine Responsibility without Divine Freedom." *Faith and Philosophy* 23.4 (2006) 381–408.

Bishop, Robert C., and Harald Atmanspacher. "The Causal Closure of Physics and Free Will." In *The Oxford Handbook of Free Will*, 2nd ed., edited by Robert Kane, 101–11. New York: Oxford University Press, 2011.

Bloom, Paul. "The Moral Life of Babies." *New York Times*, May 5, 2010, MM44.

Boling, Robert G. *Joshua*. Garden City, NY: Doubleday, 1982.

Born, Hanspeter, and Benoit Lanais. *Schuffenecker's Sunflowers: and Other van Gogh Forgeries*. 2014. http://www.amazon.com/Schuffeneckers-Sunflowers-Other-Gogh-Forgeries-ebook/dp/B00HZP3VPO#reader_B00HZP3VPO 2014).

Boyd, Gregory A. *God of the Possible: A Biblical Introduction to the Open View of God*. Grand Rapids: Baker, 2000.

Bradley, Raymond. "A Moral Argument for Atheism." In *The Impossibility of God*, edited by Michael Martin and Ricki Monnier, 129–46. Amherst, MA: Prometheus, 2003.

Bromiley, Geoffrey, ed., *The International Standard Bible Encyclopedia*. 4 vols. Grand Rapids: Eerdmans, 1989.

Brown, Colin. *Miracles and the Critical Mind*. Grand Rapids: Eerdmans, 1984.

Bruce, F. F. *The Letter of Paul to the Romans*. Tyndale New Testament Commentaries. 2nd ed. Grand Rapids: Eerdmans, 1985.

Buckhout, Robert. "Eyewitness Testimony." *Scientific American* 231.6, December 1974, 23–31.

Bultmann, Rudolph. "προγινώσκω." In *Theological Dictionary of the New Testament*, edited by G. Kittel et al., 1: 715–16. Reprint. Grand Rapids: Eerdmans, 2006.

Burge, Tyler. "Mind-Body Causation and Explanatory Practice." In *Mental Causation*, edited by John Heil and Alfred Mele, 97–120. Oxford: Clarendon, 1995.

Calvin, John. *Institutes of the Christian Religion*. Louisville, KY: Westminster John Knox, 1960.

Campbell, Keith. *Body and Mind*. Garden City, NY: Anchor, 1970.

Chapman, Stephen B. "Martial Memory, Peaceable Vision." In *Holy War in the Bible*, edited by Heath Thomas et al., 47–67. Downers Grove, IL: IVP, 2013.

Copan, Paul, and Matthew Flannagan. "The Ethics of 'Holy War' for Christian Morality and Theology." In *Holy War in the Bible*, edited by Heath Thomas et al., 201–39. Downers Grove, IL: IVP Academic, 2013.

Craig, William L., and Quentin Smith. *Theism, Atheism, and Big Bang Cosmology*. Oxford: Clarendon, 1993.

Cullmann, Oscar. *The Christology of the New Testament*. Philadelphia: Westminster, 1957.

Davies, Brian. *The Reality of God and the Problem of Evil*. New York: Continuum, 2006.

Davis, Stephen T., ed. *Encountering Evil*. Louisville, KY: Westminster John Knox, 2001.

de Lavilléon, G., et al., "Explicit Memory Creation during Sleep Demonstrates a Causal Role of Place Cells in Navigation." *Nature Neuroscience*. doi:10.1038/nn.3970, 2015.

Dennett, Daniel. *Consciousness Explained*. Boston: Little, Brown, 1991.

Dillmann, Charles N., and Nola J. Opperwall. "Thank; Thankful(ness); Thanksgiving." In *International Standard Biblical Encyclopedia*, edited by Geoffrey Bromiley, 4: 882–84. Grand Rapids: Eerdmans, 1995.

Dretske, Fred. "Mental Events as Structuring Causes of Behaviour." In *Mental Causation*, edited by John Heil and Alfred Mele, 121–36. Oxford: Clarendon, 1993.

Dunn, James D. G. *Romans 1–8*. Word Biblical Commentary, Vol. 38A. Dallas: Word, 1988.

———. *Romans 9–16*. Word Biblical Commentary, Vol. 38B. Dallas: Word, 1988.
Dworkin, Gerald, ed. *Determinism, Free Will, and Moral Responsibility*. Englewood Cliffs, NJ: Prentice-Hall, 1970.
Earl, Douglas S. "Holy War and חרם." In *Holy War in the Bible*, edited by Heath Thomas et al., 19–46. Downers Grove, IL: IVP Academic, 2013.
Edwards, Jonathan. *Freedom of the Will*. New Haven: Yale University Press, 1957.
Erickson, Millard J. *Christian Theology*. Grand Rapids: Baker, 1998.
———. *What Does God Know and When Does He Know It?* Grand Rapids: Zondervan, 2003.
Fischer, John Martin. "Responsibility and Control." *Journal of Philosophy* 89.1 (1982) 24–40.
———, ed. *God, Foreknowledge, and Freedom*. Stanford: Stanford University Press, 1989.
Flew, Antony. *Hume's Philosophy of Belief*. New York: Humanities, 1961.
Flint, Thomas. *Divine Providence: The Molinist Account*. Ithaca, NY: Cornell University Press, 1998.
Fodor, Jerry. "Making Mind Matter More." *Philosophical Topics* 17 (1989) 59–79.
———. "The Mind-Body Problem." In *The Mind-Body Problem: A Guide to the Current Debate*, edited by Richard Warner and Tadeusz Szubka, 24–40. Oxford: Blackwell, 1994.
Foster, Richard J., and James Bryan Smith, eds. *Devotional Classics: Selected Readings for Individuals and Groups*. San Francisco: Harper, 1990.
Gallagher, Shaun, and Dan Zahavi. "Phenomenological Approaches to Self-Consciousness." In *The Stanford Encyclopedia of Philosophy*, edited by Edward N. Zalta. (Spring 2015). http://plato.stanford.edu/archives/spr2015/entries/self-consciousness-phenomenological/.
Geach, Peter T. "An Irrelevance of Omnipotence." *Philosophy* 48.186 (1973) 327–33.
———. "Omnipotence." *Philosophy* 48.183 (1973) 7–20.
Geisler, Norman. *Chosen But Free*. 2nd ed. Minneapolis: Bethany, 2010.
Gibb, Sophie C. "Closure Principles and the Laws of Conservation of Momentum." *Dialectica* 64.3 (2010) 363–84.
Gibb, Sophie C., E. J. Lowe, and R. D. Ingthorsson, eds. *Mental Causation and Ontology*. New York: Oxford University Press, 2013.
Ginet, Carl. "Might We Have No Choice." In *Freedom and Determinism*, edited by Lehrer, 87–104. New York: Random House, 1966.
Grundmann, Walter. "δύναμαί, etc." *Theological Dictionary of the New Testament*, edited by G. Kittel et al., 2: 284–317. Reprint. Grand Rapids: Eerdmans, 2006.
Guleserian, Theodore. "Divine Freedom and the Problem of Evil." *Faith and Philosophy* 17 (2000) 348–66.
Hagner, Donald A. *Matthew 14–28*. Word Biblical Commentary, Vol. 33b. Dallas: Word, 1995.
Hartshorne, Charles. *Omnipotence and Other Theological Mistakes*. Albany, NY: SUNY Press, 1984.
Hasker, William "Divine Knowledge and Human Freedom." In *The Oxford Handbook of Free Will*, 2nd ed., edited by Robert Kane, 39–54. New York: Oxford University Press, 2011.
———. *The Emergent Self*. Ithaca, NY: Cornell University Press, 1999.
———. "Foreknowledge and Necessity." *Faith and Philosophy* 2.2 (1985) 121–57.

———. *God, Time, and Knowledge*. Ithaca, NY: Cornell University Press, 1989.
———. "Hard Facts and Theological Determinism." *Noûs* 22 (1988) 419–36. Reprinted in *God, Foreknowledge, and Freedom*, edited by John Martin Fischer, 159–77. Stanford: Stanford University Press, 1989.
———. "Yes, God Has Beliefs!" *Religious Studies* 24 (1988) 385–94.
———. *The Triumph of God over Evil*. Downers Grove, IL: IVP, 2008.
Heil, John. "Mental Causation in the Physical World." In *Mental Causation and Ontology*, edited by S. C. Gibb et al., 18–34. New York: Oxford University Press, 2013.
Heil, John, and Alfred Mele, eds. *Mental Causation*. Oxford: Clarendon, 1995.
Helm, Paul. *The Providence of God*. Contours of Christian Theology. Downers Grove, IL: IVP, 1994.
Hick, John. *Evil and the God of Love*. Basingstoke, UK: Macmillan, 1966.
Hjelmgaard, Kim. "Israel Revokes Travel Permits, Deploys Troops after Attack." *USA Today*, Thursday, June 9, 2016.
Hodgson, David. "Quantum Physics, Consciousness, and Free Will." In *The Oxford Handbook of Free Will*, 2nd ed., edited by Robert Kane, 57–83. New York: Oxford University Press, 2011.
Hoffman, Joshua. *Omnipotence*. Chichester, UK: Wiley Blackwell, 2010.
Hoffman, Joshua, and Gary Rosenkrantz. "Hard and Soft Facts." In *God, Foreknowledge, and Freedom*, edited by John Martin Fischer, 123–35. Stanford: Stanford University Press, 1989.
Holland, Roy F. "The Miraculous." *American Philosophical Quarterly* 2 (1965) 43–51.
Hornsby, Jennifer. "Agency and Causal Explanation." In *Mental Causation*, edited by John Heil and Alfred Mele, 161–85. Oxford: Clarendon, 1995.
Howard-Snyder, Daniel, ed. *The Evidential Argument from Evil*. Bloomington, IN: Indiana University Press, 1996.
Hume, David. *An Enquiry Concerning Human Understanding*. Indianapolis: Bobbs-Merrill, 1955.
Hunt, David P. "Divine Providence and Simple Foreknowledge." *Faith and Philosophy* 10.3 (1993) 394–414.
Johansson, Petter, et al. "Failure to Detect Mismatches between Intention and Outcome in a Simple Decision Task." *Science* 310, October 7, 2005, 116–19.
Jowers, Dennis, ed. *Four Views on Divine Providence*. Counterpoints. Grand Rapids: Zondervan, 2011.
Kane, Robert, ed. *The Oxford Handbook of Free Will*. 2nd ed. New York: Oxford University Press, 2011.
———. "Rethinking Free Will: New Perspectives on an Ancient Problem." In *The Oxford Handbook of Free Will*, 2nd ed., edited by Robert Kane, 381–404. New York: Oxford University Press, 2011.
Keller, James A. *Problems of Evil and the Power of God*. Burlington, VT: Ashgate, 2007.
Kenny, Anthony. *The God of the Philosophers*. Oxford: Clarendon, 1979.
Kilby, Clyde. *The Christian World of C. S. Lewis*. Grand Rapids: Eerdmans, 1964.
Kim, Jaegwon. *Mind in a Physical World*. Cambridge: MIT Press, 1998.
———. "The Non-Reductivist's Troubles with Mental Causation." In *Mental Causation*, edited by John Heil and Alfred Mele, 189–210. Oxford: Clarendon, 1995.

Kittel, Gerhard, and Gerhard Friedrich, eds. *Theological Dictionary of the New Testament*. 10 vols. Translated by Geoffrey Bromiley. Grand Rapids: Eerdmans, 1964–76.
Knobe, Joshua, and Shaun Nichols. "Free Will and the Bounds of the Self." In *The Oxford Handbook of Free Will*, 2nd ed., edited by Robert Kane, 530–54. New York: Oxford University Press, 2011.
Kosso, Peter. *Reading the Book of Nature*. Cambridge: Cambridge University Press, 1992.
Kuhn, Thomas S. *The Structure of Scientific Revolutions*. Chicago: University of Chicago Press, 1962.
Kvanvig, Jonathan L. *The Possibility of an All-Knowing God*. New York: St. Martin's, 1986.
Lehrer, Keith. "An Empirical Disproof of Determinism?" In *Determinism, Free Will, and Moral Responsibility*, edited by Gerald B. Dworkin, 172–95. Englewood Cliffs, NJ: Prentice-Hall, 1970.
———. *Freedom and Determinism*. New York: Random House, 1966.
Lewis, Clive S. *A Grief Observed*. New York: Bantam, 1961.
———. "Meditation in a Toolshed." In *C. S. Lewis: Essay Collection and Other Short Pieces*, edited by Lesley Walmsley, 607–10. London: HarperCollins, 2000.
———. *Miracles*. New York: Macmillan, 1947.
———. "Petitionary Prayer: A Problem without an Answer." In *Christian Reflections*, edited by Walter Hooper, 175–86. Grand Rapids: Eerdmans, 1967.
———. *The Problem of Pain*. New York: Macmillan, 1962.
Linden, Toby. "Shapere on Observation." *Philosophy of Science* 59.2 (1992) 293–99.
Lovejoy, Arthur O. *The Great Chain of Being*. New York: Harper and Row, 1936.
Lowe, Edward J. "Substance Causation, Powers, and Human Agency." In *Mental Causation and Ontology*, edited by S. C. Gibb et al, 153–72. New York: Oxford University Press, 2013.
Mackie, John L. "Evil and Omnipotence." *Mind* 64.254 (1955) 200–212.
———. *The Miracle of Theism*. Oxford: Oxford University Press, 1982.
Martens, Elmer A. "God, Names of." In *Evangelical Dictionary of Biblical Theology*, edited by Roger Elwell, 297–300. Grand Rapids: Baker, 1996.
McCann, Hugh. "Divine Sovereignty and the Freedom of the Will." *Faith and Philosophy* 12 (1995) 582–98.
McKinnon, Alastair. "Miracle." In *Miracles*, edited by Richard Swinburne, 49–52. London: Macmillan, 1989.
McLaughlin, Brian, and Karen Bennett. "Supervenience." In *Stanford Encyclopedia of Philosophy*, edited by Edward N. Zalta. http://plato.stanford.edu/archives/spr2014/entries/supervenience.
McMahon, Darrin M. *Happiness: A History*. New York: Atlantic Monthly, 2006.
Mavrodes, George. "Some Puzzles Concerning Omnipotence." *Philosophical Review* 72.2 (1963) 191–202.
Menzies, Peter. "Mental Causation in the Physical World." In *Mental Causation and Ontology*, edited by S. C. Gibb et al., 58–87. New York: Oxford University Press, 2013.
Michaelis, Wilhelm. "παντοκράτωρ." *Theological Dictionary of the New Testament*, edited by G. Kittel et al., 3: 914–15. Reprint. Grand Rapids: Eerdmans, 2006.

Molina, Luis de. *On Divine Foreknowledge*. Translated by Alfred J. Freddoso. Ithaca, NY: Cornell University Press, 1988.

Montero, Barbara. "What Does the Conservation of Energy Have to Do with Physicalism?" *Dialectica* 60.4 (2006) 383–96.

Morris, Leon. *The Gospel according to John*. Grand Rapids: Eerdmans, 1971.

Morris, Thomas. *Anselmian Explorations*. South Bend, IN: University of Notre Dame Press, 1987.

Morriston, Wes. "The Case of Divinely Mandated Genocide." *Sophia* 51.1 (2012) 117–35.

Mullen, Jethro. "New van Gogh Painting Discovered: 'Sunset at Montmajour.'" http://www.cnn.com/2013/09/09/world/europe/netherlands-van-gogh-new-painting.

Murray, Michael J. "God Responds to Prayer." In *Contemporary Debates in Philosophy of Religion*, edited by Michael L. Peterson and Raymond J. Arragon, 242–54. Oxford: Blackwell, 2004.

Murray, Michael J., and Kurt Meyers. "Ask and It Will Be Given to You." *Religious Studies* 30 (1994) 311–30.

O'Brien, Miles, and Jon Baime. "Babies and Learning." (March 28, 2011.) http://www.nsf.gov/news/special_reports/science_nation/babieslearning.jsp.

O'Connor, Timothy, ed. *Agents, Causes, Events: Essays on Indeterminism and Free Will*. New York: Oxford University Press, 1995.

———. "The Impossibility of Middle Knowledge." *Philosophical Studies* 66 (1992) 139–66.

———. *Theism and Ultimate Explanation: The Necessary Shape of Contingency*. Malden, MA: Blackwell, 2008.

O'Doherty, John. "Neural Conditioning Using Real-time fMRI." (August 20, 2014.) http://www.dana.org/Media/GrantsDetails.aspx?id=38915.

Origin. *Contra Celsum*. Translated by Henry Chadwick. Cambridge: Cambridge University Press, 1953.

Papineau, David. *Thinking about Consciousness*. Oxford: Oxford University Press, 2002.

Parfit, Derek. *Reasons and Persons*. Oxford: Oxford University Press, 1984.

Parsons, John J. "Hebrew Names of God." (2016.) http://www.hebrew4christians.com/Names_of_G-d/El/el.html.

Peterson, Michael L. *God and Evil: An Introduction to the Issues*. Boulder, CO: Westview, 2009.

———. *Problem of Evil: Selected Readings*. South Bend, IN: University of Notre Dame Press, 1992.

Peterson, Michael L., and Raymond J. Van Arragon, eds. *Contemporary Debates in Philosophy of Religion*. Oxford: Blackwell, 2004.

Pike, Nelson. "Divine Omniscience and Voluntary Action." *Philosophical Review* 74 (1965) 27–46.

———. "Omnipotence and God's Ability to Sin." *American Philosophical Quarterly* 6 (1969) 208–16.

Pinnock, Clark. *Most Moved Mover: A Theology of God's Openness*. Grand Rapids: Baker, 2001.

———, et al. *The Openness of God: A Biblical Challenge to the Traditional Understanding of God*. Downers Grove, IL: IVP, 1994.

Place, Ullin T. "Is Consciousness a Brain Process?" *British Journal of Psychology* 47 (1956) 44–50.

Plantinga, Alvin. *God, Freedom, and Evil*. New York: Harper & Row, 1974.
———. *The Nature of Necessity*. London: Oxford University Press, 1974.
Pruss, Alexander. "A New Free-Will Defence." *Religious Studies* 39.2 (2003) 211–23.
Rattner, Arye. "Convicted but Innocent: Wrongful Conviction and the Criminal Justice System." *Law and Human Behavior* 12 (1988) 283–94.
Reichenbach, Bruce R. *Epistemic Obligations*. Waco, TX: Baylor University Press, 2012.
———. *Evil and a Good God*. New York: Fordham University Press, 1982.
———. "Freedom, Justice, and Moral Responsibility." In *The Grace of God, the Will of Man*, edited by Clark Pinnock, 277–303. Grand Rapids: Zondervan, 1989.
———. "Genesis 1 as a Theological-Political Narrative of Kingdom Establishment." *Bulletin for Biblical Research* 13.1 (2003) 47–69.
———. "God Limits His Power." In *Predestination and Free Will*, edited by David Basinger and Randall Basinger, 101–24. Downers Grove, IL: IVP, 1986.
———. "Hasker on Omniscience." *Faith and Philosophy* 4.1 (1987) 86–93.
———. "The Healing View." In *The Nature of the Atonement: Four Views*, edited by James Beilby and Paul R. Eddy, 117–42. Downers Grove, IL: IVP, 2006.
———. "Mavrodes on Omnipotence." *Philosophical Studies* 37 (1980) 211–14.
Reichenbach, Bruce R., and V. Elving Anderson. *On Behalf of God: A Christian Ethic for Biology*. Grand Rapids: Eerdmans, 1995.
Rhoda, Alan. "The Philosophical Case for Open Theism." *Philosophia* 35 (2007) 301–11.
Rice, Richard. *God's Foreknowledge and Man's Free Will*. Minneapolis: Bethany, 1985.
Robb, David, and John Heil. "Mental Causation." In *The Stanford Encyclopedia of Philosophy*, edited by Edward N. Zalta. 2014. http://plato.stanford.edu/archives/spr2014/entries/mental-causation.
Robinson, Terry E., and Kent C. Berridge. "The Neural Basis of Drug Craving: An Incentivization-Theory of Addiction." *Brain Research Reviews* 18.3 (1993) 247–91.
Roy, Steven C. *How Much Does God Foreknow?* Downers Grove, IL: IVP, 2006.
Sanders, John. *The God Who Risks*. Downers Grove, IL: IVP, 2006.
Schiffer, Stephen. *Remnants of Meaning*. Cambridge: MIT Press/Bradford, 1987.
Schlier, Heinrich. "ἀνακεφαλαιόομαι." In *Theological Dictionary of the New Testament*, edited by G. Kittel et al., 3: 681–82. Reprint. Grand Rapids: Eerdmans, 2006.
Sevincer, A. Timur, P. Daniel Busatta, and Gabriele Oettingen. "Mental Contrasting and Transfer of Energization." *Personality and Social Psychology Bulletin* 40.2 (2014) 139–52.
Shapere, Dudley. "The Concept of Observation in Science and Philosophy." *Science and Philosophy* 49 (1982) 485–525.
———. *Reason and the Search for Knowledge*. Dordrecht: Reidel, 1984.
Stoljar, Daniel. "Physicalism." In *The Stanford Encyclopedia of Philosophy*, edited by Edward N. Zalta. 2009. http://plato.stanford.edu/archives/fall2009/entries/physicalism.
Stump, Eleonore. "Petitionary Prayer." *American Philosophical Quarterly* 16.4 (1979) 81–91.
Swinburne, Richard. *The Coherence of Theism*. Oxford: Clarendon, 1977.
———. *The Concept of Miracle*. London: Macmillan, 1970.
———. *The Existence of God*. Oxford: Clarendon, 1979.
———. *Is There a God?* New York: Oxford University Press, 1996.
———, ed. *Miracles*. London: Macmillan, 1989.
———. *Providence and the Problem of Evil*. Oxford: Clarendon, 1998.

Thelle, Rannfrid I. "The Biblical Conquest Account and Its Modern Hermeneutical Challenges." *Studia Theologica* 61 (2007) 61–81.
Thomas, à Kempis. *The Imitation of Christ*. Translated by Justin McCann. New York: New American Library, 1962.
Thomas, Aquinas. *Summa Contra Gentiles*, 4 vols. South Bend, IN: University of Notre Dame Press, 1991.
———. *Summa Theologica. Basic Writings of St. Thomas Aquinas*. 2 vols. Edited by Anton C. Pegis. New York: Random House, 1944.
Thomas, Heath A., Jeremy Evans, and Paul Copan, eds. *Holy War in the Bible*. Downers Grove, IL: IVP Academic, 2013.
Townsend, Tim. "'Miracle Priest Sees a Divine Plan in a Media Frenzy." *St. Louis Post-Dispatch*, January 23, 2014. http://www.stltoday.com/lifestyles/faith-and-values/miracle-priest-sees-a-divine-plan-in-a-media-frenzy/article_90298808-4d6b-5d7b-9d22-92b29cb25f6b.html.
Trevisanato, Siro Igino. *The Plagues of Egypt: Archaeology, History, and Science Look at the Bible*. Piscataway, NJ: Gorgias, 2005.
Twelftree, Graham. *Miracles: The Cambridge Companion to Miracles*. Cambridge: Cambridge University Press, 2011.
Urban, Lin, and Douglas N. Walton, eds. *The Power of God*. New York: Oxford University Press, 1978.
van Fraassen, Bas. *The Scientific Image*. New York: Oxford University Press 1980.
van Inwagen, Peter. *Metaphysics*. Boulder, CO: Westview, 2002.
Ward, Michael. *Planet Narnia*. Oxford: Oxford University Press, 2008.
Ware, Bruce A. *God's Lesser Glory: The Diminished God of Open Theism*. Wheaton, IL: Crossway, 2000.
White, James. *The Potter's Freedom*. Amityville, NY: Calvary, 2000.
Wolterstorff, Nicholas. "Reading Joshua." In *Divine Evil? The Moral Character of the God of Abraham*, edited by Michael Bergmann, Michael J. Murray, and Michael C. Rea, 236–56. New York: Oxford University Press, 2010.
Yancey, Philip. *The Bible Jesus Read*. Grand Rapids: Zondervan, 1999.
Young, Elizabeth Drummond. "God's Moral Goodness and Supererogation." *International Journal of the Philosophy of Religion* 73 (2013) 83–95.
Younger Jr., K. Lawson. *Ancient Conquest Accounts: A Study in Ancient Near Eastern and Biblical History Writing*. Supp. 98. Sheffield, UK: Journal for the Study of the Old Testament, 1990.
Zagzebski, Linda Trinkhaus. *The Dilemma of Freedom and Foreknowledge*. New York: Oxford University Press, 1991.

General Index

Abraham, 1, 46, 96–97, 121, 136, 189–90, 198, 201
agency, 38, 43, 56–58, 78–80
  God's, 85, 87, 100–101, 151, 172, 201
almighty, 104–5, 134–50, 152, 203
  and evil, 141–42
  human freedom, 142–43
  omnipotence paradox, 140–41
analogical predication, 86, 91–92
anomalies, 73, 269, 272, 295–96
Anselm, 87, 118, 123, 142, 152
Aristotle, 84, 92, 215
Audi, 69n25, 76n36
Augustine, 37, 39, 47, 93, 109, 123, 139, 143–46

Baggett, David, 81n1, 92n24, 102n40, 103n42, 104,
Basinger, David, 186n13, 195n34, 237n3, 240, 263n1
beliefs, 22, 26, 57–58, 63, 76, 264, 282–84, 292
  dispositional, 202–3
  God's, 151, 154–66, 171–72, 186, 188–89, 195, 198, 202–4, 206
  justifying, 282–83
Ben-Dahan, Eli, 115n59
Bergmann, Michael, 90n20, 100
Bloom, Paul, 93n28
Boling, Robert, 109n50
Boyd, Greg, 179n5, 183n11, 188, 195
Bruce, F. F., 35n19
Burge, Tyler, 77n36, 78

Calvin, John, 37–40, 44n39, 45–47
category mistake, 86

Catherine of Genoa, 237
Celsus, 127–28
character, 40, 88, 116, 178, 186–87, 190, 193–94, 199, 225
  God's, 86–87, 90, 92–95, 105–6, 129, 141–43
character-building, 214–22, 230
  of witnesses, 292–93
choice based on good reasoning, 63–65
communitarian, 238–39
compatibilism, see freedom
compatibilism, see foreknowledge
conservation of energy, 72–75
contemplation, 303–5
Copan, Paul, 111n53
covenant, x–xii, 12, 14–16, 34, 96–97, 250–51
Cullman, Oscar, 106, 107n44

dance, 14, 16, 48, 289, 306
David, 182, 193, 260–61
Davies, Brian, 83–87, 90, 92, 237
Descartes, Rene, 52, 59, 77
determinism, 23–25, 39, 52, 163
disposition, 17, 47, 49, 76, 88, 93–94, 147, 202–3, 206
Dunn, James, 34, 35n20, 49n47, 50n49

Earl, Douglas, 111, 112n57
Edwards, Jonathan, 41–43
election, 29–36, 46, 48–49
Elihu, 106, 214, 218
enjoyment, 303–6
epiphenomenalism, 62–63, 65, 69
Erickson, Millard, 29n13, 179n5
ethnic cleansing of Canaanites, 107–15

as punishment, 113–15
evil, problem of, 101–2, 207–31, 302, 305
   discipline/character formation theodicy, 213–18
   gratuitous, 7, 46, 144, 224–25, 230
   free will theodicy, 222–25
   miracles and evil, 226–29
   moral, 209–10, 214, 216, 219, 222–25
   morally sufficient reasons, 101, 207, 210–11, 216, 221, 229–31
   natural, 208–10, 213–14, 216–20, 222, 225–29, 231
   natural law theodicy, 225–26
   punishment theodicy, 218–22
explanation, 57, 59, 64, 66–67, 70–71, 77–80, 270, 293–96

Fischer, John Martin, 18n5
Flew, Antony, 294–96
Fodor, Jerry, 57n8, 72n5
foreordination, 13, 29–34, 36–40, 44, 48, 50n49, 146
foreknowledge, 31–34, 36, 48, 146, 151–70, 171–206, 300–301, 305
   compatibilism, 157–63
   hard and soft facts, 163–66
   incompatibilism, 155–58, 166–68, 172–75
   impracticality of, 197–200
   self-limiting, 200–204
   prophecy, see prophecy
   truth value, 152, 166–70, 174
freedom
   and agency, 56–58
   compatibilism, 37–50

   definition, 17–22
   evidence for, 22–26
   and foreordination, 29–34
   libertarianism, 17–25, 47, 51–52, 56–57, 59, 77, 79, 94, 124, 174

   morally significant, 89, 94–95, 99–101, 131–32, 143, 171, 212, 223–26
   quantum phenomena, 37n22, 59n12, 66
   scriptural account, 26–29

Gates, Bill, 239–40
Geach, Peter, 134n1, 142n13
Gibb, Sophie, 74n33
God
   almighty, see almighty
   evil, see evil, problem of
   change of mind, 181–87
   disappointment, 180–81, 183–85, 188
   experience of, 284–85
   foreknowledge, see foreknowledge
   good, see goodness of God
   and human freedom, 129–32, 142–47
   impeccability, 93–94, 102, 104–5
   knowledge, 151–52, 305; see foreknowledge
   omnipotent, see omnipotence
   omniscience, see omniscience
   power, 118–27, 135–41, 147–48
   power to do evil, 127–29, 141–42
   regret, 179–81, 183–85
   self-limitation, 129–32, 142–43, 147
   suffers, 230
   title or name, 99, 103–7, 116, 142
goodness of God, 81–117
   axiological, 96–98, 145–46
   contingent, 102–5, 116
   criteria for, 88–92, 102
   moral, 85–92
   necessary, 87–88, 98–99, 105–7
   ontological, 83–87
   supererogation, 96–98, 145–46
Hasker, William, 64n18, 151n1, 155–66, 175–79, 192n26, 193n29, 197n39, 211n2
Heil, John, 58n10, 66n19

ḥērem (ban), 109–11, 115
Helm, Paul, 16n1, 38, 44
Hezekiah, 182
Hick, John, 215–17
Holland, R. F., 273–74
human person, 54–56
Hume, David, 264–67, 292–94
Hunt, David, 200–202

identity theory, 59–61
incompatibilism, see foreknowledge

Johansson, Petter, 20n7
Job, 121
Judas, 143–44, 198

Kane, Robert, 17n2
Kim, Jaegwon, 69n25, 70–71
Knobe, Joshua, 22n8, 54n2, 55n4

law of conservation of matter and energy, 72–74
Lehrer, Keith, 23–25
Leibniz, G.W., 60
Lentz, Katie, 274–75
Lewis, C.S., 90n22, 91, 211n2, 244, 247, 266n6, 268n10, 272, 287–90, 303–4
love, *ix–xii*, 34–35, 48, 82–83, 98–99, 214–15, 217–19, 289, 304–5

Mackie, J.L., 101n39, 130, 212, 266, 292
Martens, Elmer, 136n5
Mavrodes, George, 125–26
memory, 55–56
mental causation, 58, 61–69, 72–73
mental energy, 72–74
Menzies, Peter, 62n15, 66n19, 71n28
middle knowledge, 13–14n5, 224–25
miracle, 8–10, 226–29, 262–99, 301
  definition, 263–67, 271–72
  fit, 286–90
  actuality, 275–76
  of production, 273
  of timing, 273–75
  possibility of, 267–71
  testimony about, 290–96
  world run by, 9–10, 212, 223–24, 226–27
moral accountability, 25–26, 28, 39–45, 47, 99–101
  corporate, 114–15, 221
morally significant actions, 25–26, 89–90
Morris, Leon, 259n20
Morris, Thomas, 95–98, 101–3, 145
Murray, Michael, 237n2, 250–55

natural laws 8–10, 225–28, 263–78, 294–96
Noah, 96–97
novelist, 12–14, 148, 224

Ockhamism, 168–70
O'Connor, Timothy, 127
O'Doherty, John, 79n42
omnipotence, 39–40, 102–4, 118–33
  and evil, 127–29
  see God, power
  human freedom, 129–32
  paradox of, 124–27, 140–41
  a perfection, 123–24
  scripture, 121–23
omniscience, 102–3, 152–55, 199–200, 237
  see foreknowledge
  self-limiting knowledge, 200–204
open theism, 171–206
Origen, 124, 127–28, 139n11
original sin, 93
overdetermination, 67–68

pantokrator, 137, 148
Papineau, David, 73n30
Parsons, John, 136n3, 137n7
Paul, 33–36, 46–50, 242
personal identity, 54–56
Peter, 31, 196
petitionary prayer, 182, 200, 231, 233–61, 305–6

General Index

conversational practice, 235,
  242–43, 250–54, 256–60
goods of, 250–57
how to pray, 244–47
purposes of, 234–36, 257–60
repeated petitions, 241–43
unanswered prayer, 247–50
why pray, 236–41
Piercean view, 168–70
Pike, Nelson, 95 n32, 128n15, 156n4
Pinnock, Clark, 194, 204
plagues of Egypt, 274
Plantinga, Alvin, 89, 158n10
Plotinus, 145n20
predestination, see foreordination
principle of exclusion, see principle of physical closure
principle of physical closure, 65–72
properties, mental and physical, 53–55, 58n10, 59–71
prophecy, 154, 190–97
providence
  extent of, 1–3
  and freedom, 16
  and plans, 3–8, 29–32, 34, 180–81, 193, 286–87, 297–98
  meticulous, 5–7, 13–14, 245–46, 254
Pruss, Alexander, 98–99
puzzles, *xii–xiv*, 300–305

Rawls, John, 238n5
reductionism, 69n23, 70–71
Reichenbach, Bruce, 2n1, 76n36, 107n46, 131n18, 158n8, 202n45, 222n6, 302n2
Rhoda, Alan, 168–70
Rice, Richard, 191n23
Robb, David, 62n16
Robinson, Terry, 80n43
Roy, Steven, 192, 196n38

Sabaoth, 135, 137, 148
Sanders, John, 32n15, 175n5, 181n7, 184n12, 187n15, 188, 189n18, 190n21, 191n24, 193n29, 194n24, 195–96, 198–99, 204, 205n49, 246n9
salvation, universal, 144–47
Schiffer, Stephen, 68n21
Searle, John, 75
self-consciousness, 55–56
Sevincer, A., 73n31, 74
Shaddai, 135–37
Shakespeare, William, 288
Shapere, Dudley, 280–86
sovereignty, 10–14, 38, 137, 172, 197
  God's, 147–49
  and power, 10–12, 14
stewardship, 2, 246, 302
Stoljar, Daniel, 58n11
supervenience, 58, 66, 69–71
supererogatory actions, 96–98, 145–46, 239–41
Swinburne, Richard, 201n43, 292–94, 296

testimony, see miracle
testing, by God, 189–90, 198–201
Thelle, Rannfrid, 108n49, 110n51
Thomas a Kempis, 244, 258–59
Thomas, Aquinas, 37, 84–85, 123–26, 129, 142, 272n15

Van Gogh, Vincent, 288

Ward, Michael, *x*n2, 303
Ware, Bruce, 178n3, 189, 190n22, 192n28, 205–6
weaver, 297–98

Yancey, Phillip, 29n12, 231n8

Scripture Index

OLD TESTAMENT

Genesis

1:2	302
1:31	81
2:15	259
2:16–17	27
2:18	81
3:2–3	27
3:15	81
3:17	27
4:15	2
6:6–8	180
6:7	147
6:14–17	2
9:8–17	147
12:1–3	4, 82
12:3	109
12:9–16	96
15	97
15:3	245
17:1	136
18:14	121
18:20–28	46
18:25	96
20:17	245
22:8	1
22:12	189
22:14	1
25:21	245
28:3	136
29:25	137n6
30:17, 22	245
35:11	136
37:9–10	194
43:14	136
49:25	136

Exodus

3	2, 4
3:1–3	279
3:18	194
5:1	194
6:2–3	136n3
6:3	136
7–10	11
9:16	4, 119
12	2, 114
13:21	2
15:3	109
15:6, 13	138
16	2
17:5–6	2
20:5	221
22:11	97
23:31–32	108
23:23, 32–33	113
32:9–10	30
32:10–14	180
33:19–20	130
34:15–17	113
37:7	221

Leviticus

25:23	107n46
26	114

Numbers

12:13	245
14:11–12	30
14:18	221
14:20–31	31
22–24	30
23:19	183n10

Scripture Index

Numbers (*continued*)

24:4	136n4

Deuteronomy

4:37	48
4:37–38	119
5:9	221
6:23–7:2	108
7:1–6	113
7:7–8	48
7:17–24	2
8:10, 17–19	251
9:3	108n48
11:12	305
12:31	113
13:12–17	114
18:10–11	113
20:10–18	109
20:14	112
20:17	110
24:26	221
27:10	89n17
30:11–16	27
31:16	30
31:29	153
32:6	97

Joshua

4:23–24	139
7:11	110
7:24–25	115
9:3–26	114
10	11
10:40	110
11:12, 15, 20	110
11:16–23	111
22:22	152
24:8, 12	108n48
24:14–15	27

Judges

3:2	111n55
3:4	111n55
3:5	111
3:6–7	113
3:12	112
4:1–3	112
6:25	246
7:2	108

1 Samuel

1:3	135
1:10–11	245
1:12	242
2:3	152
2:30–33	181
8:4–5	31
8:7–9	12
9:15	4
9:16	31
13:9, 13–14	31
13:13	187, 198
15:2	113
15:11	181
15:2–3, 10–11, 26	110
15:28	181
15:29	183n10
15:30	111
17:45	135
23:9–13	193
23:14	2

2 Samuel

7:4	137
12:13–18	182
12:16–23	261
24	115
24:16	182

1 Kings

8:56	87
11:4–8	113
11:34–37	192
13:2	192
16:2–4	192
17:9	192
17:15–16	268
21:19	192
21:23	192
22:19	135

2 Kings

1:16–17	192
17	112
20:1–6	154, 182, 191

1 Chronicles

22:1–20	119
28:9	189
29:11–12	12, 119

2 Chronicles

5:13	83
6:17	245

Nehemiah

1:6	242
1:8–10	139
9:6	12

Job

1:6	180n6
5:10	2
5:17	136
6:4, 14	136n5
8:3	136n5
8:5	136n5
10:13	122n4
11:7	136n5
13:3	136n5
15:25	136n5
21:15	136n5
21:20	136
26	119
27:11	136
29:5	136
32:2	106
33:4	136
33:12–13	106
33:16–20, 23–24, 29–30	214
34:10–12	87, 105, 218
34:17–28	87
34:28	106
36:11	106
36:22–24	119
36:31	2
37:23–24	106
38	121
38:41	2
38–42	120
40:6–8	211
42:2	30, 121
42:5	214n3

Psalms

1:3	82
3:7	249
15:5–6	117
16:8–11	191
17:13	245
17:13–14	249
19:1–4	16
22:2	242
22:18	191
23	149
24:9–10	135
25:7–8	82, 97
30:11–12	116
32:10	117
33:10–11	5, 6
34:8	82, 149
40:5	5, 6
36:6	87
52:9	117
54:7	83
62:11–12	119
64:1	245
66:5–7	139
66:7	119
68:28–30	119
68:35	119
69:16	83
73:4–5, 12	253
73:2–5, 13–14, 16–17, 18–24	210–11
73:18–20, 23–26	254
74:20	97
77:14–20	139
84:3	135
84:11	83
85:12	83
86:5	83

Psalms (continued)

88:1	242
89:49–50	97
92:15	97
103:2–5	82
104:29	12
105	3
105:44–45	109
106:1	82
106:34–39	108
107:8	117
110:1	191
111:6	119
111:9	2
119:137	97
136	3
139	2, 152
139:1–2	189
139:16	31n14
140:1	245
143:9	245
147:1–5, 8–9	ix
147:5	152
147:9	2
150:2	119

Proverbs

3:11–12	214
19:21	30
20:30	30

Isaiah

1:9	137
1:15	105
5:19	30
6:3	137
6:5	135
13:4–6	135
13:6	136n3
14:26	29–30
14:27	30
19:17	30
19:20–25	36
19:23–25	2
22:11–12	30
24:23	135
27:4	107n46
30:23–26	2
37:4	135
37:26	30, 31n14
38:1–6	154
40–48	196n38
40:26	138
40:28, 29, 31	119
41:14–20	194
41:21–29	104, 196
42:8–9	196
43:8–13	196
42:13	109
43:20	2
44:6–8	104, 196
44:28	4, 154
44:28—45:5	153
45:1	154
45:1–7	191
45:12–13	139
45:18–25	196
46:9–11	192, 196
46:10	30
48:3	192
48:3–8	196
61:8–9	xi
65:6–7	221

Jeremiah

1:5–9	4
3:6–7	181
3:7	188, 193
3:19–20	181, 193
7	109
10:12	119
18:7–10	182
26:2–6	181, 185
29:11	5–6
32:17	121
32:27	121
33:9	2
33:11	83
46:25–26	194
50:18, 21	113
51:15	119

Lamentations

| 3:22–23 | xi |
| 3:25 | 83 |

Ezekiel

1:24	136n3
12:10–14	192
16:36, 38, 40, 57	113
18:20	115n58, 221
18:21–29	96
26	194
33	27
33:4–6	28
34:29	2

Daniel

7–9	154
9:20–27	154
11	191

Hosea

2:2	28
4:1–2	28
11:1	196
11:8–9	183n10

Amos

| 7:1–6 | 182n8 |

Jonah

1:17	2
3:4–5	191
3:6–10	115

Micah

| 3:9–12 | 194 |
| 5:2 | 153, 191 |

Zechariah

1:6	30
8:20–22	136
14:16	136

NEW TESTAMENT

Matthew

2:6	191
2:15	196
2:23	196
4:1–11	106
5–7	28
5:28, 44	88n16
5:45	2, 8
6:5–7	235
6:7	242
6:8	237, 306
6:10, 11–13	244
7:7–8	236, 247, 249
7:9–11	248
7:11	83, 236
7:21	246
8:2–3	245n8
9:1–8	xi
9:6–8	120
9:16–20	89n17
9:27	245
10:29–30	2, 3, 153
11:4–6	120
11:21	144, 299
11:23	299
12:22–24	278
14:14	xi
14:29–30	9n4
15:32	xi
16:21	191
18:19	245
19:16–20	89n17
19:21	28
19:26	122, 123
20:1–16	12
20:30	245
21:21–23	245, 247
22:29	120
22:42	122
23:37	28
24:2	194
26:39, 42, 44	8, 122
26:53	205
26:64	120

Mark

1:27	120
2:1–12	268
2:3–12	221–22
3:15	120
4:11–12	8
7:20–23	88n15
10:27	122
14:36	122, 140
14:62	120

Luke

1:11–20	122n3
1:15	120
1:26–29	279
1:28–38	122n3
1:37	122, 123
1:38	140
1:73	97
5:12, 18-20	245
7:3–5	245
7:13	xi
7:30	31
8:41–48	245
9:37–40	245
14:16–20	8
18:1–7	241
18:7–8	242
18:27	122
21:36	242
22:42	244
24:49	120

John

1:16	145
2:3–5	245
3:16	xi, 2, 82, 147
5:27	120
9	221
11:25	245
11:35	230
11:40	230
13:19	196
14:13–14	247, 259
14:15	89n17
16:13	2
19:11	123
19:23–24	191
20:31	9, 262
21:15–17	4

Acts

1:8	120
2:23	31, 205
2:25–35	191
2:30	97
3:6, 8	272
4:27–28	31, 205
5:19	2
6:18	132
8:18	273
9:4–6	29
9:15–16	4
10	246
12:6–11	2
13:48	31
14:17	2
16:9	8
16:10	246
16:25–26	3
16:34	115
17:26	30
19:11	272

Romans

1:4	120
1:5	49n48
1:16	120
1:24–32	49
3:25–26	205
4:21	123
6:12–23	49n48
7:14–24	49
8:2, 5	49
8:13	49n48
8:27	48
8:28	206
8:28–30	33
8:28—11:36	33
8:29	48
8:35–39	48
8:39	4, 34

9:4–6	48
9:6–9	33, 34
9:10–11	33
9:11–12	48
9:11, 16	49
9:14	46
9:15	48
9:16	48
9:18–20	144
9:19–24	12
9:19–26	46
9:21	35
9:22	35, 36n21, 120
9:22–24	44
9:23	34
9:24–29	35
9:29	137
9:30–32	34, 48
10:1	36
10:3	34, 48
10:8–9	36
10:9–13	35
10:10	48
10:12–15	34
10:13	36
10:16	48
10:21	34
11:2	33, 34, 48
11:5	35n18
11:4–5	34
11:5–6	34, 48
11:7–10	35
11:11	34, 35
11:15	35, 36n21
11:20	36n21
11:22	35
11:26	35n19
11:26–32	36n21
11:28	33n16, 48
11:29	34
11:30–32	35
11:32	35n19
12:1–2	49

1 Corinthians

10:13	2
11:27–30	222

2 Corinthians

1:18	120
6:18	137
12:9	305
13:4	120

Galatians

6:15–16	12

Ephesians

1:3–15	32–33
1:5	2
1:10	4
1:22	4
2:7	4
2:8–9	32
2:13–22	4
3:2–6	31
4:15	4
4:22–24	259
4:24	92
5:25–27	xi
6:18	233, 242

Philippians

2:6–11	301
2:7	132
3:23	138
4:7	233

Colossians

1:17	12
3:10	259

1 Thessalonians

3:10	242
4:17	194
5:16–18	306
5:17	242
5:25	242

1 Timothy

2:4	8, 28, 144, 146
6:17	3

2 Timothy

3:16	2

Titus

2:11	145

Hebrews

1:2, 10	107
1:3	12
2:9	230
4:13	153
4:14–15	106
6:13–18	97
7:22	12
7:27	xi
8:13	12
12:5–11	214, 215

James

1:2–3	215
1:6–8	245
1:15	87, 106
1:17	82, 251
4:2	236, 245
4:3	236
5:4	137
5:10–11	219
5:14–15	234
5:15–16	220

1 Peter

1:2	33, 48
1:5	120
1:10	204
1:19–20	154
1:20	205n49

2 Peter

3:9	4

1 John

3:8	4
3:22	247
5:14–15	244

Revelation

1:8	137n8
2:26	120
4:8	137
4:11	138
11:15–17	137
11:17	137n8
13:8	205
15:3	137n8
16:7, 14	137n8
19:6	137
19:15	137n8
21:3–4	xii
21:22	137n8

www.ingramcontent.com/pod-product-compliance
Lightning Source LLC
Chambersburg PA
CBHW030432300426
44112CB00009B/964